THE LIFE OF NELSON

VOLUME I.

Nelson

THE

LIFE OF NELSON

THE EMBODIMENT

OF THE

SEA POWER OF GREAT BRITAIN

BY

CAPTAIN A. T. MAHAN, D.C.L., LL.D.

UNITED STATES NAVY

AUTHOR OF "THE INFLUENCE OF SEA POWER UPON HISTORY, 1660–1783," "THE
INFLUENCE OF SEA POWER UPON THE FRENCH REVOLUTION AND
EMPIRE," AND OF A "LIFE OF ADMIRAL FARRAGUT"

IN TWO VOLUMES

VOL. I.

GREENWOOD PRESS, PUBLISHERS
NEW YORK   1968

PREFACE.

THE Life of Nelson has been written so often, that an explanation — almost an apology — seems due for any renewal of the attempt; but, not to mention the attractiveness of the theme in itself, it is essential to the completeness and rounding off of the author's discussion of the Influence of Sea Power, that he present a study, from his own point of view, of the one man who in himself summed up and embodied the greatness of the possibilities which Sea Power comprehends, — the man for whom genius and opportunity worked together, to make him the personification of the Navy of Great Britain, the dominant factor in the periods hitherto treated. In the century and a half embraced in those periods, the tide of influence and of power has swelled higher and higher, floating upward before the eyes of mankind many a distinguished name; but it is not until their close that one arises in whom all the promises of the past find their finished realization, their perfect fulfilment. Thenceforward the name of Nelson is enrolled among those few presented to us by History, the simple mention of which suggests, not merely a personality or a career, but a great force or a great era concrete in a single man, who is its standard-bearer before the nations.

Yet, in this process of exaltation, the man himself, even when so very human and so very near our own time as Nelson is, suffers from an association which merges his individuality in the splendor of his surroundings; and it is perhaps pardonable to hope that the subject is not so far exhausted but that a new worker, gleaning after the reapers, may contribute something further towards disengaging the figure of the hero from the glory that cloaks it. The aim of the present writer, while not neglecting other sources of knowledge, has been to make Nelson describe himself, — tell the story of his own inner life as well as of his external actions. To realize this object, it has not seemed the best way to insert numerous letters, because, in the career of a man of action, each one commonly deals with a variety of subjects, which bear to one another little relation, except that, at the moment of writing, they all formed part of the multifold life the writer was then leading. It is true, life in general is passed in that way; but it is not by such distraction of interest among minute details that a particular life is best understood. Few letters, therefore, have been inserted entire; and those which have, have been chosen because of their unity of subject, and of their value as characteristic.

The author's method has been to make a careful study of Nelson's voluminous correspondence, analyzing it, in order to detect the leading features of temperament, traits of thought, and motives of action; and thence to conceive within himself, by gradual familiarity even more than by formal effort, the character therein revealed. The impression thus produced he has sought to convey to others, partly in the form of ordinary narrative, — daily living with his hero, — and partly by such grouping of incidents and utterances, not always, nor even nearly, simultaneous, as shall serve by their joint evidence to emphasize particular traits, or particular opinions, more forcibly than when such testimonies are scattered far apart; as they would be, if recounted in a strict order of time.

A like method of treatment has been pursued in regard to that purely external part of Nelson's career in which are embraced his military actions, as well as his public and private life. The same aim is kept in view of showing clearly, not only what he did, but the principles which dominated his military thought, and guided his military actions, throughout his life; or, it may be, such changes as must inevitably occur in the development of a man who truly lives. This cannot be done satisfactorily without concentrating the evidence from time to time; and it is therefore a duty a writer owes to his readers, if they wish such acquaintance with his subject as he thinks he has succeeded in acquiring for himself.

The author has received individual assistance from several persons. To a general expression of thanks he wishes to add his special acknowledgments to the present Earl Nelson, through whose aid he has obtained information of interest which otherwise probably would have escaped him; and to Lords Radstock and De Saumarez, both of whom have been good enough to place in his hands letters contemporary with Nelson, and touching incidentally matters that throw light on his career. Material of the same kind has also been furnished him by Professor John Knox Laughton, whose knowledge of Nelson and of the Navy of that period is second to none; it is not the least of the writer's advantages that he has had before him, to check possible errors in either fact or conclusions, the admirable, though brief, Life of Nelson published by Mr. Laughton two years since.

Illustrative anecdotes have also been supplied by Admiral Sir William R. Mends, G. C. B., who has shown his continued interest in the work by the trouble he has taken for it; by Mr. Stuart J. Reid, of Blackwell Cliff, East Grinstead; and by Mr. Edgar Goble, of Fareham, Hants. Mr. B. F. Stevens, of 4 Trafalgar Square, has also kindly exerted himself on several occasions to obtain needed information. To Mrs. F. H. B. Eccles, of Sherwell House, Plymouth, granddaughter of Josiah Nisbet, Nelson's stepson, the author is indebted for reminiscences of Lady Nelson, and for her portrait here published; and his thanks are also due to Lieutenant-Colonel W. Clement D. Esdaile, of Burley Manor, Ringwood, Hants, through whom he was brought into communication with Mrs. Eccles, and who has in other ways helped him.

Throughout the writing of the book constant assistance has been received from Mr. Robert B. Marston, to whom cordial acknowledgment is made for the untiring pains taken in prosecuting necessary inquiries, which could not have been done without great delay by one not living in England. Suggestions valuable to the completeness of the work have been given also by Mr. Marston.

For the portrait of Mrs. Philip Ward, the "Horatia" whom Nelson called generally his adopted daughter, but at times spoke of as his daughter simply, and whom, on the last morning of his life, he commended to the care of his Country, the author has to thank Mr. and Mrs. Nelson Ward, of 15 Lancaster Road, Belsize Park, London. Mr. Nelson Ward is her son.

To the more usual sources of information already in print, it is not necessary to refer in detail; but it is right to mention especially the collection of Hamilton and Nelson letters, published by Mr. Alfred Morrison, a copy of which by his polite attention was sent the writer, and upon which must necessarily be based such account of Nelson's relations with Lady Hamilton as, unfortunately, cannot be omitted wholly from a life so profoundly affected by them.

A. T. MAHAN.

MARCH, 1897.

CONTENTS OF VOL. I.

CHAPTER I.

THE FIRST TWENTY-FIVE YEARS.

CHAPTER II.

Cruise of the "Boreas." — Controversy over the Enforcement of the Navigation Act. — Return to England. — Retirement until the Outbreak of the French Revolution. — Appointed to command the "Agamemnon."

1784–1793.

CHAPTER III.

NELSON'S DEPARTURE FROM ENGLAND IN THE " AGAMEMNON." — SERVICES IN THE MEDITERRANEAN UNTIL THE RECOVERY OF TOULON BY THE FRENCH. — LORD HOOD IN COMMAND.

FEBRUARY – DECEMBER, 1793.

CHAPTER IV.

REDUCTION OF CORSICA BY THE BRITISH. — DEPARTURE OF LORD
HOOD FOR ENGLAND. — THE "AGAMEMNON" REFITTED AT
LEGHORN.

JANUARY – DECEMBER, 1794.

CHAPTER V.

NELSON'S SERVICES WITH THE FLEET IN THE MEDITERRANEAN
UNDER ADMIRAL HOTHAM. — PARTIAL FLEET ACTIONS OF
MARCH 13 AND 14, AND JULY 13. — NELSON ORDERED TO
COMMAND A DETACHED SQUADRON CO-OPERATING WITH THE
AUSTRIAN ARMY IN THE RIVIERA OF GENOA.

JANUARY – JULY, 1795.

CHAPTER VI.

NELSON'S COMMAND OF A DETACHED SQUADRON ON THE RIVIERA
OF GENOA, UNTIL THE DEFEAT OF THE AUSTRIANS AT THE
BATTLE OF LOANO. — SIR JOHN JERVIS APPOINTED COM-
MANDER-IN-CHIEF IN THE MEDITERRANEAN.

JULY – DECEMBER, 1795.

CHAPTER VII.

CHAPTER VIII.

The Evacuation of Elba. — Night Combat with Two Spanish
Frigates. — Battle of Cape St. Vincent. — Nelson Promoted to Rear-Admiral. — Services before Cadiz.

December, 1796 – June, 1797.

CHAPTER IX.

THE UNSUCCESSFUL ATTEMPT AGAINST TENERIFFE. — NELSON
LOSES HIS RIGHT ARM. — RETURN TO ENGLAND. — REJOINS
ST. VINCENT'S FLEET, AND SENT INTO THE MEDITERRANEAN
TO WATCH THE TOULON ARMAMENT.

JULY, 1797 – MAY, 1798.

CHAPTER X.

The Campaign and Battle of the Nile.

May – September, 1798.

CONTENTS.

CHAPTER XI.

NELSON'S RETURN FROM EGYPT TO NAPLES. — MEETING WITH
LADY HAMILTON. — ASSOCIATION WITH THE COURT OF NAPLES.
— WAR BETWEEN NAPLES AND FRANCE. — DEFEAT OF THE
NEAPOLITANS. — FLIGHT OF THE COURT TO PALERMO.

SEPTEMBER – DECEMBER, 1798.

CHAPTER XII.

NELSON'S CAREER, AND GENERAL EVENTS IN THE MEDITERRA-
NEAN AND ITALY, FROM THE OVERTHROW OF THE ROYAL
GOVERNMENT IN NAPLES TO THE INCURSION OF THE FRENCH
FLEET UNDER ADMIRAL BRUIX.

JANUARY – MAY, 1799.

CHAPTER XIII.

From the Incursion of the French Fleet under Bruix to the Restoration of the Royal Authority at Naples. — The Caracciolo Execution. — Nelson's Disobedience to Admiral Lord Keith.

May – July, 1799.

CONTENTS.

LIST OF ILLUSTRATIONS.

VOLUME ONE.

MAPS AND BATTLE PLANS.

VOLUME ONE.

THE LIFE OF NELSON.

CHAPTER I.

THE FIRST TWENTY-FIVE YEARS.

1758–1783.

IT is the appointed lot of some of History's chosen few to come upon the scene at the moment when a great tendency is nearing its crisis and culmination. Specially gifted with qualities needed to realize the fulness of its possibilities, they so identify themselves with it by their deeds that they thenceforth personify to the world the movement which brought them forth, and of which their own achievements are at once the climax and the most dazzling illustration. Fewer still, but happiest of all, viewed from the standpoint of fame, are those whose departure is as well timed as their appearance, who do not survive the instant of perfected success, to linger on subjected to the searching tests of common life, but pass from our ken in a blaze of glory which thenceforth forever encircles their names. In that evening light break away and vanish the ominous clouds wherewith human frailties or tyrant passions had threatened to darken their renown ; and their sun goes down with a lustre which the lapse of time is powerless to dim. Such was the privilege of the stainless Wolfe ; such, beyond all others, that of Nelson. Rarely has a man been more favored in the hour of his appearing; never one so fortunate in the moment of his death.

Yet, however accidental, or providential, this rarely allotted portion, this crowning incident of an heroic career, it is after all but an incident. It the man has not contrived; but to it he has contributed much, without which his passing hour would have faded to memory, undistinguished among those of the myriads, great and small, who have died as nobly and are forever forgotten. A sun has set; but before its setting it has run a course, be it long or short, and has gathered a radiance which fixes upon its parting beams the rapt attention of beholders. The man's self and the man's works, what he was and what he did, the nature which brought forth such fruits, the thoughts which issued in such acts, hopes, fears, desires, quick intuitions, painful struggles, lofty ambitions, happy opportunities, have blended to form that luminous whole, known and seen of all, but not to be understood except by a patient effort to resolve the great result into its several rays, to separate the strands whose twisting has made so strong a cord.

Concerning the man's external acts, it will often happen that their true value and significance can best be learned, not from his own personal recital, but from an analytic study of the deeds themselves. Yet into them, too, often enters, not only the subtile working of their author's natural qualities, but also a certain previous history of well-defined opinions, of settled principles firmly held, of trains of thought and reasoning, of intuitions wrought into rational convictions, all of which betray both temperament and character. Of these intellectual antecedents, the existence and development may be gleaned from his writings, confirming the inference reached somewhat mechanically by the scrutiny of his actions. They play to the latter the part of the soul to the body, and thus contribute to the rather anatomical result of the dissecting process a spiritual element it would otherwise lack. But if this is so even of the outward career, it is far more deeply true of the inner history, of that underlying native character, which masterfully moulds and colors every life, yet evades the last analysis except when the obscure workings of heart and mind have been laid bare by their owner's words, recording the feelings of the fleeting hour with no view to future inspection. In these revelations of self, made without thought of the world outside, is to be found, if anywhere, the clue to that complex and often contradictory mingling of qualities which go to form the oneness of the man's personality. This discordance between essential unity and superficial diversities must be harmonized, if a true conception of his being is to be formed. We know the faces of our friends, but we see each as one. The features can, if we will, be separately considered, catalogued, and valued; but who ever thus thinks habitually of one he knows well? Yet to know well must be the aim of biography, — so to present the traits in their totality, without suppression of any, and in their true relative proportions, as to produce, not the blurred or distorted outlines seen through an imperfect lens, but the vivid apprehension which follows long intimacy with its continual, though unconscious, process of correction.

For such a treatment of Nelson's character, copious, if imperfect, material is afforded in his extensive and varied correspondence. From it the author aims, first, to draw forth a distinct and living image of the man himself, as sketched therein at random and loosely by his own hand. It is sought to reach the result by keeping the reader in constant contact, as by daily acquaintance, with a personality of mingled weakness and strength, of grave faults as well as of great virtues, but one whose charm was felt in life by all who knew it. The second object, far less ambitious, is to present a clear narrative of the military career, of the mighty deeds of arms, of this first of British

seamen, whom the gifts of Nature and the course of History have united to make, in his victories and in their
results, the representative figure of the greatest sea-power
that the world has known.

It will not be thought surprising that we have, of the
first thirty years of Nelson's life, no such daily informal
record as that which illustrates the comparatively brief
but teeming period of his active fighting career, from 1793
to 1805, when he at once, with inevitable directness and
singular rapidity, rose to prominence, and established intimate relations with numbers of his contemporaries. A few
anecdotes, more or less characteristic, have been preserved
concerning his boyhood and youth. In his early manhood
we have his own account, both explicit and implied in
many casual unpremeditated phrases, of the motives which
governed his public conduct in an episode occurring when,
scarcely yet more than a youth, he commanded a frigate in
the West Indies, — the whole singularly confirmatory, it
might better be said prophetic, of the distinguishing qualities afterwards so brilliantly manifested in his maturity.
But beyond these, it is only by the closest attention and
careful gleaning that can be found, in the defective and
discontinuous collection of letters which remains from his
first thirty years, the indisputable tokens, in most important particulars, of the man that was to be.

The external details of this generally uneventful period
can be rapidly summarized. He was born on the 29th of
September, 1758, the fifth son and sixth child of Edmund
Nelson, then rector of the parish of Burnham Thorpe, in
Norfolk, a county which lies along the eastern coast of
England, bordering the North Sea. His mother, whose
name before marriage was Catherine Suckling, was grand-
niece to Sir Robert Walpole, the famous prime minister
of Great Britain during twenty years of the reigns of the
first two Georges. Sir Robert's second brother was called
Horatio; and it was from the latter, or from his son, that

the future hero took his baptismal name, which, in a more common form, was also that of Sir Robert's younger son, the celebrated letter and memoir writer, Horace Walpole.

Of the eleven children borne by Nelson's mother in her eighteen wedded years, only two lived to grow old. She herself died at forty-two; and her brother, Captain Maurice Suckling, of the Royal Navy, was also cut off in the prime of his age. As the earlier Nelsons were unusually long-lived, it seems probable that a certain delicacy of constitution was transmitted through the Sucklings to the generation to which the admiral belonged. He was himself, at various periods through life, a great sufferer, and frequently an invalid; allusions to illness, often of a most prostrating type, and to his susceptibility to the influences of climate or weather, occur repeatedly and at brief intervals throughout his correspondence. This is a factor in his career which should not be lost to mind; for on the one hand it explains in part the fretfulness which at times appears, and on the other brings out with increased force the general kindly sweetness of his temper, which breathed with slight abatement through such depressing conditions. It enhances, too, the strength of purpose that trod bodily weakness under foot, almost unconsciously, at the call of duty or of honor. It is notable, in his letters, that the necessity for exertion, even when involving severe exposure, is apt to be followed, though without apparent recognition of a connection between the two, by the remark that he has not for a long time been so well. He probably experienced, as have others, that it is not the greater hardships of the profession, much less the dangers, but its uncertainties and petty vexations, which tell most severely on a high-strung organization like his own.

The immediate occasion of his going to sea was as follows. In 1770 the Falkland Islands, a desolate and then unimportant group, lying in the South Atlantic, to the eastward of Patagonia, were claimed as a possession by both Spain and Great Britain. The latter had upon them a settlement called Port Egmont, before which, in the year named, an overwhelming Spanish squadron suddenly appeared, and compelled the British occupants to lower their flag. The insult aroused public indignation in England to the highest pitch; and while peremptory demands for reparation were despatched to Spain, a number of ships of war were ordered at once into commission. Among these was the "Raisonnable," of sixty-four guns, to the command of which was appointed Nelson's uncle, Captain Maurice Suckling. The latter had some time before promised to provide for one of his sister's children, the family being very poor; and, the custom of the day permitting naval captains, as a kind of patronage, to take into the King's service on board their own ships a certain number of lads, as midshipmen or otherwise, the opportunity of giving a nephew a start in life was now in his hands. The story is that Horatio, though then but twelve years old, realized the burden of pecuniary care that his father was carrying, and himself volunteered the wish that his uncle would take him to sea. However it happened, the suggestion staggered Suckling, who well knew the lad's puny frame and fragile constitution. "What has poor little Horatio done," cried he, "that he, being so weak, should be sent to rough it at sea? But let him come, and if a cannon-ball takes off his head, he will at least be provided for." Under such gloomy foreboding began the most dazzling career that the sea, the mother of so many heroes, has ever seen.[1]

[1] The precise date of Nelson's entering the Navy, which would be that of his being rated upon the books of the "Raisonnable," is not stated. Accepting the times during which he was borne upon the books of different ships, as given by Sir Harris Nicolas (Letters and Despatches of Lord Nelson, vol. i. p. 4, note), and with them calculating back from October 15, 1773, the day mentioned by Nelson himself as that on which he was paid off from the "Carcass" (Nicolas, p. 5), the date of entry upon the books of the "Raisonnable" would be November 27, 1770; unless, which is unlikely, there

Captain Maurice Suckling

Spain, after a short hesitation, yielded the British demands, so that war did not come, and the " Raisonnable," with other ships, was again put out of commission. The incident of the Falkland Islands, however, had served the purpose of introducing Nelson to his profession, for which otherwise the opportunity might not have offered. Being so young when thus embarked, he, in common with many of the most successful seamen of that day, got scanty schooling; nor did he, as some others did, by after application remedy the eccentricities of style, and even of grammar, which are apt to result from such early neglect. His letters, vigorous and direct as they are, present neither the polished diction of Collingwood, nor the usual even correctness of St. Vincent and Saumarez, but are, on the contrary, constantly disfigured by awkward expressions and bad English. There was rarely, however, danger of mistaking his meaning, as was sometimes charged against Lord Howe.

Here, before fairly parting with the humble home life, of which the motherless boy had seen, and was throughout his career to see so little, is a fit place to introduce two anecdotes associated with those early days which his biographers have transmitted to us. We of these critical times have learned to look with incredulity, not always unmixed with derision, upon stories relating to the childhood of distinguished men; but it can safely be said that the two now to be given are in entire keeping, not merely with particular traits, but with the great ruling tenor of Nelson's whole life. He and his elder brother were going to school one

were any lost days. The news of the Port Egmont business reached England in October, 1770. Clarke and M'Arthur (Life of Nelson, vol. i. p. 14, note) infer January 1, 1771, for his entry upon the " Raisonnable's " books; but this would not allow the times which Nicolas gives with minute exactness. For his actually joining the " Raisonnable " they give, loosely, the spring of 1771, — March or April. This is very possible, as rating back, for the sake of gaining constructive time needed to qualify for promotion, was tolerated by the practice of the day.

winter day upon their ponies. Finding the snow so deep
as to delay them seriously, they went back, and the elder
reported that they could not get on. The father very judiciously replied: "If that be so, I have of course nothing
to say; but I wish you to try again, and I leave it to your
honour not to turn back, unless necessary." On the second attempt, the elder was more than once for returning;
but Horatio stuck it out, repeating continually, "Remember it was left to our honour," and the difficult journey was
accomplished.

The children in this instance seem to have felt that there
was danger in going on. The other recorded occurrence
shows in the lad that indifference to personal benefit, as
distinguished from the sense of conspicuous achievement,
which was ever a prominent characteristic of the man.
The master of his school had a very fine pear-tree, whose
fruit the boys coveted, but upon which none dared hazard
an attempt. At last Nelson, who did not share their
desires, undertook the risk, climbed the tree by night, and
carried off the pears, but refused to eat any of them, —
saying that he had taken them only because the others
were afraid.

Trivial though these incidents may seem, they are so
merely because they belong to the day of small things. To
those accustomed to watch children, they will not appear
unworthy of note. Taken together, they illustrate, as
really as do his greatest deeds, the two forms assumed at
different times by the one incentive which always most
powerfully determined Nelson's action through life, — the
motive to which an appeal was never made in vain. No
material considerations, neither danger on the one hand,
nor gain on the other, ever affected him as did that ideal-
ized conception which presented itself, now as duty, now
as honor, according as it bore for the moment upon his relations to the state or to his own personality. "In my
mind's eye," said he to his friend Captain Hardy, who after-

wards bent over him as his spirit was parting amid the tumult of his last victory, "I ever saw a radiant orb suspended which beckoned me onward to renown." Nelson did not often verge upon the poetical in words, but to the poetry of lofty aspiration his inmost being always answered true.

To the young naval officer of a century ago, especially if without political or social influence, it was a weighty advantage to be attached to some one commanding officer in active employment, who by favorable opportunity or through professional friendships could push the fortunes of those in whom he was interested. Much of the promotion was then in the hands of the admirals on foreign stations; and this local power to reward distinguished service, though liable to abuse in many ways, conduced greatly to stimulate the zeal and efforts of officers who felt themselves immediately under the eye of one who could make or mar their future. Each naval captain, also, could in his degree affect more or less the prospects of those dependent upon him. Thus Suckling, though not going to sea himself, continued with intelligent solicitude his promised care of the young Nelson. When the "Raisonnable" was paid off, he was transferred to the command of the "Triumph," of seventy-four guns, stationed as guard-ship in the river Medway; and to her also he took with him his nephew, who was borne upon her books for the two following years, which were, however, far from being a period of inactive harbor life. Having considerable professional interest, he saw to the lad's being kept afloat, and obtained for him from time to time such service as seemed most desirable to his enterprising spirit.

The distinction between the merchant seaman and the man-of-war's man, or even the naval officer, in those days of sailing ships and simple weapons was much less sharply marked than it has since become. Skill in seamanship, from the use of the marlinespike and the sail-needle

up to the full equipping of a ship and the handling of her
under canvas, was in either service the prime essential. In
both alike, cannon and small arms were carried; and the
ship's company, in the peaceful trader as well as in the
ship of war, expected to repel force with force, when meeting upon equal terms. With a reduced number of naval
vessels in commission, and their quarter-decks consequently
over-crowded with young officers, a youth was more likely
to find on board them a life of untasked idleness than a
call to professional occupation and improvement. Nelson
therefore was sent by his careful guardian to a merchant-
ship trading to the West Indies, to learn upon her, as a
foremast hand, the elements of his profession, under conditions which, from the comparative fewness of the crew and
the activity of the life, would tend to develop his powers
most rapidly. In this vessel he imbibed, along with nautical knowledge, the prejudice which has usually existed,
more or less, in the merchant marine against the naval
service, due probably to the more rigorous exactions and
longer terms of enlistment in the latter, although the life
in other respects is one of less hardship; but in Nelson's
day the feeling had been intensified by the practice of im-
pressment, and by the severe, almost brutal discipline that
obtained on board some ships of war, through the arbitrary
use of their powers by captains, then insufficiently controlled by law. In this cruise he seems to have spent a
little over a year; a time, however, that was not lost to
him for the accomplishment of the period of service technically required to qualify as a lieutenant, his name continuing throughout on the books of the " Triumph," to
which he returned in July, 1772.

Suckling's care next insured for him a continuance of
active, semi-detached duty, in the boats of the " Triumph,"—
an employment very different from, and more responsible
than, that in which he had recently been occupied, and
particularly calculated to develop in so apt a nature the

fearlessness of responsibility, both professional and personal, that was among the most prominent features of Nelson's character. " The test of a man's courage is responsibility," said that great admiral and shrewd judge of men, the Earl of St. Vincent, after a long and varied experience of naval officers ; and none ever shone more brightly under this supreme proof than the lad whose career is now opening before us. It may be interesting, too, to note that this condition of more or less detached service, so early begun, in which, though not in chief command, he held an authority temporarily independent, and was immediately answerable for all that happened on the spot, was the singular characteristic of most of his brilliant course, during which, until 1803, two years before Trafalgar, he was only for brief periods commander-in-chief, yet almost always acted apart from his superior. Many a man, gallant, fearless, and capable, within signal distance of his admiral, has, when out of sight of the flag, succumbed with feeble knees to the burden of independent responsible action, though not beyond his professional powers. This strength, like all Nature's best gifts, is inborn ; yet, both for the happy possessor and for the merely average man, it is susceptible of high development only by being early exercised, which was the good fortune of Nelson.

Of these two years of somewhat irregular service, while nominally attached to the " Triumph," it will be well to give the account in his own words ; for, having been written a full quarter of a century later, they record the deepest and most lasting impressions made upon him during that susceptible period when first becoming familiar with the calling he was to adorn : —

" The business with Spain being accommodated, I was sent in a West India ship belonging to the house of Hibbert, Purrier, and Horton, with Mr. John Rathbone, who had formerly been in the Navy, in the Dreadnought with Captain Suckling. From this voyage I returned to the Triumph at Chatham in July,

1772; and, if I did not improve in my education, I returned a practical Seaman, with a horror of the Royal Navy, and with a saying, then constant with the Seamen, '*Aft the most honour, forward the better man!*' It was many weeks before I got the least reconciled to a Man-of-War, so deep was the prejudice rooted; and what pains were taken to instil this erroneous principle in a young mind! However, as my ambition was to be a Seaman, it was always held out as a reward, that if I attended well to my navigation, I should go in the cutter and decked long-boat, which was attached to the Commanding officer's ship at Chatham. Thus by degrees I became a good pilot, for vessels of that description, from Chatham to the Tower of London, down the Swin, and the North Foreland; and confident of myself amongst rocks and sands, which has many times since been of great comfort to me. In this way I was trained, till the expedition towards the North Pole was fitted out; when, although no boys were allowed to go in the Ships, (as of no use,) yet nothing could prevent my using every interest to go with Captain Lutwidge in the Carcass; and, as I fancied I was to fill a man's place, I begged I might be his coxswain; which, finding my ardent desire for going with him, Captain Lutwidge complied with, and has continued the strictest friendship to this moment. Lord Mulgrave, whom I then first knew, maintained his kindest friendship and regard to the last moment of his life. When the boats were fitting out to quit the two Ships blocked up in the ice, I exerted myself to have the command of a four-oared cutter raised upon, which was given me, with twelve men; and I prided myself in fancying I could navigate her better than any other boat in the Ship."

It will be recognized from this brief yet suggestive and characteristic narrative, that, however valuable and even indispensable may have been his uncle's assistance in forwarding his wishes, it was his own ambition and his own impulse that even at this early day gave direction to his course, and obtained opportunities which would scarcely have been offered spontaneously to one of his physical frailty. In this Arctic expedition he underwent the experiences common to all who tempt those icebound seas. During it occurred an incident illustrative of Nelson's recklessness of personal danger, — a very different thing from official recklessness, which he never showed even in his moments of greatest daring and highest inspiration. The story is so hackneyed by frequent repetition as to make its relation a weariness to the biographer, the more so that the trait of extreme rashness in youth is one by no means so rare as to be specially significant of Nelson's character. It will be given in the words of his first biographers : —

" There is also an anecdote recollected by Admiral Lutwidge, which marked the filial attention of his gallant cockswain. Among the gentlemen on the quarter-deck of the Carcass, who were not rated midshipmen, there was, besides young Nelson, a daring shipmate of his, to whom he had become attached. One night, during the mid-watch, it was concerted between them that they should steal together from the ship, and endeavour to obtain a bear's skin. The clearness of the nights in those high latitudes rendered the accomplishment of this object extremely difficult : they, however, seem to have taken advantage of the haze of an approaching fog, and thus to have escaped unnoticed. Nelson in high spirits led the way over the frightful chasms in the ice, armed with a rusty musket. It was not, however, long before the adventurers were missed by those on board ; and, as the fog had come on very thick, the anxiety of Captain Lutwidge and his officers was very great. Between three and four in the morning the mist somewhat dispersed, and the hunters were discovered at a considerable distance, attacking a large bear. The signal was instantly made for their return ; but it was in vain that Nelson's companion urged him to obey it. He was at this time divided by a chasm in the ice from his shaggy antagonist, which probably saved his life ; for the musket had flashed in the pan, and their ammunition was expended. ' Never mind,' exclaimed Horatio, ' do but let me get a blow at this devil with the but-end of my musket, and we shall have him.' His companion, finding that entreaty was in vain, regained the ship. The captain, seeing the young man's danger, ordered a gun to be fired to terrify the enraged animal. This had the desired effect; but Nelson was obliged to return without his bear, somewhat agitated with the apprehension of the consequence of this adventure. Captain Lutwidge, though he could not but admire so daring a disposition, reprimanded him rather sternly for such rashness, and for conduct so unworthy of the situation he occupied; and desired to know what motive he could have for hunting a bear? Being thought by his captain to have acted in a manner unworthy of his situation, made a deep impression on the high-minded cockswain; who, pouting his lip, as he was wont to do when agitated, replied, ' Sir, I wished to kill the bear, that I might carry its skin to my father.' "

Upon his return to England from the Arctic Seas, Nelson again by his own choice determined his immediate future. Within a fortnight of leaving the " Carcass," he was, through his uncle's influence, received on board by the captain of the " Seahorse," of twenty guns, one of the ships composing a squadron that was just then fitting out for the East Indies. To quote himself, " Nothing less than such a distant voyage could in the least satisfy my desire of maritime knowledge." During an absence of three years he for much of the time, as formerly in his West India cruise, did the duty of a seaman aloft, from which he was afterwards rated midshipman, and placed, this time finally, upon the quarter-deck as an officer. In the ordinary course of cruising in peace times, he visited every part of the station from Bengal to Bussorah; but the climate, trying even to vigorous Europeans, proved too much for his frail health. After a couple of years he broke down and was invalided home, reaching England in September, 1776. His escape from death was attributed by himself to the kind care of Captain Pigot of the " Dolphin," in which ship he came back. At this period we are told that, when well, he was of florid counte-

nance, rather stout and athletic; but, as the result of his
illness, he was reduced to a mere skeleton, and for some
time entirely lost the use of his limbs, — a distressing
symptom, that returned upon him a few years later after
his Central American expedition in 1780, and confirms the
impression of extreme fragility of constitution, which is
frequently indicated in other ways.

During this absence in the East Indies Captain Suckling, in April, 1775, had been named Comptroller of the
Navy, — a civil position, but one that carried with it power
and consequent influence. This probably told for much in
obtaining for Nelson, who was but just eighteen, and had
not yet passed the examinations for his first promotion,
an acting appointment as lieutenant. With this he joined
a small ship-of-the-line, the "Worcester," of sixty-four guns,
on board which he remained for six months, engaged in
convoy duty between the Channel and Gibraltar, seeing
from her decks for the first time the waters of the Mediterranean and its approaches, since then indissolubly associated with his name and his glory. He took with him a
letter from his uncle to the captain of his new ship; but
while such introduction, coming from so influential a quarter, doubtless contributed powerfully to clear from his path
the obstacles commonly encountered by young men, Nelson had gained for himself a reputation for professional
capacity, which, here as throughout his life, quickly won
him the full confidence of his superiors. In later years,
when his admiral's flag was flying, he recorded, with evident pride in the recollection, that while on board the
"Worcester," notwithstanding his youth, his captain used
to say, "He felt as easy when I was upon deck as any officer of the ship." It is doubtful, indeed, whether Nelson
ever possessed in a high degree the delicate knack of handling a ship with the utmost dexterity and precision. He
certainly had not the reputation for so doing. Codrington,
— a thorough Nelsonian, to use his own somewhat factious

expression — used to say in later years, " Lord Nelson was no seaman; even in the earlier stages of the profession his genius had soared higher, and all his energies were turned to becoming a great commander." His apprenticeship, before reaching command, was probably too short; and, as captain, his generous disposition to trust others to do work for which he knew them fitted, would naturally lead him to throw the manipulation of the vessel upon his subordinates. But although, absorbed by broader and deeper thoughts of the responsibilities and opportunities of a naval commander, to which he was naturally attracted by both his genius and his temperament, he was excelled in technical skill by many who had no touch of his own inspiration, he nevertheless possessed a thoroughly competent knowledge of his profession as a simple seaman; which, joined to his zeal, energy, and intelligence, would more than justify the confidence expressed by his early commander. Of this knowledge he gave full proof a year later, when, before a board of captains, strangers to him, he successfully passed his examinations for a lieutenancy. His uncle Suckling, as Comptroller of the Navy, was indeed on the Board; but he concealed the fact of relationship until the other members had expressed themselves satisfied.

His examination was held within a week of his leaving the " Worcester," on the 8th of April, 1777; and Suckling once more, but for the last time in his life, was able to exert his influence in behalf of his relative by promptly securing for him, not only his promotion to lieutenant, which many waited for long, but with it his commission, dated April 10, to the " Lowestoffe," a frigate of thirty-two guns. This class of vessel was in the old days considered particularly desirable for young officers, being more active than ships-of-the-line, while at the same time more comfortable, and a better school for the forming of an officer, than were the smaller cruisers; and his uncle probably felt that Nelson, whose service hitherto had been mainly upon the latter, needed yet to perfect the habits and methods distinctive of a ship of war, for he now wrote him a letter upon the proprieties of naval conduct, excellently conceived, yet embracing particulars that should scarcely have been necessary to one who had served his time on board well-ordered ships. The appointment to the " Lowestoffe " was further fortunate, both for him and for us, as in the commander of the vessel, Captain William Locker, he found, not only an admirable officer and gentleman, but a friend for whom he formed a lasting attachment, ending only with Locker's death in 1800, two years after the Battle of the Nile. To this friendship we owe the fullest record, at his own hands, of his early career; for Locker kept the numerous letters written him by Nelson while still an unknown young man. Of sixty-seven which now remain, covering the years from 1777 to 1783, all but thirty were to this one correspondent.

In another respect the appointment to the " Lowestoffe " was fortunate for Nelson. The ship was destined to the West Indies — or, to speak more precisely, to Jamaica, which was a command distinct from that of the eastern Caribbean, or Lesser Antilles, officially styled the Leeward Islands Station. Great Britain was then fully embarked in the war with her North American colonies, which ended in their independence; and the course of events was hastening her to the rupture with France and Spain that followed within a year. In this protracted contest the chief scene of naval hostilities was to be the West Indies; but beyond even the casualties of war, the baneful climate of that region insured numerous vacancies by prostration and death, with consequent chances of promotion for those who escaped the fevers, and found favor in the eyes of their commander-in-chief. The brutal levity of the old toast, " A bloody war and a sickly season," nowhere found surer fulfilment than on those pestilence-stricken coasts.

Captain Locker's health soon gave way. Arriving at Jamaica on the 19th of July, 1777, we find Nelson in the following month writing to him from the ship during an absence produced by a serious illness, from which fatal results were feared. The letter, like all those to Locker, was marked by that tone of quick, eager sympathy, of genial inclination always to say the kindest thing, that characterized his correspondence, and, generally, his intercourse with others, — traits that through life made him, beyond most men, acceptable and beloved. He was, from first to last, not merely one of those whose services are forced upon others by sheer weight of ability, because indispensable, — though this, too, he was, — but men wanted him because, although at times irritable, especially after the wounds received in later years, he was an easy yokefellow, pleasant to deal with, cordial and ready to support those above him, a tolerant and appreciative master to subordinates. It may even be said that, in matters indifferent to him, he too readily reflected the feelings, views, and wishes of those about him ; but when they clashed with his own fixed convictions, he was immovable. As he himself said in such a case, " I feel I am perfectly right, and you know upon those occasions I am not famous for giving up a point."

Of his connection with the " Lowestoffe " he himself, in the short autobiographical sketch before quoted, mentions two circumstances, which, from the very fact of their remaining so long in his memory, illustrate temperament. " Even a frigate," he says, " was not sufficiently active for my mind, and I got into a schooner, tender to the Lowestoffe. In this vessel I made myself a complete pilot for all the passages through the [Keys] Islands situated on the north side Hispaniola." This kind of service, it will be noted, was in direct sequence, as to training, to his handling of the " Triumph's " long-boat in the lower waters of the Thames, and would naturally contribute to increase

Captain William Locker

that "confidence in himself among rocks and sands," which was afterwards to be so "great a comfort" to him. In his later career he had frequent and pressing need of that particular form of professional judgment and self-reliance for which these early experiences stood him in good stead. As he afterwards wrote to the First Lord of the Admiralty, when pleading the cause of a daring and skilful officer who had run his ship ashore : " If I had been censured every time I have run my ship, or fleets under my command, into great danger, I should long ago have been *out* of the service, and never *in* the House of Peers." At the critical instants of the Nile and Copenhagen, as well as in the less conspicuous but more prolonged anxieties of the operations off Corsica and along the Riviera of Genoa, this early habit, grafted upon the singularly steady nerve wherewith he was endowed by nature, sustained him at a height of daring and achievement to which very few have been able to rise.

The other incident recorded by him as happening while on board the " Lowestoffe," he himself cites as illustrative of temperament. "Whilst in this frigate, an event happened which presaged my character; and, as it conveys no dishonour to the officer alluded to, I shall insert it. Blowing a gale of wind, and a very heavy sea, the frigate captured an American letter-of-marque. The first Lieutenant was ordered to board her, which he did not do, owing to the very heavy sea. On his return, the Captain said, ' Have I no officer in the ship who can board the prize?' On which the Master ran to the gangway, to get into the boat: when I stopped him, saying, 'It is my turn now; and if I come back, it is yours.' This little incident," he continues, "has often occurred to my mind ; and I know it is my disposition, that difficulties and dangers do but increase my desire of attempting them." An action of this sort, in its results unimportant, gives keener satisfaction in the remembrance than do greater deeds, because more

purely individual, — entirely one's own. It is upon such
as this, rather than upon his victories, that Nelson in his
narrative dwells caressingly. His personal daring at St.
Vincent, and against the gunboats off Cadiz, ministered
more directly to his self-esteem, to that consciousness of
high desert which was dear to him, than did the Battle of
the Nile, whose honors he, though ungrudgingly, shared
with his " band of brothers."

When the " Lowestoffe " had been a year upon the station, it became very doubtful whether Locker could continue in her, and finally he did go home ill. It was
probably due to this uncertainty that he obtained the
transfer of Nelson, in whom he had become most affec-
tionately interested, to the " Bristol," flagship of Sir Peter
Parker, the commander-in-chief. Here, under the admiral's
own eye, warmly recommended by his last captain, and
with a singular faculty for enlisting the love and esteem
of all with whom he was brought into contact, the young
officer's prospects were of the fairest; nor did the event
belie them. Joining the " Bristol " as her third lieutenant,
not earlier than July, 1778, he had by the end of September risen " by succession " — to use his own phrase — to be
first; a promotion by seniority whose rapidity attests the
rate at which vacancies occurred. Both Parker and his
wife became very fond of him, cared for him in illness, and
in later years she wrote to him upon each of the occasions
on which he most brilliantly distinguished himself — after
St. Vincent, the Nile, and Copenhagen. " Your mother,"
said she after the first, " could not have heard of your
deeds with more affection ; nor could she be more rejoiced
at your personal escape from all the dangers of that glorious day ; " and again, after the Nile, " Sir Peter and I
have ever regarded you as a son." The letter following
the victory at Copenhagen has not been published ; but
Nelson, whose heart was never reluctant to gratitude
nor to own obligation, wrote in reply : " Believe me

when I say that I am as sensible as ever that I owe my present position in life to your and good Sir Peter's partiality for me, and friendly remembrance of Maurice Suckling."

This last allusion indicates some disinterestedness in Parker's patronage, and its vital importance to Nelson at that time. Captain Suckling had died in July, 1778, and with him departed the only powerful support upon which the young lieutenant could then count, apart from his own merits and the friends obtained by them. There was in those days an immense difference in prospects between the nephew of the Comptroller of the Navy and a man unknown at headquarters. By what leading principles, if any, Sir Peter Parker was guided in the distribution of his favors, can scarcely now be ascertained ; but that he brought rapidly forward two men of such great yet widely differing merit as Nelson and Collingwood, is a proof that his judgment was sound and the station one where vacancies were frequent. Collingwood, who was then a lieutenant on board a sloop-of-war, went to the " Lowestoffe " in Nelson's place. When the latter, in December, 1778, was made commander into the brig " Badger," the other was transferred to the vacant room in the " Bristol ; " and when Nelson, on the 11th of June, 1779, became post-captain in the " Hinchinbrook " frigate, Collingwood again followed him as commander of the " Badger." Finally, when through a death vacancy a better frigate offered for Nelson, Collingwood also was posted into the " Hinchinbrook ; " this ship thus having the singular distinction of conferring the highest rank obtainable by selection, and so fixing the final position of the two life-long friends who led the columns at Trafalgar, the crowning achievement of the British Navy as well as of their own illustrious careers. The coincidence at the earlier date may have been partly factitious, due to a fad of the commander-in-chief ; but it assumes a different and very impressive aspect viewed in the light of their later close association, especially when it is recalled that Collingwood also succeeded, upon Nelson's death, to the Mediterranean command, and was there worn out, as his predecessor fell, in the discharge of his duty upon that important station, which thus proved fatal to them both. Few historic parallels are so complete. Sir Peter Parker, living until 1811, survived both his illustrious juniors, and at the age of eighty-two followed Nelson's coffin, as chief mourner at the imposing obsequies, where the nation, from the highest to the lowest, mingled the exultation of triumph with weeping for the loss of its best-beloved.

Of Nelson's exterior at this time, his early biographers have secured an account which, besides its value as a portrait. possesses the further interest of mentioning explicitly that charm of manner which was one of his best birth-gifts, reflecting, as it did, the generous and kindly temper of his heart. "The personal appearance of Captain Nelson at this period of his life, owing to his delicate health and diminutive figure, was far from expressing the greatness of his intellectual powers. From his earliest years, like Cleomenes, the hero of Sparta, he had been enamoured of glory, and had possessed a greatness of mind. Nelson preserved, also, a similar temperance and simplicity of manners. Nature, as Plutarch adds of the noble Spartan. had given a spur to his mind which rendered him impetuous in the pursuit of whatever he deemed honourable. The demeanour of this extraordinary young man was entirely the demeanour of a British seaman; when the energies of his mind were not called forth by some object of duty, or professional interest, he seemed to retire within himself, and to care but little for the refined courtesies of polished life." No saving sense of humor seems to have suggested that the profane might here ask, "Is this the British seaman?" "In his dress he had all the cleanliness of an Englishman, though his manner of wearing it gave him an air of negligence; and yet his general address and conversation, when he wished to please, possessed a charm that was irresistible." [1]

In June, 1779, when posted into the "Hinchinbrook," Nelson wanted still three months of being twenty-one. By the custom of the British Navy, then and now, promotions from the grade of Captain to that of Admiral are made by seniority only. Once a captain, therefore, a man's future was assured, so far as concerned the possibility of juniors passing over his head, — neither favor nor merit could procure that; his rank relatively to . others was finally fixed. The practical difficulty of getting at a captain of conspicuous ability, to make of him a flag-officer, was met by one of those clumsy yet adequate expedients by which the practical English mind contrives to reconcile respect for precedent with the demands of emergency. There being then no legal limit to the number of admirals, a promotion was in such case made of all captains down to and including the one wanted; and Lord St. Vincent, one of the most thorough-going of naval statesmen, is credited with the declaration that he would promote a hundred down the list of captains, if necessary, to reach the one demanded by the needs of the country. Even with this rough-riding over obstacles, — for the other officers promoted, however useful in their former grade, not being wanted as admirals, remained perforce unemployed, — the advantage of reaching post-rank betimes is evident enough; and to this chiefly Nelson referred in acknowledging his permanent indebtedness to Sir Peter Parker. With this early start, every artificial impediment was cleared from his path; his extraordinary ability was able to assert itself, and could be given due opportunity, without a too violent straining of service methods. He had, indeed, to wait eighteen years for his flag-rank; but even so, he obtained it while still in the very prime of

[1] Clarke and M'Arthur, vol. i. p. 31.

his energies, before he was thirty-nine, — a good fortune equalled by none of his most distinguished contemporaries.[1]

A somewhat singular feature of this early promotion of Nelson is that it was accorded without the claim of service in actual battle, — a circumstance that seems yet more remarkable when contrasted with the stormy and incessant warfare of his later career. While he was thus striding ahead, his equals in years, Saumarez and Pellew, were fighting their way up step by step, gaining each as the reward of a distinct meritorious action, only to find themselves outstripped by one who had scarcely seen a gun fired in anger. The result was mainly due to the nature of the station, where sickness made vacancies more rapidly than the deadliest engagement. But while this is true, and must be taken into the account, it was characteristic of Nelson that his value transpired through the simplest intercourse, and amid the commonplace incidents of service. Locker and Parker each in turn felt this. A little later, while he and Collingwood were still unknown captains, the latter, usually measured and formal in his language, wrote to him in these singularly strong words : " My regard for you, my dear Nelson, my respect and veneration for your character, I hope and believe, will never lessen." So, some years afterwards, but before he became renowned or had wrought his more brilliant achievements, an envious brother captain said to him, " You did just as you pleased in Lord Hood's time, the same in Admiral Hotham's, and now again with Sir John Jervis; it makes no difference to you who is Commander-in-chief." This power of winning confidence and inspiring attachment was one of the strongest elements in Nelson's success, alike as a subordinate and when himself in chief command.

With his mind ever fixed upon glory, or rather upon

---

[1] Collingwood was nearly fifty when he got his flag. Howe was forty-five, St. Vincent fifty-three, Saumarez forty-four, Exmouth (Pellew) forty-eight.

honor, — the word he himself most often used, and which more accurately expresses his desire for fame ; honor, which is to glory what character is to reputation, — the same hard fortune persisted in denying to him, during the War of the American Revolution, the opportunities for distinction which he so ardently coveted. In the " Badger " and in the " Hinchinbrook," during the year 1779, his service was confined to routine cruising about Jamaica and along the Mosquito coast of Central America. A gleam of better things for a moment shone upon him in August of that year, when the French fleet, under Count D'Estaing, appeared in Haïti, numbering twenty-two ships-of-the-line, with transports reported to be carrying twenty thousand troops. All Jamaica was in an uproar of apprehension, believing an attack upon the island to be imminent ; for its conquest was known to be one of the great objects of the enemy. Nelson was at the time living on shore, the " Hinchinbrook " seemingly [1] not having returned to the port since his appointment to her, and he eagerly accepted the duty of commanding the land batteries. The odds were great, — " You must not be surprised to hear of my learning to speak French," he wrote, laughingly, to Locker in England, — but if so, the greater the honor attendant, whether upon success or defeat. D'Estaing, however, passed on to America to encounter disaster at Savannah, and Nelson's hopes were again disappointed.

In January, 1780, an opportunity for service offered, which ended in no conspicuous or permanent result, but nevertheless conferred distinction upon one who, to use his own expression, was determined to climb to the top of the tree, and to neglect no chance, however slight, that could help him on. War with Spain had then been about seven months declared, and the British governor of Jamaica

---

[1] This appears certain from his letters of July 28 and August 12, which explicitly mention that ship's absence.

had sagaciously determined to master Lake Nicaragua, and
the course of the river San Juan, its outlet to the Caribbean Sea. The object of the attempt was twofold, both
military and commercial. The route was recognized then,
as it is now, as one of the most important, if not the most
important, of those affording easy transit from the Pacific
to the Atlantic by way of the Isthmus. To a nation of
the mercantile aptitudes of Great Britain, such a natural
highway was necessarily an object of desire. In her hands
it would not only draw to itself the wealth of the surrounding regions, but would likewise promote the development of her trade, both north and south, along the
eastern and western coasts of the two Americas. But the
pecuniary gain was not all. The military tenure of this
short and narrow strip, supported at either end, upon the
Pacific and the Atlantic, by naval detachments, all the
more easily to be maintained there by the use of the belt
itself, would effectually sever the northern and southern
colonies of Spain, both by actual interposition, and by depriving them of one of their most vital lines of intercom-
munication. To seek control of so valuable and central a
link in a great network of maritime interests was as natural and inevitable to Great Britain a century ago, as it
now is to try to dominate the Mediterranean and the Suez
Canal, which fulfil a like function to her Eastern possessions and Eastern commerce.

Preoccupied, however, with numerous and more pressing
cares in many quarters of the world, and overweighted in
a universal struggle with outnumbering foes, Great Britain
could spare but scanty forces to her West India Islands,
and from them Governor Dalling could muster but five
hundred men for his Nicaraguan undertaking. Nelson
was directed to convoy these with the "Hinchinbrook" to
the mouth of the San Juan del Norte, where was the port
now commonly called Greytown, in those days a fine and
spacious harbor. There his charge ended; but his mental

constitution never allowed him to look upon a military task as well done while anything remained to do. In the spirit of his famous saying, fifteen years later, " Were ten ships out of eleven taken, I would never call it well done if the eleventh escaped, if able to get at her," he determined to go with the troops. With his temperament it was impossible to turn his back upon the little body of soldiers, whose toilsome advance up the tropical stream might be aided and hastened by his ready seamen.

The first objective of the expedition was Fort San Juan, a powerful work controlling the river of the same name, and thereby the only natural water transit between the sea and Lake Nicaragua. Upon the possession. of this, as a position of vantage and a safe depot for supplies and re-inforcements, Dalling based his hopes of future advance, both west and south. Nelson took with him forty-seven seamen and marines from his ship's company; the former, aided by some Indians, doing most of the labor of forcing the boats against the current, through shoal and tortuous channels, under his own constant supervision and encouragement. A small outpost that withstood their progress was by him intrepidly stormed, sword in hand, by sudden assault; and upon reaching Fort San Juan he urgently recommended the same summary method to the officer commanding the troops. The latter, however, was not one of the men who recognize the necessity for exceptional action. Regular approaches, though the slower, were the surer way of reducing a fortified place, and entailed less bloodshed. Professional rule commonly demanded them, and to professional rule he submitted. Nelson argued that through delays, which, however incurred, were now past discussion, the expedition had reached its destination in April, at the end of the healthy, dry season, instead of shortly after its beginning, in January. Consequently, owing to the fall of the water, much additional trouble had been experienced in the advance, the men were pro-

portionately weakened by toil and exposure, and the wet
months, with their dire train of tropical diseases, were at
hand. Therefore, though more might fall by the enemy's
weapons in a direct attack, the ultimate loss would be less
than by the protracted and sickly labors of the spade;
while with San Juan subdued, the force could receive all the
care possible in such a climate, and under the best conditions await the return of good weather for further progress.

In military enterprises there will frequently arise the
question, Is time or life in this case of the greater value?
Those regularly ordered and careful procedures which
most economize the blood of the soldier may, by their
inevitable delays, seriously imperil the objects of the campaign as a whole; or they may even, while less sanguinary,
entail indirectly a greater loss of men than do prompter
measures. In such doubtful matters Nelson's judgment
was usually sound; and his instinct, which ever inclined
to instant and vigorous action, was commonly by itself
alone an accurate guide, in a profession whose prizes are
bestowed upon quick resolve more often than upon deliberate consultation. The same intuition that in his prime
dictated his instant, unhesitating onslaught at the Nile,
depriving the French of all opportunity for further preparation, — that caused him in the maturity of his renown,
before Copenhagen, to write, "every hour's delay makes
the enemy stronger; we shall never be so good a match
for them as at this moment," — that induced him at Trafalgar to modify his deliberately prepared plan in favor of
one vastly more hazardous, but which seized and held the
otherwise fleeting chance, — led him here also at San Juan,
unknown, and scarcely more than a boy, to press the policy
of immediate attack.

The decision was not in his hands, and he was overruled;
whereupon, with his usual readiness to do his utmost, he
accepted the course he disapproved, and, without nursing a
grievance, became at once active in erecting batteries and

serving the guns. " When unfortunate contentions," says one dispassionate narrator, " had slackened the ardour for public service, Captain Nelson did not suffer any narrow spirit to influence his conduct. He did more than his duty: where anything was to be done, he saw no difficulties." Great as his merits were, he was never insensible to them; and, in the sketch of his career, furnished by him to his chief biographers, he records his exploits with naïve self-satisfaction, resembling the sententious tablets of Eastern conquerors: " I boarded, if I may be allowed the expression, an outpost of the enemy, situated on an island in the river ; I made batteries, and afterwards fought them, and was a principal cause of our success." But this simple, almost childlike, delight in his own performances, which continually crops out in his correspondence, did not exaggerate their deserts. Major Polson, commanding the land forces, wrote to Governor Dalling : " I want words to express the obligations I owe to Captain Nelson. He was the first on every service, whether by day or night. There was not a gun fired but was pointed by him, or by Captain Despard, Chief Engineer." Dalling, after some delay, wrote in the same sense to the Minister of War in London, warmly recommending Nelson to the notice of the home Government.

While the siege was in progress, Nelson received word of his appointment to a better ship, the " Janus," of forty-four guns, and it became necessary for him to join her. He left Fort San Juan only the day before it surrendered, and returned to Jamaica; but his health now gave way wholly, and his command of the " Janus," for the most part merely nominal, soon came to an end altogether. Dalling had truly said, " Captain Nelson's constitution is rather too delicate for service in this northern ocean." [1] Before

---

[1] The Caribbean was formerly thus styled in contradistinction to the South Sea, the Pacific, which was so called because its first discoverers saw it to the south from the Isthmus.

starting on the expedition, he had himself written to his friend Locker : " If my health is not much better than it is at present, I shall certainly come home after this trip, as all the doctors are against my staying so long in this country. You know my old complaint in my breast : it is turned out to be the gout got there. I have twice been given over since you left this country with that cursed disorder. the gout." In such weakness he lived and worked through a month of a short campaign, in which, of the " Hinchinbrook's " crew of two hundred, one hundred and forty-five were buried in his time or that of his successor, Collingwood, — a mortality which he justly cites as a further proof of the necessity for expedition in such climates. But, though he survived, he escaped by the skin of his teeth. Worn out by dysentery and fatigue, he was carried ashore in his cot, and soon after taken to Sir Peter Parker's house, where Lady Parker herself nursed him through. Her kindness to him and his own debility are touchingly shown by a note written from the mountains, where he was carried in his convalescence : " Oh, Mr. Ross, what would I give to be at Port Royal! Lady Parker not here, and the servants letting me lay as if a log, and take no notice." By September, 1780, it was apparent that perfect restoration, without change of climate, was impossible, and in the autumn, having been somewhat over three years on the station, he sailed for home in the " Lion," of sixty-four guns, Captain Cornwallis,[1] to whose careful attention, as formerly to that of Captain Pigot, he gratefully attributed his life. The expedition with which he had been associated ended in failure, for although a part of the force pushed on to Lake Nicaragua, sickness compelled the abandonment of the conquests, which were repossessed by the Spaniards.

---

[1] Cornwallis was an officer of marked gallantry and conduct, who distinguished himself on several occasions, as captain, during the War of 1778, and as admiral during the wars of the French Revolution. He was brother to Lord Cornwallis, who surrendered at Yorktown, in 1781.

Arriving in England, Nelson went to Bath, and there
passed through a period of extreme suffering and tedious
recovery. " I have been so ill since I have been here,"
says one of his letters, " that I was obliged to be carried
to and from bed, with the most excruciating tortures."
Exact dates are wanting; but he seems to have been under treatment near three months, when, on the 28th of January, 1781, he wrote to Locker, in his often uncouth style :
" Although I have not quite recovered the use of my limbs,
yet my inside is a new man ; " and again, three weeks later,
" I have now the perfect use of all my limbs, except my left
arm, which I can hardly tell what is the matter with it.
From the shoulder to my fingers' ends are as if half dead."
He remained in Bath until the middle of March, latterly
more for the mild climate than because feeling the necessity of prosecuting his cure; yet that his health was far
from securely re-established is evident, for a severe relapse
followed his return to London. On the 7th of May, 1781,
he writes to his brother: " You will say, why does not he
come into Norfolk ? I will tell you : I have entirely lost
the use of my left arm, and very near of my left leg and
thigh." In estimating Nelson's heroism, the sickly fragility of his bodily frame must be kept in memory; not to
excuse shortcomings of nerve or enterprise, for there
were none, but to exalt duly the extraordinary mental
energy which rather mocked at difficulties than triumphed
over them.

While yet an invalid he had again applied for employment, and, as the war was still raging, was appointed in
August, 1781, to the " Albemarle," a small frigate of
twenty-eight guns. He was pleased with the ship, the
first commissioned by himself at home, with a long cruise
in prospect; and, together with his expressions of content
with her, there appears that manifestation of complete satisfaction with his officers and crew, with those surrounding
him as subordinates, that so singularly characterized his

habit of mind. "I have an exceeding good ship's company. Not a man or officer in her I would wish to change.
. . . I am perfectly satisfied with both officers and ship's company." Down to the month before Trafalgar, when, to the bidding of the First Lord of the Admiralty to choose his own officers, he replied, "Choose yourself, my lord; the same spirit actuates the whole profession, you cannot choose wrong," there is rarely, it might almost be said never, anything but praise for those beneath him. With the "Agamemnon," "We are all well; indeed, nobody can be ill with my ship's company, they are so fine a set." At the Nile, "I had the happiness to command a band of brothers; therefore night was to my advantage. Each knew his duty, and I was sure each would feel for a French ship. *My friends* readily conceived my plan." His ships in the Mediterranean, in 1803, "are the best commanded and the very best manned" in the navy. So his frequent praise of others in his despatches and letters has none of the formal, perfunctory ring of an official paper; it springs evidently from the warmest appreciation and admiration, is heartfelt, showing no deceptive exterior, but the true native fibre of the man, full of the charity which is kind and thinketh no evil. It was not always so toward those above him. Under the timid and dilatory action of Hotham and Hyde Parker, under the somewhat commonplace although exact and energetic movements of Lord Keith, he was restive, and freely showed what he felt. On the other hand, around Hood and Jervis, who commanded his professional respect and esteem, he quickly threw the same halo of excellence, arising from his tendency to idealize, that colored the medium through which he invariably saw the men whom he himself commanded. The disposition to invest those near to him with merits, which must in part at least have been imaginary, is a most noteworthy feature of his character, and goes far to explain the attraction he exerted over others, the enthusiasm

which ever followed him; the greatness of his success, and also, unhappily, the otherwise almost inexplicable but enduring infatuation which enslaved his later years, and has left the most serious blot upon his memory.

Though thus pleased with his surroundings, his own health continued indifferent. He excuses himself for delay in correspondence, because "so ill as to be scarce kept out of bed." In such a state, and for one whose frame had been racked and weakened by three years spent in the damp heat of the tropics, a winter's trip to the Baltic was hardly the best prescription; but thither the "Albemarle" was sent, — "it would almost be supposed," he wrote, "to try my constitution." He was away on this cruise from October to December, 1781, reaching Yarmouth on the 17th of the latter month, with a large convoy of a hundred and ten sail of merchant-ships, all that then remained of two hundred and sixty that had started from Elsinore on the 8th. "They behaved, as all convoys that ever I saw did, shamefully ill; parting company every day." After being several days wind-bound in Yarmouth Roads, he arrived in the Downs on the first day of 1782. The bitter cold of the North had pierced him almost as keenly as it did twenty years later in the Copenhagen expedition. "I believe the Doctor has saved my life since I saw you," he wrote to his brother. The ship was then ordered to Portsmouth to take in eight months' provisions, — a sure indication that she was intended for a distant voyage. Nelson himself surmised that she would join the squadron of Sir Richard Bickerton, then fitting out to reinforce the fleet in the East Indies. Had this happened, he would have been on hand to hear much and perchance see something of one of his own professional forerunners, the great French Admiral Suffren, as well as of the latter's doughty antagonist, Sir Edward Hughes; for Bickerton arrived in time to take part in the last of the five pitched battles between those two hard fighters. Unluckily, a severe accident had

befallen the "Albemarle," — a large East Indiaman having
dragged down upon her during a heavy gale in the Downs.
The injuries received by this collision were so extensive
that the ship was under repairs at Portsmouth for six
weeks, during which time Bickerton sailed.

While thus detained in one of the principal dockyards
and naval stations of the kingdom, another large detachment, belonging to the Channel fleet, assembled before
Nelson's eyes. It comprised twelve sail-of-the-line, under
Admiral Barrington; and among these was the "Foudroyant," the most famous ship of her time, then commanded by Captain John Jervis, with whom, as the Earl
of St. Vincent, Nelson was afterwards closely associated;
but the young frigate captain did not now come in contact
with his stately superior, who in later years so highly valued and loved him. It was for him still the day of small
things. Though thus thrown in the midst of the din and
bustle of extensive naval preparations, he had not the fortune to be directly connected with them; and consequently
no occasion arose for becoming known to admirals who
could recognize his worth, and give him the opportunities
without which distinction cannot be achieved. It is, however, a significant and instructive fact that, while thus
persistently dissociated from the great operations then in
progress, and employed wholly in detached service, Nelson's natural genius for war asserted itself, controlling the
direction of his thoughts and interests, and fixing them to
that broad field of his profession from which he was as yet
debarred. "The height of his ambition," an acquaintance
of this period tells us, "was to command a line-of-battle
ship; as for prize money," for which frigates offered the
best chances, "it never entered his thoughts." A few
months later, while still in the "Albemarle," it was said
of him by Lord Hood, the most original tactician of the
day, that he knew as much about naval tactics as any
officer in the fleet. When this high encomium was be-

stowed, Nelson had barely passed his twenty-fourth birthday.

Meanwhile the " Albemarle " was again ordered upon convoy duty, this time to Quebec. This destination also was distasteful on account of the climate. " I want much to get off from this d——d voyage," he wrote. " Mr. Adair," an eminent London surgeon, who the year before had treated him for the paralysis of his limbs, " has told me that if I was sent to a cold damp climate it would make me worse than ever." He himself had scruples about applying for an exchange, and the efforts of some friends who interfered proved useless. The " Albemarle " started with a convoy of thirty-odd vessels on the 10th of April, 1782; and after a short stop at Cork, anchored at St. John's, Newfoundland, on May 27, whence she reached Quebec July 1. Three days later she again sailed on a cruise that lasted over two months, spent chiefly about Boston Bay and Cape Cod. During this time several enemy's vessels were taken or destroyed; but, with the bad luck that so often followed Nelson in the matter of prize-money, none of the captures reached port, and the cruise was pecuniarily unprofitable. It afforded him, however, an opportunity for displaying conduct and gaining deserved reputation, which he valued more highly. On the 14th of August the sudden lifting of a fog showed the " Albemarle " within gunshot of a French squadron, of four ships-of-the-line and a frigate, that had just come out of Boston. A close chase followed, lasting nine or ten hours; but Nelson threw off the heavy ships by running among the shoals of George's Bank, which he ventured to do, trusting to the cool head and aptitude for pilotage acquired in earlier life. The frigate followed warily, watching for a chance to strike at advantage; but when the ships-of-the-line had been dropped far enough to be unable to help their consort, the British vessel hove-to [1] in defiance. and the enemy fell back upon his supports.

[1] That is, stopped.

Shortly after this escape, so many of the ship's company fell ill with scurvy that Nelson decided to go back to Quebec, where he arrived on the 17th of September. " For eight weeks," he wrote, " myself and all the officers lived upon salt beef; nor had the ship's company had a fresh meal since the 7th of April." The fears for his health that he had expressed before sailing from England had happily proved groundless, and a month's stay in port which now followed, at the most delightful and invigorating of the American seasons, wrought wonders for him. His letters to Locker state that the voyage agreed with him better than he had expected; while from the St. Lawrence he wrote to his father, " Health, that greatest of blessings, is what I never truly enjoyed until I saw *Fair* Canada. The change it has wrought, I am convinced, is truly wonderful." This happy result had been due, in part at least, to surroundings that told favorably upon his sensitive nervous system, and not to the bracing climate alone. He had been actively occupied afloat, and had fallen desperately in love with a fair Canadian, around whom his ardent imagination threw that glamour of exaggerated charm in which he saw all who were dear to him, except his wife. Her he seems from the first to have looked upon with affection indeed, but without rapture or illusion. The Canadian affair came near ending in an imprudent offer, from which he was with difficulty deterred by a cool-headed friend. The story runs that, the ship being ordered to New York and ready for sea, he had bidden her good-bye and gone on board, expecting to sail next day; but that, unable to bear the approaching separation, he returned to the city, and was on his way to the lady's home when his friend met him.

Tearing himself away from his mistress by a violent effort, Nelson, on the 20th of October, sailed for New York. Arriving on the 13th of November, he found there a large part of the West India fleet, under Lord Hood, who

had been second in command to Rodney on the occasion
of the latter's celebrated victory over De Grasse in the
previous April. Rodney had since then been recalled to
England, while Hood had gone to Boston to look after a
division of the beaten French fleet, which was there refitting. He was now on his return to the islands, where
the enemy was expected to make a vigorous aggressive
campaign the following spring. Extensive preparations
were in fact on foot for the reduction of Jamaica, frustrated six months before by De Grasse's mishap. Nelson
thus found himself again in tantalizing contact with the
stirring circumstance that preludes hostilities, in which he
himself had little hope to share; for the "Albemarle" belonged to the North American station, where all active
naval operations had ceased with the surrender of Cornwallis the year before. He went, therefore, to Hood, and
begged to be transferred to his squadron. In vain did
Admiral Digby, his own commander-in-chief, tell him that
he was on a good station for prize-money. "Yes," he replied, "but the West Indies is the station for honour."

Digby was reluctant to part with a frigate, as all admirals were; but Hood, either from an intuitive faculty for
judging men, or from his conversations with Nelson elicit-
ing the latter's singular knowledge of the higher part of
his profession, wished to push an officer of so much promise, and succeeded in obtaining the transfer of the "Albemarle" to his squadron. "I am a candidate with Lord
Hood for a line-of-battle ship," wrote Nelson to Locker;
"he has honoured me highly, by a letter, for wishing to
go off this station to a station of service, and has promised
me his friendship." A few months later he wrote again:
"My situation in Lord Hood's fleet must be in the highest
degree flattering to any young man. He treats me as if
I were his son, and will, I am convinced, give me anything
I can ask of him." This was really the beginning, the
outstart, of Nelson's great career; for Hood's interest in

him, then aroused, and deepened by experience to the
utmost confidence and appreciation, made itself felt the
instant the French Revolutionary War began. Nelson
then came at once under his orders, went with him to the
Mediterranean, and there speedily made his mark, being
transferred from admiral to admiral with ever-growing
tokens of reliance. Despite the lapse of time, and the long
interval of peace, it is no exaggeration to say that there is
a direct connection of cause and effect between his transfer to Hood's fleet, in the harbor of New York, and the
battle of Cape St. Vincent, in 1797, when he emerged from
merely professional distinction to national renown, standing head and shoulders above all competitors. In the four
days that followed his arrival in New York, Nelson took
the tide at the flood, and was borne on to fortune. Yet in
this, as in many other instant and happy decisions, we may
not see the mere casting of a die, the chance result of an
irreflective impulse. The determination to change into
Hood's squadron, with its powerful, far-reaching effect
upon his future, was in necessary logical sequence to Nelson's whole habit of thought, and wish, and previous preparation. He was swept into the current that carried him
on to fame by the irresistible tendency of his own conscious will and cherished purpose. Opportunity flitted by;
he was ready, and grasped it.

At this turning-point the commendable diligence of his
principal biographers has again secured for us a striking
description of the young captain's personal appearance,
and of the impression produced by his manner upon an
interested acquaintance, who afterwards became a warm
friend and admirer as well as a frequent correspondent.
The narrator — then Prince William Henry, afterwards
King William IV.— gave the following account, apparently
at some period between 1805, when Nelson fell, and 1809,
when the first edition of Clarke and M'Arthur's Life appeared. "I was then a midshipman on board the Bar-

fleur," Lord Hood's flagship, "lying in the Narrows off
Staten Island, and had the watch on deck, when Captain
Nelson, of the Albemarle, came in his barge alongside,
who appeared to be the merest boy of a captain I ever beheld; and his dress was worthy of attention. He had on
a full-laced uniform; his lank unpowdered hair was tied
in a stiff Hessian tail, of an extraordinary length; the
old-fashioned flaps of his waistcoat added to the general
quaintness of his figure, and produced an appearance which
particularly attracted my notice; for I had never seen anything like it before, nor could I imagine who he was, nor
what he came about. My doubts were, however, removed
when Lord Hood introduced me to him. There was something irresistibly pleasing in his address and conversation;
and an enthusiasm, when speaking on professional subjects,
that showed he was no common being." The Countess of
Minto, in her Life of Lord Minto, speaks of Nelson's
"shock head" at the time (1794) when he was a frequent
visitor at the house of Minto, then Sir Gilbert Elliott, and
Viceroy of Corsica; a trivial detail, but confirmatory, so
far, of the picture drawn by the prince. The latter continued: "Nelson, after this, went with us to the West
Indies, and served under Lord Hood's flag during his inde-
fatigable cruise off Cape François. . . . I found him warmly
attached to my father [King George III.], and singularly
humane. He had the honour of the King's service and the
independence of the British navy particularly at heart;
and his mind glowed with this idea as much when he was
simply captain of the Albemarle, and had obtained none
of the honours of his Country, as when he was afterwards
decorated with so much well-earned distinction."

The war of 1778 was now fast drawing to its close; the
preliminaries of peace being signed in January, 1783,
though not ratified till the following September. Hood
cruised off Cap François, a naval station of the French at
the west end of Haïti, to intercept the fleet from Boston,

which was understood to be on its way to the Caribbean; but the enemy, learning his whereabouts, went through the Mona Passage, east of the island, thus avoiding a meeting, and was next heard of by the British as being off Curaçoa, far to the southward. Nelson, therefore, had no opportunity to show his prowess in battle; and as only three letters remain covering this uneventful period, little is known of his movements, except that he made an abortive attempt to recapture Turk's Island from the French with a small force of ships he was able to gather at short notice. An interesting indication of the spirit which animated him transpires in the first of the three letters mentioned. He had received unexpected orders to wait in New York after Hood's leaving. "I was to have sailed with the fleet this day, but for some private reasons, when my ship was under sail from New York to join Lord Hood, at Sandy Hook, I was sent for on shore, and told I was to be kept forty-eight hours after the sailing of the fleet. It is much to my private advantage," allowing more latitude for picking up prizes, without having to share with the other ships, "but I had much rather have sailed with the fleet." "Money," he continues, "is the great object here," on the North American Station, "nothing else is attended to," — a motive of action which he always rejected with disdain, although by no means insensible to the value of money, nor ever thoroughly at his ease in the matter of income, owing largely to the lavish liberality with which he responded to the calls upon his generosity or benevolence. A year later he wrote in the same strain: "I have closed the war without a fortune; but I trust, and, from the attention that has been paid to me, believe, that there is not a speck in my character. True honour, I hope, predominates in my mind far above riches."

When news of the peace reached the West Indies, Hood was ordered to return with his fleet to England. Nelson went home at the same time, being directed first to accompany Prince William Henry in a visit to Havana. The "Albemarle" reached Spithead on the 25th of June, 1783, and was paid off a week later, her captain going on half-pay until the following April. The cruise of nearly two years' duration closed with this characteristic comment: "Not an officer has been changed, except the second lieu-tenant, since the Albemarle was commissioned; therefore, it is needless to say, I am happy in my ship's company." And again he writes: "My ship was paid off last week, and in such a manner that must flatter any officer, in par-ticular in these turbulent times. The whole ship's company offered, if I could get a ship, to enter for her immediately." Nelson was keenly alive to the impolicy and injury to the service involved in the frequent changes of officers and men from ship to ship. "The disgust of the seamen to the Navy," he wrote immediately after leaving the Albemarle, "is all owing to the infernal plan of turning them over from ship to ship, so that men cannot be attached to their offi-cers, or the officers care twopence about them." This element of personal attachment is never left out of calcu-lation safely.

Nelson was now nearly twenty-five. In direct achieve-ment he had accomplished little, and to most he was un-known; but he did not deceive himself in believing that his reputation was established, and his promise, as a capable man of action, understood by those who knew him, and especially by the brilliant admiral under whom he had last served. Within a week of his release from the ship Hood carried him to Court, and presented him to the King, — an evident proof of his approbation; and Nelson notes that the sovereign was exceedingly attentive. The next few months were spent in London, or at his old home in Norfolk, to which and to his family he was always fondly attached. Toward the end of October he obtained a leave of absence, in order to visit France and acquire the French language. His impressions of that country, as far as he went, — from Calais to St. Omer, — are given in lively enough style in a few letters; but they differ little from what might be expected from any very young man deeply tinged with insular prejudice. "I hate their country and their manners," he wrote, soon after his return; and his biographers were quite right in saying that he had been brought up in the old anti-Gallican school, with prejudices not to be eradicated by a flying visit. He duly records his disgust with two British naval captains, one of whom was afterwards among his most valued and valuable friends, for wearing epaulettes, at that time confined to the French service. "I hold them a little *cheap*," he said, "for putting on any part of a Frenchman's uniform."

It is more interesting to notice that his impressionable fancy was again taken by an attractive young Englishwoman, the daughter of a clergyman named Andrews, living at St. Omer. "Two very beautiful young ladies," he writes to Locker and to his brother; "I must take care of my heart, I assure you." "My heart is quite secured against the French beauties; I almost wish I could say as much for an English young lady, the daughter of a clergyman, with whom I am just going to dine, and spend the day. She has such accomplishments that, had I a million of money, I am sure I should at this moment make her an offer of them." "The most accomplished woman my eyes ever beheld," he repeats, a month later. The sentimental raptures of a young man about a handsome girl have in themselves too much of the commonplace to justify mention. What is remarkable, and suggests an explanation of the deplorable vagary of his later years, is that his attachment to his wife, even in the days of courtship, elicited no such extravagance of admiration as that into which he freely lapses in his earlier fancies, and yet more in his last absorbing passion. Respect and tenderness for her he certainly felt and expressed; but there is no indication that she ever enkindled his ardent imagination, or filled for him the place of an ideal, which his mental constitution imperatively demanded as an object of worship. The present attachment went so far with him that he wrote to his uncle William Suckling, asking for an allowance to enable him to marry. "If nothing can be done for me," said he, gloomily, "I know what I have to trust to. Life is not worth preserving without happiness; and I care not where I may linger out a miserable existence. I am prepared to hear your refusal, and have fixed my resolution if that should happen. . . . I pray you may never know the pangs which at this instant tear my heart." If, as is said by the gentlemen into whose hands this letter passed, Suckling consented to help him, as he certainly did at the time of his actual marriage, it seems probable that the lady refused him.

CHAPTER II.

1784–1793. AGE, 26–34.

WHATEVER the cause, Nelson's visit to France ended prematurely and abruptly. Early in January, 1784, after an absence of two months, he went back to England, announcing to his friends that his coming was only temporary, partly on business, partly for treatment; for his delicate health again occasioned him anxiety. "The frost, thank God, is broke," he wrote; "cold weather is death to me." But even while speaking confidently of his speedy return to the Continent, he dropped a hint that he was disposed to resume the active pursuit of his profession, although on leaving the "Albemarle," six months before, he had said that he could not afford to live afloat, in peace times, in the style then prevalent. "My stay in England will be but very short, without the First Lord in the Admiralty thinks proper to employ me. I shall offer my services." He did see Lord Howe, at that time First Lord, asking him for a ship; and he renewed his cordial relations with Hood, then living in London. On the 18th of March Howe appointed him to the command of the frigate "Boreas." Occupation in peace, with a reduced establishment, was not easy to get, and his brother, an inveterate wirepuller, must needs know to whose favor Nelson owed it. "You ask," replied the hero, "by what interest did I get a ship? I answer, having served with credit was my recommendation to Lord Howe. Anything in reason that I can ask, I am sure of obtaining from his justice." The statement was no more than fair to Howe; but in his knowledge of the merits of Nelson, whose claim lay rather in evident promise than in conspicuous performance, we can probably trace the friendly intervention of Lord Hood.

Nelson's wish was that the "Boreas" should go to the East Indies. To this he inclined, apparently, because the station was to be under the command of Commodore Cornwallis, in whose ship he had returned from Jamaica as an invalid in 1780, and to whom on that occasion he was indebted for the most friendly care. He was not long allowed to indulge this hope, for five days after receiving his appointment he wrote that the ship was bound to the Leeward Islands, and that he had been asked to take as passengers the wife and family of the commander-in-chief, Sir Richard Hughes, who had already gone out. In a small vessel, for such the "Boreas" was, the request, which he could not well refuse, gave Nelson cause of reasonable discontent, entailing crowding and a large outlay of money. "I shall be pretty well filled with *lumber*," he wrote; and later, on the voyage out, "I shall not be sorry to part with them, although they are very pleasant, good people; but they are an incredible expense." The incident, annoying though it was, was not without compensations. After arriving on the station, he soon became involved in a serious difference with Sir Richard Hughes; and the latter, though a weak man and in the wrong, might have acted more peremptorily, had he not laid himself under such obligations. On the other hand, Lady Hughes, many years later, shortly after Nelson's death, committed to writing some recollections of his personal traits and actions during the passage, so characteristic, even though trivial, that we could ill have spared them.

" I was too much affected when we met at Bath," wrote
she to Mr. Matcham, Nelson's brother-in-law, " to say every
particular in which was always displayed the infinite cleverness and goodness of heart of our dearly beloved Hero.   As
a woman, I can only be a judge of those things that I could
comprehend — such as his attention to the young gentlemen who had the happiness of being on his quarter-deck.
It may reasonably be supposed that among the number of
thirty, there must be timid as well as bold; the timid he
never rebuked, but always wished to show them he desired
nothing of them that he would not instantly do himself :
and I have known him say, ' Well, Sir, I am going a
race to the masthead, and beg I may meet you there.'
No denial could be given to such a wish, and the poor
fellow instantly began his march.   His Lordship never
took the least notice with what alacrity it was done, but
when he met in the top, instantly began speaking in the
most cheerful manner, and saying how much a person was
to be pitied that could fancy there was any danger, or
even anything disagreeable, in the attempt.   After this
excellent example, I have seen the timid youth lead another, and rehearse his captain's words.   In like manner,
he every day went into the school-room, and saw them do
their nautical business, and at twelve o'clock he was the
first upon deck with his quadrant.   No one there could be
behindhand in their business when their captain set them
so good an example.   One other circumstance I must
mention which will close the subject, which was the day
we landed at Barbadoes.   We were to dine at the Governor's.   Our dear captain said, ' You must permit me,
Lady Hughes, to carry one of my aid-de-camps with me; '
and when he presented him to the Governor, he said, ' Your
Excellency must excuse me for bringing one of my midshipmen, as I make it a rule to introduce them to all the good
company I can, as they have few to look up to besides
myself during the time they are at sea.'   This kindness

and attention made the young people adore him; and even
his wishes, could they have been known, would have been
instantly complied with."

The charm and wisdom of such a bearing is patent;
but it was the natural character of the man that thus shone
out, and no mere result of conscientious care. To the last,
through all his ill-health, anxiety, and sufferings, the same
genial sweetness of manner, the outcome of an unaffected,
cordial good-will to all, was shown to those who came in
contact with him. Captain Duff, who met him for the
first time three weeks before Trafalgar, and who fell in
the battle, wrote to his wife in almost the same words as
Lady Hughes: "You ask me about Lord Nelson, and
how I like him. I have already answered that question
as every person must do that ever served under him. He
is so good and pleasant a man, that we all wish to do what
he likes, without any kind of orders. I have been myself
very lucky with most of my admirals, but I really think
the present the pleasantest I have met with." There do,
it is true, occur in Nelson's letters occasional, though very
rare, expressions of that passing annoyance with individuals which is inseparable from the close and long-
continued contact of ship life. Thus, shortly before leaving the "Boreas," he writes: "I begin to be very strict in
my Ship. Whenever I may set off in another, I shall be
indifferent whether I ever speak to an Officer in her, but
upon duty." One wonders what passing and soon forgotten
breeze was responsible for this most un-Nelson-like outburst. But to the end it remained true that between the
officers and crews under Nelson's command and their
chief, there was always that cordial regard which can only
spring from the hearty sympathy of the commander with
those beneath him.

While thoughtful and considerate, even to gentleness,
for the weak and dependent, the singular energy that
quickened Nelson's frail and puny frame showed itself on

occasion in instant resentment of any official slight to himself or his ship, or injury to the interests of the country. During the " Boreas's " stay at Madeira, the British Consul neglected to return his visit, on the plea that the Government allowed him no boat. Nelson declined any further intercourse with him. While lying in the Downs, he learns that sixteen British seamen are detained by force on board a Dutch Indiaman. He requires their delivery to him ; and when their effects were withheld, on the alleged ground of their being in debt to the ship, he stops all intercourse between it and the shore, sending an armed cutter to enforce his order. " The Admiralty," he wrote, " have fortunately approved my conduct in the business," and added grimly, " a thing they are not very guilty of where there is a likelihood of a scrape." When entering the harbor of Fort Royal, Martinique, the principal French island in the Lesser Antilles, the officer at the citadel neglected to hoist the colors, a ceremonial observance customary when a ship of war approached. Nelson at once demanded an explanation and received ample amends ; the offending party being placed under arrest. To the governor of some of the British West India islands, he wrote making suggestions for the better discharge of certain duties, in which both of them were interested. He received, it is said, a testy message that " old generals were not in the habit of taking advice from young gentlemen." " I have the honour, Sir," replied Nelson, " of being as old as the prime minister of England, and think myself as capable of commanding one of his majesty's ships as that minister is of governing the state ; " and throughout he held to the stand he had taken.

The most remarkable instance, however, of this promptness to assert the dignity and rights of his official position, allowing no man to despise his youth, occurred very soon after his arrival upon the station, and brought him to a direct issue with his commander-in-chief, — if not, indeed,

with an authoritative precedent set by so great a man as
Lord Rodney. Young though he still was in years, — only
twenty-six, — Nelson was by date of commission the senior
captain in the small squadron, of some half-dozen vessels,
to which the economies of the administration had reduced
the Leeward Islands station. Being thus next in rank to
the admiral, the latter, who made his headquarters at Barbadoes in the southern part of the station, sent him to the
northern division, centring about the island of Antigua.
Having remained in harbor, as was usual, during the hurricane months, Nelson cruised during the winter and until
February, 1785, when some damage received compelled the
" Boreas " to put into Antigua for repairs. Here he found
a vessel of the squadron, whose own captain was of course
junior to him, flying a Commodore's broad pendant, which
asserted the official presence of a captain superior to himself in rank and command, and duly qualified to give him
orders. He at once asked the meaning of this from the
ship's proper commander, and was informed by him that
Captain Moutray, an old officer, twenty years his senior
on the post list, and then acting as Commissioner of the
Navy, a civil office connected with the dockyard at Antigua,
had directed it to be hoisted, and claimed to exercise control over all men-of-war in the harbor, during the admiral's
absence.

Nelson was not wholly unprepared for this, for Hughes
had notified him and the other captains that Moutray was
authorized by himself to take this step. Being then away
from the island, he had replied guardedly that if Commissioner Moutray *was put into commission,* he would have
great pleasure in serving under him, — thus reserving his
decision to the moment for action. He now took the
ground that an officer not commissioned afloat, but holding
only a civil appointment, could not exercise naval command, — that an order authorizing him to do so was invalid, — that to entitle him to such command he must be

put into military commission by being attached to a ship
in commission. He therefore flatly declined to obey
Moutray's orders, refusing to admit his claim to be considered a commodore, or entitled to military obedience,
unless he produced a commission. This he held to when
Moutray gave him a written order to put himself under his
command.

On technical points of this kind Nelson was a clear and
accurate thinker, and in the admiral he had to do with a
muddle-headed, irresolute superior. Hughes had already
been badly worried and prodded, on matters concerning
his own neglected duties, by his unquiet young subordinate, who was never satisfied to leave bad enough alone,
but kept raising knotty points to harass an easy-going old
gentleman, who wanted only to be allowed to shut his eyes
to what went on under his nose. He was now exasperated
by Nelson's contumacy, but he was also a little afraid of
him, and supported his own order by no more decisive action than laying the case before the Admiralty, who informed Nelson that he should have referred his doubts to
the admiral, instead of deciding for himself in a matter
that concerned " the exercise of the functions of his [the
admiral's] appointment." This was rather begging the
question, for Nelson expressed no doubts, either to Hughes
or in his explanatory letter to the Admiralty. The latter
in turn shirked thus the decision of the question, — for, if
Nelson was right, Hughes's order was illegal and not entitled to obedience; if he was wrong, he had been guilty
of flagrant insubordination, and should have been sharply
dealt with. The Government probably thought that the
admiral had blundered in undertaking to give military
authority to a civil official, — a step so generally disastrous
in experience that it is now explicitly forbidden by the
regulations of most navies. It is worthy of note that
twenty years later, when commander-in-chief in the Mediterranean, Nelson directed the captains of ships cruising

in the Straits of Gibraltar to consult on all occasions with the Commissioner of the Navy resident in Gibraltar, as well as to receive his advice, if proffered, — adding that the commissioner's opinion of their conduct would have great weight with himself; but he did not put them under his orders.[1]

Reasoning from Nelson's position, as the pendant was flying without proper authority on board a ship under his immediate command, he should, as senior captain afloat, have gone further and hauled it down. Of his authority to do so he felt no doubt, as is evident from his letter to the Admiralty; but his motive for refraining was characteristic. He was unwilling to wound Moutray; just as, before Trafalgar, in direct disregard of the Admiralty's orders, he allowed an admiral going home under charges to take with him his flagship, a vessel of the first force and likely to be sorely needed in the approaching battle, because he was reluctant to add to the distress the officer was undergoing already. "I did not choose to order the Commissioner's pendant to be struck, as Mr. Moutray is an old officer of high military character; and it might hurt his feelings to be supposed wrong by so young an officer." The question solved itself shortly by the Commissioner's returning to England; but the controversy seems to have made no change in the friendly and even affectionate relations existing between him and his wife and Nelson. For Mrs. Moutray the latter had formed one of those strong idealizing attachments which sprang up from time to time along his path. "You may be certain," he writes to his brother at the very period the discussion was pending, "I never passed English Harbour without a call, but alas! I am not to have much comfort. My dear, sweet friend is going home. I am really an April day; happy on her account, but truly grieved were I only to consider myself. Her equal I never saw in any country or in any situation.

[1] Nicolas, vol. v. p. 356.

If my dear Kate [his sister] goes to Bath next winter she
will be known to her, for my dear friend promised to make
herself known.   What an acquisition to any female to be
acquainted with, what an example to take pattern from."
" My sweet, amiable friend sails the 20th for England.   I
took my leave of her three days ago with a heavy heart.
What a treasure of a woman."   Returning to Antigua a
few weeks later, he writes again in a sentimental vein very
rare in him : " This country appears now intolerable, my
dear friend being absent.   It is barren indeed.   English
Harbour I hate the sight of, and Windsor I detest.   I went
once up the hill to look at the spot where I spent more
happy days than in any one spot in the world.   E'en the
trees drooped their heads, and the tamarind tree died : — all
was melancholy : the road is covered with thistles ; let them
grow.   I shall never pull one of them up."   His regard
for this attractive woman seems to have lasted through his
life ; for she survived him, and to her Collingwood addressed a letter after Trafalgar, giving some particulars of
Nelson's death.   Her only son also died under the latter's
immediate command, ten years later, when serving in
Corsica.

The chief interest of the dispute over Moutray's position lies not in the somewhat obscure point involved, but
in the illustration it affords of Nelson's singular independence and tenacity in a matter of principle.   Under a conviction of right he throughout life feared no responsibility
and shrank from no consequences.   It is difficult for the
non-military mind to realize how great is the moral effort
of disobeying a superior, whose order on the one hand
covers all responsibility, and on the other entails the most
serious personal and professional injury, if violated without due cause ; the burden of proving which rests upon
the junior.   For the latter it is, justly and necessarily, not
enough that his own intentions or convictions were honest :
he has to show, not that he meant to do right, but that

he actually did right, in disobeying in the particular instance. Under no less rigorous exactions can due military subordination be maintained. The whole bent of advantage and lifelong training, therefore, draws in one direction, and is withstood by nothing, unless either strong personal character supplies a motive, or established professional standing permits a man to presume upon it, and to exercise a certain right to independence of action. At this time Nelson was practically unknown, and in refusing compliance with an order he took a risk that no other captain on the station would have assumed, as was shown by their failure a few months later to support their convictions in an analogous controversy, upon which Nelson had entered even before the Moutray business. In both cases he staked all upon legal points, considered by him vital to the welfare of the navy and the country. The spirit was identically the same that led him to swing his ship out of the line at Cape St. Vincent without waiting for signals. After that day and the Nile he could afford to take liberties, and sometimes took them with less justification than in his early career.

When the Moutray question arose, Nelson was already engaged in a more far-reaching dispute, not only with his commander-in-chief, but with the colonial authorities and the popular sentiment of the West India Islands. Like most men, great and small, he shared the prepossessions of his day and generation; differing, however, from others, in that he held his opinions as principles, from asserting which he was not to be deterred by the ill-will or dislike of those immediately about him. Upon arriving in the West Indies he found flourishing a system of trade extremely beneficial to the islands, but which his education condemned as hurtful to Great Britain, as it certainly was contrary to then existing laws that had for a century previous regulated the commerce of the kingdom. In 1784, a year only had elapsed since the United States had been

formally recognized as independent, thereby becoming, in
British estimation as well as in their own, a nation foreign
to the British flag.   By the Navigation Laws, first established by Cromwell, but continued under the restored
monarchy without serious modification until 1794, trade
with the Colonies was reserved to vessels built in Great
Britain or her dependencies, and manned in three-fourths
part by British subjects.   The chief object and advantage
of the law were conceived to be, not merely a monopoly of
the trade, — concerning the economical wisdom of which
serious doubts began to be felt, — but the fostering of the
British merchant service as a nursery of seamen, upon
whom, in time of war, the navy could draw.   The military strength of the Empire was thought to be involved in
the enforcement of the Navigation Act.[1]

Before the United States declared their independence,
they, as British colonies, enjoyed the privilege of trading
with their fellow-colonists under what was then the common flag; and the nearness of the two regions contributed
to the advantage of both in this traffic, in which the continental communities were the chief suppliers of many articles essential to the islands, notably provisions and lumber.
This mutual intercourse and dependence promoted a sympathy which was scarcely disguised in the West Indies
during the War of Independence; indeed, Nelson wrote
that many of the inhabitants were as arrant rebels as those
who had renounced their allegiance.   Under these conditions, when peace was restored, the old relations were
readily resumed; and as there had really been considerable
inconvenience and loss to the islanders from the depriva-
tion of American products, the renewal was eagerly promoted by popular sentiment.   The local authorities, as

---

[1] Thus Collingwood, rarely other than sober and restrained in his language, wrote to Hughes: " It is from the idea that the greatness and superiority of the British navy very much depends upon preserving inviolate the
Act of Navigation, excluding foreigners from access to the colonies, that I
am induced to make this representation to you."   Nicolas, vol. i. p. 172

usual and natural, yielded to the pressure around them, and in entire disregard of the known policy of the home government permitted American vessels to trade openly under their own colors. In Jamaica the governor had even gone so far as to authorize formally a free trade, during pleasure, with the United States, contrary to the explicit orders of his superiors in Great Britain. Where scruples were felt or hesitation was shown, advantage was taken of the exceptions of the law, which allowed vessels in distress to sell so much of their cargoes as would pay for necessary repairs. With the tendency of commerce to evade restrictions by liberal stretching of the conscience, the merchant-captain and the colonial officer found little difficulty in arranging that the damage should be great enough to cover the sale of the whole lading.

After laying up in Antigua during the hurricane season of 1784, Nelson was summoned to Barbadoes in November, with the other captains, to receive orders for the winter's cruising. These, when issued, were found to direct only the examination of anchorages, and the gathering of information about supplies of wood and water. Nelson's attention had been drawn already to the American traffic; and he, with his friend Collingwood, who was again on the station, went to the admiral, and urged that it was the duty of ships of war to enforce the Navigation Laws. The admiral professed ignorance of these; and Nelson himself remarks that British vessels up to that time had been so much cheaper built than others, that they had, without artificial protection, naturally absorbed their own colonial trade, — the question, therefore, had dropped out of sight till it was revived by American competition. A copy of the Act being then produced, Hughes gave an order requiring his vessels to enforce it; making special mention of the changed relations of the United States to Great Britain, whereby they were "to be considered as foreigners, and excluded from all commerce with the islands in these seas."

With these instructions Nelson sailed again for the north, where the Virgin Islands, with those of Montserrat, Nevis, and St. Christopher, were put under his especial charge, — the sloop " Rattler," Captain Wilfred Collingwood, a brother of the well-known admiral, being associated with the " Boreas." At first the two officers confined their action to warning off American vessels, and at times forcing them to leave ports where they had anchored; but they found that either the vessels returned during the absence of the ships of war, or that permissions to land, upon what they thought trivial grounds, were given by the Customs' officials, in virtue of the exceptions to the law above mentioned.

There matters stood until the 11th of January, 1785, Nelson acting by the authority of the commander-in-chief, but exercising his own discretion, and with forbearance, in carrying out his instructions. On the day named he received another order from the admiral, modifying the first upon the grounds of a more mature consideration, and of " the opinion of the King's Attorney-General " in the islands. Nelson was now directed, in case of a foreign merchant-ship coming within the limits of his station, to cause her to anchor near his own vessel and to report her arrival, and situation in all respects, to the governor of the colony where he then was ; " and if, after such report shall have been made and received, the governor or his representative shall think proper to admit the said foreigner into the port or harbour of the island where you may be, *you are on no account to hinder or prevent such foreign vessel from going in accordingly, or to interfere any further in her subsequent proceedings."*

Here the admiral not only raised, but also decided, the point as to whether the enforcement of the Navigation Act rested with naval officers, or was vested only in the

civil authorities of the islands. Nelson was convinced
that an essential part of the duty of ships of war, and
especially when peace took from them so much of their
military function, was to afford to the commerce of the
nation proper protection, of which a necessary feature,
according to the ideas of the age, was the interdiction of
foreign traders. A seaman, he plausibly argued, could decide better than an unprofessional man the questions of
injuries and distress upon which the unlawful traffic largely
hinged. "In judging of their distress, no person can
know better than the sea officers," he wrote to Hughes.
"The governors may be imposed upon by false declara-
tions; we, who are on the spot, cannot." He was aware,
also, that a petition for relaxing the Act in favor of the
American trade with the West Indies had been referred to
the home government, by which it had been explicitly rejected. Strengthened by this knowledge, but actuated,
after all, chiefly by his invariable resoluteness to assume
responsibility where he felt he was right, he replied to the
admiral's letter with a clear statement of the facts, concluding with the words: "Whilst I have the honour to
command an English man-of-war, I never shall allow myself to be subservient to the will of any Governor, nor
coöperate with him in doing *illegal acts.* . . . If I rightly
understand your order of the 29th of December, it is
founded upon an Opinion of the King's Attorney-General, viz.: 'That it is legal for Governors or their representatives to admit foreigners into the ports of their
government, if they think fit.' How the King's Attorney-
General conceives he has a right to give an illegal opinion,
which I assert the above is, he must answer for. I know
the Navigation Laws." As he summed up the matter in a
letter to his friend Locker: "Sir Richard Hughes was a
delicate business. I must either disobey my orders, or
disobey Acts of Parliament, which the admiral was disobeying. I determined upon the former, trusting to the

uprightness of my intention. In short, I wrote the Admiral that I should decline obeying his orders, till I had an opportunity of seeing and talking to him, at the same time making him an apology."

Hughes's first impulse was to supersede his recalcitrant subordinate, and bring him to trial. He learned, however, that many of the other captains, of whom the court must be formed, shared his junior's views, although they shrank, with the submissiveness of military men, from the decisive act of disobedience. The result of a trial must therefore be doubtful. He was, moreover, a fiddler, as Nelson continually styled him, shifting back and forth, from opinion to opinion, and to be relied upon for only one thing, — to dodge responsibility, if possible. Consequently, no official action was taken; the commander-in-chief contented himself with washing his hands of all accountability. He had given orders which would clear himself, in case Nelson's conduct was censured in England. If, on the contrary, it was approved, it would redound to the credit of the station.

The matter was soon brought to a test. The governors and all the officials, particularly of the Custom House, resented the action of the naval officers; but the vigilance of the latter so seriously interrupted the forbidden traffic under American colors, that recourse was had to giving British registers to the vessels concerned, allowing them to trade under British flags. This, however, was equally contrary to the Navigation Act, which forbade British registry to foreign-built ships, except when prizes taken in war; and the disguise was too thin to baffle men like Collingwood and Nelson. The latter reported the practice to the home Government, in order that any measures deemed necessary might be taken. Meanwhile he patiently persisted in turning away all vessels, not British built, which he encountered, confining himself for the time to this merely passive prevention; but finding at last that this was not a sufficient deterrent, he gave notice that after the 1st of May, 1785, he would seize all American vessels trading to the islands, " let them be registered by whom they might." Accordingly, on the 2d of May he arrested an American-built schooner, owned in Philadelphia and manned entirely by Americans, but having a British register issued at the island of St. Christopher.

The Crown lawyer was now called upon to prosecute the suit. He expressed grave doubts as to a naval captain's power to act by virtue simply of his commission, the sole authority alleged by the captor; and, although he proceeded with the case, his manner so betrayed his uncertainty that Nelson felt it necessary to plead for himself. To the confusion of all opponents the judge decided in his favor, saying he had an undoubted right to seize vessels transgressing the Navigation Laws. The principle thus established, Nelson on the 23d of the same month, at the island of Nevis, upon the same grounds, seized four vessels, — one of which had been registered at Dominica by Governor Orde, a naval captain senior in rank to himself, and with whom he came into unpleasant contact upon several occasions in his later life.

There was no serious question as to the condemnation of the four last seizures, the facts being clear and the principle settled;[1] but the rage of the inhabitants of Nevis led them to seek revenge upon Nelson for the injury they could no longer prevent. He had summoned the masters of the ships on board the " Boreas," and, after satisfying himself that the vessels were not entitled to British regis-

---

[1] Nelson's letters are contradictory on this point. In a letter to Locker of March 3, 1786, he says, " Before the first vessel was tried I had seized four others ; " whereas in the formal and detailed narrative drawn up — without date, but later than the letter to Locker — he says the first vessel was tried and condemned May 17, the other four seized May 23. (Nicolas, vol. i. pp. 177, 178.) The author has followed the latter, because from the particularity of dates it seems to have been compiled from memoranda, that of Locker written from memory, — both nearly a year after the events.

ters, had sent marines to hold them, and to prevent essential witnesses from leaving them, until the cases were tried. Upon these circumstances was based an accusation of assault and imprisonment, the masters swearing that they had made their statements under bodily fear. Writs were issued against Nelson, damages being laid at four thousand pounds, a sum which to him meant ruin. Although he asserted that there was absolutely no truth in the charges, which are certainly in entire contradiction to the general, if not invariable, tenor of his life and conduct, he was advised by the Crown lawyers not to subject himself to trial, as in the state of public feeling he could not expect a fair verdict. To avoid arrest, he was forced to confine himself to the ship for seven weeks, during which the marshal made several attempts to serve the writ, but without success. On the day that the case of the seized ships came up, he was able to be present in court only by the safe conduct of the judge.

Two days after the seizure of the four vessels, Sir Richard Hughes, who was making a tour of the station under his command, arrived at Nevis; but he had no support to give his zealous lieutenant. " He did not appear to be pleased with my conduct," wrote Nelson to Locker. " At least he did not approve it, but told me I should get into a scrape. Seven weeks I was kept a close prisoner to my ship; nor did I ever learn that the admiral took any steps for my release. He did not even acquaint the Admiralty Board how cruelly I had been treated; nor of the attempts which had been made to take me out of my ship by force, and that indignity offered under the fly of his flag." " I had the governor, the Customs, all the planters upon me; subscriptions were soon filled to prosecute; and my admiral stood neuter, although his flag was then in the roads." To this lack of countenance on the part of his superior, and direct persecution by those injuriously affected by his action, there was added a general social ostracism, to which he frequently alludes, and which was particularly emphasized by its contrast with the habits of hospitality prevalent among the small and wealthy planter community. One friend, however, stood by him, and offered to become his bail in the sum of ten thousand pounds, — Mr. Herbert, the President of Nevis, and one of the wealthiest men in the island. He had, Nelson said, suffered more than any one else from the interruption of the trade, but he considered that the young captain had done only his duty. Possibly there may have been a warmer feeling underlying this esteem, for he was the uncle of the lady whom Nelson afterwards married, and to whom he seems to have been paying attention already.

Despite his indomitable pluck and resolve, the confinement, uncertainty, and contention told heavily on Nelson's health and spirits. His temper was too kindly and social not to feel the general alienation. It could not affect his purpose; but the sense of right-doing, which sustained him in that, did not make his road otherwise easier. It is, indeed, especially to be noticed that there was not in him that hard, unyielding fibre, upon which care, or neglect, or anxiety, makes little impression. He was, on the contrary, extremely sympathetic, even emotional; and although insensible to bodily fear, he was by no means so to censure, or to risk of other misfortune. To this susceptibility to worry, strong witness is borne by an expression of his, used at the very time of which we are now writing. One of his friends — Captain Pole of the Navy — had detained and sent in a neutral vessel for breach of belligerent rights. After long legal proceedings, extending over five years, she was condemned, and proved to be a very valuable prize to the captors. "Our friend Charles Pole," he writes, "has been fortunate in his trial; but the lottery is so very much against an officer, that never will I knowingly involve myself in a doubtful cause. Prize-money is doubtless very acceptable; but my mind would have suffered so much, that no pecuniary compensation, at so late a period, would have made me amends." Contrasting this utterance with the resolution shown by him at this time, in fighting what he considered the cause of his country in the West Indies, it can be seen how much stronger with him was the influence of duty than that exercised by any considerations of merely material advantage. In the one he could find support; in the other not. But in neither case was he insensible to care, nor could he escape the physical consequences of anxiety upon a delicate frame and nervous organization. Of this, his harassment in the pursuit of the French fleet in 1798, during Bonaparte's Egyptian expedition, gave a very conspicuous illustration.

With such a temperament, being now very much in the position of an individual fighting a corporation, he appealed to the home Government; addressing, on the 29th of June, 1785, a memorial to the King, setting forth the facts of the case, as already given, adding that his health was much impaired, and asking for assistance. He received a reply to this in the following September, informing him that the King had directed that he should be defended by the Crown lawyers. This implied approval of his course was succeeded, in November, by a letter from the Secretary of the Treasury, through the usual official channels of the Admiralty, acquainting him that the Government was "of opinion that the commander-in-chief of the Leeward Islands, and officers under him, have shown a very commendable zeal, in endeavouring to put a stop to the very illicit practices which were carrying on in the islands, in open violation of the law, and to the great detriment of the navigation and trade of his Majesty's dominions." Verily, Hughes had his reward. Here he was commended in express terms for doing that which he had been too prudent to do, for zeal which he had never shown, for maintaining a law which he had given orders not to maintain. "I own I was surprised," wrote Nelson, "that the commander-in-chief should be thanked for an act which he did not order, but which, if I understand the meaning of words, by his order of the 29th December, 1784, he ordered not to be." "To the end of the station,[1] his order of the 29th of December was never repealed, so that I always acted with a rod over me." How heavily the responsibility he assumed was felt by others, is clearly shown in another statement made by him. "The Captains Collingwood were the only officers, with myself, who ever attempted to hinder the illicit trade with America; *and I stood singly with respect to seizing*, for the other officers were fearful of being brought into scrapes."

Backed by the royal approval, and with his legal expenses guaranteed, Nelson's course was now smooth. He continued in all parts of the station to suppress the contraband trade, and his unpopularity, of course, also continued; but excitement necessarily subsided as it became clear that submission was unavoidable, and as men adapted themselves to the new conditions. The whole procedure now looks somewhat barbarous and blundering, but in no essential principle differs from the methods of protection to which the world at present seems again tending. It is not for us to throw stones at it. The results, then, were completely successful, judged by the standards of the time. "At this moment," wrote Nelson some few months later, "there are nearly fifty sail employed in the trade between the Islands of St. Kitts, Nevis, and America, which are truly British built, owned, and navigated. Had I been an idle spectator, my firm belief is that not a single vessel would have belonged to those islands in the foreign trade." His own action was further endorsed by the ministry, which now gave captains of ships-of-war much more extensive

---

[1] This word is used by Nelson, apparently, as equivalent to "season."—the cruising period in the West Indies. "The admiral wishes to remain another station," he writes elsewhere.

powers, thereby justifying his contention that it was within their office to enforce the Navigation Act. Nor was this increased activity of the executive branch of the government the only result of Nelson's persistence. His sagacious study of the whole question, under the local conditions of the West Indies, led to his making several suggestions for more surely carrying out the spirit of the Law; and these were embodied the next year in a formal Act of the Legislature.

With so vivid a career as that of Nelson ahead, the delay imposed by this wrangling episode is somewhat dreary; but it undeniably shows his characteristics in the strongest light. Duty, not ease; honor, not gain; the ideal, not the material, — such, not indeed without frailty and blemish, were ever his motives. And, while he craved his reward in the approval and recognition of those around and above him, he could find consolation for the lack of them in his own sense of right-doing. "That thing called Honour," he writes to a friend soon after the "Boreas" cruise, "is now, alas! thought of no more. My integrity cannot be mended, I hope; but my fortune, God knows, has grown worse for the service; so much for serving my country. But I have invariably laid down, and followed close, a plan of what ought to be uppermost in the breast of an officer: that it is much better to serve an ungrateful Country than to give up his own fame. Posterity will do him justice; a uniform conduct of honour and integrity seldom fails of bringing a man to the goal of fame at last."

This struggle with Sir Richard Hughes, in which Nelson took the undesirable, and to a naval officer invidious, step of disobeying orders, showed clearly, not only the loftiness of his motives, but the distinguishing features which constituted the strength of his character, both personal and military. There was an acute perception of the right thing to do, an entire readiness to assume all the responsibility of doing it, and above all an accurate judgment of the best way to do it, — to act with impunity to himself and with most chances of success to his cause. Its analogy to a military situation is striking. There was a wrong condition of things to be righted — a victory to be won. To achieve this a great risk must be taken, and he was willing to take it; but in so doing he made such choice of his ground as to be practically unassailable — to attain his end without lasting harm to himself. That Nelson would have managed better had he been ten years older is very probable. Likely enough he betrayed some of the carelessness of sensibilities which the inexperience of youth is too apt to show towards age; but, upon a careful review of the whole, it appears to the writer that his general course of action was distinctly right, judged by the standards of the time and the well-settled principles of military obedience, and that he pursued an extremely difficult line of conduct with singular resolution, with sound judgment, and, in the main, with an unusual amount of tact, without which he could scarcely have failed, however well purposing, to lay himself open to serious consequences. Certainly he achieved success.

It was in the midst of this legal warfare, and of the preoccupations arising from it, that Nelson first met the lady who became his wife. She was by birth a Miss Frances Woolward, her mother being a sister of the Mr. Herbert already mentioned as President of the Council in Nevis. She was born in the first half of 1758,[1] and was therefore a few months older than Nelson. In 1779 she had married Dr. Josiah Nisbet, of Nevis, and the next year was left a widow with one son, who bore his father's full name. After her husband's death, being apparently

---

[1] Lady Nelson's tombstone in Littleham Churchyard, Exmouth, reads that she died May 6, 1831, "aged 73." She would then have been born before May 6, 1758. Nicolas (vol. i. p. 217) says that she died May 4, 1831, aged 68, but does not mention his authority.

portionless, she came to live with Herbert, who looked upon and treated her as his own child, although he also had an only daughter. When Nelson first arrived at Nevis, in January, 1785,[1] she was absent, visiting friends in a neighboring island, so that they did not then meet, — a circumstance somewhat fortunate for us, because it led to a description of him being sent to her in a letter from a lady of Herbert's family, not improbably her cousin, Miss Herbert. Nelson had then become a somewhat conspicuous factor in the contracted interests of the island society, owing to the stand he had already publicly assumed with reference to the contraband trade. People were talking about him, although he had not as yet enforced the extreme measures which made him so unpopular. "We have at last," so ran the letter, "seen the little captain of the Boreas of whom so much has been said. He came up just before dinner, much heated, and was very silent; but seemed, according to the old adage, to think the more. He declined drinking any wine; but after dinner, when the president, as usual, gave the three following toasts, ' the King,' ' the Queen and Royal Family,' and ' Lord Hood,' this strange man regularly filled his glass, and observed that those were always bumper toasts with him; which, having drank, he uniformly passed the bottle, and relapsed into his former taciturnity. It was impossible, during this visit, for any of us to make out his real character; there was such a reserve and sternness in his behaviour, with occasional sallies, though very transient, of a superior mind. Being placed by him, I endeavoured to rouse his attention by showing him all the civilities in my power; but I drew out little more than ' Yes ' and ' No.' If you, Fanny, had been there, we think you would have made something of him, for you

---

[1] Prior to May, 1785, the only stops of the "Boreas" at Nevis were January 6-8, February 1-4, and March 11-15. (Boreas's Log in Nicolas's Letters and Despatches of Lord Nelson, vol. vii. Addenda, pp. viii, ix.)

have been in the habit of attending to these odd sort of people."

Mrs. Nisbet very quickly made something of him. Little direct description has been transmitted to us concerning the looks or characteristics of the woman who now, at the time when marriage was possible to him, had the misfortune to appear in the line of succession of Nelson's early fancies, and to attract the too easily aroused admiration and affection of a man whose attachment she had not the inborn power to bind. That Nelson was naturally inconstant, beyond the volatility inherent in youth, is sufficiently disproved by the strength and endurance of his devotion to the one woman, in whom he either found or imagined the qualities that appealed to the heroic side of his character. How completely she mastered all the approaches to his heart, and retained her supremacy, once established, to the end, is evidenced by the whole tenor of his correspondence with her, by his mention of her in letters to others, by the recorded expressions he used in speaking to or about her. Despite all that he certainly knew of her, and much more that it is unreasonable to doubt he must have known of her history, there is no mistaking the profound emotions she stirred in his spirit, which show themselves continually in spontaneous outbreaks of passionate fondness and extravagant admiration, whose ring is too true and strong for doubt concerning their reality to find a place.

Many men are swayed by strong and wayward impulses; but to most the fetters imposed by social conventions, by inherited or implanted standards of seemliness and decorum, suffice to steady them in the path of outward propriety. Of how great and absorbing a passion Lord Nelson was capable is shown by the immensity of the sacrifice that he made to it. Principle apart, — and principle wholly failed him, — all else that most appeals to man's self-respect and regard for the esteem of others was powerless to exert

control. Loyalty to friendship, the sanctity which man is
naturally fain to see in the woman he loves, and, in
Nelson's own case, a peculiar reluctance to wound another,
— all these were trampled under foot, and ruthlessly piled
on the holocaust which he offered to her whom he wor-
shipped. He could fling to the winds, as others cannot,
considerations of interest or expediency, as he flung them
over and over in his professional career. My motto, he
said once and again, is "All or nothing." The same
disregard of consequences that hazarded all for all, in
battle or for duty, broke through the barriers within which
prudence, reputation, decency, or even weakness and cowardice, confine the actions of lesser men. And it must be
remembered that the admitted great stain upon Nelson's
fame, which it would be wicked to deny, lies not in a
general looseness of life, but in the notoriety of one relation, — a notoriety due chiefly to the reckless singleness of
heart which was not ashamed to own its love, but rather
gloried in the public exhibition of a faith in the worthi-
ness of its object, and a constancy, which never wavered
to the hour of his death.[1] The pitifulness of it is to see
the incongruity between such faith, such devotion, and
the distasteful inadequacy of their object.

To answer the demands of a nature capable of such
energetic manifestation — to fulfil the imagination of one
who could so cast himself at the feet of an ideal — was
beyond the gentle, ·well-ordered, and somewhat prosaic
charms with which alone Mrs. Nisbet was invested by
Nelson, even when most loverlike in tone. "My greatest
wish," he writes in the first of his letters to her that has
been preserved, "is to be united to you; and the founda-

---

[1] The author is satisfied, from casual expressions in Nelson's letters to
Lady Hamilton, that his famous two years' confinement to the ship, 1803–
1805, and, to a less extent, the similar seclusion practised in the Baltic and
the Downs, proceeded, in large part at least, from a romantic and chivalrous
resolve to leave no room for doubt, in the mind of Lady Hamilton or of the
world, that he was entirely faithful to her.

tion of all conjugal happiness, real love and esteem, is, I trust, what you believe I possess in the strongest degree toward you." Fifteen months later, and but a short time before their wedding, he says again: " His Royal Highness often tells me, he believes I am married; for he never saw a lover so easy, or say so little of the object he has a regard for. When I tell him I certainly am not, he says, ' Then he is sure I must have a great esteem for you, and that it is not what is (vulgarly), I do not much like the use of that word, called love.' He is right: my love is founded on esteem, the only foundation that can make the passion last." But general maxims, even when less disputable than this, do not admit of universal application; and if an affection was to hold its own in a nature enthusiastic and imaginative as that of Nelson, it had need to strike root deeper than that surface soil indicated by mere esteem, at least when the latter rests simply upon an assemblage of upright and amiable qualities, and not upon that force of character which compels dependence as well as appreciation. At their last parting he solemnly avowed that his esteem was not lessened; while he was destined also to afford a conspicuous illustration of how enduring a passion may flourish where no just title to esteem exists.

The progress of his wooing was rapid enough. On the 12th of May he mentions their first meeting; on the 28th of June he writes to his brother: " *Entre nous.* — Do not be surprised to hear I am a *Benedict*, for if at all, it will be before a month. Do not tell." On the 11th of September is dated his first letter to her, already quoted, in which he addresses her as " My dear Fanny," and alludes to the understanding existing between them. At the expiration of six months he wrote, formally announcing his engagement, to Mr. William Suckling, his mother's brother. He anticipates the latter's doubts as to the permanence of this fancy: " This Horatio, you will say, is for ever in love;" but he considers that six months without

change settles that question. "My present attachment is
of pretty long standing; but I was determined to be fixed
before I broke this matter to any person." He then
explains the situation, — that the lady herself has little or
nothing; that Mr. Herbert, though rich, is not likely to
help the young couple much, and he asks his uncle's
assistance. This Suckling consented to give, and for
several years continued liberally to extend. But still,
impatient though Nelson always was to complete whatever
he had on hand, various causes delayed the wedding for
another year. Even with Suckling's help the question of
means was pressing; and while, with pardonable self-
justification, he gloried to his betrothed that "the world is
convinced that I am superior to pecuniary considerations
in my public and private life, as in both instances I might
have been rich," he nevertheless owned to regretting that
he "had not given greater attention to making money."
Besides, as he wrote to his brother, "What should I do
carrying a wife in a ship, and when I marry I do not mean
to part with my wife." The cruising duty of the "Boreas"
took her from port to port of the limited area embraced in
the Leeward Islands Station, and Nevis was among the
least important of the points demanding his attention. He
was, therefore, frequently away from his betrothed during
this period, and absence rather fanned than cooled the
impetuous ardor which he carried into all his undertakings. Whether it were the pursuit of a love affair, or the
chase of an enemy's fleet, delays served only to increase
the vehemence with which Nelson chafed against difficulties. "Duty," he tells Mrs. Nisbet, "is the great business
of a sea officer, — all private considerations must give way
to it, however painful it is;" but he owns he wishes "the
American vessels at the Devil, and the whole continent
of America to boot," because they detain him from her
side.

There is no singularity in the experience that obstacles

tend rather to inflame than to check a lover's eagerness. What is noteworthy in Nelson's letters at this time is the utter absence of any illusions, of any tendency to exaggerate and glorify the qualities of the woman who for the nonce possessed his heart. There is not a sign of the perturbation of feeling, of the stirring of the soul, that was afterwards so painfully elicited by another influence. "The dear object," he writes to his brother, "you must like. Her sense, polite manners, and, to you I may say, beauty, you will much admire. She possesses sense far superior to half the people of our acquaintance, and her manners are Mrs. Moutray's." The same calm, measured tone pervades all his mention of her to others. His letters to herself, on the other hand, are often pleasing in the quiet, simple, and generally unaffected tenderness which inspires them. In a more ordinary man, destined to more commonplace fortunes, they might well be regarded as promising that enduring wedded love which strikes root downward and bears fruit upward, steadily growing in depth and devotion as the years roll by. But Nelson was not an ordinary man, and from that more humble happiness a childless marriage further debarred him. He could rise far higher, and, alas! descend far lower as he followed the radiant vision, — the image of his own mind rather than an external reality, — the ideal, which, whether in fame or in love, beckoned him onward. The calm, even, and wholly matter-of-fact appreciation of his wife's estimable traits can now be seen in the light of his after career, and its doubtful augury descried; for to idealize was an essential attribute of his temperament. Her failure, even in the heyday of courtship, to arouse in him any extravagance of emotion, any illusive exaltation of her merits, left vacant that throne in his mind which could be permanently occupied only by a highly wrought excellence, — even though that were the purely subjective creation of his own enthusiasm. This hold Lady Nelson never gained; and the long absence from 1793 to 1797, during the opening period of the war of the French Revolution, probably did to death an affection which owed what languid life it retained chiefly to propinquity and custom. Both Saumarez and Codrington, who served under him, speak passingly of the lightness with which his family ties sat upon Nelson in the years following his short stay at home in 1797. The house was empty, swept, and garnished, when the simple-minded, if lion-hearted, seaman came under the spell of one whose fascinations had overpowered the resistance of a cool-headed man of the world, leading him in his old age, with open eyes, to do what every prepossession and every reasonable conviction of his life condemned as folly.

In the summer of 1786 Sir Richard Hughes was recalled to England. During the later part of his association with Nelson, the strain which had characterized their earlier relations had not only disappeared, but had been succeeded by feelings approaching cordiality. The Government's approval of his subordinate's action, and of himself as credited with supporting it, had removed that element of apprehension which in timid men induces irritation; and Hughes, who, though irresolute, was naturally kindly, had been still farther placated by the prize-money falling to him from the vessels condemned through the zeal of Nelson. The latter, who never harbored malice, easily forgave the past, and responded to this change of tone. "I have been upon the best terms with the Admiral," he wrote from Barbadoes to his intended wife in April, 1786, "and I declare I think I could ever remain so. He is always remarkably kind and civil to every one;" and again, a few days earlier, "The admiral is highly pleased with my conduct here, as you will believe, by sending me such fine lines with a white hat. I well know I am not of abilities to deserve what he has said of me: but I take it as they are meant, to show his regard for me; and his politeness and attention to me are great: nor shall I forget it. I like the man, although not all his acts." He then directs that the lines shall not be shown to any one, "as the compliment is paid to me at the expense of the officers of the squadron," an injunction thoroughly characteristic of the man's kindly consideration for others. It was creditable to Hughes that, after being so braved, and his instructions set at naught, by his junior, he had candor enough to see and acknowledge his merit; but the fact still remained that in the hour of trial he had failed Nelson, nor did the latter, though he forgave, forget it. As he wrote to Locker in September, 1786, after the admiral's departure, "Instead of being supported by my admiral, I was obliged to keep him up, for he was frightened at this business;" of which business he truly said, emphasizing, but not at all exaggerating, the gravity of the responsibility he had taken in defiance of his superior: "After loss of health and risk of fortune, another is thanked for what I did against his orders. *Either I deserved to be sent out of the service,*[1] or at least to have had some little notice taken of me."

Nelson indeed, in the West Indies, as an unknown captain, had done that which as a junior admiral he did later at Copenhagen, at a moment far more critical to Great Britain. By his own unusual powers of impulse and resolve he had enforced, as far as was possible against the passive, inert lethargy — not to say timidity — of his superior, the course of action which at the moment was essential to the interests of his country. Truly great in his strength to endure, he knew not the perturbations nor the vacillations that fret the temper, and cripple the action, of smaller men; and, however harassed and distressed

---

[1] The author has italicized these words because they accurately express the just penalty that military law would have required of Nelson, had he not shown adequate grounds for his disobedience. They measure, therefore, the responsibility he shouldered, and the reward he deserved.

externally, the calmness of a clear insight and an unshaken purpose guided his footsteps, unwavering, in the path of duty, through all opposition, to the goal of success.   It is reported that an officer of the "Boreas," speaking to him of the vexations and odium he had undergone, used the word "pity." Nelson's reply showed the profound confidence which throughout had animated him, keenly as he had undoubtedly felt the temporary anxieties. "Pity, did you say? I shall live, Sir, to be envied; and to that point I shall always direct my course."

By the departure of Sir Richard Hughes Nelson was left senior officer upon the station until his own return home, a twelvemonth later.   In November he renewed his acquaintance with Prince William Henry, whom he had known as a midshipman in 1782, and who now came to the Leeward Islands a post-captain, in command of the frigate "Pegasus." The two young men were not far apart in age, and an intimacy between them soon arose, which ended only with the death of Nelson.   The latter had a profound reverence for royalty, both as an institution and as represented in its members; and to this, in the present case, was added a strong personal esteem, based upon the zeal and efficiency in the discharge of official duties, which he recognized in one whose rank would assure him impunity for any mere indifference.   The prince, on the other hand, quickly yielded to the charm of Nelson's intercourse, so vividly felt by most who knew him, and to the contagious enthusiasm which animated his conversation when talking of his profession.   This, also, his ardent imagination endowed with possibilities and aspirations, not greater, indeed, than its deserts, but which only the intuitions of a genius like his could realize and vivify, imparting to slower temperaments something of his own fire.   To this association the prince afterwards attributed the awakening of that strong interest in maritime affairs which he retained to the day of his death.

The two friends dined alternately one with the other, and, in their association of some six months at this time, they together fought over all the naval battles that during the recent war had illustrated the waters through which they were then cruising.

The incessant energy displayed by Nelson, and the agitations through which he passed during the three years of this stay upon the West Indian station, again produced distressing symptoms in his general health. To use his own words, the activity of the mind was "too much for my puny constitution." "I am worn to a skeleton," he writes to Mr. Suckling in July, 1786; and three months later to Locker, "I have been since June so very ill that I have only a faint recollection of anything which I did. My complaint was in my breast, such a one as I had going out to Jamaica [in 1777]. The Doctor thought I was in a consumption, and quite gave me up." This fear, however, proved unfounded; nor does there appear at any time to have been any serious trouble with his lungs.

On the 11th[1] of March, 1787, the marriage of Captain Nelson to Mrs. Nisbet took place at Nevis. Prince William Henry, whose rule it was never to visit in any private house, made an exception on this occasion, having exacted from Nelson a promise that the wedding should wait until he could be present; and he gave away the bride. Three months later, on the 7th of June, the "Boreas" sailed for England, and on the 4th of July anchored at Spithead. Whether Mrs. Nelson accompanied him in the ship does not appear certainly; but from several expressions in his letters it seems most probable that she did. Five days after his arrival he sent a message from

[1] Sir Harris Nicolas (Nelson's Despatches and Letters, vol. i. p. 217) gives March 12 as the day of the wedding, upon the ground of a letter of Lady Nelson's. Her mention of the date is, however, rather casual; and March 11 is given in the parish register of the church in Nevis.

her to Locker, in terms which indicate that she was with him.

A newly married man, who had just concluded a full cruise of such arduous and unremitting exertions, might reasonably have wished and expected a period of relaxation; but the return of the "Boreas" coincided with a very disturbed state of European politics. In the neighboring republic of Holland two parties were striving for the mastery; one of which was closely attached to France, the other, that of the Stadtholder, to Great Britain. In 1785 the former had gained the upper hand; and, by a treaty signed on Christmas Day of that year, a decided preponderance in the councils of the United Provinces had been given to France. The enfeebled condition of the latter country, however, had allowed little prospect of permanence to this arrangement; and, in the summer of 1787, an insult offered by the French party to the wife of the Stadtholder led to a forcible intervention by the King of Prussia, whose sister she was. Louis XVI. prepared to support his partisans, and notified his purpose to Great Britain; whereupon the latter, whose traditional policy for over a century had been to resist the progress of French influence in the Low Countries, replied that she could not remain a quiet spectator, and at once began to arm. "The Dutch business," wrote Nelson, "is becoming every day more serious; and I hardly think we can keep from a war, without giving forever the weight of the Dutch to the French, and allowing the Stadtholdership to be abolished, — things which I should suppose hardly possible." Already his eager spirit was panting for the fray. "If we are to have a bustle, I do not want to come on shore; I begin to think I am fonder of the sea than ever." Only five months married!

The threatening aspect of affairs necessitated the "Boreas" being kept in commission, — the more so because the economies introduced by Mr. Pitt into the administra-

tion of the two military services had reduced the available
naval force below that which France could at once send
out. "The Boreas is kept in readiness to go to sea
with the squadron at Spithead," wrote Nelson; "but in
my poor opinion we shall go no further at present. The
French have eight sail in Brest water ready for sea: therefore I think we shall not court the French out of port," —
a singular illustration of the unreadiness of Great Britain
in the years immediately preceding the French Revolution.
He looks for war, however, the following summer. As
not only ships, but men also, were urgently needed, the
impress service was hastily organized. His friend Locker
was summoned from his long retirement to superintend
that work in Exeter, and the "Boreas" was ordered to the
Thames on the same business, arriving on the 20th of
August at the Nore. There her duty was to board passing
vessels, and take from them as many of their crew as were
above the number barely necessary for the safety of the
ship. She herself, besides acting as receiving ship for
the men thus pressed, was to be kept in readiness to sail
at a moment's warning. Mrs. Nelson had therefore to
leave her and go to London. "Here we are," wrote
Nelson on the 23d of September, "laying seven miles from
the land on the Impress service, and I am as much separated
from my wife as if I were in the East Indies;" and he
closes the letter with the words, "I am this moment
getting under sail after some ships."

His early biographers say that Nelson keenly felt and
resented the kind of service in which he was then engaged;
so much so that, moved also by other causes of irritation,
he decided at one time to quit the Navy. No indication
of such feeling, however, appears in his letters. On the
contrary, one of the surest signs with him of pleasurable,
or at least of interested, excitement, was now manifested
in his improving health. As he himself said, many years
later, "To say the truth, when I am actively employed I

am not so bad." [1] A month after reaching England, though
then midsummer, he wrote: "It is not kind in one's native
air to treat a poor wanderer as it has me since my arrival.
The rain and cold at first gave me a sore throat and its
accompaniments; the hot weather has given me a slow
fever, not absolutely bad enough to keep my bed, yet
enough to hinder me from doing anything;" and again, "I
have scarcely been able to hold up my head." In bluster-
ing October, on the other hand, while in the midst of the
detested Impress work, he says: "My health, thank God,
was never better, and I am fit for any quarter of the
globe;" although "it rains hard, and we have had very
bad weather of late." Whatever momentary vexation he
may have vented in a hasty expression, it was entirely
inconsistent with his general tone to take amiss an employment whose vital importance he would have been the first
to admit. Lack of zeal, or haggling about the duty
assigned him, was entirely foreign to his character; that
the country needed the men who were to be pressed was
reason sufficient for one of his temper. If, indeed, there
had been an apparent intention to keep him in such inglorious occupation, and out of the expected war, he might
have chafed; but his orders to be constantly ready indicated the intention to send him at once to the front, if
hostilities began. Doubtless he was disappointed that
the application he made for a ship-of-the-line was not
granted; but he knew that, being still a very young captain, what he asked was a favor, and its refusal not a
grievance, nor does he seem to have looked upon it
otherwise.

There were, however, some annoyances, which, joined
to the lack of appreciation for his eminent services to the

---

[1] The same symptom will be noted in the anxious pursuit of Villeneuve
to the West Indies in 1805, where he grew better, although for some months
he had had in his hands the Admiralty's permission to return home on
account of his health.

interests of the nation in the West Indies, must have
keenly stung him. Without the slightest necessity, except
that laid upon him by his own public spirit, he had fought
and struggled, and endured three years of hot water to
serve the Government. He might have gone easy, as did
the admiral and the other captains; but instead of so doing
he had destroyed the contraband trade, and re-established
the working of laws upon which the prosperity and security of the kingdom were thought to depend. For this he
had received a perfunctory, formal acknowledgment,
though none apparently from the Admiralty, the head of
his own service. But he soon found that, if slow to
thank, they were prompt to blame, and that with no light
hand nor disposition to make allowances. He had run his
head against various regulations of the bureaucracy; and
this let him know, with all the amenities of official censure,
that if they could not recognize what he had done well,
they were perfectly clear-sighted as to where he had gone
wrong.

So far from appreciation, there seems even to have been
a prejudice against Nelson in high quarters, due not only
to the discomposure felt by the routine official, at the rude
irregularities of the man who is more concerned to do his
work than nice about the formalities surrounding it, but
also to misrepresentation by the powerful interests he had
offended through his independent course in the West
Indies. After Hughes had gone home, Nelson, as senior
officer on the station, began to examine the modes of con-
ducting government business, and especially of making
purchases. Conceiving that there were serious irregularities in these, he suggested to the Civil Department of the
Navy, under whose cognizance the transactions fell, some
alterations in the procedure, by which the senior naval
officer would have more control over the purchases than
simply to certify that so much money was wanted. The
Comptroller of the Navy replied that the old forms were

sufficient, — "a circumstance which hurt me," wrote
Nelson; while all the civil functionaries resented his
interference with their methods, and seem to have received
the tacit support, if not the direct sympathy, of the Navy
Board, as the Civil Department was then called. His
disposition to look into matters, however, had become
known, and the long struggle over the contraband trade
had given him in the islands a reputation for.tenacity and
success. It was probably in dependence upon these that
two merchants came to him, two months before he left the
station, and told him of the existence of very extensive
frauds, dating back several years, in which were implicated
both civil officials of the Navy and private parties on shore.
It is possible that the informants themselves had shared
in some of these transactions, and they certainly demanded
in payment a part of the sums recovered; but, as Nelson
truly said, the question was not as to their character, but
how to stop the continuance of embezzlements which had
then amounted to over two millions sterling.

The reports made by him upon this subject reached
London about a month before the return of the "Boreas;"
but the war scare, and the urgent call upon all depart-
ments of the Navy to mobilize the available force, prevented any immediate steps being taken. His letters
were acknowledged, and the intention expressed to investi-
gate the matter, but nothing more was then done. In
October, however, the Prussian troops occupied Amster-
dam, reinstating the Stadtholder in all his privileges, and
restoring to power the partisans of Great Britain; while
France remained passive, her power for external action
paralyzed by the dying convulsions of the monarchy. The
curtain had just risen upon the opening scene in the great
drama of the Revolution, — the first Assembly of Notables.
Warlike preparations consequently ceased, and on the 30th
of November, 1787, the cruise of the "Boreas" came to
an end.

It was during this last month of servitude, and immediately before quitting the ship, that Nelson is said to have used the vehement expressions of discontent with "an ungrateful service," recorded by his biographers, concluding with his resolve to go at once to London and resign his commission. In the absence of the faintest trace, in' his letters, of dissatisfaction with the duty to which the ship was assigned, it is reasonable to attribute this exasperation to his soreness under the numerous reprimands he had received, — a feeling which plainly transpires in some of his replies, despite the forms of official respect that he scrupulously observed. Even in much later days, when his distinguished reputation might have enabled him to sustain with indifference this supercilious rudeness, he winced under it with over-sensitiveness. "Do not, my dear lord," he wrote to Earl Spencer a year after the battle of the Nile, "let the Admiralty write harshly to me — my generous soul cannot bear it, being conscious it is entirely unmerited." This freedom of censure, often felt by him to be undeserved, or at least excessive, and its sharp contrast with the scanty recognition of his unwearied efforts, — of whose value he himself was by no means forgetful, — though not unusual in the experience of officers, are quite sufficient to account for the sense of neglect and unjust treatment by which he was then outraged. This feeling was probably accentuated, also, by a renewal of the legal persecution which had been begun in the West Indies; for towards the end of the year he received formal notice of suits being instituted against him for the seizure of the American vessels, and it is likely enough that some intimation of what was coming reached him before leaving the "Boreas." Scanty thanks, liberal blame, and the prospect of an expensive lawsuit based upon his official action, constituted, for a poor man lately married, causes of disturbance which might well have upset his equanimity.

Lord Howe, who was then at the head of the Admiralty, though formal and unbending in outward bearing, was a just and kind man, and one fully appreciative of professional worth. A mutual friend acquainted him with Nelson's irritation, and Howe wrote a private letter asking that he would call upon him as soon as he came to town. Though quick to resent, Nelson was easily soothed by attention and pleased by compliment, even when it rose to flattery, — which Howe's was not likely to do. A short interview gave the First Lord a clearer idea than he before had of the extent, value, and wholly voluntary character of the services rendered by the young captain in the West Indies; and he indicated the completeness of his satisfaction by offering to present him to the King, which was accordingly done at the next levee. George III. received him graciously; and the resentment of Nelson, whose loyalty was of the most extreme type, melted away in the sunshine of royal favor.

Thus reconciled to the service, and convinced, as in his less morbid moods he often said, that gratitude and honor, though long deferred, were sure to follow upon steadfast performance of duty, he speedily renewed his efforts to bring to light the frauds practised in the colonies. His letters on the subject to Mr. Pitt, the Prime Minister, had been turned over to the Secretary of the Treasury, Mr. George Rose, and upon the latter Nelson now called. Rose received him at first with that courteous nonchalance which is the defensive armor of the beset official, — the name of his visitor, and the business with which it was connected, had for the moment slipped his mind. Nelson's mastery of his subject, however, and his warmth in it, soon roused the attention of his hearer, who, being then pressed for time, asked to see him again the next day, stipulating only that the interview should be early, before office hours. "It cannot be too early for me," replied Nelson, whose habit, in his career as admiral, was to get through his correspondence before eight o'clock, — "six o'clock, if you please."

The arrangement was so made, and the consequent meeting lasted from six to nine the next morning. Of its general nature and results we have an authentic outline, given in later years to Nelson's biographers by Rose, who became, and to the last remained, his warm personal friend. The conversation ranged, apparently, over all the chief occurrences in the West Indies during the cruise of the "Boreas," including both the naval frauds and the contraband trade. The breadth and acuteness of Nelson's intellect have been too much overlooked, in the admiration excited by his unusually grand moral endowments of resolution, dash, and fearlessness of responsibility. Though scarcely what could be called an educated man, he was one of close and constant observation, thereby gaining a great deal of information; and to the use of this he brought a practical sagacity, which coped with the civil or political questions placed before it, *for action*, much as it did with military questions — for, after all, good generalship, on its intellectual side, is simply the application, to the solution of a military problem, of a mind naturally gifted therefor, and stored with experience, either personal or of others. As a strategist and tactician, Nelson made full proof of high native endowments, of wisdom garnered through fruitful study and meditation, and of clear insight into the determining conditions of the various military situations with which he had to deal. To Mr. Rose, the young captain of barely thirty years displayed a precise knowledge of several political subjects, connected with the commerce of the country, that would not naturally come under his notice as an officer, and which therefore the mere seaman would probably not have imbibed. Not only so, but his suggestions for dealing practically with the interests at stake were so judicious, that Rose, a valued associate of Pitt and intimately acquainted with the financial measures of that brilliant administrator, complimented him warmly upon the justice and correctness of his views, the result, as they were, of reflection based upon a mastery of the data involved. With Nelson's consent, he undertook to lay them before the prime minister, as the direct testimony of a singularly competent first-hand observer.

It is to be noted, however, of Nelson, that this accuracy of mental perception, this power of penetrating to the root of a matter, disregarding unessential details and fastening solely on decisive features, was largely dependent upon the necessity laid upon him for action; which is probably equivalent to saying that it was usually elicited by a sobering sense of responsibility. In his letters and despatches may be found many wild guesses, inconsistent from week to week, colored by changing moods and humors, — the mere passing comments of a mind off guard, — the records of evanescent impressions as numerous, fickle, and unfounded as those of the most ordinary mortal. It is when urgency presses and danger threatens, when the need for action comes, that his mental energies are aroused, and he begins to speak, as it were, *ex cathedra*. Then the unsubstantial haze rolls away, and the solid features of the scene one by one appear, until, amid all the unavoidable uncertainties of imperfect information, it becomes plain that the man has a firm grasp upon the great landmarks by which he must guide his course. Like the blind, who at first saw men as trees walking, and then saw everything clearly, so his mental illumination gradually reduces confusion to order, and from perplexity evolves correct decision. But what shall be said of those flashes of insight, as at Cape St. Vincent, elicited in a moment, as by the stroke of iron on rock, where all the previous processes of ordered thought and labored reasoning are condensed into one vivid inspiration, and transmuted without a pause into instant heroic action? Is that we call "genius" purely a mystery, of which our only account is to give it a name? Or is it true, as Napoleon said, that "on the field of battle the happiest inspiration is often but a recollection"?

From Rose Nelson went to the Comptroller of the Navy, Sir Charles Middleton, who afterwards, as Lord Barham, sent him forth to Trafalgar. Middleton had replied promptly to the first report of the fraudulent transactions, giving assurance of his readiness to act, and urging that all the information possible should be secured, as he feared that the allegations were substantially true. He now showed the instructions of the Navy Board, under which its colonial employees acted, to Nelson, who said that, if honestly followed, they must prevent the unlawful practices; but that he believed they were habitually violated, and that he himself, though senior officer on the station, had never before seen the instructions. This failure to intrust supervision to the one person upon whom all responsibility should ultimately have rested, practically neutralized the otherwise laudable methods prescribed by the Board. It was simply another instance of the jealousy between the civil and military branches of the naval organization, which, as is well known, resulted in constant strained relations between the Admiralty and the Naval Commissioners, until the latter Board was at last abolished.

It is, fortunately, unnecessary to follow farther this dreary record of old-time dishonesty. Nelson continued to interest himself strenuously in the matter for two years after his return to England, both by letter and interview with persons in authority. His own position and influence were too insignificant to effect anything, except by moving the home officials, whose administration was compromised and embarrassed by the malpractices of their representatives. Though up-hill work, it was far from fruitless. "His representations," said Mr. Rose, in a memorandum furnished to his biographers, "were all attended to, and every step which he recommended was adopted. He thus put the investigation into a proper course; which ended in the detection and punishment of some of the parties whose conduct was complained of." The broad result appears to have been that the guilty for the most part escaped punishment, unless, indeed, some of them lost their positions, of which no certain information exists; but the corrupt combination was broken up, and measures were adopted to prevent the recurrence of the same iniquities. Upon Nelson himself the effect was twofold. His energy and intelligence could not fail to impress the powerful men with whom he was in this way brought into contact. The affair increased his reputation, and made him more widely known than as a simple captain in the Navy he would otherwise have been. As the various public Boards whose money had been stolen realized the amount of the thefts, and the extent of the conspiracy to rob the Government, they felt their obligations to him, and expressed them in formal, but warm, letters of thanks. On the other hand, the principal culprits had command of both money and influence; and by means of these, as so often happens, they not only impeded inquiry, but, according to Southey, who wrote not very long after the events, "succeeded in raising prejudices against Nelson at the Board of Admiralty which it was many years before he could subdue." Clarke and M'Arthur make the same assertion.

That these prejudices did at one time exist is beyond doubt, and that they should have been fostered by this means is perfectly in keeping with common experience. Such intrigues, however, work in the dark and by indirection; it is not often easy to trace their course. The independence and single-mindedness with which Nelson followed his convictions, and the outspoken frankness with which he expressed his views and feelings, not improbably gave a handle to malicious misrepresentation. His known intimacy with Prince William Henry, upon whose favor he to some extent relied, was also more likely to do him harm than good; and he entertained for the royal captain prepossessions not far removed from partisanship, at a time when the prince avowed himself not a friend to the present minister. "Amidst that variety of business which demanded his attention on his return to England," say his biographers, "he failed not, by every means in his power, to fulfil the promise which he had made to his Royal Highness Prince William of counteracting whatever had been opposed to the merited reputation of his illustrious pupil, and to the friendship they had invariably preserved for each other." It was a difficult task. Opinionated and headstrong as the King, his father, the young man was an uneasy subordinate to the Admiralty, and made those above him realize that he was full as conscious of his personal rank as of his official position as a captain in the Navy. It was, indeed, this self-assertive temperament that afterwards frustrated his natural ambition to be the active head of the service. Having such an ally, there is something ominous for Nelson's own prospects to find him writing in evident sympathy: "The great folks above now see he will not be a cypher, therefore many of the rising people must submit to act subordinate to him, which is not so palatable; and I think a Lord of the Admiralty is hurt to see him so able, after what he has said about him. He has certainly not taken a leaf out of his book, for he is steady in his command and not violent." Upon this follows, "He has wrote Lord Hood what I cannot but approve," — a sentence unquestionably vague, but which sounds combative. Nelson had already felt it necessary to caution the prince to be careful in the choice of those to whom he told his mind.

In fact, at the time when the letter just quoted was written, the conduct of the prince had been such as necessarily, and not wholly unjustly, to prejudice an officer who displayed marked partisanship for him, such as certainly was indicated by Nelson's expressions. He had brought

his ship from Newfoundland to Ireland in flat disobedience
of orders, issued by the commander of the station, to go to
Quebec. When this action became known to the Admiralty by his arrival at Cork, in December, 1787, it was at
once reported to the King, who himself directed that the
prince should proceed to Plymouth with his ship, should
remain within the limits of the port for as many months
as he had been absent from his station, and should then
be sent back to Halifax. The Prince of Wales, afterwards
George IV., who was already at variance with the King,
took advantage of this flagrant breach of discipline to
flaunt his opposition before the world. In company with
his second brother, the Duke of York, he went down to
Plymouth, and paid a ceremonious visit to Prince William
on board his ship. The round of festivities necessitated by
their presence emphasized the disagreement between the
sovereign and the heir to the throne, and drew to it public
attention. Immediately after this, in January, 1788, Nelson
also visited the prince, having been summoned by him from
London. He could, indeed, scarcely decline, nor was he
at all the man to turn his back on a friend in difficulty;
but, in his fight against corruption, the matter could scarcely
fail to be represented by his opponents under the worst
light to the King, to whom corruption was less odious than
insubordination. If, in conversation, Nelson uttered such
expressions as he wrote to his friend Locker, he had only
himself to blame for the disfavor which followed; for, to
a naval officer, the prince's conduct should have appeared
absolutely indefensible. In the course of the same year
the King became insane, and the famous struggle about
the Regency took place. The prince had meantime returned to America, in accordance with his orders, and by
the time he again reached England the King had recovered. He could, therefore, have refrained from any indication of his own sympathies; but instead of this he openly
associated himself with the party of the Prince of Wales,

whose course throughout, when it became known to his father, had bitterly displeased the latter, and accentuated the breach between them. At a banquet given by the Spanish ambassador in celebration of the King's recovery, the three princes sat at a table separate from the rest of the royal family. A formal reconciliation took place in September, 1789; but the Duke of Clarence, as he had then become, continued attached to the Prince of Wales's clique. Those who know how party considerations influenced naval appointments at that time, will in these facts find at least a partial explanation of the cloud which then hung over Nelson.

Lord Chatham, brother of the minister to whom Prince William was not a friend, became head of the Admiralty in July, 1788, and so remained until after the war with France began in 1793. With him was associated Lord Hood, between whom and Nelson there arose what the latter called "a difference of opinion," which led to a cessation of "familiar correspondence." The exact date at which this occurred does not appear, but it was probably before May, 1790; for Hood refused to use his influence to get Nelson a ship, in the armament which was then ordered on account of a difficulty with Spain, whereas eighteen months before he had assured him that in case of hostilities he need not fear not having a good ship. This refusal was the more marked, because "almost the whole service was then called out." On the same occasion, Nelson wrote, "he made a speech never to be effaced from my memory, viz.: that the King was impressed with an unfavourable opinion of me." Knowing Nelson's value as an officer as well as Hood did, there can scarcely remain a doubt that some serious indiscretion, real or imagined, must have caused this alienation; but of what it was there is no trace, unless in his evident siding with the prince, who was then out of favor with both the King and the administration.

The five years — from 1788 to 1792 inclusive — intervening between the cruise of the "Boreas" and the outbreak of war with the French Republic, were thus marked by a variety of unpleasant circumstances, of which the most disagreeable, to a man of Nelson's active temperament, was the apparently fixed resolve of the authorities to deny him employment. He was harassed, indeed, by the recurring threats of prosecution for the West India seizures; but both the Admiralty and the Treasury agreed that he should be defended at the expense of the Crown, — a fact which tends to show that his subsequent disfavor arose from some other cause than disapproval of his official action, however some incidents may have been misrepresented. On its private side, his life during this period seems to have been happy, though uneventful; but in the failure of children he was deprived, both then and afterwards, of that sweetest of interests, continuous yet ever new in its gradual unfolding, which brings to the most monotonous existence its daily tribute of novelty and incident. The fond, almost rapturous, expressions with which he greeted the daughter afterwards born to him out of wedlock, shows the blank in his home, — none the less real because not consciously realized.

The lack of stimulus to his mind from his surroundings at this time is also manifested by the fewness of his letters. But thirty remain to show his occupation during the five years, and seventeen of these are purely official in character. From the year 1791 no record survives. His wife being with him, one line of correspondence was thereby closed; but even to his brother, and to his friend Locker, he finds nothing to write. For the ordinary country amusements and pursuits of the English gentry he had scant liking; and, barring the occasional worry over his neglect by the Admiralty, there was little else to engage his attention. The first few months after his release from the "Boreas" were spent in the West of England, chiefly at

Bath, for the recovery of Mrs. Nelson's health as well as his own; but toward the latter part of 1788 the young couple went to live with his father at the parsonage of Burnham Thorpe, and there made their home until he was again called into active service. "It is extremely interesting," say his biographers, "to contemplate this great man, when thus removed from the busy scenes in which he had borne so distinguished a part to the remote village of Burnham Thorpe;" but the interest seems by their account to be limited to the energy with which he dug in the garden, or, from sheer want of something to do, reverted to the bird-nesting of his boyhood. His favorite amusement, we are told, was coursing, and he once shot a partridge; but his habit of carrying his gun at full cock, and firing as soon as a bird rose, without bringing the piece to his shoulder, made him a dangerous companion in a shooting-party. His own account is somewhat different: "Shoot I cannot, therefore I have not taken out a license; but notwithstanding the neglect I have met with I am happy;" and again, to his brother, he says: "It was not my intention to have gone to the coursing meeting, for, to say the truth, I have rarely escaped a wet jacket and a violent cold; besides, to me, even the ride to the Smee is longer than any pleasure I find in the sport will compensate for." The fact is that Nelson cared for none of these things, and the only deduction of real interest from his letters at this time is the absolute failure of his home life and affections to content his aspirations, — the emptiness both of mind and heart, which caused his passionate eagerness for external employment to fill the void. Earnestness appears only when he is brooding over the slight with which he was treated, and the resultant thwarting of his career. For both mind and heart the future held in store for him the most engrossing emotions, but it did not therefore bring him happiness.

Of his frames of mind during this period of neglect and disfavor, his biographers give a very strongly colored picture, for which, it is to be presumed, they drew upon contemporary witnesses that were to them still accessible. "With a mortified and dejected spirit, he looked forward to a continuance of inactivity and neglect. . . . During this interval of disappointment and mortification, his latent ambition would at times burst forth, and despise all restraint. At others, a sudden melancholy seemed to overshadow his noble faculties, and to affect his temper; at those moments the remonstrances of his wife and venerable father alone could calm the tempest of his passions." That Nelson keenly felt the cold indifference he now underwent, is thoroughly in keeping with the sensitiveness to censure, expressed or implied, which his correspondence frequently betrays, while his frail organization and uncertain health would naturally entail periods of depression or nervous exasperation; but the general tenor of his letters, few as they at this time were, shows rather dignified acceptance of a treatment he had not merited, and a steady resolve not to waver in his readiness to serve his country, nor to cease asking an opportunity to do so. Many years later, at a time of still more sickening suspense, he wrote: "I am in truth half dead, but what man can do shall be done, — I am not made to despair;" and now, according to a not improbable story, he closed an application for employment with the words, "If your Lordships should be pleased to appoint me to a cockle boat, I shall feel grateful!" Hood, whose pupil he in a sense was, and who shared his genius, said of himself, when under a condition of enforced inactivity: "This proves very strongly the different frames of men's minds; some are full of anxiety, impatience, and apprehension, while others, under similar circumstances, are perfectly cool, tranquil, and indifferent."

The latter half of the year 1792 was marked by the rapid progress in France of the political distemper, which was so soon to culminate in the worst excesses of the

Revolution. The quick succession of symptoms, each more alarming' than the other, — the suspension of the royal power at the tumultuous bidding of a mob, the September massacres, the abolition of royalty, the aggressive character of the National Convention shown by the decrees of November 19 and December 15, — roused the apprehensions of most thoughtful men throughout Europe; and their concern was increased by the growing popular effervescence in other countries than France. The British cabinet, as was natural, shifted more slowly than did the irresponsible members of the community; nor could Pitt lightly surrender his strong instinctive prepossessions in favor of peace, with the continuance of which was identified the exercise of his own best powers.

During this stormy and anxious period, Nelson shared the feelings of his day and class. It is noteworthy, however, that, in regarding the perils of the time, he was no mere panic-monger, but showed the same discriminating carefulness of observation that had distinguished him as captain of the "Boreas," and had elicited the admiration of Mr. Rose. Strenuous and even bigoted royalist as he always was, satisfied of the excellence of the British Constitution, and condemning utterly the proceedings of the more or less seditious societies then forming throughout the kingdom, he yet recognized the substantial grievances of the working-men, as evident in the district immediately under his eye. The sympathetic qualities which made him, fortune's own favorite in his profession, keenly alive to the hardships, neglect, and injustice undergone by the common seaman, now engaged him to set forth the sad lot of the ill-paid rural peasantry. In his letters to the Duke of Clarence, he on the one hand strongly blames the weakness and timidity of the justices and country gentlemen, in their attitude towards the abettors of lawlessness; but, on the other, he dwells upon the sufferings of the poor, prepares a careful statement of their earnings

and unavoidable expenses, and insists upon the necessity
of the living wage.   The field laborers, he said, "do not
want loyalty, many of their superiors, in many instances,
might have imitated their conduct to advantage; but
hunger is a sharp thorn, and they are not only in want
of food sufficient, but of clothes and firing."

Under the threatening outlook, he considers that every
individual will soon "be called forth to show himself;"
and for his own part, he writes on the 3d of November,
he sees no way so proper as asking for a ship.   But, even
at that late moment, neither Pitt nor his associates had
abandoned the hope of peace, and this, as well as other
applications of Nelson's, received only a formal acknowledgment without encouragement.   Roused, however, by
the Convention's decree of November 19, which extended
the succor of France to all people who should wish to recover their liberty, and charged the generals of the republic
to make good the offer with the forces under their command, the ministry decided to abandon their guarded attitude; and their new resolution was confirmed by the
reception, on the 28th of November, of deputations from
British revolutionary societies at the bar of the Convention, on which occasion the president of the latter affected
to draw a dividing line between the British government
and the British nation.   On the 1st of December the mili-
tia was called out by proclamation, and Parliament summoned to meet on the 15th of the month.   On the latter
day the Convention put forth another decree, announcing
in the most explicit terms its purpose to overthrow all existing governments in countries where the Republican
armies could penetrate.   Pitt now changed his front with
an instantaneousness and absoluteness which gave the
highest proof of his capacity as a leader of men.   It was
not so much that war was then determined, as that the
purpose was formed, once for all, to accept the challenge
contained in the French decree, unless France would dis-

continue her avowed course of aggression. Orders were immediately given to increase largely the number of ships of war in commission.

When danger looms close at hand, the best men, if known, are not left in the cold shade of official disfavor. "Post nubila Phœbus," was the expression of Nelson, astonished for a rarity into Latin by the suddenness with which the sun now burst upon him through the clouds. "The Admiralty so smile upon me, that really I am as much surprised as when they frowned." On the 6th of January, 1793, the First Lord, with many apologies for previous neglect, promised to give him a seventy-four-gun ship as soon as it was in his power to do so, and that meanwhile, if he chose to take a sixty-four, he could have one as soon as she was ready.. On the 30th he was appointed to the "Agamemnon," of the latter rate. Within the preceding fortnight Louis XVI. had been beheaded, and the French ambassador ordered to leave England. On February 1, 1793, two days after Nelson's orders were issued, the Republic declared war against Great Britain and Holland.

CHAPTER III.

Nelson's Departure from England in the "Agamemnon." — Services in the Mediterranean until the Recovery of Toulon by the French. — Lord Hood in Command.

February–December, 1793. Age, 34.

NELSON'S page in history covers a little more than twelve years, from February, 1793, to October, 1805. Its opening coincides with the moment when the wild passions of the French Revolution, still at fiercest heat, and which had hitherto raged like flame uncontrolled, operative only for destruction, were being rapidly mastered, guided, and regulated for efficient work, by the terrors of the Revolutionary Tribunal and the Committee of Public Safety. In the object to which these tremendous forces were now about to be applied lay the threat to the peace of Europe, which aroused Great Britain to action, and sent into the field her yet unknown champion from the Norfolk parsonage. The representatives of the French people had imparted to the original movement of their nation, — which aimed only at internal reforms, however radical, — a new direction, of avowed purposeful aggression upon all political institutions exterior to, and differing from, their own. This became the one characteristic common to the successive forms of government, which culminated in the pure military despotism of Napoleon.

To beat back that spirit of aggression was the mission of Nelson. Therein is found the true significance of his career, which mounts higher and higher in strenuous effort and gigantic achievement, as the blast of the Revolution swells fiercer and stronger under the mighty impulse of the great Corsican. At each of the momentous crises, so far·removed in time and place, — at the Nile, at Copenhagen, at Trafalgar, — as the unfolding drama of the age reveals to the onlooker the schemes of the arch-planner about to touch success, over against Napoleon rises ever Nelson; and as the latter in the hour of victory drops upon the stage where he has played so chief a part, his task is seen to be accomplished, his triumph secured. In the very act of dying he has dealt the foe a blow from which recovery is impossible. Moscow and Waterloo are the inevitable consequences of Trafalgar; as the glories of that day were but the fit and assured ending of the illustrious course which was begun upon the quarter-deck of the " Agamemnon."

With the exception of the " Victory," under whose flag he fell after two years of arduous, heartbreaking uncertainties, no ship has such intimate association with the career and name of Nelson as has the " Agamemnon." And this is but natural, for to her he was the captain, solely, simply, and entirely; identified with her alone, glorying in her excellences and in her achievements, one in purpose and in spirit with her officers and seamen; sharing their hopes, their dangers, and their triumphs; quickening them with his own ardor, moulding them into his own image, until vessel and crew, as one living organism, reflected in act the heroic and unyielding energy that inspired his feeble frame. Although, for a brief and teeming period, he while in command of her controlled also a number of smaller vessels on detached service, it was not until after he had removed to another ship that he became the squadron-commander, whose relations to the vessel on which he himself dwelt were no longer immediate, nor differed, save in his bodily presence, from those he bore to others of the same division. A personality such as Nelson's makes itself indeed felt throughout its entire sphere of action, be that large or

small; but, withal, diffusion contends in vain with the
inevitable law that forever couples it with slackening
power, nor was it possible even for him to lavish on the
various units of a fleet, and on the diverse conflicting
claims of a great theatre of war, the same degree of
interest and influence that he concentrated upon the "Agamemnon," and upon the brilliant though contracted services through which he carried her.   Bonds such as these
are not lightly broken, and to the "Agamemnon" Nelson
clave for three long years and more, persistently refusing
larger ships, until the exhausted hulk could no longer re-
spond to the demands of her masters, and separation became
inevitable.   When he quitted her, at the moment of her
departure for England, it was simply a question whether he
would abandon the Mediterranean, and the prospect of a
great future there opening before him, or sever a few weeks
earlier a companionship which must in any event end upon
her arrival home.

There is yet another point of view from which his command of the "Agamemnon" is seen to hold a peculiar relation to Nelson's story.   This was the period in which
expectation passed into fulfilment, when development, long
arrested by unpropitious circumstances, resumed its outward progress under the benign influence of a favoring
environment, and the bud, whose rare promise had long
been noted by a few discerning eyes, unfolded into the
brilliant flower, destined in the magnificence of its maturity to draw the attention of a world.   To the fulness of
his glorious course these three years were what the days of
early manhood are to ripened age; and they are marked
by the same elasticity, hopefulness, and sanguine looking
to the future that characterize youth, before illusions
vanish and even success is found to disappoint.   Happiness was his then, as at no other time before or after; for
the surrounding conditions of enterprise, of difficulties
to be overcome, and dangers to be met, were in complete

correspondence with those native powers that had so long struggled painfully for room to exert themselves. His health revived, and his very being seemed to expand in this congenial atmosphere, which to him was as life from the dead. As with untiring steps he sped onward and upward, — counting naught done while aught remained to do, forgetting what was behind as he pressed on to what was before, — the ardor of pursuit, the delight of achievement, the joy of the giant running his course, sustained in him that glow of animation, that gladness in the mere fact of existence, physical or moral, in which, if anywhere, this earth's content is found. Lack of recognition, even, wrung from him only the undaunted words: "Never mind! some day I will have a gazette of my own." Not till his dreams were realized, till aspiration had issued in the completest and most brilliant triumph ever wrought upon the seas, and he had for his gazette the loud homage of every mouth in Europe, — not till six months after the battle of the Nile, — did Nelson write: "There is no true happiness in this life, and in my present state I could quit it with a smile. My only wish is to sink with honour into the grave."

The preparation of the Mediterranean fleet, to which the "Agamemnon" was assigned, was singularly protracted, and in the face of a well-ordered enemy the delay must have led to disastrous results. Nelson himself joined his ship at Chatham on the 7th of February, a week after his orders were issued; but not until the 16th of March did she leave the dockyard, and then only for Sheerness, where she remained four weeks longer. By that time it seems probable, from remarks in his letters, that the material equipment of the vessel was complete; but until the 14th of April she remained over a hundred men short of her complement. "Yet, I think," wrote Nelson, "that we shall be far from ill-manned, even if the rest be not so good as they ought to be." Mobilization in those days

had not been perfected into a science, even in theory, and
the difficulty of raising crews on the outbreak of war was
experienced by all nations, but by none more than by
Great Britain. Her wants were greatest, and for supply
depended upon a merchant service scattered in all quarters
of the globe. "Men are very hard to be got," Nelson said
to his brother, "and without a press I have no idea that
our fleet can be manned." It does not appear that this
crude and violent, yet unavoidable, method was employed
for the "Agamemnon," except so far as her crew was
completed from the guard-ship. Dependence was placed
upon the ordinary wiles of the recruiting-sergeant, and
upon Nelson's own popularity in the adjacent counties of
Suffolk and Norfolk, from which the bulk of his ship's
company was actually drawn. "I have sent out a lieutenant and four midshipmen," he writes to Locker, "to
get men at every seaport in Norfolk, and to forward them
to Lynn and Yarmouth; my friends in Yorkshire and the
North tell me they will send what men they can lay hands
on;" but at the same time he hopes that Locker, then
Commander-in-chief at the Nore, will not turn away any
who from other districts may present themselves for the
"Agamemnon." Coming mainly from the same neighborhood gave to the crew a certain homogeneousness of character, affording ground for appeal to local pride, a most
powerful incentive in moments of difficulty and emulation;
and this feeling was enhanced by the thought that their
captain too was a Norfolk man. To one possessing the
sympathetic qualities of Nelson, who so readily shared the
emotions and gained the affections of his associates, it was
easy to bind into a living whole the units animated by this
common sentiment.

His step-son, Josiah Nisbet, at this time about thirteen
years old, now entered the service as a midshipman, and
accompanied him on board the "Agamemnon." The
oncoming of a great war naturally roused to a yet higher

pitch the impulse towards the sea, which in all generations has stirred the blood of English boys. Of these, Nelson, using his captain's privilege, received a number as midshipmen upon his quarter-deck, among them several from the sons of neighbors and friends, and therefore, like the crew, Norfolk lads. It is told that to one, whose father he knew to be a strong Whig, of the party which in the past few years had sympathized with the general current of the French Revolution, he gave the following pithy counsels for his guidance in professional life: "First, you must always implicitly obey orders, without attempting to form any opinion of your own respecting their propriety; secondly, you must consider every man as your enemy who speaks ill of your king; and thirdly, you must hate a Frenchman as you do the devil." On the last two items Nelson's practice was in full accord with his precept; but to the first, his statement of which, sound enough in the general, is open to criticism as being too absolute, he was certainly not obedient. Not to form an opinion is pushing the principle of subordination to an indefensible extreme, even for a junior officer, though the caution not to express it is wise, as well as becoming to the modesty of youth. Lord Howe's advice to Codrington, to watch carefully all that passed and to form his own conclusions, but to keep them to himself, was in every respect more reasonable and profitable. But in fact this dictum of Nelson's was simply another instance of hating the French as he did the devil. The French were pushing independence and private judgment to one extreme, and he instinctively adopted the other.

It was not till near the end of April that the "Agamemnon" finally left the Thames, anchoring at Spithead on the 28th of that month. Still the fleet which Lord Hood was to command was not ready. While awaiting her consorts, the ship made a short cruise in the Channel, and a few days later sailed as one of a division of five ships-of-the-line under Admiral Hotham, to occupy a station fifty to a hundred miles west of the Channel Islands. Nelson's disposition not to form any opinion of his own respecting the propriety of orders was thus evidenced: " What we have been sent out for is best known to the great folks in London: to us, it appears, only to hum the nation and make tools of us, for where we have been stationed no enemy was likely to be met with, or where we could protect our own trade." There can be no doubt that not only was the practical management of the Navy at this time exceedingly bad, but that no sound ideas even prevailed upon the subject. Hotham's squadron gained from neutral vessels two important pieces of information, — that Nantes, Bordeaux, and L'Orient were filled with English vessels, prizes to French cruisers; and that the enemy kept eight sail-of-the-line, with frigates in proportion, constantly moving in detachments about the Bay of Biscay. Under the dispositions adopted by the British Admiralty, these hostile divisions gave, to the commerce destroying of the smaller depredators, a support that sufficiently accounts for the notorious sufferings of British trade during the opening years of the war. Nelson had no mastery of the terminology of warfare, — he never talked about strategy and little about tactics, — but, though without those valuable aids to precision of thought, he had pondered, studied, and reasoned, and he had, besides, what is given to few, — real genius and insight. Accordingly he at once pierced to the root of the trouble; — the enemy's squadrons, rather than the petty cruisers dependent upon them, to which the damage was commonly attributed. " They are always at sea, and England not willing to send a squadron to interrupt them." But, while instancing this intuitive perception of a man gifted with rare penetration, it is necessary to guard against rash conclusions that might be drawn from it, and to remark that it by no means follows that education is unnecessary to the common run of men, because a genius is in advance of his times. It is well also to note that even in him this flash of insight, though unerring in its indications, lacked the definiteness of conviction which results from ordered thought. However accurate, it is but a glimmer, — not yet a fixed light. _

Hotham's division joined the main body under Lord Hood, off the Scilly Islands, on the 23d of May, the total force then consisting of eleven sail-of-the-line, with the usual smaller vessels. It remained cruising in that neighborhood until the 6th of June, keeping the approaches of the Channel open for a homeward-bound convoy of merchantmen, which passed on that day. The fleet then bore up for the Straits, and on the 14th six ships, the "Agamemnon" among them, parted company for Cadiz, there to fill up with water, in order to avoid the delays which would arise if the scanty resources of Gibraltar had to supply all the vessels. On the 23d this division left Cadiz, reaching Gibraltar the same evening; and on the 27th Hood, having now with him fifteen of the line, sailed for Toulon.

Nelson's mind was already busy with the prospects of the campaign, and the various naval factors that went to make up the military situation. "Time must discover what we are going after," he writes to his brother; while to Locker he propounds the problem which always has perplexed the British mind, and still does, — how to make the French fight, if they are unwilling. So long as that question remains unsolved, the British government has to bear the uncertainties, exposure, and expense of a difficult and protracted defensive. "We have done nothing," he says, "and the same prospect appears before us: the French cannot come out, and we have no means of getting at them in Toulon." In "cannot come out," he alludes to the presence of a Spanish fleet of twenty-four ships-of-the-line. This, in conjunction with Hood's force, would

far exceed the French in Toulon, which the highest estimate then placed at twenty-one of the line. He had,
however, already measured the capabilities of the Spanish
Navy. They have very fine ships, he admits, but they
are shockingly manned, — so much so that if only the
barges' crews of the six British vessels that entered Cadiz,
numbering at the most seventy-five to a hundred men, but
all picked, could have got on board one of their first-rates,
he was certain they could have captured her, although her
ship's company numbered nearly a thousand. "If those
we are to meet in the Mediterranean are no better manned,"
he continues, "much service cannot be expected of them."
The prediction proved true, for no sooner did Hood find
the Spanish admiral than the latter informed him he must
go to Cartagena, having nineteen hundred sick in his fleet.
The officer who brought this message said it was no
wonder they were sickly, for they had been sixty days
at sea. This excited Nelson's derision — not unjustly.
"From the circumstance of having been longer than that
time at sea, do we attribute our getting healthy. It has
stamped with me the extent of their nautical abilities:
long may they remain in their present state." The last
sentence reveals his intuitive appreciation of the fact that
the Spain of that day could in no true sense be the ally
of Great Britain; for, at the moment he penned the
wish, the impotence or defection of their allies would leave
the British fleet actually inferior to the enemy in those
waters. He never forgot these impressions, nor the bung-
ling efforts of the Spaniards to form a line of battle. Up
to the end of his life the prospect of a Spanish war
involved no military anxieties, but only the prospect of
more prize money.

Among the various rumors of that troubled time, there
came one that the French were fitting their ships with
forges to bring their shot to a red heat, and so set fire to
the enemy's vessel in which they might lodge. Nelson

was promptly ready with a counter and quite adequate tactical move. "This, if true," he wrote, "I humbly conceive would have been as well kept secret; but as it is known, we must take care to get so close that their red shots may go *through* both sides, when it will not matter whether they are hot or cold." It is somewhat odd that the extremely diligent and painstaking Sir Harris Nicolas, in his version of this letter, should have dropped the concluding sentence, one of the most important and characteristic occurring in Nelson's correspondence at this time.

On the 14th of July Nelson notes that the fleet had received orders to consider Marseilles and Toulon as invested, and to take all vessels of whatever nation bound into those ports. He at once recognized the importance of this step, and the accurate judgment that dictated it. The British could not, as he said, get at the enemy in his fortified harbor; but they might by this means exercise the pressure that would force him to come out. Undoubtedly, whether on a large or on a small scale, whether it concern the whole plan of a war or of a campaign, or merely the question of a single military position, the best way to compel an unwilling foe to action, and to spoil his waiting game which is so onerous to the would-be assailant, is to attack him elsewhere, to cut short his resources, and make his position untenable by exhaustion. "This has pleased us," Nelson wrote; "if we make these red-hot gentlemen hungry, they may be induced to come out."

The investment by sea of these two harbors, but especially of Toulon, as being an important dockyard, was accordingly the opening move made by the British admiral. On the 16th of July he approached the latter port, and from that time until August 25 a close blockade was maintained, with the exception of a very few days, during which Hood took the fleet off Nice, and thence to Genoa, to remonstrate with that republic upon its supplying the south of France with grain, and bringing back French property under neutral papers. "Our being here is a farce if this trade is allowed," said Nelson, and rightly; for so far as appearances then went, the only influence the British squadrons could exert was by curtailing the supplies of southern France. That district raised only grain enough for three months' consumption; for the remainder of the year's food it depended almost wholly upon Sicily and Barbary, its communications with the interior being so bad that the more abundant fields of distant French provinces could not send their surplus.

In the chaotic state in which France was then plunged, the utmost uncertainty prevailed as to the course events might take, and rumors of all descriptions were current, the wildest scarcely exceeding in improbability the fantastic horrors that actually prevailed throughout the land during these opening days of the Reign of Terror. The expectation that found most favor in the fleet was that Provence would separate from the rest of France, and proclaim itself an independent republic under the protection of Great Britain; but few looked for the amazing result which shortly followed, in the delivery of Toulon by its citizens into the hands of Lord Hood. This Nelson attributed purely to the suffering caused by the strictness of the blockade. "At Marseilles and Toulon," wrote he on the 20th of August, "they are almost starving, yet nothing brings them to their senses. Although the Convention has denounced them as traitors, yet even these people will not declare for anything but Liberty and Equality." Three days later, Commissioners from both cities went on board Hood's flagship to treat for peace, upon the basis of re-establishing the monarchy, and recognizing as king the son of Louis XVI. The admiral accepted the proposal, on condition that the port and arsenal of Toulon should be delivered to him for safe keeping, until the restoration of the young prince was effected.

On the 27th of August the city ran up the white flag of the Bourbons, and the British fleet, together with the Spanish, which at this moment arrived on the scene, anchored in the outer port. The allied troops took possession of the forts commanding the harbor, while the dockyards and thirty ships-of-the-line were delivered to the navies.

"The perseverance of our fleet has been great," wrote Nelson, "and to that only can be attributed our unexampled success. Not even a boat could get into Marseilles or Toulon, or on the coast, with provisions; and the old saying, ' that hunger will tame a lion,' was never more strongly exemplified." In this he deceived himself, however natural the illusion. The opposition of Toulon to the Paris Government was part of a general movement of revolt, which spread throughout the provinces in May and June, 1793, upon the violent overthrow of the Girondists in the National Convention. The latter then proclaimed several cities outlawed, Toulon among them; and the bloody severities it exercised were the chief determining cause of the sudden treason, the offspring of fear more than of hunger, — though the latter doubtless contributed, — which precipitated the great southern arsenal into the arms of the Republic's most dangerous foe. Marseilles fell before the Conventional troops, and the resultant panic in the sister city occasioned the hasty step, which in less troubled moments would have been regarded with just horror. But in truth Nelson, despite his acute military perceptions, had not yet developed that keen political sagacity, the fruit of riper judgment grounded on wider information, which he afterwards showed. His ambition was yet limited to the sphere of the "Agamemnon," his horizon bounded by the petty round of the day's events. He rose, as yet, to no apprehension of the mighty crisis hanging over Europe, to no appreciation of the profound meanings of the opening strife. "I hardly think the War can last," he writes to his wife, "for what are we at war about?" and again, "I think we shall be in England in the winter or spring." Even some months later, in December, before Toulon had reverted to the French, he is completely blind to the importance of the Mediterranean in the great struggle, and expresses a wish to exchange to the West Indies, "for I think our Sea War is over in these seas."

It is probable, indeed, that in his zeal, thoroughness, and fidelity to the least of the duties then falling to him, is to be seen a surer indication of his great future than in any wider speculations about matters as yet too high for his position. The recent coolness between him and Lord Hood had been rapidly disappearing under the admiral's reviving appreciation and his own aptitude to conciliation. "Lord Hood is very civil," he writes on more than one occcasion, "I think we may be good friends again;" and the offer of a seventy-four-gun ship in place of his smaller vessel was further proof of his superior's confidence. Nelson refused the proposal. "I cannot give up my officers," he said, in the spirit that so endeared him to his followers; but the compliment was felt, and was enhanced by the admiral's approval of his motives. The prospective occupation of Toulon gave occasion for a yet more flattering evidence of the esteem in which he was held. As soon as the agreement with the city was completed, but the day before taking possession, Hood despatched him in haste to Oneglia, a small port on the Riviera of Genoa, and thence to Naples, to seek from the latter court and that of Turin[1] a reinforcement of ten thousand troops to hold the new acquisition. The "Agamemnon" being a fast sailer undoubtedly contributed much to this selection; but the character of the commanding officer could not but be considered on so important,

[1] Turin was capital of the Kingdom of Sardinia, which embraced the island of that name and the Province of Piedmont.

and in some ways delicate, a mission. "I should have liked to have stayed one day longer with the fleet, when they entered the harbour," he wrote to Mrs. Nelson, "but service could not be neglected for any private gratification," — a sentiment she had to hear pretty often, as betrothed and as wife, but which was no platitude on the lips of one who gave it constant demonstration in his acts. "Duty is the great business of a sea officer," he told his intended bride in early manhood, to comfort her and himself under a prolonged separation. "Thank God! I have done my duty," was the spoken thought that most solaced his death hour, as his heart yearned towards those at home whom he should see no more.

About this time he must have felt some touch of sympathy for the effeminate Spaniards, who were made ill by a sixty days' cruise. "All we get here," he writes, "is honour and salt beef. My poor fellows have not had a morsel of fresh meat or vegetables for near nineteen weeks; and in that time I have only had my foot twice on shore at Cadiz. We are absolutely getting sick from fatigue." "I am here [Naples] with news of our most glorious and great success, but, alas! the fatigue of getting it has been so great that the fleet generally, and I am sorry to say, my ship most so, are knocked up. Day after day, week after week, month after month, we have not been two gun shots from Toulon." The evident looseness of this statement, for the ship had only been a little over a month off Toulon, shows the impression the service had made upon his mind, for he was not prone to such exaggerations. "It is hardly possible," he says again, "to conceive the state of my ship; I have little less than one hundred sick." This condition of things is an eloquent testimony to the hardships endured; for Nelson was singularly successful, both before and after these days, in maintaining the health of a ship's company. His biographers say that during the term of three years that he commanded the "Boreas"

in the West Indies, not a single officer or man died out of
her whole complement, — an achievement almost incredible
in that sickly climate;[1] and he himself records that in his
two months' chase of Villeneuve, in 1805, no death
from sickness occurred among the seven or eight thousand
persons in the fleet. He attributed these remarkable
results to his attention, not merely to the physical surroundings of the crews, but also to the constant mental
stimulus and interest, which he aroused by providing the
seamen with occupation, frequent amusements, and change
of scene, thus keeping the various faculties in continual
play, and avoiding the monotony which most saps health,
through its deadening influence on the mind and spirits.

The "Agamemnon" reached Naples on the 12th of
September, and remained there four days. Nelson pressed
the matter of reinforcements with such diligence, and
was so heartily sustained by the British minister, Sir
William Hamilton, that he obtained the promise of six
thousand troops to sail at once under the convoy of the
"Agamemnon." "I have acted for Lord Hood," he wrote,
"with a zeal which no one could exceed;" and a few
weeks later he says: "The Lord is very much pleased with
my conduct about the troops at Naples, which I undertook
without any authority whatever from him; and they
arrived at Toulon before his requisition reached Naples."
It appears, therefore, that his orders were rather those of
a despatch-bearer than of a negotiator; but that he, with
the quick initiative he always displayed, took upon himself diplomatic action, to further the known wishes of his
superior and the common cause of England and Naples.
It was upon this occasion that Nelson first met Lady

[1] This statement, which apparently depends upon a memoir supplied
many years later by the first lieutenant of the "Boreas," is not strictly
accurate, for Nelson himself, in a letter written shortly after her arrival in
the West Indies, mentions that several of her ship's company had been
carried off by fever (Nicolas, vol. i. p. 111); but it can doubtless be accepted
as evidence of an unusually healthy condition.

Hamilton, who exercised so marked an influence over his later life; but, though she was still in the prime of her singular loveliness, being yet under thirty, not a ripple stirred the surface of his soul, afterward so powerfully perturbed by this fascinating woman. "Lady Hamilton," he writes to his wife, "has been wonderfully kind and good to Josiah [his step-son]. She is a young woman of amiable manners, and who does honour to the station to which she is raised." His mind was then too full of what was to be done; not as after the Nile, when, unstrung by reaction from the exhausting emotions of the past months, it was for the moment empty of aspiration and cloyed with flattery only.

The prospect of sailing with the convoy of troops, as well as of a few days' repose for the wearied ship's company, was cut short by the news that a French ship of war, with some merchant vessels in convoy, had anchored on the Sardinian coast. Although there were at Naples several Neapolitan naval vessels, and one Spaniard, none of them moved; and as the Prime Minister sent the information to Nelson, he felt bound to go, though but four days in port. "Unfit as my ship was, I had nothing left for the honour of our country but to sail, which I did in two hours afterwards. It was necessary to show them what an English man-of-war would do." The expected enemy was not found, and, after stretching along the coast in a vain search, the "Agamemnon" put into Leghorn on the 25th of September, nine days after leaving Naples, — "absolutely to save my poor fellows," wrote her captain to his brother. But even so, he purposed staying at his new anchorage but three days, "for I cannot bear the thought of being absent from the scene of action" at Toulon. In the same letter he mentions that since the 23d of April — five months — the ship had been at anchor only twenty days.

The unwavering resolution and prompt decision of his

character thus crop out at every step. In Leghorn he found a large French frigate, which had been on the point of sailing when his ship came in sight. "I am obliged to keep close watch to take care he does not give me the slip, which he is inclined to do. I shall pursue him, and' leave the two Courts [Great Britain and Tuscany] to settle the propriety of the measure, which I think will not be strictly regular. Have been up all night watching him — ready to cut the moment he did." The enemy, however, made no movement, and Nelson was not prepared to violate flagrantly the neutrality of the port. On the 30th of September he sailed, and on the 5th of October rejoined Lord Hood off Toulon, where four thousand of the Neapolitan troops, for which he had negotiated, had already arrived.

The high favor in which the admiral had held him ten years before in the West Indies, though slightly overcast by the coolness which arose during the intervening peace, had been rapidly regained in the course of the present campaign; and the customary report of his proceedings during the six weeks' absence could not but confirm Hood in the assurance that he had now to deal with a very exceptional character, especially fitted for separate and responsible service. Accordingly, from this time forward, such is the distinguishing feature of Nelson's career as a subordinate. He is selected from among many competitors, frequently his seniors, for the performance of duty outside the reach of the commander-in-chief, but requiring the attention of one upon whose activity, intelligence, and readiness, the fullest dependence could be placed. Up to the battle of the Nile, — in which, it must always be remembered, he commanded a squadron detached from the main fleet, and was assigned to it in deliberate preference to two older flag-officers, — Nelson's life presents a series of detached commands, independent as regarded the local scene of operations, and his method of attaining the pre-

scribed end with the force allotted to him, but dependent, technically, upon the distant commanders-in-chief, each of whom in succession, with one accord, recognized his singular fitness. The pithy but characteristic expression said to have been used by Earl St. Vincent, when asked for instructions about the Copenhagen expedition, — "D—n it, Nelson, send them to the devil your own way," — sums up accurately enough the confidence shown him by his superiors. He could not indeed lift them all to the height of his own conceptions, fearlessness, and enterprise; but when they had made up their minds to any particular course, they were, each and all, perfectly willing to intrust the execution to him. Even at Copenhagen he was but second in command, though conspicuously first in achievement. It was not till the opening of the second war of the French Revolution, in May, 1803, that he himself had supreme charge of a station, — his old familiar Mediterranean.

Being held in such esteem, it was but a short time before Nelson was again sent off from Toulon, to which he did not return during the British occupation. He was now ordered to report to Commodore Linzee, then lying with a detachment of three ships-of-the-line in the harbor of Cagliari, at the south end of Sardinia. On her passage the "Agamemnon" met and engaged a French squadron, of four large frigates and a brig. Though without decisive results, Nelson was satisfied with his own conduct in this affair, as was also Lord Hood when it came to his knowledge; for, one of the frigates being badly crippled, the whole force, which was on its way to Nice, was compelled to take refuge in Corsica, where it was far from secure. Two days later, on the 24th of October, Cagliari was reached, and the "Agamemnon" accompanied the division to Tunis, arriving there on the 1st of November.

Linzee's mission was to try and detach the Bey from the French interest, and it was hoped he could be induced to

allow the seizure of a number of French vessels which had
entered the port, under the convoy of a ship-of-the-line
and four frigates. When the British entered, the frigates
had disappeared, being in fact the same that Nelson had
fought ten days before. In accordance with his instructions, Linzee strove to persuade the Bey that the Republican government, because of its revolutionary and
bloodthirsty character, should receive no recognition or
support from more regular states, not even the protection
usually extended by a neutral port, and that in consequence he should be permitted to seize for Great Britain
the vessels in Tunis. The Turk may possibly have overlooked the fallacy in this argument, which assumed that
the protection extended by neutral governments was
rather for the benefit of the belligerent than for the quiet
and safety of its own waters; but he was perfectly clear-
sighted as to his personal advantage in the situation, for
the French owners, in despair of getting to France, were
selling their cargoes to him at one third their value. To
the argument that the French had beheaded their king,
he drily replied that the English had once done the same;
and he decisively refused to allow the ships to be molested.
Nelson was disgusted that his consent should have been
awaited. "The English seldom get much by negotiation
except the being laughed at, which we have been; and I
don't like it. Had we taken, which in my opinion we
ought to have done, the men-of-war and convoy, worth at
least £300,000, how much better we could have negotiated:
—given the Bey £50,000, he would have been glad to
have put up with the insult offered to his dignity;" and
he plainly intimates his dissatisfaction with Linzee. This
irresponsible and irreflective outburst was, however, only
an instance of the impatience his enterprising, energetic
spirit always felt when debarred from prompt action,
whether by good or bad reasons; for almost on the same
day he expresses the sounder judgment: "Had we latterly

attempted to take them I am sure the Bey would have declared against us, and done our trade some damage." No advantage could have accrued from the seizure of the French vessels, at all proportioned to the inconvenience of having the hostility of Tunis, flanking as it did the trade routes to the Levant. The British had then quite enough on their hands, without detaching an additional force from the north coast of the Mediterranean, to support a gratuitous quarrel on the south. As a matter of mere policy it would have been ill-judged.

Nelson, however, did not as yet at all realize the wideness of the impending struggle, for it was in these very letters that he expressed a wish to exchange to the West Indies. "You know," he writes to his old friend Locker, "that Pole is gone to the West Indies. I have not seen him since his order, but I know it was a thing he dreaded. Had I been at Toulon I should have been a candidate for that service, for I think our sea war is over in these seas." Perhaps his intrinsic merit would have retrieved even such a mistake as we can now see this would have been, and he would there have come sooner into contact with Sir John Jervis — to whom, if to any one, the name of patron to Nelson may be applied — for Jervis then had the West India command; but it is difficult to imagine Nelson's career apart from the incidents of his Mediterranean service. The Mediterranean seems inseparable from his name, and he in the end felt himself identified with it beyond all other waters.

His longing for action, which prompted the desire for the West Indies, was quickly gratified, for orders were received from Hood, by Linzee, to detach him from the latter's command. The admiral sent him a very handsome letter upon his single-handed combat with the French frigates, and directed him to go to the north end of Corsica, to take charge of a division of vessels he would there find cruising, and to search for his late enemies along that coast and through the neighboring waters, between the island and the shores of Italy. He was also to warn off neutral vessels bound to Genoa, that port being declared blockaded, and to seize them if they persisted in their voyage thither. "I consider this command as a very high compliment," wrote Nelson to his uncle Suckling, "there being five older captains in the fleet." This it certainly was, — a compliment and a prophecy as well.

In pursuance of these orders Nelson left Tunis on the 30th of November, and on the 8th of December discovered the French squadron, protected by shore batteries, in San Fiorenzo Bay, in Corsica. This island, which during the middle ages, and until some twenty years before the beginning of the French Revolution, was a dependency of Genoa, had then by the latter been ceded to France, against the express wishes of the inhabitants, whose resistance was crushed only after a prolonged struggle. Although it was now in open revolt against the Revolutionary government, the troops of the latter still held three or four of the principal seaports, among them the northern one in which the frigates then lay, as well as Bastia upon the east coast of the island, and Calvi on the west. His force being insufficient to engage the works of any of these places, there was nothing for Nelson to do but to blockade them, in hopes of exhausting their resources and at least preventing the escape of the ships of war. In this he was successful, for the latter either were destroyed or fell into the hands of Great Britain, when the ports were reduced.

Meanwhile affairs at Toulon were approaching the crisis which ended its tenure by the British and their allies. The garrison had never been sufficient to man properly the very extensive lines, which the peculiar configuration of the surrounding country made it necessary to occupy for the security of the town ; and the troops themselves were not only of different nations, but of very varying degrees of efficiency. Under these conditions the key of the position, accurately indicated by Napoleon Bonaparte, then a major and in command of the artillery, was held in insufficient force, and was successfully stormed on the night of December 16, 1793. It was immediately recognized that the ships could no longer remain in the harbor, and that with them the land forces also must depart. After two days of hurried preparations, and an attempt, only partially successful, to destroy the dockyard and French ships of war, the fleets sailed out on the 19th of December, carrying with them, besides the soldiery, as many as possible of the wretched citizens, who were forced to fly in confusion and misery from their homes, in order to escape the sure and fearful vengeance of the Republican government. The "Agamemnon" was in Leghorn, getting provisions, when the fugitives arrived there, and Nelson speaks in vivid terms of the impression made upon him by the tales he heard and the sights he saw. "Fathers are here without families, and families without fathers, the pictures of horror and despair." "In short, all is horror. I cannot write all: my mind is deeply impressed with grief. Each teller makes the scene more horrible." He expressed the opinion that the evacuation was a benefit to England, and it unquestionably was. He had not always thought so; but it must be allowed that the hopes and exultation with which he greeted the acquisition of the place had sufficient foundation, in the reported attitude of the people of Southern France, to justify the first opinion as well as the last. The attempt was worth making, though it proved unsuccessful. As it was, the occupation had resulted in a degree of destruction to the French ships and arsenal in Toulon, which, though then over-estimated, was a real gain to the allies.

CHAPTER IV.

REDUCTION OF CORSICA BY THE BRITISH. — DEPARTURE OF LORD
HOOD FOR ENGLAND. — THE "AGAMEMNON" REFITTED AT
LEGHORN.

JANUARY – DECEMBER, 1794.   AGE, 35.

B Y the loss of Toulon the British fleet in the Mediterranean was left adrift, without any secure harbor to
serve as a depot for supplies and a base for extended operations.   Hood took his ships to Hyères Bay, a few miles
east of Toulon, a spot where they could lie safely at anchor,
but which was unsuitable for a permanent establishment, —
the shores not being tenable against French attack.   He now
turned his eyes upon Corsica, whence the celebrated native
chieftain, Paoli, who had led the natives in their former
struggle against France, had made overtures to him, looking to the union of the island to the British crown.   Nelson
in person, or, during his brief absence in Leghorn, his division, had so closely invested the shores, that neither troops
nor supplies of any kind had been able to enter since the
early part of December, nor had the blockaded vessels been
able to get out.   The thoroughness with which this work
was done brought him, on the 6th of January, 1794, yet
further compliments from Hood, who wrote him that "he
looked upon these frigates as certain, trusting to my zeal
and activity, and knows, if it is in the power of man to
have them, I will secure them."   At the same time he was
instructed to enter into communication with Paoli, and
settle plans for the landing of the troops.   In attending to
this commission his intermediary was Lieutenant George

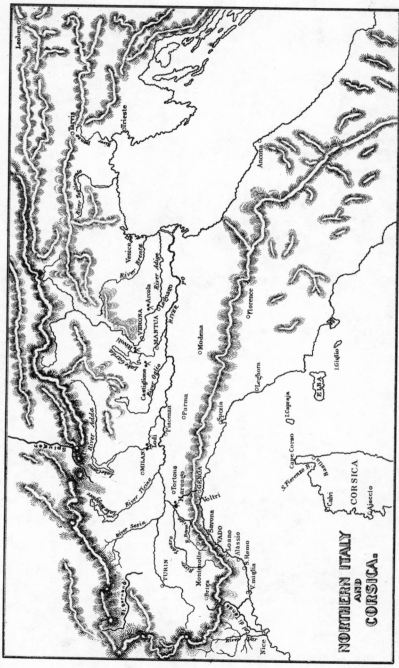

NORTHERN ITALY
AND
CORSICA.

(For Life of Nelson.)

Andrews, brother to the lady to whom he had become attached at St. Omer, and who had afterwards been a midshipman with him on board the "Boreas." " This business going through my hands," he wrote with just pride, " is a proof of Lord Hood's confidence in me, and that I shall pledge myself for nothing but what will be acceptable to him." It was indeed evident that Hood was more and more reposing in him a peculiar trust, a feeling which beyond most others tends to increase by its own action. Nelson repaid him with the most unbounded admiration. " The Lord is very good friends with me," he writes ; " he is certainly the best officer I ever saw. Everything from him is so clear it is impossible to misunderstand him." " His zeal, his activity for the honour and benefit of his country," he says at another time, " are not abated. Upwards of seventy, he possesses the mind of forty years of age. He has not a thought separated from honour and glory." The flattering proofs of his superior's esteem, and the demand made upon his natural powers to exert themselves freely, had a very beneficial effect upon his health and spirits. It was not effort, however protracted and severe, but the denial of opportunity to act, whether by being left unemployed or through want of information, that wore Nelson down. " I have not been one hour at anchor for pleasure in eight months ; but I can assure you I never was better in health."

Meanwhile a commission from the fleet arrived in Corsica. Sir Gilbert Elliot, the representative of the British government in the island, was at its head, and with him were associated two army officers, one of whom afterwards became widely celebrated as Sir John Moore. A satisfactory agreement being concluded, Hood sailed from Hyères Bay with the ships and troops, and operations began against San Fiorenzo, terminating in the evacuation of the place by the French, who upon the 19th of February retreated by land to Bastia. Nelson was not immediately

connected with this undertaking; but he had the satisfaction of knowing that two of the four frigates, of whose
detention in the island he was the immediate cause, were
here lost to the enemy. He was during these weeks actively employed harrying the coast — destroying depots of
stores on shore, and small vessels laden with supplies.
These services were mainly, though not entirely, rendered
in the neighborhood of Bastia, a strongly fortified town,
which was to become the next object of the British efforts,
and the scene of his own exertions. There, also, though
on a comparatively small scale, he was to give striking evidence of the characteristics which led him on, step by step,
to his great renown.

When Hood himself took command at San Fiorenzo, he
relieved Nelson from that part of his charge, and sent him
on the 7th of February to blockade Bastia, — a strictly detached service, and one of the utmost importance, as upon
the intercepting of supplies the issue of the siege largely
turned. Three weeks later, on the 1st of March, Nelson
wrote: "We are still in the busy scene of war, a situation
in which I own I feel pleasure, more especially as my actions have given great satisfaction to my commander-in-
chief. The blocking up of Corsica he left to me: it has
been accomplished in the most complete manner, not a boat
got in, nor a soldier landed, although eight thousand men
were embarked at Nice;" and, he might have added, although a vessel was said to sail from Nice every thirty-six
hours. Nor was his activity confined to blockading. He
continually reconnoitered the town and the works, in doing
which on the 23d of February he engaged the batteries at
short range, with the "Agamemnon" and two frigates, —
the action lasting for nearly two hours. While it was at
its height, the heads of the British columns, coming from
San Fiorenzo, only twelve miles distant by land, were seen
upon the heights overlooking Bastia from the rear. "What
a noble sight it must have been" to them! wrote Nelson

enthusiastically, in the ardor of his now opening career, — for it must be remembered that this hero of a hundred fights was even then but beginning to taste that rapture of the strife, in which he always breathed most freely, as though in his native element.

Bastia, as he saw it and reported to Lord Hood, was a walled town with central citadel, of some ten thousand inhabitants, on the east coast of Corsica, and twenty miles south of Cape Corso, the northern extremity of the island. The main fortifications were along the sea-front; but there was, besides, a series of detached works on either flank and to the rear. The latter not only guarded the approaches from the interior, but also, being situated on the hills, much above the town, were capable of commanding it, in case of an enemy gaining possession. Nelson, while modestly disclaiming any presumptuous dependence upon his own judgment, expressed a decided opinion, based upon the engagement of the 23d, that the " Agamemnon " and the frigates could silence the fire of the sea-front, batter down the walls, and that then five hundred troops could carry the place by assault. " That the works on the hills would annoy the town afterwards is certain, but the enemy being cut off from all supplies — the provisions in the town being of course in our possession — would think of nothing but making the best terms they could for themselves." To his dismay, however, and to the extreme annoyance of the admiral, General Dundas, commanding the army, refused to move against Bastia, condemning the attempt as visionary and rash. Meantime the French, unmolested except by the desultory efforts of the insurgent Corsicans, were each day strengthening their works, and converting the possibilities Nelson saw into the impossibilities of the cautious general.

Hood on the 25th of February came round from San Fiorenzo to Bastia; but he purposely brought with him no captain senior to Nelson, in order that the latter might

remain in charge of the operations he had begun so well.
When Dundas retreated again to San Fiorenzo, Hood on
the 3d of March followed him there with the flagship, to
urge his co-operation; leaving Nelson with six frigates
to conduct the blockade and take such other steps as the
opportunities might justify. By the middle of March,
nearly three months having elapsed since her last hasty
visit to Leghorn, the "Agamemnon" was wholly destitute
of supplies. "We are really," wrote Nelson to Hood,
" without firing, wine, beef, pork, flour, and almost without water: not a rope, canvas, twine, or nail in the ship.
The ship is so light she cannot hold her side to the wind.
. . . We are certainly in a bad plight at present, not a
man has slept dry for many months. Yet," he continues,
with that indomitable energy which made light of mere
difficulties of material, and conveys so impressive a les-
son to our modern days, when slight physical defects appear insurmountable, and ships not wholly up to date are
counted obsolete, — "yet if your Lordship wishes me to
remain off Bastia, I can, by going to Porto Ferrajo, get
water and stores, and twenty-four hours in Leghorn will
give us provisions; and our refitting, which will take some
time, can be put off a little. My wish is to be present at
the attack of Bastia."

On the 18th of March Hood summoned him to San
Fiorenzo. The difference between him and Dundas had
become a quarrel, and the latter had quitted his command.
Hood wished to strengthen the argument with his successor, by a report of the observations made by Nelson; but
the latter records that, after expressing his opinion that
eight hundred troops with four hundred seamen could re-
duce the place, it was found that all the army was united
against an attack, declaring the impossibility of taking
Bastia, even if all the force were united, — and this, notwithstanding that an engineer and an artillery officer had
visited the scene, and agreed with Nelson that there was a

probability of success. On the north side both they and he considered the place weak, and at the same time found the ground favorable for establishing the siege guns. Moreover, even during the winter gales, he had succeeded in so closing the sea approaches, while the revolted Corsicans intercepted those by land, that a pound of coarse bread was selling for three francs. The spring equinox was now near at hand, and with better weather the blockade would be yet more efficient. Between actual attack and famine, he argued, the place must fall. "Not attacking it I could not but consider as a national disgrace. If the Army will not take it, we must, by some way or other."

If every particular operation of war is to be considered by itself alone, and as a purely professional question, to be determined by striking a balance between the arguments pro and con, it is probable that the army officers were right in their present contention. In nothing military was scientific accuracy of prediction so possible as in forecasting the result and duration of a regular siege, where the force brought to bear on either side could be approximately known. But, even in this most methodical and least inspired of processes, the elements of chance, of the unforeseen, or even the improbable, will enter, disturbing the most careful calculations. For this reason, no case must be decided purely on its individual merits, without taking into account the other conditions of the campaign at large. For good and sufficient reasons, the British had undertaken, not to conquer a hostile island, but to effect the deliverance of a people who were already in arms, and had themselves redeemed their country with the exception of two or three fortified seaports, for the reduction of which they possessed neither the materials nor the technical skill. To pause in the movement of advance was, with a half-civilized race of unstable temperament, to risk everything. But besides, for the mere purpose of the blockade, it was imperative to force the enemy as far as possible to contract his lines. Speaking of a new work thrown up north of the town, Nelson said with accurate judgment: "It must be destroyed, or the Corsicans will be obliged to give up a post which the enemy would immediately possess; and of course throw us on that side at a greater distance from Bastia." The result would be, not merely so much more time and labor to be expended, nor yet only the moral effect on either party, but also the uncovering of a greater length of seaboard, by which supplies might be run into the town.

The strength of the place, in which, when it fell, were found "seventy-seven pieces of ordnance with an incredible amount of stores," was far superior to that estimated by the eye of Nelson, untrained as an engineer. Not only so, but the force within the walls was very much larger than he thought, when he spoke with such confidence. "I never yet told Lord Hood," he wrote nearly a year later, "that after everything was fixed for the attack of Bastia, I had information given me of the enormous number of troops we had to oppose us; but my own honour, Lord Hood's honour, and the honour of our Country must have all been sacrificed, had I mentioned what I knew; therefore you will believe what must have been my feelings during the whole siege, when I had often proposals made to me by men, now rewarded, to write to Lord Hood to raise the siege." "Had this been an English town," he said immediately after the surrender, "I am sure it would not have been taken by them. The more we see of this place, the more we are astonished at their giving it up, but the truth is, the different parties were afraid to trust each other." The last assertion, if correct, conveys just one of those incidents which so frequently concur to insure the success of a step rightly taken, as that of Nelson and Hood in this instance certainly was. "Forty-five hundred men," he continues, "have laid down their arms to under twelve hundred troops and seamen. If proofs were wanting to show that perseverance, unanimity, and gallantry, can accomplish almost incredible things, we are an additional instance."

"I always was of opinion," he wrote in the exultation of reaction from the weight of responsibility he had assumed by his secrecy, — "I always was of opinion, have ever acted up to it, and never have had any reason to repent it, that one Englishman was equal to three Frenchmen." This curious bit of the gasconade into which Nelson from time to time lapsed, can scarcely be accepted as a sound working theory, or as of itself justifying the risk taken; and yet it undoubtedly, under a grossly distorted form, portrays the temperament which enabled him to capture Bastia, and which made him what he was, — a man strong enough to take great chances for adequate ends. "All naval operations undertaken since I have been at the head of the government," said Napoleon, "have always failed, because the admirals see double, and have learned — where I do not know — that war can be made without running risks." It is not material certainty of success, the *ignis fatuus* which is the great snare of the mere engineer, or of the merely accomplished soldier, that points the way to heroic achievements. It is the vivid inspiration that enables its happy possessor, at critical moments, to see and follow the bright clear line, which, like a ray of light at midnight, shining among manifold doubtful indications, guides his steps. Whether it leads him to success or to failure, he may not know; but that it is the path of wisdom, of duty, and of honor, he knows full well by the persuasion within, — by conviction, the fortifier of the reason, though not by sight, the assurance of demonstration. Only a man capable of incurring a disaster like that at Teneriffe could rise to the level of daring, which, through hidden perils, sought and wrought the superb triumph of Aboukir Bay. Such is genius, that rare but hazardous gift, which separates a man from his fellows by a chasm not to be bridged by human will. Thus endowed, Nelson before the walls of Bastia showed, though in a smaller sphere, and therefore with a lighter hazard, the same keen perception, the same instant decision, the same unfaltering resolve, the same tenacity of purpose, that, far over and beyond the glamour of mere success, have rendered eternally illustrious the days of St. Vincent, of the Nile, and of Copenhagen.

Of the spirit which really actuated him, in his unwavering support of Lord Hood's inclination to try the doubtful issue, many interesting instances are afforded by his correspondence. "I feel for the honour of my Country, and had rather be beat than not make the attack. If we do not try we can never be successful. I own I have no fears for the final issue: it will be conquest, certain we will deserve it. My reputation depends on the opinion I have given; but I feel an honest consciousness that I have done right. We must, we will have it, or some of our heads will be laid low. I glory in the attempt." "What would the immortal Wolfe have done?" he says again, refreshing his own constancy in the recollection of an equal heroism, crowned with success against even greater odds. "As he did, beat the enemy, if he perished in the attempt." Again, a fortnight later: "We are in high health and spirits besieging Bastia; the final event, I feel assured, will be conquest." When the siege had already endured for a month, and with such slight actual progress as to compel him to admit to Hood that the town battery had been "put in such a state, that firing away many shot at it is almost useless till we have a force sufficient to get nearer," his confidence remains unabated. "I have no fears about the final issue," he writes to his wife; "it will be victory, Bastia will be ours; and if so, it must prove an event to which the history of England can hardly boast an equal." Further on in the same letter he makes a prediction, so singularly accurate as to excite curiosity about its source: "I will tell you as a secret, Bastia will be ours between the 20th and 24th of this month" — three weeks after the date of writing — "if succours do not get in." It surrendered actually on the 22d. One is tempted to speculate if there had been any such understanding with the garrison as was afterwards reached with Calvi; but there is no other token of such an arrangement. It is instructive also to compare this high-strung steadfastness of purpose to dare every risk, if success perchance might be won thereby, with his comment upon his own impulses at a somewhat later date. "My disposition cannot bear tame and slow measures. Sure I am, had I commanded our fleet on the 14th, that either the whole French fleet would have graced my triumph, or I should have been in a confounded scrape." Surely the secret of great successes is in these words.

The siege of Bastia was not in its course productive of striking events. Having reasoned in vain with the two successive generals, Hood demanded that there should be sent back to him a contingent of troops, which had originally been detailed to serve as marines in the fleet, but which he had loaned to the army for the operations against San Fiorenzo. Having received these, he returned to Bastia, and on the 4th of April, 1794, the besieging force, twelve hundred troops and two hundred and fifty seamen, landed to the northward of the town. They at once began to throw up batteries, while the Corsicans harassed the landward approaches to the place. Nelson being with the troops, the "Agamemnon" with some frigates was anchored north of the city, Hood with his ships south of it. During the nights, boats from the fleet rowed guard near to the sea-front, with such diligence that few of the craft that attempted to run in or out succeeded in so doing. When darkness covered the waters, British gunboats crept close to the walls, and by an intermitting but frequent fire added much to the distress of the enemy. On the 11th of April

the garrison was formally summoned, and, the expected
refusal having been received, the British batteries opened.
There was not force enough, however, to bring the place
to terms as a consequence of direct attack, and after three
weeks Nelson, while betraying no apprehension of failure,
practically admitted the fact.   "Although I have no
doubt but even remaining in our present situation, and by
strict guard rowing close to the town, and the Corsicans
harassing them on the hills, and the gunboats by night,
but that the enemy must surrender before any great length
of time, yet, if force can be spared, a successful attack on
the heights must much facilitate a speedy capture.   I
own it will give me the highest pleasure to assist in the
attack."

It was by such an attack, or rather by the fear of it,
coming upon the long and exhausting endurance of cannonade and hunger, that Bastia finally fell.   "We shall
in time accomplish the taking of Bastia," wrote Nelson on
the 3d of May.   "I have no doubt in the way we proposed
to attempt it, by bombardment and cannonading, joined
to a close blockade of the harbour."   "If not," he adds,
"our Country will, I believe, sooner forgive an officer for
attacking his enemy than for letting it alone."   On the
12th a large boat was captured coming out from the port;
and on her were found letters from the governor, Gentili,
confessing the annoyance caused by the British fire, and
saying that if relief did not arrive by the 29th, the place
must be looked upon as lost.   Three nights later another
boat was caught attempting to enter.   On board her was
a brother of the Mayor of Bastia.   This man, while talking with Hood's secretary, expressed his fears for the
result to his relatives, if the town were carried by assault.
The secretary replied that Hood could not prevent those
evils, if the garrison awaited the attack, and gave the
Corsican to understand that it was imminent, troops being
expected from San Fiorenzo.   At the urgent request of

the prisoner, one of the seamen taken with him was permitted to land with a letter, stating the impending danger. By a singular coincidence, or by skilful contrivance, the San Fiorenzo troops appeared on the heights upon the evening, May 19, following this conversation. Flags of truce had already been hoisted, negotiations were opened, and on the 22d the French colors were struck and the British took possession. "When I reflect what we have achieved," confessed the hitherto outwardly unmoved Nelson, "I am all astonishment. The most glorious sight that an Englishman can experience, and which, I believe, none but an Englishman could bring about, was exhibited, — 4,500 men laying down their arms to less than 1,000 British soldiers, who were serving as marines." As towards the French this account is perhaps somewhat less than fair; but it does no more than justice to the admirable firmness and enterprise shown by Hood and Nelson. As a question of Bastia only, their attempt might be charged with rashness; but having regard to the political and military conditions, to the instability of the Corsican character, and to the value of the island as a naval station, it was amply justified, for the risks run were out of all proportion less than the advantage to be gained.

Thus the siege of Bastia ended in triumph, despite the prior pronouncement of the general commanding the troops, that the attempt was "most visionary and rash." These epithets, being used to Hood after his own expressions in favor of the undertaking, had not unnaturally provoked from him a resentful retort; and, as men are rarely conciliated by the success of measures which they have ridiculed, there arose a degree of strained relations between army and navy, that continued even after the arrival of a new commander of the land forces, and indeed throughout Hood's association with the operations in Corsica.

During this busy and laborious period, despite his burden of secret anxiety, Nelson's naturally delicate health

VOL. I. — 9

showed the favorable reaction, which, as has before been noted, was with him the usual result of the call to exertion. His letters steadily reflect, and occasionally mention, the glow of exultation produced by constant action of a worthy and congenial nature. "We are in high health and spirits besieging Bastia," he writes to his wife soon after landing; and shortly before the fall of the place he says again: "As to my health, it was never better, seldom so well." Yet, although from beginning to end the essential stay of the enterprise, the animating soul, without whose positive convictions and ardent support Lord Hood could scarcely have dared so great a hazard, he was throughout the siege left, apparently purposely, in an anomalous position, and was at the end granted a recognition which, though probably not grudging, was certainly scanty. No definition of his duties was ever given by the commander-in-chief. He appears as it were the latter's unacknowledged representative ashore, a plenipotentiary without credentials. "What my situation is," he writes to a relative, "is not to be described. I am everything, yet nothing ostensible; enjoying the confidence of Lord Hood and Colonel Villettes, and the captains landed with the seamen obeying my orders." A fortnight later he writes to Hood: "Your Lordship knows exactly the situation I am in here. With Colonel Villettes I have no reason but to suppose I am respected in the highest degree; nor have I occasion to complain of want of attention to my wishes from any parties; but yet I am considered as not commanding the seamen landed. My wishes may be, and are, complied with; my orders would possibly be disregarded. Therefore, if we move from hence, I would wish your Lordship to settle that point. Your Lordship will not, I trust, take this request amiss: I have been struggling with it since the first day I landed."

Hood apparently gave him full satisfaction as regards his own view of the situation. "I am happy," Nelson wrote, when acknowledging his reply, "that my ideas of the situation I am in here so perfectly agree with your Lordship's;" but he did not settle the matter by a decisive order. His object, as he seems to have explained, was to bestow a certain amount of prominence upon a young captain, Hunt, who had recently lost his ship, and who, Hood thought, would be sooner provided with another, if he appeared as in command at the guns. Nelson acceded to this arrangement with his usual generosity. "Your kind intention to Captain Hunt," he wrote, "I had the honour of telling your Lordship, should be furthered by every means in my power; and my regard for him, I assure you, is undiminished. He is a most exceeding good young man, nor is any one more zealous for the service. I don't complain of any one, but an idea has entered into the heads of some under him, that his command was absolutely distinct from me; and that I had no authority over him, except as a request." Unfortunately, Hood, in his desire to serve Hunt, not only unduly but absurdly minimized Nelson's relations to the whole affair. His despatch ran: "Captain Nelson, of his Majesty's ship Agamemnon, who had the command and directions of the seamen *in landing the guns, mortars and stores,*[1] and Captain Hunt *who commanded at the batteries,*[1] . . . have an equal claim to my gratitude." To limit Nelson's share in the capture of Bastia to the purely subsidiary though important function of landing the guns, was as unjust as it was unnecessary to the interests of Hunt. The latter, being second in command ashore, and afterwards sent home with the despatches, was sure to receive the reward customarily bestowed upon such services.

The incident singularly and aptly illustrates the difference, which in a military service cannot be too carefully kept in mind, between individual expressions of opinion, which may be biassed, and professional reputation, which,

[1] The italics are the author's.

like public sentiment, usually settles at last not far from the truth. Despite this curious inversion of the facts by Lord Hood, there probably was no one among the naval forces, nor among the soldiery, who did not thoroughly, if perchance somewhat vaguely, appreciate that Nelson was the moving spirit of the whole operation, even beyond Hood himself. As the Greek commanders after Salamis were said to have voted the award of merit each to himself first, but all to Themistocles second, so at Bastia, whatever value individuals might place on their own services, all probably would have agreed that Nelson came next.

The latter meantime was happily unconscious of the wrong done him, so that nothing marred the pleasure with which he congratulated the commander-in-chief, and received the latter's brief but hearty general order of thanks, wherein Nelson's own name stood foremost, as was due both to his seniority and to his exertions. When the despatch reached him, he freely expressed his discontent in letters to friends; but being, at the time of its reception, actively engaged in the siege of Calvi, the exhilaration of that congenial employment for the moment took the edge off the keenness of his resentment. "Lord Hood and myself were never better friends — nor, *although his Letter does,*[1] did he wish to put me where I never was — in the rear. Captain Hunt, who lost his ship, he wanted to push forward for another, — a young man who never was on a battery, or ever rendered any service during the siege; if any person ever says he did, then I submit to the character of a story-teller. Poor Serocold, who fell here,[2] was determined to publish an advertisement, as he commanded a battery under my orders. The whole operations of the siege were carried on through Lord Hood's letters to me. I was the mover of it — I was the cause of its success. Sir Gilbert Elliot will be my evi-

[1] The italics are Nelson's.
[2] Written at the siege of Calvi.

dence, if any is required. I am not a little vexed, but shall not quarrel." "I am well aware," he had written to Mrs. Nelson a few days before, "my poor services will not be noticed: I have no interest; but, however services may be received, it is not right in an officer to slacken his zeal for his Country."

These noble words only voiced a feeling which in Nelson's heart had all the strength of a principle; and this light of the single eye stood him in good stead in the moments of bitterness which followed a few months later, when a lull in the storm of fighting gave the sense of neglect a chance to rankle. "My heart is full," he writes then to his uncle Suckling, speaking not only of Bastia, but of the entire course of operations in Corsica, "when I think of the treatment I have received: every man who had any considerable share in the reduction has got some place or other — I, only I, am without reward. . . . Nothing but my anxious endeavour to serve my Country makes me bear up against it; but I sometimes am ready to give all up." "Forgive this letter," he adds towards the end: "I have said a great deal too much of myself; but indeed it is all too true." In similar strain he expressed himself to his wife: "It is very true that I have ever served faithfully, and ever has it been my fate to be neglected; but that shall not make me inattentive to my duty. I have pride in doing my duty well, and a self-approbation, which if it is not so lucrative, yet perhaps affords more pleasing sensations." Thus the consciousness of duty done in the past, and the clear recognition of what duty still demanded in the present and future, stood him in full stead, when he failed to receive at the hands of others the honor he felt to be his due, and which, he never wearied in proclaiming, was in his eyes priceless, above all other reward. "Corsica, in respect of prizes," he wrote to Mrs. Nelson, "produces nothing but honour, far above the consideration of wealth: not that I despise riches, quite the contrary, yet I would not sacrifice a good name to obtain them. Had I attended less than I have done to the service of my Country, I might have made some money too: however, I trust my name will stand on record when the money-makers will be forgot," — a hope to be abundantly fulfilled.

At the moment Bastia fell there arrived from England a new commander-in-chief for the land forces, General Stuart, an officer of distinguished ability and enterprise. Cheered by the hope of cordial co-operation, Hood and Nelson resumed without delay their enthusiastic efforts. Within a week, on the 30th of May, the latter wrote that the "Agamemnon" was taking on board ammunition for the siege of Calvi, the last remaining of the hostile strongholds. In the midst of the preparations, at eleven P. M. of June 6, word was received that nine French ships-of-the-line had come out of Toulon, and were believed to be bound for Calvi, with reinforcements for the garrison. At seven the next morning the squadron was under way; the "Agamemnon," which had two hundred tons of ordnance stores to unload, sailing only half an hour after her less encumbered consorts, whom she soon overtook.

Hood shaped his course for Calvi, being constrained thereto, not only by the rumor of the enemy's destination, but also by the military necessity of effecting a junction with the rest of his fleet. Admiral Hotham, who commanded the British division of seven ships in front of Toulon, instead of waiting to verify the report brought to him of the enemy's force, — which was actually the same, numerically, as his own, — bore up hastily for Calvi, intending, so wrote Nelson at the time, to fight them there, rather than that they should throw in succors. Whatever their numbers, thus to surrender touch of them at the beginning was an evident mistake, for which, as for most mistakes, a penalty had in the end to be paid; and in fact, if the relief of Calvi was the object of the sortie, the place to fight was evidently as far from there as possible. Off Toulon, even had Hotham been beaten, his opponents would have been too roughly handled to carry out their mission. As it was, this precipitate retirement lost the British an opportunity for a combat that might have placed their control of the sea beyond peradventure; and a few months later, Nelson, who at first had viewed Hotham's action with the generous sympathy and confident pride which always characterized his attitude towards his brother officers, showed how clearly he was reading in the book of experience the lessons that should afterwards stand himself in good stead. "When ' Victory ' is gone," he wrote, "we shall be thirteen sail of the line [to the French fifteen], when the enemy will keep our new Commanding Officer [Hotham] in hot water, who missed, unfortunately, the opportunity of fighting them, last June." Ten years later, in his celebrated chase of Villeneuve's fleet, he said to his captains: "If we meet the enemy we shall find them not less than eighteen, I rather think twenty, sail of the line, and therefore do not be surprised if I should not fall on them immediately [he had but eleven] — *we won't part*[1] without a battle; " and he expressed with the utmost decision his clear appreciation that even a lost battle, if delivered at the right point or at the right moment, would frustrate the ulterior objects of the enemy, by crippling the force upon which they depended. As will be seen in the sequel, Hotham, throughout his brief command as Hood's successor, suffered the consequences of permitting so important a fraction of the enemy's fleet to escape his grasp, when it was in his power to close with it.

The British divisions met off the threatened port two days after leaving Bastia, and two hours later a lookout frigate brought word that the French fleet had been seen by her the evening before, to the northward and westward,

---

[1] Author's italics.

some forty miles off its own coast.   Hood at once made
sail in pursuit, and in the afternoon of the 10th of June
caught sight of the enemy, but so close in with the shore
that they succeeded in towing their ships under the protection of the batteries in Golfe Jouan, where, for lack of
wind, he was unable to follow them for some days, during
which they had time to strengthen their position beyond
his powers of offence.   Hotham's error was irreparable.
The "Agamemnon" was then sent back to Bastia, to
resume the work of transportation, which Nelson pushed
with the untiring energy that characterized all his movements.   Arriving on the 12th, fifteen hundred troops were
embarked by eight the next morning, and at four in the
afternoon he sailed, having with him two smaller ships of
war and twenty-two transports.   On the 15th he anchored
at San Fiorenzo.

Here he met General Stuart.   The latter was anxious
to proceed at once with the siege of Calvi, but asked
Nelson whether he thought it proper to take the shipping
to that exposed position; alluding to the French fleet that
had left Toulon, and which Hood was then seeking.
Nelson's reply is interesting, as reflecting the judgment
of a warrior at once prudent and enterprising, concerning
the influence of a hostile "fleet in being" upon a contemplated detached operation.   "I certainly thought it right,"
he said, "placing the firmest reliance that we should be
perfectly safe under Lord Hood's protection, who would
take care that the French fleet at Gourjean[1] should not
molest us."   To Hood he wrote a week later: "I believed
ourselves safe under your Lordship's wing."   At this
moment he thought the French to be nine sail-of-the-line
to the British thirteen, — no contemptible inferior force.
Yet that he recognized the possible danger from such a
detachment is also clear; for, writing two days earlier,
under the same belief as to the enemy's strength, and

[1] Golfe Jouan; on the coast of France between Toulon and Nice.

speaking of the expected approach of an important convoy, he says: "I hope they will not venture up till Lord Hood can get off Toulon, or wherever the French fleet are got to." When a particular opinion has received the extreme expression now given to that concerning the "fleet in being," and apparently has undergone equally extreme misconception, it is instructive to recur to the actual effect of such a force, upon the practice of a man with whom moral effect was never in excess of the facts of the case, whose imagination produced to him no paralyzing picture of remote contingencies. Is it probable that, with the great issues of 1690 at stake, Nelson, had he been in Tourville's place, would have deemed the crossing of the Channel by French troops impossible, because of Torrington's "fleet in being"?

Sailing again on June 16, the expedition arrived next day off Calvi. Although it was now summer, the difficulties of the new undertaking were, from the maritime point of view, very great. The town of Calvi, which was walled and had a citadel, lies upon a promontory on the west side of an open gulf of the same name, a semicircular recess, three miles wide by two deep, on the northwest coast of Corsica. The western point of its shore line is Cape Revellata; the eastern, Point Espano. The port being fortified and garrisoned, it was not practicable to take the shipping inside, nor to establish on the inner beach a safe base for disembarking. The "Agamemnon" therefore anchored outside, nearly two miles south of Cape Revellata, and a mile from shore, in the excessive depth of fifty-three fathoms; the transports coming-to off the cape, but farther to seaward. The water being so deep, and the bottom rocky, the position was perilous for sailing-ships, for the prevailing summer wind blows directly on the shore, which is steep-to and affords no shelter. Abreast the "Agamemnon" was a small inlet, Porto Agro, about three miles from Calvi by difficult

approaches. Here Nelson landed on the 18th with
General Stuart; and, after reconnoitring both the beach
and the town, the two officers decided that, though a very
bad landing, it was the best available. On the 19th, at
7 A. M., the troops disembarked. That afternoon Nelson
himself went ashore to stay, taking with him two hundred
and fifty seamen. The next day it came on to blow so
hard that most of the ships put to sea, and no intercourse
was had from the land with those which remained. The
"Agamemnon" did not return till the 24th. Lord Hood
was by this time in San Fiorenzo Bay, having abandoned
the hope of attacking the French fleet in Golfe Jouan.
On the 27th he arrived off Calvi, and thenceforth Nelson
was in daily communication with him till the place
fell.

As the army in moderate, though not wholly adequate,
force conducted the siege of Calvi, under a general officer
of vigorous character, the part taken by Nelson and his
seamen, though extremely important, and indeed essential
to the ultimate success, was necessarily subordinate. It
is well to notice that his journal, and correspondence with
Lord Hood, clearly recognize this, his true relation to the
siege of Calvi; for it makes it probable that, in attributing
to himself a much more important part at Bastia, and in
saying that Hood's report had put him unfairly in the
background, he was not exaggerating his actual though
ill-defined position there. That Nelson loved to dwell
in thought upon his own achievements, that distinction in
the eyes of his fellows was dear to him, that he craved
recognition, and was at times perhaps too insistent in
requiring it, is true enough; but there is no indication
that he ever coveted the laurels of others, or materially
misconceived his own share in particular events. Glory,
sweet as it was to him, lost its value, if unaccompanied by
the consciousness of desert which stamps it as honor. It
is, therefore, not so much for personal achievement as for

revelation of character that this siege has interest in his life.

Besides the defences of the town proper, Calvi was protected by a series of outworks extending across the neck of land upon which it lay. Of these the outermost was on the left, looking from the place. It flanked the approaches to the others, and commanded the communications with the interior. It was, by Nelson's estimate, about twenty-two hundred yards from the town, and had first to be reduced. By the 3d of July thirteen long guns, besides a number of mortars and howitzers, had been dragged from the beach to the spot by the seamen, who also assisted in placing them in position, and for the most part worked them in battle, an artillerist from the army pointing. Nelson, with Captain Hallowell, already an officer of mark and afterwards one of distinction, took alternate day's duty at the batteries, a third captain, Serocold, having fallen early in the siege. Fearing news might reach his wife that a naval captain had been killed, without the name being mentioned, he wrote to her of this sad event, adding expressively: "I am very busy, yet own I am in all my glory; except with you, I would not be anywhere but where I am, for the world." On July 7th the first outwork fell. The attack upon the others was then steadily and systematically prosecuted, until on the 19th all had been captured, and the besiegers stood face to face with the town walls.

During this time Nelson, as always, was continually at the front and among the most exposed. Out of six guns in the battery which he calls "ours," five were disabled in six days. On the 12th at daylight, a heavy fire opened from the town, which, he says, "seldom missed our battery;" and at seven o'clock a shot, which on the ricochet cleared his head by a hair's breadth, drove sand into his face and right eye with such violence as to incapacitate him. He spoke lightly and cheerfully of the incident to

Lord Hood, "I got a little hurt this morning: not much, as you may judge by my writing," and remained absent from duty only the regular twenty-four hours; but, after some fluctuations of hope, the sight of the eye was permanently lost to him. Of General Stuart's conduct in the operations he frequently speaks with cordial admiration. "He is not sparing of himself on any occasion, he every night sleeps with us in the advanced battery. If I may be allowed to judge, he is an extraordinary good judge of ground. No officer ever deserved success more." At the same time he expresses dissatisfaction with some of the subordinate army officers, to whose inefficiency he attributes the necessity for undue personal exertion on the general's part: "The General is not well. He fatigues himself too much, but I can't help seeing he is obliged to do it. He has not a person to forward his views, — the engineer sick, the artillery captain not fit for active service; therefore every minute thing must be done by himself, or it is not done at all."

The work was tedious and exhausting, and the malaria of the hot Corsican summer told heavily on men's health and patience. The supply of ammunition, and of material of war generally, for the army seems to have been inadequate; and heavy demands were made upon the fleet, not only for guns, which could be returned, but for powder and shot, the expenditure of which might prove embarrassing before they could be renewed. The troops also were not numerous enough, under the climatic conditions, to do all their own duty. In such circumstances, when two parties are working together to the same end, but under no common control, each is prone to think the other behindhand in his work and exacting in his demands. "Why don't Lord Hood land 500 men to work?" said Colonel Moore, the general's right-hand man. "Our soldiers are tired." Nelson, on the other hand, thought that Moore wanted over-much battering done to the breach of·a work, before he led the stormers to it; and Hood, who was receiving frequent reports of the preparations of the French fleet in Toulon, was impatient to have the siege pushed, and thought the army dilatory. "The rapidity with which the French are getting on at Toulon," he wrote confidentially to Nelson, "makes it indispensably necessary for me to put the whole of the fleet under my command in the best possible state for service; and I must soon apply to the general for those parts of the regiments now on shore, ordered by his Majèsty to serve in lieu of marines, to be held in readiness to embark at the shortest notice. I shall delay this application as long as possible."

Nelson, being a seaman, sympathized of course with his own service, and with Hood, for whom he had most cordial admiration, both personal and professional. But at the same time he was on the spot, a constant eye-witness to the difficulties of the siege, a clear-headed observer, with sound military instincts, and fair-minded when facts were before him. The army, he wrote to Hood, is harassed to death, and he notices that it suffers from sickness far more than do the seamen. He repeats the request for more seamen, and, although he seems to doubt the reasonableness of the demand, evidently thinks that they should be furnished, if possible. Hood accordingly sent an additional detachment of three hundred, raising the number on shore to the five hundred suggested by Moore. "I had much rather," he wrote, "that a hundred seamen should be landed unnecessarily, than that one should be kept back that was judged necessary." On the other hand, when the general, after a work bearing on the bay had been destroyed, suggests that the navy might help, by laying the ships against the walls, Nelson takes "the liberty of observing that the business of laying wood before walls was much altered of late," and adds the common-sense remark, that "the quantity of powder and shot which

would be fired away on such an attack could be much
better directed from a battery on shore." This conversation took place immediately after all the outworks had
been reduced. It was conducted "with the greatest
politeness," he writes, and "the General thanked me for
my assistance, but it was necessary to come to the point
whether the siege should be persevered in or given up.
If the former, he must be supplied with the means, which
were more troops, more seamen to work, and more ammunition." Nelson replied that, if the requisite means could
not be had on the spot, they could at least hold on where
they were till supplied from elsewhere.

It will be noticed that Nelson was practically the intermediary between the two commanders-in-chief. In fact,
there appears to have been between them some constraint,
and he was at times asked to transmit a message which
he thought had better go direct. In this particularly
delicate situation, one cannot but be impressed with the
tact he for the most part shows, the diplomatic ability,
which was freely attributed to him by his superiors in
later and more influential commands. This was greatly
helped by his cordial good-will towards others, combined
with disinterested zeal for the duty before him; the whole
illumined by unusual sagacity and good sense. He sees
both sides, and conveys his suggestions to either with a
self-restraint and deference which avert resentment; and
he preserves both his calmness and candor, although he
notices in the camp some jealousy of his confidential communication with his immediate superior, the admiral.
Though never backward to demand what he thought the
rights of himself or his associates, Nelson was always
naturally disposed to reconcile differences, to minimize
causes of trouble, and this native temperament had not
yet undergone the warping which followed his later
wounds — especially that on the head received at the Nile
— and the mental conflict into which he was plunged by

his unhappy passion for Lady Hamilton. At this time, in the flush of earlier enthusiasm, delighting as few men do in the joy of battle, he strove to promote harmony, to smooth over difficulties by every exertion possible, either by doing whatever was asked of him, or by judicious representations to others. Thus, when Hood, impatient at the disturbing news from Toulon, wishes to hasten the conclusion by summoning the garrison, in the hope that it may yield at once, the general objected, apparently on the ground that the statement of their own advantages, upon which such a summons might be based, would be prejudicial, if, as was most probable, the demand was rejected. Whatever his reason, Nelson, though indirectly, intimates to Hood that in this matter he himself agrees, upon the whole, with the general, and Hood yields the point, — the more so that he learns from Nelson that the outposts are to be stormed the next night; and sorely was the captain, in his judicious efforts thus to keep the peace, tried by the postponement of the promised assault for twenty-four hours. "*Such things are,*" he wrote to Hood, using a favorite expression. "I hope to God the general, who seems a good officer and an amiable man, is not led away; but Colonel Moore is his great friend."

The feeling between the land and sea services was emphasized in the relations existing between Lord Hood and Colonel Moore, who afterwards, as Sir John Moore, fell gloriously at Corunna. To these two eminent officers fortune denied the occasion to make full proof of their greatness to the world; but they stand in the first rank of those men of promise whose failure has been due, not to their own shortcomings, but to the lack of opportunity. Sir John Moore has been the happier, in that the enterprise with which his name is chiefly connected, and upon which his title to fame securely rests, was completed, and wrought its full results; fortunate, too, in having received the vindication of that great action at the hands of the most eloquent of military historians. His country and his profession may well mourn a career of such fair opening so soon cut short. But daring and original in the highest degree as was the march from Salamanca to Sahagun, it did not exceed, either in originality or in daring, the purposes nourished by Lord Hood, which he had no opportunity so to execute as to attract attention. Condemned to subordinate positions until he had reached the age of seventy, his genius is known to us only by his letters, and by the frustrated plans at St. Kitts in 1782, and at Golfe Jouan in 1794, in the former of which, less fortunate than Moore, he failed to realize his well-grounded hope of reversing, by a single blow, the issues of a campaign.

It is to be regretted that two such men could not understand each other cordially. Hood, we know from his letters, was " of that frame and texture that I cannot be indifferent," — " full of anxiety, impatience, and apprehension," — when service seemed to him slothfully done. Moore, we are told by Napier, " maintained the right with vehemence bordering upon fierceness." Had he had the chief command on shore, it is possible that the two, impetuous and self-asserting though they were, might have reached an understanding. But in the most unfortunate disagreement about Bastia, — wherein it •is to a naval officer of to-day scarcely possible to do otherwise than blame the sullen lack of enterprise shown by the army, — and afterwards at Calvi, Moore appeared to Hood, and to Nelson also, as the subordinate, the power behind the throne, who was prompting a line of action they both condemned. No position in military life is more provocative of trouble than to feel you are not dealing with the principal, but with an irresponsible inferior; and the situation is worse, because one in which it is almost impossible to come to an issue. Moore's professional talent and force of character naturally made itself felt, even with a man of

Lord Hood

Stuart's ability. Hood and Nelson recognized this, and they resented, as inspired by a junior, what they might have combated dispassionately, if attributed to the chief. There was friction also between Moore and Elliot, the viceroy of the island. Doubtless, as in all cases where suspicion, not to say jealousy, has been begot, much more and worse was imagined by both parties than actually occurred. The apportionment of blame, or prolonged discussion of the matter, is out of place in a biography of Nelson. To that it is of moment, only because it is proper to state that Nelson, on the spot and in·daily contact,— Nelson, upon whose zeal and entire self-devotion at this period no doubt is cast, — agreed in the main with Hood's opinion as to what the latter called the San Fiorenzo leaven, of which Moore was to them the exponent. It is true that Nelson naturally sympathized with his profession and his admiral, whom he heartily admired; but some corrective, at least, to such partiality, was supplied by his soreness about the latter's omission duly to report his services at Bastia, of which he just now became aware. The estrangement between the two commanders-in-chief was doubtless increased by the apparent reluctance, certainly the lack of effort, to see one another frequently.

The principal work, called by Nelson the Mozelle battery, was carried before daylight of July 19, and before dark all the outposts were in the hands of the British. "I could have wished to have had a little part in the storm," wrote Nelson, characteristically covetous of strenuous action, "if it was only to have placed the ladders and pulled away the palisadoes. However, we did the part allotted to us." That day a summons was sent to the garrison, but rejected, and work upon batteries to breach the town walls was then pushed rapidly forward; for it was becoming more and more evident that the siege must be brought to an end, lest the entire force of besiegers should become disabled by sickness. On the 28th the batteries were ready, and General Stuart sent in word that he would not fire upon the hospital positions, where indicated by black flags. The besieged then asked for a truce of twenty-five days, undertaking to lay down their arms, if not by them relieved. The general and admiral refused, but were willing to allow six days. This the garrison in turn rejected; and on the night of the 30th four small vessels succeeded in eluding the blockading frigates and entering supplies, which encouraged the besieged. On the 31st the batteries opened, and after thirty-six hours' heavy cannonade the town held out a flag of truce. An arrangement was made that it should surrender on the 10th of August, if not relieved; the garrison to be transported to France without becoming prisoners of war.

No relief arriving, the place capitulated on the day named. It was high time for the besiegers. "We have upwards of one thousand sick out of two thousand," wrote Nelson, "and the others not much better than so many phantoms. We have lost many men from the season, very few from the enemy." He himself escaped more easily than most. To use his own quaint expression, "All the prevailing disorders have attacked me, but I have not strength enough for them to fasten upon. I am here the reed amongst the oaks: I bow before the storm, while the sturdy oak is laid low." The congenial moral surroundings, in short, — the atmosphere of exertion, of worthy and engrossing occupation, — the consciousness, to him delightful, of distinguished action, of heroic persistence through toil and danger, — prevailed even in his physical frame over discomfort, over the insidious climate, and even over his distressing wound. "This is my ague day," he writes when the batteries opened; "I hope so active a scene will keep off the fit. It has shaken me a good deal; but I have been used to them, and now don't mind them much." "Amongst the wounded, in a slight manner, is

myself, my head being a good deal wounded and my right
eye cut down; but the surgeons flatter me I shall not
entirely lose the sight. It confined me, thank God, only
one day, and at a time when nothing particular happened
to be doing." "You must not think my hurts confined
me," he tells his wife; "no, nothing but the loss of a
limb would have kept me from my duty, and I believe
my exertions conduced to preserve me in this general mortality." In his cheery letters, now, no trace is percep-
tible of the fretful, complaining temper, which impaired,
though it did not destroy, the self-devotion of his later
career. No other mistress at this time contended with
honor for the possession of his heart; no other place than
the post of duty before Calvi distracted his desires, or
appealed to his imagination through his senses. Not
even Lord Hood's report of the siege of Bastia, which here
came to his knowledge, and by which he thought himself
wronged, had bitterness to overcome the joy of action and
of self-contentment.

Not many days were required, after the fall of Calvi, to
remove the fleet, and the seamen who had been serving on
shore, from the pestilential coast. Nelson seems to have
been intrusted with the embarkation of the prisoners in
the transports which were to take them to Toulon. He
told his wife that he had been four months landed, and
felt almost qualified to pass his examination as a besieging
general, but that he had no desire to go on with campaigning. On the 11th of August, the day after the delivery of the place, he was again on board the "Agamemnon,"
from whose crew had been drawn the greatest proportion
of the seamen for the batteries. One hundred and fifty
of them were now in their beds. "My ship's company are
all worn out," he wrote, "as is this whole army, except
myself; nothing hurts me, — of two thousand men I am
the most healthy. Every other officer is scarcely able to
crawl." Among the victims of the deadly climate was

Lieutenant Moutray, the son of the lady to whom, ten years before, he had been so warmly attracted in the West Indies. Nelson placed a monument to him in the church at San Fiorenzo.

On the 15th of August the "Agamemnon" sailed from Calvi, and after a stop at San Fiorenzo, where Hood then was, reached Leghorn on the 18th. Now that the immediate danger of the siege was over, Nelson admitted to his wife the serious character of the injury he had received. The right eye was nearly deprived of sight, — only so far recovered as to enable him to distinguish light from darkness. For all purposes of use it was gone; but the blemish was not to be perceived, unless attention was drawn to it.

At Leghorn the ship lay for a month, — the first period of repose since she went into commission, a year and a half before. While there, the physician to the fleet came on board and surveyed the crew, finding them in a very weak state, and unfit to serve. This condition of things gave Nelson hopes that, upon the approaching departure of Lord Hood for England, the "Agamemnon" might go with him: for he was loath to separate from an admiral whose high esteem he had won, and upon whom he looked as the first sea-officer of Great Britain. Hood was inclined to take her, and to transfer the ship's company bodily to a seventy-four. This he considered no more than due to Nelson's distinguished merit and services, and he had indeed offered him each ship of that rate whose command fell vacant in the Mediterranean; but the strong sense of attachment to those who had shared his toils and dangers, of reluctance that they should see him willing to leave them, after their hard work together, — that combination of sympathy and tact which made so much of Nelson's success as a leader of men, — continued to prevent his accepting promotion that would sever his ties to them.

The exigencies of the war in the Mediterranean forbade the departure, even of a sixty-four with a disabled crew.

A full month later her sick-list was still seventy-seven, out of a total of less than four hundred. " Though certainly unfit for a long cruise," Nelson said, "we are here making a show," — a military requirement not to be neglected or despised. He accepted the disappointment, as he did all service rubs at this period, with perfect temper and in the best spirit. " We must not repine," he wrote to his wife on the 12th of October, the day after Hood sailed for England. " Lord Hood is very well inclined towards me, but the service must ever supersede all private consideration. I hope you will spend the winter cheerfully. Do not repine at my absence; before spring I hope we shall have peace, when we must look out for some little cottage." She fretted, however, as some women will; and he, to comfort her, wrote more sanguinely about himself than the facts warranted. " Why you should be uneasy about me, so as to make yourself ill, I know not. I feel a confident protection in whatever service I may be employed upon; and as to my health, I don't know that I was ever so truly well. I fancy myself grown quite stout." To his old captain, Locker, he admitted that he could not get the better of the fever.

Corsica being now wholly in the power of its inhabitants, allied with and supported by Great Britain, his attention and interest were engrossed by the French fleet centring upon Toulon, the dominant factor of concern to the British in the Mediterranean, where Vice-Admiral Hotham had succeeded Hood as commander-in-chief. Nelson realizes more and more the mistake that was made, when a fraction of it was allowed to escape battle in the previous June. The various reasons by which he had at first excused the neglect to bring it to action no longer weigh with him. He does not directly blame, but he speaks of the omission as an " opportunity lost," — a phrase than which there are few more ominous, in characterizing the closely balanced, yet weighty, decisions, upon which the issues of war depend.

Nothing, he thinks, can prevent the junction of the two fragments, — then in Golfe Jouan and Toulon, — one of which, with more resolution and promptitude on Hotham's part, might have been struck singly at sea a few months before; and if they join, there must follow a fleet action, between forces too nearly equal to insure to Great Britain the decisive results that were needed. The thought he afterwards expressed, " Numbers only can annihilate," was clearly floating in his brain, — inarticulate, perhaps, as yet, but sure to come to the birth. " If we are not completely victorious, — I mean, able to remain at sea whilst the enemy must retire into port, — if we only make a Lord Howe's victory, take a part, and retire into port, Italy is lost." Criticism clearly is going on in his mind; and not mere criticism, (there is enough and to spare of that in the world, and not least in navies), but criticism judicious, well considered, and above all fruitful. The error of opportunity lost he had seen; the error of a partial victory — "a Lord Howe's victory," another opportunity lost — he intuitively anticipated for the Mediterranean, and was soon to see. He was already prepared to pass an accurate judgment instantly, when he saw it. May we not almost hear, thundering back from the clouds that yet veiled the distant future of the Nile, the words, of which his thought was already pregnant, " You may be assured I will bring the French fleet to action the moment I can lay my hands upon them."

The year closed with the British fleet watching, as best it could, the French ships, which, according to Nelson's expectation, had given the blockaders the slip, and had made their junction at Toulon. There was now no great disparity in the nominal force of the two opponents, the British having fourteen ships-of-the-line, the French fifteen; and it was quite in the enemy's power to fulfil his other prediction, by keeping Hotham in hot water during the winter. In the middle of November the " Agamemnon " had to go to Leghorn for extensive repairs, and remained there, shifting her main and mizzen masts, until the 21st of December. Nelson, who had endured with unyielding cheerfulness the dangers, exposure, and sickliness of Calvi, found himself unable to bear patiently the comfort of quiet nights in a friendly port, while hot work might chance outside. " Lying in port is misery to me. My heart is almost broke to find the Agamemnon lying here, little better than a wreck. I own my sincere wish that the enemy would rest quiet until we are ready for sea, and a gleam of hope sometimes crosses me that they will." " I am uneasy enough for fear they will fight, and Agamemnon not present, — it will almost break my heart; but I hope the best, — that they are only boasting at present, and will be quiet until I am ready." " It is misery," he repeats, " for me to be laid up dismantled."

It was during this period of comparative inactivity in port, followed by monotonous though arduous winter cruising off Toulon, which was broken only by equally dreary stays at San Fiorenzo, that Nelson found time to brood over the neglect of which he thought himself the victim, in the omission of Lord Hood to notice more markedly his services in Corsica. It is usually disagreeable to the uninterested bystander to see an excessive desire for praise, even under the guise of just recognition of work done. Words of complaint, whether heard or read, strike a discord to one who himself at the moment is satisfied with his surroundings. We all have an instinctive shrinking from the tones of a grumbler. Nelson's insistence upon his grievances has no exemption from this common experience; yet it must be remembered that these assertions of the importance of his own services, and dissatisfaction with the terms in which they had been mentioned, occur chiefly, if not solely, in letters to closest relations, — to his wife and uncle, — and that they would never have become known but for the after fame, which has caused all his most private correspondence to have interest and to be brought to light. As a revelation of character they have a legitimate interest, and they reveal, or rather they confirm, what is abundantly revealed throughout his life, — that intense longing for distinction, for admiration justly earned, for conspicuous exaltation above the level of his kind, which existed in him to so great a degree, and which is perhaps the most potent — certainly the most universal — factor in military achievement. They reveal this ambition for honor, or glory, on its weak side; on its stronger side of noble emulation, of self-devotion, of heroic action, his correspondence teems with its evidence in words, as does his life in acts. To quote the words of Lord Radstock, who at this period, and until after the battle of Cape St. Vincent, was serving as one of the junior admirals in the Mediterranean, and retained his friendship through life, "a perpetual thirst of glory was ever raging within him." " He has ever showed himself as great a despiser of riches as he is a lover of glory; and I am fully convinced in my own mind that he would sooner defeat the French fleet than capture fifty galleons."

After all allowance made, however, it cannot be denied that there is in these complaints a tone which one regrets in such a man. The repeated "It was I" jars, by the very sharpness of its contrast, with the more generous expressions that abound in his correspondence. "When I reflect that I was the cause of re-attacking Bastia, after our *wise* generals gave it over, from not knowing the force, fancying it 2,000 men; that it was I, who, landing, joined the Corsicans, and with only my ship's party of marines, drove the French under the walls of Bastia; that it was I, who, knowing the force in Bastia to be upwards of 4,000 men, as I have now only ventured to tell Lord Hood, landed with only 1,200 men, and kept the secret till within this week past; — what I must have felt during the whole siege may be easily conceived. Yet I am scarcely mentioned. I freely forgive, but cannot forget. This and much more ought to have been mentioned. It is known that, for two months, I blockaded Bastia with a squadron; only fifty sacks of flour got into the town. At San Fiorenzo and Calvi, for two months before, nothing got in, and four French frigates could not get out, and are now ours. Yet my diligence is not mentioned; and others, for keeping succours out of Calvi for a few summer months, are handsomely mentioned. *Such things are.* I have got upon a subject near my heart, which is full when I think of the treatment I have received. . . . The taking of Corsica, like the taking of St. Juan's, has cost me money. St. Juan's cost near £500; Corsica has cost me £300, an eye, and a cut across my back; and my money, I find, cannot be repaid me."

As regards the justice of his complaints, it seems to the author impossible to read carefully Hood's two reports, after the fall of Bastia and that of Calvi, and not admit, either that Nelson played a very unimportant part in the general operations connected with the reduction of Corsica, with which he became associated even before it was effectively undertaken, and so remained throughout; or else that no due recognition was accorded to him in the admiral's despatches. Had he not become otherwise celebrated in his after life, he would from these papers be inferred to stand, in achievement, rather below than above the level of the other captains who from time to time were present. That this was unfair seems certain; and notably at Calvi, where, from the distance of the operations from the anchorage, and the strained relations which kept Hood and Stuart apart, he was practically the one naval man upon whose discretion and zeal success depended. It is probable, however, that the failure to do him justice proceeded as much from awkward literary construction, phrases badly turned, as from reluctance to assign due prominence to one subordinate among several others.

How readily, yet how keenly, he derived satisfaction,

even from slight tributes of recognition, is shown by the simplicity and pleasure with which he quoted to Mrs. Nelson the following words of Sir Gilbert Elliot, the Viceroy of Corsica, then and always a warm friend and admirer: "I know that you, who have had such an honourable share in this acquisition, will not be indifferent at the prosperity of the Country which you have so much assisted to place under His Majesty's government." "Whether these are words of course and to be forgotten," wrote Nelson, "I know not; they are pleasant, however, for the time." Certainly his demands for praise, if thus measured, were not extreme.

CHAPTER V.

JANUARY – JULY, 1795. AGE, 36.

FROM the naval point of view, as a strategic measure, the acquisition of Corsica by the British was a matter of great importance. It was, however, only one among several factors, which went to make up the general military and political situation in the Mediterranean at the end of the year 1794. Hitherto the exigencies of the well-nigh universal hostilities in which France had been engaged, and the anarchical internal state of that country, had prevented any decisive operations by her on the side of Italy, although she had, since 1792, been formally at war with the Kingdom of Sardinia, of which Piedmont was a province.

At the close of 1794 the conditions were greatly modified. In the north, the combined forces of Great Britain, Austria, and Holland had been driven out of France and Belgium, and the United Provinces were on the point of submission. On the east, the Austrians and Prussians had retreated to the far bank of the Rhine, and Prussia was about to withdraw from the coalition, which, three years before, she had been so eager to form. On the south, even greater success had attended the French armies, which had crossed the Pyrenees into Spain, driving

before them the forces of the enemy, who also was soon
to ask for peace. It was therefore probable that operations in Italy would assume greatly increased activity,
from the number of French soldiers released elsewhere,
as well as from the fact that the Austrians themselves,
though they continued the war in Germany, had abandoned other portions of the continent which they had
hitherto contested.

The political and military conditions in Italy were,
briefly, as follows. The region north of the Maritime
Alps and in the valley of the Po was, for the most part,
in arms against France, — the western province, Piedmont, as part of the Kingdom of Sardinia, whose capital
was at Turin, and, to the eastward of it, the duchies of
Milan and Mantua, as belonging to Austria. The governments of the numerous small states into which Northern
and Central Italy were then divided — Venice, Genoa,
Tuscany, the States of the Church, and others — sympathized generally with the opponents of France, but, as far
as possible, sought to maintain a formal though difficult
neutrality. The position of Genoa was the most embarrassing, because in direct contact with all the principal
parties to the war. To the westward, her territory along
the Riviera included Vintimiglia, bordering there on the
county of Nice, and contained Vado Bay, the best anchorage between Nice and Genoa. To the eastward, it embraced the Gulf of Spezia, continually mentioned by Nelson
as Porto Especia.

The occupation of the Riviera was of particular moment
to the French, for it offered a road by which to enter
Italy, — bad, indeed, but better far than those through
the passes of the upper Alps. Skirting the sea, it afforded
a double line of communications, by land and by water;
for the various detachments of their army, posted along it,
could in great degree be supplied by the small coasting-
vessels of the Mediterranean. So long, also, as it was in

their possession, and they held passes of the Maritime
Alps and Apennines, as they did in 1794, there was the
possibility of their penetrating through them, to turn the
left flank of the Sardinian army in Piedmont, which was,
in fact, what Bonaparte accomplished two years later.
These inducements had led the French to advance into
the county of Nice, then belonging to Sardinia, which in
the existing state of war it was perfectly proper for them
to do; but, not stopping there, they had pushed on past
the Sardinian boundary into the neutral Riviera of Genoa,
as far as Vado Bay, which they occupied, and where they
still were at the end of 1794.

Genoa submitted under protest to this breach of her neutrality, as she did both before [1] and after to similar insults
from parties to the war. She derived some pecuniary
benefit from the condition of affairs, — her ports, as well as
those of Tuscany, immediately to the southward, becoming
depots of a trade in grain, which supplied both the French
army and the southern provinces of France. These food
stuffs, absolutely essential to the French, were drawn
chiefly from Sicily and the Barbary States, and could not
be freely taken into French ports by the larger class of
sea-going vessels, in face of the British fleet. They were,
therefore, commonly transshipped in Leghorn or Genoa,
and carried on by coasters. As so much Genoese sea-
coast was occupied by French divisions, it was practically
impossible for British cruisers to distinguish between vessels carrying corn for the inhabitants and those laden for
the armies, and entirely impossible to know that what was
intended for one object would not be diverted to another.
If, too, a vessel's papers showed her to be destined for
Vintimiglia, near the extreme of the Genoese line, there
could be no certainty that, having got so far, she might
not quietly slip by into a French port, either Nice or be-

---

[1] In the year 1793 the French frigate " Modeste " had been forcibly taken
from the harbor of Genoa by an English squadron.

yond. The tenure of the neutral Riviera of Genoa by the French army was a threat to the allies of Great Britain in Piedmont and Lombardy, as well as to the quasi-neutrals in Genoa, Tuscany, Venice, and the Papal States. Its further advance or successes would imperil the latter, and seriously affect the attitude of Naples, hostile to the Republic, but weak, timid, and unstable of purpose. On the other hand, the retention of its position, and much more any further advance, depended upon continuing to receive supplies by way of the sea. To do so by the shore route alone was not possible. Southern France itself depended upon the sea for grain, and could send nothing, even if the then miserable Corniche road could have sufficed, as the sole line of communications for forty thousand troops.

Thus the transfer of Corsica to Great Britain had a very important bearing upon the military and political conditions. At the moment when Italy was about to become the scene of operations which might, and in the event actually did, exercise a decisive influence upon the course of the general war, the British position was solidified by the acquisition of a naval base, unassailable while the sea remained in their control and the Corsicans attached to their cause, and centrally situated with reference to the probable scenes of hostilities, as well as to the points of political interest, on the mainland of Italy. The fleet resting upon it, no longer dependent upon the reluctant hospitality of Genoese or Tuscan ports, or upon the far distant Kingdom of Naples, was secure to keep in its station, whence it menaced the entire seaboard trade of France and the Riviera, as well as the tenure of the French army in the latter, and exerted a strong influence upon the attitude of both Genoa and Tuscany, who yielded only too easily to the nearest or most urgent pressure. The fleet to which Nelson belonged had spent the greater part of the year 1794 in securing for itself, as a base of operations, this position, by far the most suitable among those that could be considered at all. It remained now to utilize the advantage obtained, to make the situation of the French army in Italy untenable, by establishing an indisputable control of the sea. To this the holding of Corsica also contributed, indirectly; for the loss of the island forced the French fleet to go to sea, in order, if possible, to expedite its re-conquest. In all the operations resulting from these various motives, Nelson bore a part as conspicuous and characteristic as he had done in the reduction of Corsica. Almost always on detached service, in positions approaching independent command, he was continually adding to his reputation, and, what was far more important, maturing the professional character, the seeds of which had been so bountifully bestowed upon him by nature. His reputation, won hard and step by step, obtained for him opportunity; but it was to character, ripened by experience and reflection, that he owed his transcendent successes.

The scheme for the government of the island as a British dependency, stated broadly, was that it should be administered by the Corsicans themselves, under a viceroy appointed by the British crown. Its military security was provided for by the control of the sea, and by British soldiers holding the fortified ports, — a duty for which the Corsicans themselves had not then the necessary training. Nelson, who did not yet feel the impossibility of sustaining a successful over-sea invasion, when control of the sea was not had, was anxious about the expected attempts of the French against the island, and urged the viceroy, by private letter, to see that Ajaccio, which he regarded as the point most favorable to a descent, was garrisoned sufficiently to keep the gates shut for a few days. This caution did not then proceed from a distrust of the Corsicans' fidelity, without which neither France nor England could hold the island, as was shown by the quickness of its

transfer two years later, when the inhabitants again revolted to France. "With this defence," he wrote, "I am
confident Ajaccio, and I believe I may say the island of
Corsica, would be perfectly safe until our fleet could get
to the enemy, when I have no doubt the event would be
what every Briton might expect."

The repairs of the "Agamemnon" were completed before Nelson's anxious apprehensions of a battle taking
place in his absence could be fulfilled. On the 21st of
December, 1794, he sailed from Leghorn with the fleet, in
company with which he remained from that time until the
following July, when he was sent to the Riviera of Genoa
on special detached service. He thus shared the severe
cruising of that winter, as well as the abortive actions of
the spring and early summer, where the admiral again contrived to lose opportunities of settling the sea campaign,
and with it, not improbably, that of the land also. There
were plain indications in the port of Toulon that a maritime enterprise of some importance was in contemplation.
In the outer road lay fifteen sail-of-the-line, the British
having then fourteen; but more significant of the enemy's
purpose was the presence at Marseilles of fifty large transports, said to be ready. "I have no doubt," wrote Nelson,
"but Porto Especia is their object." This was a mistake,
interesting as indicating the slight weight that Nelson at
that time attributed to the deterrent effect of the British
fleet "in being" upon such an enterprise, involving an
open-sea passage of over a hundred miles, though he
neither expressed nor entertained any uncertainty as to
the result of a meeting, if the enemy were encountered.
The French Government, not yet appreciating the inefficiency to which its navy had been reduced by many con-
current circumstances, was ready to dispute the control
of the Mediterranean, and it contemplated, among other
things, a demonstration at Leghorn, similar to that successfully practised at Naples in 1792, which might com-

pel the Court of Tuscany to renounce the formally hostile
attitude it had assumed at the bidding of Great Britain;
but it does not appear that there was any serious purpose
of exposing a large detachment, in the attempt to hold
upon the Continent a position, such as Spezia, with which
secure communication by land could not be had.

Though none too careful to proportion its projects to the
force at its disposal, the Directory sufficiently understood
that a detachment at Spezia could not be self-dependent,
nor could, with any certainty, combine its operations with
those of the army in the Riviera; and also that, to be
properly supported at all, there must be reasonably secure
and unbroken communication, either by land or water,
neither of which was possible until the British fleet was
neutralized. The same consideration dictated to it the
necessity of a naval victory, before sending out the expedition, of whose assembling the British were now hearing,
and which was actually intended for Corsica; although it
was known that in the island there had already begun the
revulsion against the British rule, which culminated in
open revolt the following year. Owing to the dearth of
seamen, the crews of the French ships were largely composed of soldiers, and it was thought that, after beating
the enemy, four or five thousand of these might be at once
thrown on shore at Ajaccio, and that afterwards the main
body could be sent across in safety. First of all, however,
control of the sea must be established by a battle, more or
less decisive.

On the 24th of February, 1795, the British fleet arrived
at Leghorn, after a very severe cruise of over a fortnight.
On the 2d of March Nelson mentioned, in a letter to his
wife, that the French were said then to have a hundred
and twenty-four transports full of troops, from which he
naturally argued that they must mean to attempt something. On the evening of the 8th, an express from Genoa
brought Hotham word that they were actually at sea,

fifteen ships-of-the-line, with half a dozen or more smaller vessels. He sailed in pursuit early the next morning, having with him thirteen [1] British ships-of-the-line and one Neapolitan seventy-four. Of the former, four were three-decked ships, carrying ninety-eight to one hundred guns, a class of vessel of which the French had but one, the "Sans Culottes," of one hundred and twenty, which, under the more dignified name of "L'Orient," afterwards met so tragic a fate at the Battle of the Nile; but they had, in compensation, three powerful ships of eighty guns, much superior to the British seventy-fours. As, however, only partial engagements followed, the aggregate of force on either side is a matter of comparatively little importance in a Life of Nelson.

Standing to the northward and westward, with a fresh easterly wind, the British fleet through its lookouts discovered the enemy on the evening of the day of sailing, and by the same means kept touch with them throughout the 10th and 11th; but the baffling airs, frequent in the Mediterranean, prevented the main body seeing them until the morning of the 12th. At daylight, then, they were visible from the "Agamemnon," in company with which were five British ships and the Neapolitan; the remainder of the fleet being so far to the eastward that their hulls were just rising out of the water. The British lying nearly becalmed, the French, who were to windward, bore down to within three miles; but although, in Nelson's judgment, they had a fair opportunity to separate the advanced British ships, with which he was, from the main body, they failed to improve it. Nothing happened that day, and, a fresh breeze from the west springing up at dusk, both fleets stood to the southward with it, the French being to windward. That night one of the latter, a seventy-four, having lost a topmast, was permitted to return to port.

[1] The "Berwick," seventy-four, had been left in San Fiorenzo for repairs. Putting to sea at this time, she fell in with the French fleet, and was taken.

The next morning the wind was still southwest and squally. Hotham at daylight ordered a general chase, which allowed each ship a certain freedom of movement in endeavoring to close with the French. The "Agamemnon" had been well to the westward, from the start; and being a very handy, quick-working ship, as well as, originally at least, more than commonly fast, was early in the day in a position where she had a fair chance for reaching the enemy. A favorable opportunity soon occurred, one of those which so often show that, if a man only puts himself in the way of good luck, good luck is apt to offer. At 8 A. M. the eighty-gun ship "Ça Ira," third from the rear in the French order, ran on board the vessel next ahead of her, and by the collision lost her fore and main topmasts. These falling overboard on the lee side — in this case the port,[1] — not only deprived her of by far the greater part of her motive power, but acted as a drag on her progress, besides for the time preventing the working of the guns on that side. The "Ça Ira" dropped astern of her fleet. Although this eighty-gun ship was much bigger than his own, — "absolutely large enough to take Agamemnon in her hold," Nelson said, — the latter saw his chance, and instantly seized it with the promptitude characteristic of all his actions. The "Agamemnon," if she was not already on the port tack, opposite to that on which the fleets had been during the night, must have gone about at this time, and probably for this reason. She was able thus to fetch into the wake of the crippled vessel, which a frigate had already gallantly attacked, taking advantage of the uselessness of the Frenchman's lee batteries, encumbered with the wreckage of the masts.

At 10 A. M., the "Ça Ira" and the "Agamemnon" having passed on opposite tacks, the latter again went about and stood in pursuit under all sail, rapidly nearing the enemy,

---

[1] The port side, or, as it was called in Nelson's day, the larboard side, is the left, looking from the stern to the bow of a ship.

who at this time was taken in tow by a frigate. But although in this position the French ship could not train her broadside guns upon her smaller opponent, she could still work freely the half-dozen stern guns, and did so with much effect. "So true did she fire," noted Nelson, "that not a shot missed some part of the ship, and latterly the masts were struck every shot, which obliged me to open our fire a few minutes sooner than I intended, for it was my intention to have touched his stern before a shot was fired." At quarter before eleven, the "Agamemnon" was within a hundred yards of the "Ça Ira's" stern, and this distance she was able to keep until 1 P. M. Here, by the use of the helm and of the sails, the ship alternately turned her starboard side to the enemy to fire her batteries, and again resumed her course, to regain the distance necessarily lost at each deviation. This raking fire not only killed and wounded many of the "Ça Ira's" crew, and injured the hull, but, what was tactically of yet greater importance, preventing the replacing of the lost spars. Thus was entailed upon the French that night a crippled ship, which they could not in honor abandon, nor yet could save without fighting for her, — a tactical dilemma which was the direct cause of the next day's battle.

Brief and cursory as is the notice of this action of the "Agamemnon" in Hotham's despatches, he mentions no other ship-of-the-line as engaged at this time, and states that she and the frigate were so far detached from the fleet, that they were finally obliged to retire on account of other enemy's vessels approaching. Nelson's journal says that two French ships, one of one hundred and twenty guns and a seventy-four, were at gun-shot distance on the bow of the "Ça Ira" when he began to attack her. These, with several others of their fleet, went about some time before one, at which hour the frigate, towing the disabled ship, tacked herself, and also got the latter around. The "Agamemnon" standing on, she and the "Ça Ira" now crossed

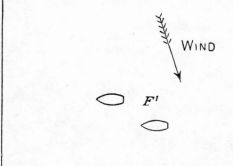

WIND

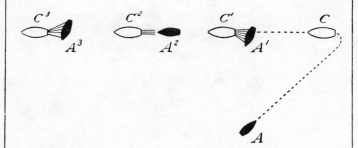

Agamemnon & Ça Ira
March 13, 1795.

A – Agamemnon
C – Ça Ira
F – French Ships of Line
B – Nearest British do.

within half pistol-range; but, the French guns being too much elevated, the shot passed over their antagonist, who lost in this day's work only seven men wounded. Nelson then again tacked to follow, but by this time the French admiral had apparently decided that his crippled vessel must be rescued, and his fleet no longer defied by a foe so inferior in strength. Several of the enemy were approaching, when Hotham made a signal of recall, which Nelson on this occasion at least had no hesitation in obeying, and promptly. There was no pursuit, the hostile commander-in-chief being apparently satisfied to save the " Ça Ira " for the moment, without bringing on a general engagement.

In this affair, what is mainly to be noted in Nelson is not the personal courage, nor yet even the professional daring, or the skill which justified the daring. It may be conceded that all these were displayed in a high degree, but they can scarcely be claimed to have exceeded that shown by other officers, not a few, when equally tried. What is rather striking, account for it how we will, is that Nelson, here as always, was on hand when opportunity offered ; that after three days of chase he, and he only, was so far to the front as to be able to snatch the fleeting moment. " On looking round," he says at ten o'clock, when about to begin the action, " I saw no ship-of-the-line within several miles to support me ; the Captain was the nearest on our lee-quarter." With the looseness and lack of particularity which characterize most logs and despatches remaining from those days, and make the comprehension of naval engagements, other than the greatest, a matter of painful and uncertain inference, it is impossible accurately to realize the entire situation ; but it seems difficult to imagine that among all the other thirteen captains, " where emulation was common to all and zeal for his Majesty's service the general description of the fleet," to use Hotham's words, none could have been on the spot to support so promising an attempt, had there been " common " that sort of emulation which takes a man ever to the front, not merely in battle but at all times, — the spirit that will not and cannot rest while anything remains to be done, ever pressing onward to the mark. To this unquestionably must be added the rapid comprehension of a situation, and the exceeding promptitude with which Nelson seized his opportunity, as well as the tenacious intrepidity with which he held to his position of advantage, despite the imminent threat to his safety from the uninjured and gigantic " Sans Culottes," barely out of gunshot to windward. It is right also to note the accessibility to advice, a feature of his genial and kindly temperament, to which he admitted much of the success was due. The trait is not rare in mankind in general, but it is exceptional in men of a character so self-reliant and decided as Nelson. " If the conduct of the Agamemnon on the 13th," he generously wrote, " was by any means the cause of our success on the 14th, Lieutenant Andrews has a principal share in the merit, for a more proper opinion was never given by an officer than the one he gave me on the 13th, in a situation of great difficulty."

The same hot spirit, the same unwearying energy, made itself still more manifest the next day, when were to be garnered the results of his own partial, yet, in its degree, decisive action of the 13th. " Sure I am," said he afterwards, " had I commanded our fleet on the 14th, that either the whole French fleet would have graced my triumph, or I should have been in a confounded scrape." A confounded scrape he would have been in on the 13th, and on other days also, great and small, had there been a different issue to the risks he dared, and rightly dared, to take. Of what man eminent in war, indeed, is not the like true? It is the price of fame, which he who dare not pay must forfeit; and not fame only, but repute.

During the following night the " Sans Culottes " quitted the French fleet. The wind continued southerly, both

fleets standing to the westward, the crippled " Ça Ira "
being taken in tow by the " Censeur," of seventy-four
guns. At daylight of March 14, being about twenty miles
southwest from Genoa, these two were found to be much
astern and to leeward of their main body, — that is, northeast from it. The British lay in the same direction, and
were estimated by Nelson to be three and a half miles
from the disabled ship and her consort, five miles from the
rest of the French. At 5.30 A. M. a smart breeze sprang
up from the northwest, which took the British aback, but
enabled them afterwards to head for the two separated
French ships. Apparently, from Nelson's log, this wind
did not reach the main body of the enemy, a circumstance
not uncommon in the Mediterranean. Two British seventy-
fours, the " Captain " and the " Bedford," in obedience to
signals, stood down to attack the " Censeur " and the " Ça
Ira; " and, having in this to undergo for twenty minutes a
fire to which they could not reply, were then and afterwards
pretty roughly handled. They were eventually left behind, crippled, as their own fleet advanced. The rest of
the British were meantime forming in line and moving
down to sustain them. The French main body, keeping
the southerly wind, wore in succession to support their
separated ships, and headed to pass between them and
their enemies. The latter, having formed, stood also towards these two, which now lay between the contestants
as the prize to the victor.

Apparently, in these manœuvres, the leading British
ships ran again into the belt of southerly wind, — which
the French kept throughout, — while part of the centre and
rear were left becalmed, and had little or no share in the
cannonade that followed. Under these conditions the resolution of the French admiral seems to have faltered, for
instead of passing to leeward — north — of his endangered
ships, which was quite in his power, and so covering them
from the enemy, he allowed the latter to cut them off, thus

insuring their surrender. His fleet kept to windward of the British, passing fairly near the two leading ships, the "Illustrious" and the "Courageux," who thus underwent a "concentration by defiling," that took the main and mizzen masts out of both, besides killing and wounding many of their people. The "Princess Royal" and "Agamemnon," which came next, could only engage at long range. "The enemy's fleet kept the southerly wind," wrote Nelson in his journal, "which enabled them to keep their distance, which was very great. At 8 A. M. they began to pass our line to windward, and the Ça Ira and Le Censeur were on our lee side; therefore the Illustrious, Courageux, Princess Royal, and Agamemnon were obliged to fight on both sides of the ship." At five minutes past ten A. M. both the French vessels struck, the "Ça Ira" having lost her three masts, and the "Censeur" her mainmast. It was past one P. M. when firing wholly ceased; and the enemy then crowded all possible sail to the westward, the British fleet lying with their heads to the southeast.

When the British line was forming, between seven and eight in the morning, Nelson was directed by Vice-Admiral Goodall, the second in command, to take his station astern of his flagship, the "Princess Royal," of ninety guns. Immediately behind the "Agamemnon" came the "Britannia," carrying Hotham's flag. This position, and the lightness of the wind, serve to explain how Nelson came to take the step he mentions in several letters; going on board the "Britannia," after the two French vessels struck, and urging the commander-in-chief to leave the prizes in charge of the British frigates and crippled ships-of-the-line, and vigorously to pursue the French, who having lost four ships out of their fleet, by casualty or capture, were now reduced to eleven sail. "I went on board Admiral Hotham as soon as our firing grew slack in the van, and the Ça Ira and the Censeur had struck, to propose to him leaving our two crippled ships, the two prizes, and four frigates, to

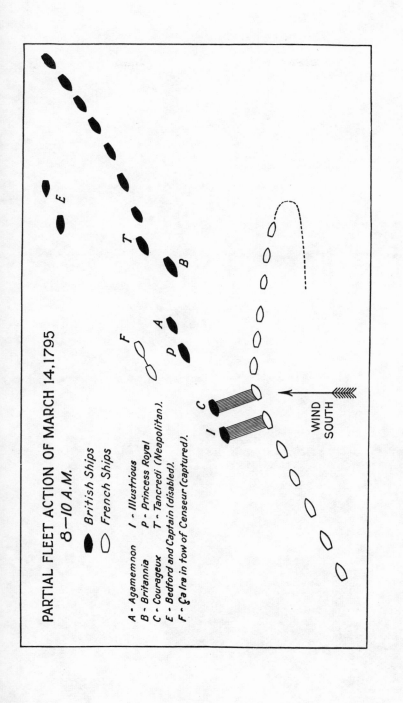

PARTIAL FLEET ACTION OF MARCH 14, 1795
8–10 A.M.

◣ British Ships
◇ French Ships

A - Agamemnon   I - Illustrious
B - Britannia   P - Princess Royal
C - Courageux   T - Tancredi (Neapolitan).
E - Bedford and Captain (disabled).
F - Ça Ira in tow of Censeur (captured).

WIND
SOUTH

themselves, and to pursue the enemy; but he, much cooler than myself, said, ' We must be contented, we have done very well.' Now, had we taken ten sail, and had allowed the eleventh to escape, when it had been possible to have got at her, I could never have called it well done. Goodall backed me ; I got him to write to the admiral, but it would not do : we should have had such a day as I believe the annals of England never produced."

Nelson here evidently assumes that it was possible to have got at the French fleet. After a man's reputation has been established, there is always the danger of giving undue weight to his opinions, expressed at an earlier time, somewhat casually, and not under the sobering sense of responsibility. Hotham. may have questioned the possibility of getting at the French effectively, having regard to the fickle lightness of the wind then prevalent, and to the fact that, besides the two ships partially dismasted and for the moment useless, two others, the " Captain " and the " Bedford," had suffered severely in sails and rigging. He would also doubtless consider that the three-decked ships, of which he had four, were notoriously bad sailers, and sure to drop behind if the chase lasted long, leaving to eight ships, including the " Neapolitan," the burden of arresting the enemy, who had shown very fair offensive powers in the morning. Nelson was not blind to these facts, and not infrequently alludes to them. " Had we only a breeze, I have no doubt we should have given a destructive blow to the enemy's fleet." " Sure I am, that had the breeze continued, so as to have allowed us to close with the enemy, we should have destroyed their whole fleet." Whether these remarks apply to the heat of the engagement, or to the proposed chase, which Hotham declined to permit, is not perfectly clear ; but inasmuch as the second part of the action of the 14th consisted, actually, in the French filing by the " Courageux " and the " Illustrious," upon whom their fire was thus concentrated, while the rest of the British were becalmed out of gunshot, it is very possible he was thinking of that incident only, which doubtless would have taken a very different turn had the main body been able to come down. His wish to pursue is unquestionable, both from his assertion and from the whole character of his career before and after; and a casual remark, written ten days after the affair, shows his opinion confirmed by time. "Had our good admiral followed the blow, we should probably have done more, but the risk was thought too great."

The question attracts attention, both impersonally, as of military interest, and also as bearing upon Nelson's correctness of judgment, and professional characteristics, at this time. As regards the amount of wind, it is sufficient to say that the French fleet, having borne away to the westward in the afternoon, was next day out of sight.[1] Most of the British might equally have been out of sight from the position in which they remained. As for the risk — of course there was risk; but the whole idea of a general chase rests upon the fact that, for one reason or another, the extreme speed of the ships in each fleet will vary, and that it is always probable that the fastest of the pursuers can overtake the slowest of the pursued. The resulting combats compel the latter either to abandon his ships, or to incur a general action, which, from the fact of his flight, it is evident he has reason to avoid. In this case many of the retreating French were crippled, — some went off towed by frigates, and some without bowsprits. Unquestionably, the pursuers who thus engage may be overpowered before those following them come up; but the balance of chances is generally in their favor, and in the particular instance would have been markedly so, as was shown by the results of the two days' fighting, which had proved the superior quality of the British ships' companies.

The fact is, neither Hotham nor his opponent, Martin,

was willing to hazard a decisive naval action, but wished merely to obtain a temporary advantage, — the moment's safety, no risks. "I have good reason," wrote Hotham in his despatch, "to hope, from the enemy's steering to the westward after having passed our fleet, that whatever might have been their design, *their intentions are for the present frustrated.*" It is scarcely necessary to say that a man who looks no further ahead than this, who fails to realize that the destruction of the enemy's fleet is the one condition of permanent safety to his cause, will not rise to the conception presented to him on his quarter-deck by Nelson. The latter, whether by the sheer intuition of genius, which is most probable, or by the result of well-ordered reasoning, which is less likely, realized fully that to destroy the French fleet was the one thing for which the British fleet was there, and the one thing by doing which it could decisively affect the war. As he wrote four years later to St. Vincent, "Not one moment shall be lost in bringing the enemy to battle; for I consider the best defence for his Sicilian Majesty's dominions is to place myself alongside the French."

Yet Nelson was far from unconscious of the difficulties of Hotham's position, or from failing duly to allow for them. "Admiral Hotham has had much to contend with, a fleet half-manned, and in every respect inferior to the enemy; Italy calling him to her defence, our newly acquired kingdom [1] calling might and main, our reinforcements and convoy hourly expected; and all to be done without a force by any means adequate to it." Add to this the protection of British trade, of whose needs Nelson was always duly sensible. Yet, as one scans this list of troubles, with the query how to meet them running in his mind, it is scarcely possible not to see that each and every difficulty would have been solved by a crushing pursuit of the beaten French, preventing their again taking the sea.

[1] Corsica.

The British admiral had in his control no means to force
them out of port.   Therefore, when out, he should by no
means have allowed them to get back.   It is only just to
Hotham, who had been a capable as well as gallant captain, to say that he had objected to take the chief command, on account of his health.

Nelson was delighted with his own share in these affairs,
and with the praise he received from others for his conduct, — especially that on the 13th.   He was satisfied, and
justly, that his sustained and daring grapple with the "Ça
Ira," in the teeth of her fleet, had been the effective cause
of the next day's action and consequent success.   It was
so, in truth, and it presented an epitome of what the 14th
and 15th ought to have witnessed, — a persistent clinging
to the crippled ships, in order to force their consorts again
into battle.   "You will participate," he wrote to his
uncle, "in the pleasure I must have felt in being the great
cause of our success.   Could I have been supported, I
would have had Ça Ira on the 13th."   Elliot, the Viceroy
of Corsica, wrote to him: "I certainly consider the business of the 13th of March as a very capital feature in the
late successful contest with the French fleet; and the part
which the Agamemnon had in it must be felt by every
one to be one of the circumstances that gave lustre to this
event, and rendered it not only useful, but peculiarly
honourable to the British arms."   "So far," added Nelson,
in quoting this to his wife, "all hands agree in giving me
the praises which cannot but be comfortable to me to the
last moment of my life."   He adds then a reflection,
evincing that he was assimilating some of the philosophy
of life as well as of fighting.   "The time of my being left
out here by Lord Hood," which he had so much regretted,
"I may call well spent; had I been absent, how mortified
should I now be.   What has happened may never happen
to any one again, that only one ship-of-the-line out of
fourteen should get into action with the French fleet for

so long a time as two hours and a half, and with such a ship as the Ca Ira." It may be of interest to mention that the French fleet, upon this occasion, was largely composed of the vessels which three years later were destroyed by him at the Battle of the Nile.

In all his interests, ambitions, and gratification with success and praise, he at this period writes fully and intimately to his wife, between whom and himself there evidently still existed, after these two years of absence, a tender and affectionate confidence. "It is with an inexpressible pleasure I have received your letters, with our father's. I rejoice that my conduct gives you pleasure, and I trust I shall never do anything which will bring a blush on your face. Rest assured you are never absent from my thoughts." When looking forward to the action of March 14, he tells her: "Whatever may be my fate, I have no doubt in my own mind but that my conduct will be such as will not bring a blush on the face of my friends: the lives of all are in the hands of Him who knows best whether to preserve mine or not; to His will do I resign myself. My character and good name are in my own keeping. Life with disgrace is dreadful. A glorious death is to be envied;" and he signs himself with unwonted tenderness, "Ever your most faithful and affectionate husband." Save of the solemn hours before Trafalgar, when another image occupied his thoughts, this is the only personal record we have of the feelings with which this man, dauntless above his fellows, went into battle. He refrains thoughtfully from any mention of his health that may cause her anxiety, which she had shown herself over weak and worrying to bear; but he speaks freely of all that passes, confiding that with her he need have no reserves, even in a natural self-praise. "This I can say, that all I have obtained I owe to myself, and to no one else, and *to you* I may add, that my character stands high with almost all Europe. Even the Austrians knew my name perfectly." While silent on the subject of illness, he admits now that his eye had grown worse, and was in almost total darkness, besides being very painful at times; "but never mind," he adds cheeringly, "I can see very well with the other."

It is instructive to note, in view of some modern debated questions, that, despite the recent success, Nelson was by no means sure that the British fleet could defend Corsica. "I am not even now certain Corsica is safe," he wrote on the 25th of March, "if they undertake the expedition with proper spirit." The threat, never absent while the French fleet remained, was emphasized by the arrival of six ships-of-the-line from Brest, which reached Toulon on the 4th of April, materially altering the complexion of affairs in the Mediterranean, and furnishing an instructive instance of the probable punishment for opportunity imperfectly utilized, as on the 14th of March. Great discontent was felt at the apparent failure of the Admiralty to provide against this chance. "Hotham is very much displeased with them," wrote Nelson, "and certainly with reason;" and doubtless it is satisfactory to believe, rightly or wrongly, that our disadvantages are due to the neglect of others, and not to our own shortcomings.

Although the nominal force of the French was thus raised to twenty of the line, the want of seamen, and the absence of discipline, prevented their seizing the opportunity offered by the temporary inferiority of the British, reduced to thirteen besides two Neapolitans, in whose efficiency, whether justly or not, Nelson placed little confidence. At this critical moment, with a large British military convoy expected, and the fleet, to use his' impatient expression, "skulking in port," a Jacobin outbreak occurred in Toulon, and the seamen assumed the *opérabouffe* rôle of going ashore to assist in deliberations upon the measures necessary to save the country. Before they were again ready to go to sea, the convoy had arrived.

On the 7th of June, however, the French again sailed from Toulon, seventeen ships-of-the-line; and the following day Nelson, writing to his brother, thus gave vent to the bitterness of his feelings: "We have been cruising off Minorca for a long month, every moment in expectation of reinforcements from England. Great good fortune has hitherto saved us, what none in this fleet could have expected for so long a time. Near two months we have been skulking from them. Had they not got so much cut up on the 14th of March, Corsica, Rome, and Naples would, at this moment, have been in their possession, and may yet, if these people [the Admiralty] do not make haste to help us. I am out of spirits, although never better in health."

His depression was due less to the inadequacy of the British fleet than to the dismissal of Lord Hood from the command, news of which was at this time received. When about to sail from England, to resume his duty as commander-in-chief, he got into a controversy with the Government about the force necessary in the Mediterranean, and, giving offence by the sharpness of his language, was ordered to haul down his flag. He never again went to sea. Nelson deplored his loss in terms unusually vivacious: "Oh, miserable Board of Admiralty! They have forced the first officer in our service away from his command." In more temperate but well-weighed words, he said: "This fleet must regret the loss of Lord Hood, the best officer, take him altogether, that England has to boast of. Lord Howe is certainly a great officer in the management of a fleet, but that is all. Lord Hood is equally great in all situations which an admiral can be placed in." In the judgment of the present writer, this estimate of Hood is as accurate as it is moderate in expression. It was nothing less than providential for the French that he was not in command on the 14th of March, or in the yet more trivial and discreditable affair of July 13th, when, to use again Nelson's words, "To say how much we wanted Lord Hood at that time, is to say, will you have all the French fleet or no action?"

On the 14th of June the expected reinforcement from England, nine ships-of-the-line, joined the fleet off Minorca; and a few days later a large convoy also arrived, with which the whole body of ships of war put into San Fiorenzo Bay on the 29th. This concluded for Nelson a period of three months, counting from the action of March 14th, of pretty monotonous cruising with the fleet, the last in which he was to take part until his admiral's flag was hoisted, two years later. Though unmarked by any event of importance, the time was passed not unprofitably to himself, for his correspondence bears marks of fruitful reflection, not merely upon the evident inadequacy of his commander-in-chief to the position he unwillingly occupied, but upon the character of the operations and the line of conduct that ought to be followed. If he does criticise the former's want of head for enterprise, he formulates for himself a general principle which showed its vital influence in his future career. "After all my complaints, I have no doubt but, if we can get close to the enemy, we shall defeat any plan of theirs; *but we ought to have our ideas beyond mere defensive measures.*"

Among other matters for reflection, he had at this time a curious cause of anxiety, lest he should be promoted to flag rank, or rather that, being promoted, he should be obliged to return to England at once, as there would be too many admirals in the Mediterranean to permit his retention. A rumor was current, which proved to be correct, that there would be a large promotion on the 1st of June, the first anniversary of the victory celebrated by that name. Being then forty-six on the list of captains, Nelson feared that it might include him; in which case, if not permitted to hoist his flag where he was, not only would he lose his ardently desired opportunities for dis-

tinction, — " not an hour this war will I, if possible, be
out of active service," — but he would be put to much inconvenience and loss. " If they give me my flag, I shall
be half ruined: unless I am immediately employed in this
country, I should, by the time I landed in England, be a
loser, several hundred pounds out of pocket." To be
taken " from actual service would distress me much, more
especially as I almost believe these people will be mad
enough to come out." He escaped this disappointment,
however, for the promotion left him still on the post-
captains' list, seven from its head; but he received, what
was both complimentary and profitable, the honorary rank
of Colonel of Marines, — a sinecure appointment, of which
there were then four, given to post-captains of distinguished services, and vacated by them upon promotion.
These are now discontinued, and replaced, as a matter of
emolument, by Good Service Pensions. Nelson heard later
that this reward had been conferred upon him, not merely
as a favor, but with a full recognition of all his claims to it.
" The Marines have been given to me in the handsomest
manner. The answer given to many was, the King knew
no officer who had served so much for them as myself."

These promotions came timely to insure for him an employment particularly suited to his active temperament
and fearlessness of responsibility, but which, though the
fittest man for it, he might, with less seniority, not have
received from Hotham, despite the well-known confidence
in him shown by Hood. Since the spring opened, the
Austrians and their allies, the Sardinians, had been waiting, ostensibly at least, for assistance from the Navy, to
begin a forward movement, the first object of which was
the possession of Vado Bay as a safe anchorage for the
fleet. Until the arrival of Man and the convoy, Hotham
had not felt strong enough to spare the required force;
but now, after the ships had filled ·their wants from the
transports, he, on the 4th of July, detached Nelson, with

the "Agamemnon" and six smaller vessels, to co-operate
with the Austrian commander-in-chief. The latter had
begun his movement on the 13th of June, passing through
Genoese territory despite the remonstrances of the Republic, whose neutrality could claim but slight regard from
one belligerent, when she had already permitted the occupation of so much of her shore line by the other. The
French had fallen back, when attacked, abandoning Vado
Bay to the enemy, whose headquarters were established at
that point.

Nelson, having sailed with four of his squadron, fell in
with the French fleet of seventeen of the line, off the Riviera, on the 6th of July. He had, of course, to retreat, which
he did upon San Fiorenzo, to join the body of the fleet.
On the morning of the 7th the "Agamemnon" and her
followers, with the French in close pursuit, were sighted
from the anchorage, much to the surprise of the admiral,
who knew the enemy had come out, but, upon the information of the Austrian general, believed them returned to
Toulon. Why he had not more accurate news from lookout frigates is not clear; but, as Nelson said, he took
things easy, and he had persuaded himself that they had
left harbor only to exercise their men. As it was, the
"Agamemnon" was hard pressed, but escaped, chiefly
through the enemy's lack of seamanship. The fleet, when
she arrived, was in the midst of refitting and watering, but
succeeded in getting to sea the following morning in search
of the enemy, who meantime had disappeared.

Precise information of the French whereabouts could
not be obtained until the evening of the 12th, when two
of the British lookout ships reported that they had been
seen a few hours before to the southwest, south of the
Hyères Islands. The fleet made sail in that direction.
During the night a heavy gale came on from west-north-
west, out of the Gulf of Lyons, which split the main-
topsails of several British ships. At daybreak the enemy

were discovered in the southeast, standing north to close the land. After some elaborate manœuvring — to reach one of those formal orders, often most useful, but which the irregular Mediterranean winds are prone to disarrange as soon as completed — the admiral at 8 A. M. signalled a general chase. The British being to windward, and the breeze fresh, the half-dozen leading ships had at noon closed the enemy's rear within three-quarters of a mile; but, from their relative positions, as then steering, the guns of neither could be used effectively. At this time a shift of wind to north headed off both fleets, which put their bows to the eastward, throwing the British advanced vessels, to use Nelson's expression, into line abreast, and bringing to bear the broadsides of the ships, of both fleets, that were within range. The action then began, the British fire being directed mainly upon the French rear ship, the "Alcide," which surrendered at about 2 P. M., and soon afterwards blew up. The wind had meanwhile changed again to the eastward, giving the weather-gage to the French, most of whom were considerably nearer the shore than their opponents, and better sailers.

Up to this time Nelson, who in the forenoon had thought there was every prospect of taking every ship in the French fleet, still felt almost certain that six would be secured; but, to use his own words, it was now "impossible to close." In the space between the ships engaged, and to leeward, the light air seems to have been killed by the cannonading; whereas the French, who were now to windward, still received enough to draw slowly away. Hotham, being in one of the very worst sailers in the fleet, if not in the Navy, had fallen eight miles astern, and not seeing clearly how things were going, made at this time a signal of recall, which was certainly premature. It seems a not improper comment that, in light and baffling weather, such as that of the Mediterranean, the commander-in-chief should have been in a fast and handy ship, able at the least to keep him within eyeshot of the decisive scene. Remaining in the " Britannia " may have been due to the natural unwillingness of an invalid to quit his well-ordered surroundings, by which even St. Vincent was led to take a first-rate ship away with himself at a critical moment; but, if so, it only emphasizes the absolute necessity of physical vigor to a commander-in-chief.

Nelson had again managed to keep the " Agamemnon " well to the front, for the other ships that succeeded in getting into action were almost wholly from among those which had recently arrived from England with Rear-Admiral Man. These, being fresh from home, should naturally outsail a ship now two and a half years in commission, and which, not long after, had to be wrapped with hawsers to hold her together. In his comments on the action he says comparatively little of the signal of recall, which, though ill-timed, he does not seem to have thought affected the result materially; but he was utterly dissatisfied with the previous management of the business, and into the causes of this dissatisfaction it is desirable to look, as bearing at once upon his natural military characteristics, and the development they received from time and thought. " The scrambling distant fire was a farce," he wrote ; " but if one fell by such a fire, what might not have been expected had our whole fleet engaged? Improperly as the part of the fleet which fired got into action, we took one ship; but the subject is unpleasant, and I shall have done with it." The criticism, though far from explicit, evidently bears upon the manner in which the fleet was handled, from the moment the enemy was sighted until the firing began. During the latter, Man was the senior officer on the spot, and Nelson does not blame him ; on the contrary, punning on the name, says, " He is a good *man* in every sense of the word."

The precise working of his thought can only be inferred. " The whole fleet " failed to get into action. Why ? Be-

cause the signal for a general chase was delayed from 4
to 8 A. M., pending certain drill-ground manœuvres, upon
whose results, however well intended, no dependence could
be placed in Mediterranean weather. During these four
hours the wind was fresh, — the heel of a short summer's
gale, invaluable to both sides, — and the enemy were using
it to close the shore, where wind, the sole dependence for
motive power, baffles most. Had the fastest British ships,
under a competent flag-officer, utilized that time and that
wind, there was, to put the case most mildly, the chance
that they could repeat, upon the French rear, the same
part the "Agamemnon" alone had played with the "Ça
Ira," — and such a chance, were it no more, should not
have been dawdled with. "Missed the opportunity," —
the fatal words, "it might have been." Is it far-fetched
to see in his reflections upon "this miserable action," as it
is styled independently by James and himself, the forecast of the opening sentence of his celebrated order before
Trafalgar? — "Thinking it almost impossible to bring a
fleet of forty sail-of-the-line [1] into a line of battle in variable
winds, thick weather, and other circumstances which must
occur, *without such a loss of time that the opportunity would
probably be lost of bringing the enemy to battle in such a manner as to make the business decisive,* I have therefore made
up my mind — " Or, again, as he saw Man dragged off
— with too little remonstrance, it may be — by a superior,
who could by no means see what was the state of the action, is there not traceable a source of the feeling, partly
inborn, partly reasoned, that found expression in the generous and yet most wise words of the same immortal order? — "The second in command will [in fact command
his line and],[2] after my intentions are made known to him,

---

[1] There were twenty-three present on July 13, 1795.
[2] The words in brackets were erased in the rough draft, but are here inserted, because they emphasize the underlying thought, that the second was
to have real command, not wait nor look for signals, nor yet fear them.

have the entire direction of his line to make the attack upon the enemy, and to follow up the blow until they are captured or destroyed." Whether such words be regarded as the labored result of observation and reflection, or whether as the flashes of intuition, with which genius penetrates at once to the root of a matter, without the antecedent processes to which lesser minds are subjected, — in either case they are instructive when linked with the events of his career here under discussion, as corroborative indications of natural temperament and insight, which banish altogether the thought of mere fortuitous valor as the one explanation of Nelson's successes.

With this unsatisfactory affair, Nelson's direct connection with the main body of the fleet came to an end for the remainder of Hotham's command. It is scarcely necessary to add that the prime object of the British fleet at all times, and not least in the Mediterranean in 1795, — the control of the sea, — continued as doubtful as it had been at the beginning of the year. The dead weight of the admiral's having upon his mind the Toulon fleet, undiminished in force despite two occasions for decisive action, was to be clearly seen in the ensuing operations. On this, also, Nelson did much thinking, as passing events threw light upon the consequences of missing opportunities. "The British fleet," he wrote, five years later, and no man better knew the facts, "could have prevented the invasion of Italy; and, if our friend Hotham had kept his fleet on that coast, I assert, and you will agree with me, no army from France could have been furnished with stores or provisions; even men could not have marched." But how keep the fleet on the Italian coast, while the French fleet in full vigor remained in Toulon? What a curb it was appeared again in the next campaign, and even more clearly, because the British were then commanded by Sir John Jervis, a man not to be checked by ordinary obstacles. From the decks of his flagship Nelson, in the following April, watched a convoy passing close in shore. " To get at them was impossible before they anchored under such batteries as would have crippled our fleet; and, had such an event happened, *in the present state of the enemy's fleet*, Tuscany, Naples, Rome, Sicily, &c., would have fallen as fast as their ships could have sailed along the coast. Our fleet is the only saviour at present for those countries."

CHAPTER VI.

Nelson's Command of a Detached Squadron on the Riviera
of Genoa, until the Defeat of the Austrians at the Battle of Loano. — Sir John Jervis appointed Commander-
in-Chief in the Mediterranean.

July–December, 1795. Age, 37.

AFTER the action of July 13, Nelson was again despatched upon his mission to co-operate with the
Austrians on the Riviera. His orders, dated July 15,
were to confer first with the British minister at Genoa,
and thence to proceed with his squadron to the Austrian
headquarters at Vado Bay. The seniority he had now attained made his selection for this detached and responsible
service less evidently flattering than Hood's preferment of
him to such positions when he was junior in rank; but the
duty had the distinction of being not only arduous from
the purely naval standpoint, but delicate in the diplomatic
management and tact required. Although Great Britain
at that period was rarely slack in resorting to strong and
arbitrary measures in dealing with neutrals, when her interests seemed to demand it, she was always exceedingly
desirous to avoid causes of needless offence. The exigencies of Southern France, and of both the opposing armies in
the Riviera, had created a busy neutral trade, occupied in
supplying all parties to the war, as well as the inhabitants
of Genoese towns then in military occupation by the
French. Although the latter and the Austrians had both
openly disregarded the neutrality of Genoa, it was the
policy of Great Britain now to manifest respect for it as

far as possible, and at the same time not to raise causes of diplomatic contention over the neutral trade, although this was well known to be supporting the enemy's army.

When Nelson left the fleet, he had, besides his special orders for his own mission, a circular letter from the admiral to all vessels under his command, framed upon instructions received from England a month before, directing special care " not to give any just cause of offence to the foreign powers in amity with his Majesty, and whenever any ships or vessels belonging to the subjects of those powers shall be detained, or brought by you into port, you are to transmit to the Secretary of the Admiralty a complete specification of their cargoes, and not to institute any legal process against such ships or vessels until their lordships' further pleasure shall be known."

To the naval officers on the spot this order was calculated to increase vastly the perplexities, which necessarily arose from the occupation of the Genoese coast by French troops. But, besides questions of trade, the weaker States, Genoa and Tuscany, —the latter of which had recently made peace with France, — were driven to manifold shifts and compromises, in order to maintain in their ports such semblance of impartial neutrality as would save them from reprisals by either party. These measures, while insuring to some extent the end in view, gave rise also to a good deal of friction and recrimination between the neutral and the belligerents. The vessels of the latter were admitted, under certain limitations as to number, into the neutral port, where they lay nearly side by side, jealously watching each other, and taking note of every swerving, real or presumed, from an exact and even balance. Each sailed from the neutral port to carry on war, but it is obvious that the shelter of such a port was far more useful to the belligerent who did not control the water, who moved upon it only by evasion and stealth, and who was therefore tempted, in order to improve such advantages, to stretch

to the verge of abuse the privileges permitted to him by
the neutral. "The Genoese allow the French," wrote
Nelson, "to have some small vessels in the port of Genoa,
that I have seen towed out of the port, and board vessels
coming in, and afterwards return into the mole; the conduct of the English is very different." He elsewhere
allows, however, that, "in the opinion of the Genoese, my
squadron is constantly offending; so that it almost appears
a trial between us, who shall first be tired, they of complaining, or me of answering them."

After the first successes of the Austrians and Sardinians,
in the previous June, the French commander-in-chief, Kel-
lerman, feeling his inferiority to be such as compelled him
to a defensive attitude, had carefully selected the most
advanced line that he thought could be held. His right
rested upon the sea, near the village of Borghetto, some
fifty or sixty miles east of Nice, extending thence to and
across the mountains, to Ormea. The Austrian front was
parallel, in a general sense, to that of the enemy, and a
couple of leagues to the eastward; thus securing for the
British Vado Bay, considered the best anchorage between
Genoa and Nice. In rear of Vado, to the eastward, and on
the coast road, lay the fortress of Savona, esteemed by
Bonaparte of the first importance to an army operating in
the Riviera and dependent upon the control of the road.
The town was occupied by the Austrians, but they were
excluded from the citadel by Genoese troops, — a condition
of weakness in case of sudden retreat. It ought, said
Bonaparte, to be the object of all the enemy's efforts. In
these positions, both armies depended for supplies partly
upon the sea, partly upon the land road along the Riviera.
Across the mountains, in Piedmont, lay the Sardinian
forces, extending perpendicularly to the main front of the
French operations, and, so far as position went, threatening their communications by the narrow land road. The
character of the ground intervening between the French

and Austrians rendered an attack upon either line, once fairly established, very difficult; and it was doubtless a fault in the Austrian commander, De Vins, while superior in force, to allow the enemy to strengthen himself in a position which at the first had its weak points; the more so as the plainly approaching peace between Spain and France foretold that the Army of Italy would soon be reinforced. Having, however, made this mistake, the Austrian settled himself in his works, shrugged the responsibility off his own shoulders, and awaited that either the Sardinians by land, or the British by sea, should, by choking the communications of the French, compel them to abandon their lines.

Such was the situation when Nelson, on the 21st of July, had his first interview with De Vins; on the 22d peace between Spain and France was formally concluded. Within a month, Bonaparte, who then occupied a prominent position in Paris, as military adviser to the Government, was writing: " Peace with Spain makes offensive war in Piedmont certain; my plan is being discussed; Vado will soon be taken; " and a few days later, on the 25th of August, "Troops from Spain are marching to Italy." It was incumbent upon the French to repossess Vado, for, by affording safe anchorage to small hostile cruisers, it effectually stopped the trade with Genoa. De Vins had there equipped several privateers, under the Austrian flag. Of it Bonaparte said: " By intercepting the coasters from Italy, it has suspended our commerce, stopped the arrival of provisions, and obliged us to supply Toulon from the interior of the Republic. It is recognized that our commerce and subsistence require that communication with Genoa be promptly opened." Having in view Bonaparte's remarkable campaign of the following year, and the fact that Vado was now held in force by the Austrians, the importance of British co-operation by the fleet, at this critical moment, becomes strikingly apparent. The future thus throws back a ray of illuminating significance upon the otherwise paltry and obscure campaign of 1795, dragging out into broad daylight the full meaning of lost opportunities in the early year, and of Nelson's strenuous efforts in his detached command.

Immediately upon his arrival in Genoa, on July 17, the effect of the neutral trade, if unchecked, upon the operations of both armies, was brought before him by the British minister. Unless the supplies thus received by the French could be stopped, the Austrian general would not only be unable to advance, but feared he could not hold his present position. If, on the other hand, the forage and grain thus brought to them could be intercepted, they would be forced to retreat, and there were hopes that the Austrians might reach Nice before winter, thus covering the excellent and advanced harbor of Villefranche as an anchorage for their British allies. Nelson readily understood the situation, and admitted the necessity of the service demanded of his squadron, which was simply a blow at the enemy's communications; but he pointed out to the minister that the circular instructions, before quoted, tied his hands. Not only would the ordinary difficulties of proving the ownership and destination of a cargo give rise to the usual vexatious disputes, and irritate neutrals, contrary to the spirit of the order; but there was a particular complication in this instance, arising from the occupation of Genoese towns by French troops, and from the close proximity of the neutral and hostile seaboards. These embarrassments might be met, were it permissible to sell the cargoes, and hold the money value, subject to the decision of an admiralty court upon the propriety of the seizure; but this the circular explicitly forbade, until the case was referred to England. If the decision there was adverse to the captors, the other party would look to the responsible naval officer for pecuniary redress, and as, during the delay, the cargo would be spoiled, costs could come only out of the captor's pocket.

Nelson's experiences in the West Indies, ten years before, naturally made him cautious about further legal annoyances.

All this he stated with his usual lucidity; but the case was one in which his course could have been safely predicted by a person familiar with his character. The need for the proposed action was evident. " The whole of the necessity of stopping all the vessels is comprised in a very few words that, if we will not stop supplies of corn, etc., going to France, the armies will return from whence they came, and the failure of this campaign, from which so much is expected, will be laid to our want of energy; for the only use of the naval co-operation is the keeping out a supply of provisions." He therefore, after a night's reflection, told the minister that if he would tell him, officially, that it was for the benefit of his Majesty's service that he should stop all trade between the neutral towns and France, and places occupied by the armies of France, he would give the proper directions for that purpose. It would have been possible for him, though with some delay, to refer the matter to Hotham, but he knew the latter's temperament, and distrusted it. " Our admiral has no political courage whatever," he wrote to Collingwood, "and is alarmed at the mention of any strong measure; but, in other respects, he is as good a man as can possibly be." With a superior so little decided, it was better, by his own independent initiative, to create a situation, which the former would be as backward to reverse as he would have been to change the previous and wholly different state of things. Like the American frontiersman, whose motto was, " Be sure you're right, then go ahead," Nelson, when convinced, knew no hesitations; but further, he unquestionably derived keen enjoyment from the sense that the thing done involved risk to himself, appealed to and brought into play his physical or moral courage, in the conscious exercise of which he delighted. " I am acting, not only without the orders of my commander-in-chief, but in some measure

contrary to them. However, I have not only the support
of his Majesty's ministers, both at Turin and Genoa, but a
consciousness that I am doing what is right and proper for
the service of our King and Country. Political courage in
an officer abroad is as highly necessary as military courage." " The orders I have given are strong, and I know
not how my admiral will approve of them, for they are, in
a great measure, contrary to those he gave me; but the
service requires strong and vigorous measures to bring the
war to a conclusion."

The case bore some resemblance to that in which he had
disobeyed Hughes in the West Indies; but the disregard
of the superior's orders on the earlier occasion was more
direct, and the necessity for it less urgent. In both he
disobeyed first, and referred afterwards, and in both his
action was practically sustained; for, whatever the technical fault, the course taken was the one demanded by the
needs of the situation. It is possible to recognize the
sound policy, the moral courage, and the correctness of
such a step in the particular instance, without at all sanc-
tioning the idea that an officer may be justified in violat-
ing orders, because he thinks it right. The justification
rests not upon what he thinks, but upon the attendant
circumstances which prove that he *is* right; and, if he is
mistaken, if the conditions have not warranted the infraction
of the fundamental principle of military efficiency, — obedience, — he must take the full consequences of his error,
however honest he may have been. Nor can the justification of disobedience fairly rest upon any happy consequences that follow upon it, though it is a commonplace to
say that the result is very apt to determine the question of
reward or blame. There is a certain confusion of thought
prevalent on this matter, most holding the rule of obedience too absolutely, others tending to the disorganizing
view that the integrity of the intention is sufficient; the
practical result, and for the average man the better result,

being to shun the grave responsibility of departing from the letter of the order. But all this only shows more clearly the great professional courage and professional sagacity of Nelson, that he so often assumed such a responsibility, and so generally — with, perhaps, but a single exception — was demonstrably correct in his action.

Hotham in this case very heartily approved what had been done, and issued, to the fleet in general, orders similar to those given by Nelson; but he did not like the difficulties that surrounded the question of co-operation, and left the conduct of affairs on the spot wholly to his eager and enterprising subordinate. The latter directed the seizure of all vessels laden with corn for France or the French armies, an order that was construed to apply to the Genoese towns occupied by them. The cargoes appear to have been sold and the money held. The cruisers in his command were stationed along the Riviera, east and west of Genoa itself. Those to the eastward, in the neighborhood of Spezia, where no French were, gave great offence to the Government of the Republic, which claimed that their chief city was blockaded; but Nelson refused to remove them. They are not blockading Genoa, he said, but simply occupying the station best suited to intercept a contraband trade. The various British vessels displayed the full activity that might have been expected from the character of their leader, and the pressure was speedily felt by the enemy, and by the neutrals whose lucrative trade was summarily interrupted. The traffic in vessels of any considerable size, sea-going vessels, soon ceased, and Nelson entertained at first great hopes of decisive results from the course adopted by him. "We have much power here at present to do great things, if we know how to apply it," he wrote, after being ten days on the ground; and at the end of a month, "The strong orders which I judged it proper to give on my first arrival, have had an extraordinary good effect; the French army is now supplied

with almost daily bread from Marseilles; not a single boat
has passed with corn." The enemy themselves admitted
the stringency of their situation. But Nelson had yet to
learn how ingenuity and enterprise could find a way of
eluding his care. The coasting-trade soon began to take on
a large development. The Spaniards, now at peace with
France, supplied Marseilles, and from both that port and
Genoa grain was carried by small boats, that could be
moved by oar as well as sail, could hug closely the rocky
shore, and run readily under the batteries with which the
French had covered the small bays of the western Riviera,
whither the cruisers could not follow. The operations of
the latter, dependent only upon their canvas, could not
always be extended to within easy gunshot of the beach,
along which the blockade-runners kept, usually under
cover of night.

Hence, although seriously inconvenienced, the French
did not find their position untenable. There were two
ways by which the pressure might be increased. A flotilla
of small vessels, similar to the coasters themselves, but
armed and heavily manned, might keep close in with the
points which the latter had to round, and prevent their
passage; but the British had no such vessels at their disposal, and, even if they had, the operations would be exposed to danger from the weather upon a hostile, iron-bound
coast, whose shelter was forbidden them by the enemy's
guns. The Neapolitans had such a flotilla, and it seems
probable that its co-operation was asked, for Nelson speaks
of it as a desirable aid on the 23d of August; but it did
not actually join him until the 15th of September, when the
season for its acting was almost past. "Had I the flotilla," wrote he, "nothing should be on this coast. A few
weeks more and they will not stay a night at sea to save
an empire." Prior to its arrival the British attempted to
harass the traffic with their ships' boats, but these were un-
decked, and of limited capacity compared to those against

which they were to act. They were occasionally successful, but the results were too uncertain and hazardous to
warrant perseverance, although Bonaparte had to admit
that "The audacity of the English boats and the indolence
of the Genoese, who allow their own vessels to be taken
in their own roads, make it necessary to erect a battery for
hot shot at a proper point, which you will exact shall be
done by the governor of San Remo."

Nelson's active mind, clinging with its usual accurate insight to the decisive factor in the situation, now fixed upon
the idea of seizing a suitable point upon the Riviera to the
westward of the French, upon their line of communication
with Nice. A body of troops there, strong enough to hold
the position, would stop the passage of supplies by land,
and, if they controlled an anchorage, a condition indispensable to their support, — and to their retreat, if necessary
to retire, — the small vessels based upon that could better
interrupt the coasting business. In pursuance of this plan,
he in the first week of September made a cruise with the
"Agamemnon" as far to the westward as Nice, reconnoitring carefully all recesses of the shore line that seemed
available for the purpose. Upon his return, he wrote to
De Vins what he had done, and described San Remo as the
only available spot. He mentioned its disadvantages as
well as its advantages, but undertook positively to land
there five thousand men with field-guns, and provisions for
a few days, to maintain their supplies by sea, and to cover
their embarkation in case retreat became imperative. In
short, he guaranteed to land such a force safely, and to be
responsible for its communications; for both which he
practically pledged his professional reputation. He added,
what was indisputable, that the French army must abandon
its present lines for want of supplies, if San Remo were
held for some time.

De Vins replied on the 14th of September, expressing his
interest in the matter thus broached to him, but carefully

evading the issue. He addressed his remarks to the comparative merits of Vado and San Remo as anchorages, upon which Nelson had touched barely, and only incidentally, for the gist of his proposal was simply to intercept the enemy's communications; if this were feasible, all other considerations were subsidiary and matters of detail. San Remo was admitted to be the poorer anchorage, unfit for the fleet, but open to small vessels, which could carry the supplies to the Austrian detachment, and stop those of the enemy. The move proposed was intended to effect by sea, substantially, the object which De Vins himself had told Nelson, three weeks before, that he was trying to secure through the co-operation of the Sardinian land forces. "He has been long expecting," wrote Nelson on the 13th of August, "an attack by General Colli with the Piedmontese, near Ormea, directly back from Vintimiglia. This is the great point to be carried, as the Piedmontese army would then get Vintimiglia, and . . . probably, unless the enemy are very active, their retreat to Nice will be cut off. De Vins says he has flattered and abused the Piedmontese and Neapolitans, but nothing will induce them to act." Colli was a good soldier, but his relations with the Austrian were very strained, and coalitions rarely act cordially. This plan, however, becoming known to the French, was commended by Bonaparte as well conceived. "We have examined attentively the project attributed to the enemy in the enclosed note. We have found it conformable to his real interests, and to the present distribution of his troops. The heights of Briga are in truth the key to the Department of the Maritime Alps, since from there the high-road may be intercepted and we be obliged to evacuate Tende. We charge you to pay serious attention to this matter." [1] Disappointed in Sardinian support, Nelson and De Vins had then discussed a plan, of

[1] Correspondance de Napoléon, August 30, 1795. The letter was from Bonaparte's hand, though signed by the Committee of Public Safety.

which the former's present proposal was the very clear and practical outcome. Some risk must be run, he said; but De Vins, when it came to the point, saw the dangers too plainly. He did not distinctly refuse, but talked only, and instead of San Remo proposed to land west of Nice, between it and the Var. Nothing, however, was done, or even attempted, and Hotham refused co-operation.

Having regard to the decisive effect exercised upon any strategic position, or movement, by a valid threat against the communications, — considering, for example, the vital influence which the French occupation of Genoa in 1800 had upon the campaign which terminated at Marengo, — it is impossible to speak otherwise than with respect of this proposal of Nelson's. Nevertheless, serious reflection can scarcely fail to affirm that it was not really practicable. There is an immeasurable difference between the holding of a strongly fortified city with an army corps, and the mere seizure of a comparatively open position by a detachment, which, if it means to remain, must have time to fortify itself, in order to withstand the overwhelming numbers that the enemy must at once throw upon it. The time element, too, is of the utmost importance. It is one thing to grasp a strong position with a few men, expecting to hold it for some hours, to delay an advance or a retreat until other forces can come into play, and quite another to attempt to remain permanently and unsupported in such a situation. In the case before us, De Vins would have landed five thousand men in a comparatively exposed position; for, although the town of San Remo was in possession of the French, who might be driven out for the moment, the only strong point, the citadel, was occupied — as in the case of Savona, to the eastward of the Austrians — by the Genoese, who would doubtless have refused admission. Before his main body would still lie the works which the French had been diligently strengthening for more than two months, and which, with his whole force in hand, he

did not care to assail. The enemy, knowing him thus
weakened, could well afford to spare a number greatly
superior to the detachment he had adventured, certain that,
while they were dislodging it, he could make no serious
impression upon their lines. As for retreat and embarkation
under cover of the guns of a squadron, when pressed by
an enemy, the operation is too critical to be hazarded for
less than the greatest ends, and with at least a fair possibility of success for the undertaking whose failure would
entail it.

Nelson's confidence in himself and in his profession, and
his accurate instinct that war cannot be made without running risks, combined with his lack of experience in the difficulties of land operations to mislead his judgment in the
particular instance. In a converse sense, there may be
applied to him the remark of the French naval critic, that
Napoleon lacked " le sentiment exact des difficultés de la
marine." It was not only to British seamen, and to the
assured control of the sea, that Nelson thought such an
attempt offered reasonable prospect of success. He feared
a like thing might be effected by the French, — by evasion.
" If the enemy's squadron comes on this coast, and lands
from three to four thousand men between Genoa and
Savona, I am confident that either the whole Austrian
army will be defeated, or, must inevitably retreat into
Piedmont, and abandon their artillery and stores." These
words, the substance of which he frequently repeats, though
written immediately before the disastrous Battle of Loano,
do not apply to the purpose entertained by the French on
that occasion, of endeavoring, by a small detachment at
Voltri, to check the Austrian retreat till their pursuers
came up. He is contemplating a much more considerable
and sustained effort, strategic in character, and identical in
aim with his own proposal to De Vins about San Remo. It
is clear that Nelson, in his day, did not attach absolute
deterrent effect to a fleet in being, even to such an one as

the British then had in the Mediterranean. Important a factor as it was, it might conceivably be disregarded, by a leader who recognized that the end in view justified the risk.

There was yet another motive actuating Nelson in his present proposals. Justly impatient of the delays and colorless policy of both De Vins and the British leaders, he foresaw that the latter would be made to take the blame, if the campaign proved abortive or disastrous. The Austrians had at least something to show. They had advanced, and they had seized Vado Bay, cutting off the intercourse between Genoa and France, which Bonaparte deemed so important, and at the same time securing an anchorage for the fleet. The latter had done nothing, although its co-operation had been promised; except Nelson's little squadron, in which was but one small ship-of-the-line out of the twenty-three under Hotham's command, it had not been seen.[1] Nelson was determined, as far as in him lay, to remove all grounds for reproach. He urged the admiral to send him more ships, and abounded in willingness towards De Vins. For the latter he had at first felt the esteem and confidence which he almost invariably showed, even to the point of weakness, towards those associated with him; but he now became distrustful, and devoted himself to stopping every loophole of excuse which might afterwards be converted into reproaches to the navy.

The cause for the inadequacy of the force left under his command, of which he often complains, is not apparent. The question was put direct to the admiral whether he would co-operate with the fleet in the proposed descent of the Austrians. He said that he could not, owing to the nature of his instructions from home; but that he would

---

[1] The fleet passed once, August 14, in sight of Vado Bay. Nelson went on board, and tried to induce Hotham to go in and meet De Vins. He refused, saying he must go to Leghorn, but would return, and water the fleet in Vado; but he never came.

answer for it that the French navy should not interfere.
Six weeks later the question was repeated; but the admiral
replied that, after a consultation with the flag-officers under
his command, he refused co-operation in what he considered
a wild scheme.   In this opinion he was probably right,
though Nelson possibly was reminded of Dundas's objections to besieging Bastia.   Nelson then went in person to
Leghorn, and saw Hotham.   He asked to be given two
seventy-fours and the transports, to make the attempt himself.   Hotham again refused a single ship; but not only
so, reduced Nelson's squadron, and ordered him, in addition
to his present duties, to reconnoitre Toulon continually,
" whilst he," said Nelson, scornfully, " lies quiet in Leghorn
Roads."   It would almost seem as if the admiral thought
that the time had come for a little judicious snubbing, and
repression of ardor in the uncomfortable subordinate, whose
restless energy conflicted so much with his repose of mind.
The fleet spent its time chiefly in San Fiorenzo Bay or in
Leghorn, making occasional cruises off Toulon to observe the
French navy in that port.   The latter was undoubtedly its
principal care; but, being distinctly inferior to the British,
it is impossible to say why Nelson should not have been reinforced.   If it was due to the wish to continue so largely
superior in numbers, it certainly illustrates with singular
appositeness the deterrent effect of an inferior " fleet in
being," and that that effect lies less in the nature of things
than in the character of the officer upon whom it is produced.   Moreover, the employment of adequate force upon
the Riviera, in active aggressive work under Nelson during
the summer, when it was practicable to do so, would have
compelled the French fleet to come out and fight, or the
French army to fall back.

On the 1st of November Hotham struck his flag in
Genoa, and departed, bequeathing to his successors a military estate encumbered by the old mortgage of the French
fleet, still in being, which he might have cleared off, and

by a new one in the numerous and powerful batteries of
the Riviera, built and controlled by troops whose presence
to erect them might have been prevented by a timely action
on his part. The harm, being done, was thenceforth irreparable. As time passed, the situation became more and
more favorable to the French. The reinforcements from
Spain arrived, and gunboats and flatboats, fitted out at
Toulon, began to come upon the scene. Their appearance
revived in Nelson the apprehension, so consonant to his
military ideas at this time, of an attempt upon the coast
road in rear of the Austrians. He even feared for Genoa
itself, and for the "Agamemnon," while she lay there, as
the result of such a dash. The recurrence of this prepossession is illustrative of his view of possibilities. The true
and primary object of the French was to consolidate their
communications; nor, with Bonaparte in the influential
position he then occupied, was any such ex-centric movement likely. For useful purposes, Genoa was already at
his disposal; the French subsistence department was, by
his plans, to collect there rations of corn for sixty thousand
men for three months, preparatory to an advance. For
the same object the coasting activity redoubled along the
Riviera, from Toulon to the French front. By November
1st a hundred sail — transports and small ships of war —
had assembled fifteen miles behind Borghetto, in Alassio
Bay, whither Nelson had chased them. Depots and supplies were collecting there for the prospective movement.
Nelson offered to enter the bay with three ships-of-the-line,
specified by name, and to destroy them; but this was declined by Sir Hyde Parker, who had temporarily succeeded
Hotham in command, and who at a later day, in the Baltic,
was to check some of Nelson's finest inspirations. " I pretend not to say," wrote the latter, a month afterwards, when
the Austrians had been driven from their lines, " that the
Austrians would not have been beat had not the gunboats
harassed them, for, on my conscience, I believe they would;

but I believe the French would not have attacked had we destroyed all the vessels of war, transports, etc." As to the practicability of destroying them, Nelson's judgment can safely be accepted, subject only to the chances which are inseparable from war.

So far from reinforcing the squadron on the Riviera, Sir Hyde Parker first reduced it, and then took away the frigates at this critical moment, when the indications of the French moving were becoming apparent in an increase of boldness. Their gunboats, no longer confining themselves to the convoy of coasters, crept forward at times to molest the Austrians, where they rested on the sea. Nelson had no similar force to oppose to them, except the Neapolitans, whom he ordered to act, but with what result is not clear. At the same time the French partisans in Genoa became very threatening. On the 10th of November a party of three hundred, drawn from the ships in the port, landed at Voltri, about nine miles from Genoa, seized a magazine of corn, and an Austrian commissary with £10,000 in his charge. The place was quickly retaken, but the effrontery of the attempt from a neutral port showed the insecurity of the conditions. At the same time a rumor spread that a force of between one and two thousand men, partly carried from Genoa in the French ships of war then lying there, partly stealing along shore in coasters from Borghetto, was to seize a post near Voltri, and hold it. Nelson was informed that men were absolutely being recruited on the Exchange of Genoa for this expedition. When the attack at Voltri was made, the "Agamemnon" was lying in Vado Bay. Leaving a frigate there, Nelson started immediately for Genoa, in order, by the presence of a superior naval force and the fear of retaliation, both to compel the Republic to have its neutrality observed, and to check similar undertakings in the future. The "Agamemnon" was laid across the harbor's mouth, and no French vessel was allowed to sail. Urgent representations were made to Nelson by the Austrian minister and commander-in-chief, that, if the ship were withdrawn, the consequences to the army would be most serious. Contrary, therefore, to his personal inclinations, which were always to be at the front, he remained, although the demonstrations of the gunboats continued, and it was evident that they would at least annoy the Austrian flank in case of an assault. The latter evil, however, was much less disquieting than a descent on the army's line of retreat, at the same moment that it was assailed in front in force; and it was evident that the Austrian general was feeling an uneasiness, the full extent of which he did not betray. De Vins had by this time quitted his command, ill, and had been succeeded by General Wallis.

In this condition of affairs, a general attack upon the Austrian positions was made by the French on the morning of November 24. As had been feared, the gunboats took part, in the absence of any British ships, — the frigate having been removed, Nelson asserts, without his knowledge; but the matter was of very secondary importance, for the weight of the enemy's attack fell upon the positions in the mountains, the centre and right, which were routed and driven back. Swinging round to their own right, towards the sea, the victorious French pushed after the disordered enemy, seeking to intercept their retreat by the coast. Had there then been established, in a well-chosen point of that narrow road, a resolute body of men, even though small, they might well have delayed the fliers until the main body of the pursuers came up; but the presence of the "Agamemnon" controlled the departure of the intended expedition from Genoa, upon which alone, as an organized effort, the projected obstruction depended. Thus she was the efficient cause, as Nelson claimed, that many thousands of Austrians escaped capture. As it was, they lost in this affair, known as the Battle of Loano, seven thousand men, killed, wounded, or prisoners. The entire Riviera was abandoned, and they retreated across the Apennines into Piedmont.

When things go wrong, there is always a disposition on the part of each one concerned to shift the blame. The Austrians had complained before the action, and still more afterwards, of the failure of the fleet to aid them. Nelson thought their complaint well founded. "They say, and true, they were brought on the coast at the express desire of the English, to co-operate with the fleet, which fleet nor admiral they never saw." On his own part he said : " Our admirals will have, I believe, much to answer for in not giving me that force which I so repeatedly called for, and for at last leaving me with Agamemnon alone. Admiral Hotham kept my squadron too small for its duty; and the moment Sir Hyde took the command of the fleet he reduced it to nothing, — only one frigate and a brig; whereas I demanded two seventy-four-gun ships and eight or ten frigates and sloops to insure safety to the army."

It is unnecessary to inquire into the motives of the two admirals for the distribution of their force. Unquestionably, the first thing for them to do was to destroy or neutralize the French fleet; and next to destroy, or at least impede, the communications of the French army. That it was possible to do this almost wholly may be rested upon the authority of Nelson, whose matured opinion, given five years later, has already been quoted. Two opportunities to cripple the Toulon fleet were lost; but even so, after the junction of Man, in June, the superiority over it was so great that much might have been spared to the Riviera squadron. The coast was not at this time so extensively fortified that coasting could not, in Nelson's active hands, have been made a very insufficient means of supply. As an illustration of the operations then possible, on the 26th of August, six weeks after the naval battle of July 13, the "Agamemnon," with her little squadron, anchored in the Bay of Alassio, three cables' length from the fort in the centre of the town, and with her boats took possession of all the French vessels in the harbor. Two months later, so much had the place been strengthened, he could not vouch for success with less than three ships-of-the-line; but had the pressure been consistently applied during those months, the French position would long before have become untenable. That a shore line, by great and systematic effort, could be rendered secure throughout for coasters, was proved by Napoleon's measures to cover the concentration of the Boulogne flotilla in 1803–5; but such conditions did not obtain between Nice and Vado in 1795.

Despite the abortive and ignominious ending to the campaign, Nelson's own reputation issued from it not only unscathed, but heightened; and this is saying much, for, although due public recognition of his services had scarcely been extended, — except in conferring the Marines upon him, — he had already, before its beginning, made upon all who were brought into contact with him that impression of unusual efficiency, zeal, and sound judgment, to which subsequent employment and opportunity apply a sure and searching test. As he entered upon his detached duties, the Viceroy of Corsica, who had necessarily seen and known much of his past conduct, wrote to him thus : " Give me leave, my dear Sir, to congratulate you on the Agamemnon's supporting uniformly, on all occasions, the same reputation which has always distinguished that ship since I have been in the Mediterranean. It gives me great pleasure also to see you employed in your present important service, which requires zeal, activity, and a spirit of accommodation and co-operation, qualities which will not be wanting in the Commodore of your squadron. I consider the business you are about, I mean the expulsion of the enemy from the Genoese and Piedmontese territories, as the most important feature in the southern campaign." These anticipations of worthy service and exceptional merit were confirmed, after all the misfortunes and disappointments of the campaign, by the singularly competent judgment of the new commander-in-chief, Sir John Jervis. The latter at his first interview with Nelson, nearly two months after his arrival on the station, so that time enough had elapsed to mature his opinion, asked him to remain under his command, as a junior admiral, when he received his promotion. Having regard to Jervis's own high endowments, it was not then in the power of the British Navy to pay an officer of Nelson's rank a higher compliment.

During these months of service upon the Riviera, there occurred an incident, which, from the reflection made upon Nelson's integrity, drew from him a letter, struck off at such white heat, and so transparently characteristic of his temperament, aspirations, and habit of thought, as to merit quotation. A report had been spread that the commanders of the British ships of war connived at the entry of supply-vessels into the ports held by the French, and a statement to that effect was forwarded to the Secretary of State for Foreign Affairs. The latter sent the paper, for investigation, to the Minister to Genoa, who mentioned its tenor to Nelson. The latter, justly stigmatizing the conduct imputed to him and his officers as "scandalous and infamous," requested a copy of the accusation, in order that by his refutation he might convince the King, that he was "an officer who had ever pursued the road of honour, very different from that to wealth." Having received the copy, he wrote to the Secretary as follows: —

AGAMEMNON, GENOA ROAD, 23d November, 1795.

MY LORD, — Having received, from Mr. Drake, a copy of your Lordship's letter to him of October, enclosing a paper highly reflecting on the honour of myself and other of His Majesty's Officers employed on this Coast under my Orders, it well becomes me, as far as in my power lies, to wipe away this ignominious stain on our characters. I do, therefore, in behalf of myself, and much injured Brethren, demand, that the person, whoever he may be, that wrote, or gave that paper to your Lordship, do fully, and expressly bring home his charge; which, as he states that this agreement is made by numbers of people on both sides, there can be no difficulty in doing. We dare him, my Lord, to the proof. If he cannot, I do most humbly implore, that His Majesty will be most graciously pleased to direct his Attorney-General to prosecute this infamous libeller in His Courts of Law; and I likewise feel, that, without impropriety, I may on behalf of my brother Officers, demand the support of His Majesty's Ministers: for as, if true, no punishment can be too great for the traitors; so, if false, none can be too heavy for the villain, who has dared to allow his pen to write such a paper. Perhaps I ought to stop my letter here; but I feel too much to rest easy for a moment, when the honour of the Navy, and our Country, is struck at through us; for if nine [ten] Captains, whom chance has thrown together, can instantly join in such a traitorous measure, it is fair to conclude we are all bad.

As this traitorous agreement could not be carried on but by concert of all the Captains, if they were on the Stations allotted them, and as they could only be drawn from those Stations by orders from me, I do most fully acquit all my brother Captains from such a combination, and have to request, that I may be considered as the only responsible person for what is done under my command, if I approve of the conduct of those under my orders, which in this most public manner I beg leave to do: for Officers more alert, and more anxious for the good, and honour, of their King and Country, can scarcely ever fall to the lot of any Commanding Officer: their Names I place at the bottom of this letter.

For myself, from my earliest youth I have been in the Naval Service; and in two Wars, have been in more than one hundred and forty Skirmishes and Battles, at Sea and on shore: have lost an eye, and otherwise blood, in fighting the Enemies of my King and Country; and, God knows, instead of riches, my little fortune has been diminished in the Service: but I shall not trouble your Lordship further at present, than just to say — that at the close of this Campaign, where I have had the pleasure to receive the approbation of the Generals of the Allied Powers; of his Excellency Mr. Drake, who has always been on the spot; of Mr. Trevor, who has been at a distance; when I expected and hoped, from the representation of His Majesty's Ministers, that His Majesty would have most graciously condescended to have favourably noticed my earnest desire to serve Him, and when, instead of all my fancied approbation, to receive an accusation of a most traitorous nature — it has almost been too much for me to bear. Conscious innocence, I hope, will support me.

> I have the honour to be,
> My Lord,
> Your Lordship's most obedient, humble servant,
> HORATIO NELSON.

Except this vexatious but passing cloud, his service upon the Riviera, despite the procrastinations and final failure of his associates in the campaign, was pleasant both personally and officially. He earned the warm esteem of all with whom he acted, notably the British ministers at Turin and Genoa; and though necessarily in constant collision with the Genoese authorities upon international questions, he upheld the interests and policy of his own government, without entailing upon it serious cause of future reclamations and disputes.[1] Hotham's very indifference and lethargy, while crippling his enterprise, increased his independence. " I cannot get Hotham

---

[1] A year later, when all his transactions with Genoa as an independent republic were concluded, Nelson received from the British Minister of Foreign Affairs, through the Admiralty, the following strong and comprehensive endorsement of his political conduct : —

"I esteem it an act of justice due to that officer, to inform your lordships that His Majesty has been graciously pleased entirely to approve of the conduct of Commodore Nelson in all his transactions with the Republic of Genoa. I have the honour to be, &c., &c. GRENVILLE."

The First Lord of the Admiralty about the same time expressed "the great satisfaction derived here from the very spirited, and at the same time dignified and temperate manner, in which your conduct has been marked both at Leghorn and Genoa."

on the coast," he said, "for he hates this co-operation;" but he owns to the fear that the admiral, if he came, might overrule his projects. The necessity for exertion delighted him. "My command here is so far pleasant," he wrote to his friend Collingwood, "as it relieves me from the inactivity of our fleet, which is great indeed, as you will soon see." "At present," he tells his wife, "I do not write less than from ten to twenty letters every day; which, with the Austrian general, and aide-de-camps, and my own little squadron, fully employ my time: this I like; active service or none." As usual, when given room for the exercise of his powers, he was, for him, well. He had a severe attack of illness very soon after assuming the duty — "a complaint in the breast" — the precursor perhaps of the similar trouble from which he suffered so much in later years; but it wore off after an acute attack of a fortnight, and he wrote later that, except being at home, he knew no country so pleasant to serve in, nor where his health was so good. This well-grounded preference for the Mediterranean, as best suited to his naturally frail constitution, remained with him to the end.

Besides his official correspondence, he wrote freely and fully to those at home, unburdening to them the thoughts, cares, and disappointments of his career, as well as the commendations he received, so dear to himself as well as to them. Mrs. Nelson and his father lived together, and to her most of his home letters were addressed. "I have been very negligent," he admits to her, "in writing to my father, but I rest assured he knows I would have done it long ago, had you not been under the same roof. . . . Pray draw on me," he continues, "for £200, my father and myself can settle our accounts when we meet; at present, I believe I am the richer man, therefore I desire you will give my dear father that money." One wonders whether, in the slightly peremptory tone of the last sentence, is to be seen a trace of the feeling she is said, by one biographer, to have shown, that he was too liberal to his relatives; an indication of that lack of sympathy, which, manifested towards other traits of his, no less marked than openhandedness, struck a jarring note within him, and possibly paved the way to an indifference which ended so unfortunately for both. An absent husband, however, very possibly failed to realize what his extreme generosity might mean, to one who had to meet household expenses with narrow means.

The political surmises with which his correspondence at this period abounds were often crude, though not infrequently also characterized by the native sagacity of his intellect, as yet undisciplined, and to some extent deficient in data for accurate forecasts. The erroneous military conception which colored much of his thought, the propositions for ex-centric movements in an enemy's rear, by bodies comparatively small, out of supporting distance from the rest of the army, and resting upon no impregnable base, contributed greatly to the faulty anticipations entertained and expressed by him from time to time. When applied to operations directed by the consummate and highly trained genius of Bonaparte, speculations so swayed naturally flew wide of the mark. His sanguine disposition to think the best of all persons and all things — except Frenchmen — made him also a ready prey to the flattering rumors of which war is ever fertile. These immaturities will be found to disappear, as his sphere widens and his responsibilities increase.

After the close of the campaign, Nelson made a short cruise from Genoa to the westward, seeing the French on November 29 in full possession of Vado Bay. He then went to Leghorn, where he arrived on the 6th of December and remained till the middle of January, repairing, to make the "Agamemnon" "as fit for sea as a rotten ship can be." The longing for rest and for home, after nearly three years' absence, was again strong upon him in this moment of relaxation. "I fear our new admiral is willing to keep me with him," he wrote to his brother. "He has wrote me, I am sorry to say, a most flattering letter, and I hear I am to be offered St. George or Zealous [much larger ships], but, in my present mind, I shall take neither. My wish is to see England once more, and I want a few weeks' rest." But here again, having regard to that fame which was to him most dear, he was mistaken, as he now owned he had been in the wish, a year before, to accompany Lord Hood on his return. In Sir John Jervis he was to meet, not only one of the most accomplished and resolute officers of the British Navy, closely akin to himself in enterprise and fearlessness, though without his exceptional genius, but also a man capable of appreciating perfectly the extraordinary powers of his subordinate, and of disregarding every obstacle and all clamor, in the determination to utilize his qualities to the full, for the good of the nation.

CHAPTER VII.

NELSON'S SERVICES IN THE MEDITERRANEAN DURING THE YEAR 1796. — BONAPARTE'S ITALIAN CAMPAIGN. — THE BRITISH ABANDON CORSICA, AND THE FLEET LEAVES THE MEDITERRANEAN.

JANUARY–DECEMBER, 1796. AGE, 38.

WHILE the "Agamemnon" was refitting in Leghorn, the sensitive mind of her captain, no longer preoccupied with the cares of campaigning and negotiations, dwelt with restless anxiety upon the reflections to which the British Navy was liable, for its alleged failure to support the Austrians throughout the operations, and especially at the critical moment of the Battle of Loano, when the left flank of their army was harassed with impunity by the French gunboats. Nelson felt rightly that, with the British superiority at sea, this should have been impossible; and he feared that his own name might be unpleasantly involved, from the fact that the "Agamemnon" had remained throughout at Genoa, instead of being where the fighting was. He was by nature, and at all times, over-forward to self-vindication, — an infirmity springing from the innate nobility of his temperament, which was impatient of the faintest suspicion of backwardness or negligence, and at the same time resolved that for any shortcoming or blunder, occurring by his order or sanction, no other than himself should bear blame, directly or indirectly.

After the first unsuccessful pursuit of Bonaparte's expedition to Egypt, in 1798, in the keenness of his emotions over a failure that might by some be charged to a precipi-

tate error of judgment, he drew up for Lord St. Vincent a
clear and able statement of all the reasons which had determined his action, arraigning himself, as it were, at the bar
of his lordship's opinion and that of the nation, and assuming entire responsibility for the apparent mistake, while at
the same time justifying the step by a review of the various considerations which at the time had occasioned it.
His judicious friend and subordinate, Captain Ball, whom
he consulted, strongly advised him not to send the paper.
" I was particularly struck," he wrote, " with the clear and
accurate style, as well as with the candour of the statement
in your letter, but I should recommend a friend never to
begin a defence of his conduct before he is accused of
error." Nevertheless, in February, 1805, when he once
more went to Alexandria in search of Villeneuve, this time
really misled by the elaborate mystifications of Napoleon,
he again brought himself before the Admiralty. " I am
entirely responsible to my King and Country for the whole
of my conduct . . . I have consulted no man, therefore
the whole blame of ignorance in forming my judgment
must rest with me. I would allow no man to take from
me an atom of my glory, had I fallen in with the French
fleet, nor do I desire any man to partake any of the responsibility — all is mine, right or wrong."

In 1795, being a much younger man, of less experience
of the world, and with a reputation, already brilliant indeed, but still awaiting the stamp of solidity which the
lapse of time alone can give, Nelson felt strongly, and not
improperly, that it was necessary to be vigilant against any
possible imputations upon his action. This was the more
true, because blame certainly did attach to the service of
which he was the representative on the spot, and the course
he had been obliged to follow kept him to the rear instead
of at the front. There would have been no greater personal danger to a man on board the " Agamemnon " in one
place than in the other ; but current rumor, seeking a vic-

tim, does not pause to analyze conditions. Not only, there-fore, did he draw up for Sir John Jervis a succinct synopsis of·occurrences subsequent to his taking command of the operations along the Riviera, in which he combined a justi-fication of his own conduct with the general information necessary for a new commander-in-chief, but to all his principal correspondents he carefully imparted the facts necessary to clear him from blame, and to show just what the Navy had effected, and where it had fallen short through inadequate force.

To the British minister to Genoa, who was constantly at the Austrian headquarters, he wrote with clear emphasis, as to one cognizant of all the truth, and so a witness most important to himself. Having first asked certain certifi-cates, essential to be presented in the Admiralty Courts when Genoese prizes came to be adjudicated, he continued characteristically: "The next request much more concerns my honour, than the other does my interest — it is to prove to the world, to my own admiral, or to whoever may have a right to ask the question, why I remained at Genoa. I have therefore to desire that you will have the goodness to express, in writing, what you told me, that the Imperial minister and yourself were assured, if I left the port of Genoa unguarded, not only the Imperial troops at St. Pierre d'Arena and Voltri would be lost, but that the French plan for taking post between Voltri and Savona would certainly succeed; and also, that if the Austrians should be worsted in the advanced posts, the retreat by the Bocchetta would be cut off: to which you added, that if this happened, the loss of the Army would be laid to my leaving Genoa, and recommended me most strongly not to think of it. I am anxious, as you will believe, to have proofs in my possession, that I employed to the last the Agamemnon as was judged most beneficial to the com-mon cause."

A week later he wrote again, having heard that the Aus-

trian commander-in-chief, General Wallis, had declared that
the defeat was due to the failure of the British to co-
operate. Nelson thought that they had a strong hold on
Wallis, and he therefore enclosed a letter to him, which he
asked might be forwarded by the minister. The experience
and training of the latter, however, here interposed to prevent his sensitive uneasiness leading to a false step, and
one that might involve him farther than he foresaw.
While bearing the clearest and strongest witness to the
facts which Nelson had asked him to establish, he hinted
to him, tactfully and with deference, that it was scarcely
becoming a public servant to justify his conduct to a foreign official, he being accountable only to his own government. Nelson accepted the suggestion, and in so doing
characterized aptly enough the temperament which then
and at other times carried him farther than discretion warranted. " My feelings ever alive, perhaps, to too nice a
sense of honour, are a little cooled."

Along with this care for the stainless record of the past,
there went on in his mind a continual reasoning upon the
probable course of the next year's operations. In his forecasts it is singular to notice how, starting from the accurate premise that it is necessary for the French to get into
the plains of Italy, — "the gold mine," — he is continually
misled by his old prepossession in favor of landing in rear
of the enemy a body of troops, supported neither by sure
communication with their main army, nor by a position in
itself of great strength. The mistake, if mistake it was,
illustrates aptly the errors into which a man of great genius
for war, of quick insight, such as Nelson indisputably had,
can fall, from want of antecedent study, of familiarity with
those leading principles, deduced from the experience of
the past, which are perhaps even more serviceable in warning against error than in prompting to right. Everything
assures him that the French will carry some twenty thousand men to Italy by sea. "If they mean to carry on the

war, they must penetrate into Italy. I am convinced in
my own mind, that I know their very landing-place."
This, it appears afterwards, he believed would be between
Spezia and Leghorn, in the districts of Massa and Carrara,
whence also they would doubtless turn upon Leghorn,
though neutral, as a valuable and fortified seaport. "The
prevention," he continues, "requires great foresight; for,
if once landed, our fleet is of no use."

The importance of Vado Bay, so discreditably lost the
year before, strikes him from this point of view, as it did
also Bonaparte from his more closely coherent plan of
operations. Nelson reasoned that, if Vado were possessed
by the allies, the French, in their attempt to reach the
Tuscan coast, would be compelled to put to sea, where
they would be exposed to the British fleet, while such an
anchorage would enable the latter, when necessary, to keep
the coast close aboard, or would provide a refuge to a small
squadron, if threatened by the sudden appearance of a superior force. Bonaparte thought Vado important, because,
on the one hand, essential to uninterrupted coasting-trade
with Genoa, and on the other as advancing his water line
of communications — that by land being impassable for
heavy articles, such as siege-guns and carriages — to
Savona, from which point the mountains could be crossed
at their lowest elevation, and by their most practicable
passes.

Nelson's analysis of the conditions, in other respects than
the one mentioned, was not unworthy of his great natural
aptitudes. There are three things to be guarded against,
he says. One is that pet scheme of his imagination, the
transport of a corps by sea to Tuscany; the other two are
an invasion of Piedmont, and the entrance into Italy by
the pass of the Bocchetta, behind Genoa. "If three are to
be attended to, depend upon it one will fall, and the Emperor, very possibly, may be more attentive to the Milanese
than to Piedmont." Upon this divergence of interests in

a coalition Bonaparte also explicitly counted; and his plan, in its first inception, as laid before the Directory in the summer of 1795, looked primarily to the subjugation of Piedmont, by separating it from the support of the Austrian Army. The bearing of Vado Bay upon this project is not definitely recognized by Nelson. He sees in the possession of it only the frustration of both the enemy's supposed alternatives, — invasion of Italy by the Bocchetta, and of Tuscany by sea.

With these views Nelson arrived, at San Fiorenzo, on the 19th of January, and had his first interview with Jervis. His reception by the latter, whom he never before had met, was not only cordial but flattering. He was at once offered the choice of two larger ships, which were declined, "but with that respect and sense of obligation on my part which such handsome conduct demanded of me." The admiral then asked him if he would have any objection to remain on the station, when promoted, as he soon must be. Nelson's longing to go home had worn off with his disgust, occasioned by the impotent conclusions of last year's work. Then he was experiencing the feeling voiced by the great Frenchman, Suffren, some dozen years before: "It was clear that, though we had the means to impose the law, all would be lost. I heartily pray you may permit me to leave. War alone can make bearable the weariness of certain things." Now his keen enjoyment of active service revived as the hour of opening hostilities drew near. With these dispositions, the graciousness of his reception easily turned the scale, and before long he was not only willing to remain, but fearful lest he should be disappointed, despite the application for his retention which the admiral hastened to make.

"The credit I derive from all these compliments," he wrote to his wife, "must be satisfactory to you; and, should I remain until peace, which cannot be very long, you will, I sincerely hope, make your mind easy." But more grateful than open flattery, to one so interested in, and proud of, his military activities, was the respect paid by Jervis to his views and suggestions relative to the approaching operations. " He was so well satisfied with my opinion of what is likely to happen, and the means of prevention to be taken, that he had no reserve with me respecting his information and ideas of what is likely to be done;" or, as he wrote a month later, " he seems at present to consider me more as an associate than a subordinate officer; for I am acting without any orders. This may have its difficulties at a future day; but I make none, knowing the uprightness of my intentions. 'You must have a larger ship,' continued the admiral, 'for we cannot spare you, either as captain or admiral.'" Such were the opening relations between these two distinguished officers, who were in the future to exert great influence upon each other's career.

It is far from improbable that the ready coincidence of Jervis's views with those of Nelson, as to future possibilities, arose, partly indeed from professional bias and prepossession as to the potency of navies, but still more from the false reports, of which Bonaparte was an apt promoter, and which a commission of the allies in Genoa greedily swallowed and transmitted. The deterrent effect of their own fleet, " in being," seems not to have prevented either of them from believing that the attempt upon Tuscany by sea was seriously intended. True, Nelson does at times speak of the French as being so unreasonable that one may expect anything from them; but this scheme, which probably had not even a paper existence in France, was accepted by him as imminent, because he thought it suitable. As he cogently remarked to Beaulieu, it is likely that your enemy will not do the thing which you wish him to do; and conversely, in this case, what to him appeared most threatening to his own cause was just what he expected to occur. Jervis, sharing his views, and already knowing his

Earl of St. Vincent

man, despatched him again to the Gulf of Genoa, within forty-eight hours of his arrival in San Fiorenzo, somewhat to the disgust of the other captains, weary of being ever under the eye of an observant and exacting admiral. "You did as you pleased in Lord Hood's time," said one grumbler, "the same in Admiral Hotham's, and now again with Sir John Jervis; it makes no difference to you who is commander-in-chief." The tone of these words, which in the reading are almost flattering, is evident from Nelson's comment: "I returned a pretty strong answer to this speech."

The object of his present mission was to ascertain what preparations for the expected descent were being made along the Riviera, and to frustrate them as far as lay in the power of his squadron. He soon reported to Jervis that there was as yet no collection of vessels between Nice and Genoa. He then went on to reconnoitre Toulon, where he saw thirteen sail-of-the-line and five frigates lying in the outer roads, ready for sea, while five more of the line he learned were fitting at the arsenal. During the six days he remained off the port he noted that continual progress was being made in the enemy's preparations. At the end of this time, on the 23d of February, 1796, the admiral joined with the fleet, and the same afternoon the "Agamemnon" again parted company for Genoa, where she anchored on the 2d of March.

The bustle on board the French ships confirmed Nelson's belief in the descent upon Tuscany; and it is interesting here to quote his words upon the possibilities of the operation, regarded from the naval point of view by one of the ablest of sea-generals. His opinion throws light upon the vexed question of the chances for and against Napoleon's projected invasion of England in 1805, — so far, that is, as the purely naval part of the latter project is concerned. He imagines as perfectly feasible ("I firmly believe," are his words) a combination at Toulon, of the fleet already there with divisions arriving from Cadiz and

Brest, giving a total much superior to that actually with Jervis. This anticipates Napoleon's projected concentration under Villeneuve in the Channel. Nelson then continues: "One week's very superior fleet will effect a landing between Port Especia and Leghorn, I mean on that coast of Italy. . . . We may fight their fleet, but unless we can destroy them [i. e. the transports], their transports will push on and effect their landing. What will the French care for the loss of a few men-of-war? It is nothing if they can get into Italy." "Make us masters of the channel for three days, and we are masters of the world," wrote Napoleon to his admirals, with preparations far more complete than those Nelson was considering in 1796, and the distance across the Channel is less than from Vado to Spezia.[1]

With these convictions, Nelson immediately began to urge the necessity of again occupying Vado upon the Austrian commander-in-chief, through the medium of the British ministers to Genoa and Turin, with whom he was in frequent correspondence. If this were not done, he assured them, the enemy's fleet could with ease convoy a body of troops in transports to Italy, which they could not do with their present force unless they held Vado. It was also the only means, he added, by which the French could be prevented from receiving plenty of provisions from Genoa. "Unless the Austrians get possession of a point of land, we cannot stop the coasting-trade." The latter argument, at any rate, was incontestable; and it was also true that only by an advance to Vado could communication between

---

[1] This indicates no opinion as to the fortune of the military operations in England, a landing once effected. It has, however, seemed to the author singular that men fail to consider that Napoleon would not have hesitated to abandon an army in England, as he did in Egypt and in Russia. A few hours' fog or calm, and a quick-pulling boat, would have landed himself again in France; while the loss of 150,000 men, if it came to that, would have been cheaply bought with the damage such an organized force could have done London and the dockyards, not to speak of the moral effect.

the army and the British fleet be restored and maintained. Beaulieu, who had lately acquired a high reputation on the battle-fields of Belgium, had now succeeded De Vins in the command. He was averse to opening the campaign by an advance to the sea, a feeling shared by the Austrians generally. He wished rather to await the enemy in the plains of Lombardy, and to follow up by a decisive blow the victory which he confidently expected there. It was in this connection that Nelson warned him, that he must not reckon upon the French following the line of action which he himself would prefer.

The time for hostilities had now arrived; from February to August being the period that Bonaparte, who knew the wars of Italy historically, considered the most proper for operations in the field, because the least sickly. But for the backwardness of the spring, — for snow that year lay upon the mountains late into March, — the campaign doubtless would have been begun before. At the same time came fresh reports, probably set afloat by the French, of large reinforcements of seamen for the fleet and transports, in Toulon and Marseilles; and Nelson furthermore received precise information that the enemy's movement would be in three columns, — one upon Ceva, which was Bonaparte's original scheme, one by the Bocchetta, and the third either to march through Genoese territory to Spezia, or to be carried thither by sea. Nelson felt no doubt that the last was the real plan, aiming at the occupation of Leghorn and entrance into the plains of Italy. The others he considered to be feints. There will in this opinion be recognized the persistency of his old ideas. In fact, he a month later revived his proposal of the previous year, to occupy San Remo, — this time with British troops.

The urgency of the British, aided, perhaps, by the reports of the French designs, prevailed at last upon Beaulieu to advance as requested; nor can it be denied that the taking of Vado was in itself a most proper and desirable accessory object of the campaign. Unfortunately, the Austrian general, as is well known, fastening his eyes too exclusively upon the ulterior object of his movement, neglected to provide for the immediate close combination and mutual support of the organized forces, — his own and the Piedmontese, — upon which final success would turn. Manœuvring chiefly by his own left, towards the Riviera, and drawing in that direction the efforts of the centre and right, he weakened the allied line at the point where the Austrian right touched the Sardinian left. Through this thin curtain Bonaparte broke, dividing the one from the other, and, after a series of combats which extended over several days, rendering final that division, both political and military, for the remainder of the war.

To one who has accustomed himself to see in Nelson the exponent of the chief obstacle Napoleon had to meet, — who has recognized in the Nile, in Copenhagen, and in Trafalgar, the most significant and characteristic incident attending the failure of each of three great and widely separated schemes, — there is something impressive in noting the fact, generally disregarded, that Nelson was also present and assisting at the very opening scene of the famous campaign in Italy. This was not, certainly, the beginning of Napoleon's career any more than it was of Nelson's, who at the same moment hoisted for the first time his broad pendant as commodore ; but it was now that, upon the horizon of the future, toward which the world was fast turning, began to shoot upward the rays of the great captain's coming glory, and the sky to redden with the glare from the watchfires of the unseen armies which, at his command, were to revolutionize the face of Europe, causing old things to pass away, never to be restored.

The Austrians had asked for a clear assurance that their movement to the seashore should receive the support of the fleet, whether on the Riviera or at Spezia, upon the possession of which also Nelson had laid stress, as a precaution against the invasion of Tuscany. These engagements he readily made. He would support any movement, and provide for the safety of any convoys by water. He told the aid-de-camp whom Beaulieu sent to him that, whenever the general came down to the sea-coast, he would be sure to find the ships; and to the question whether his squadron would not be risked thereby, he replied that it would be risked at all times to assist their allies, and, if lost, the admiral would find another. "If I find the French convoy in any place where there is a probability of attacking them," he wrote about this time, "you may depend they shall either be taken or destroyed at the risk of my squadron, . . . which is built to be risked on proper occasions." Here was indeed a spirit from which much might be expected. The fleet, doubtless, must be husbanded in coastwise work so long as the French fleet remained, the legacy of past errors, — this Nelson clearly maintained; but such vessels as it could spare for co-operation were not to be deterred from doing their work by fear of harm befalling them. Warned by the recriminations of the last campaign, he had minutes taken of his interview with the Austrian officer, of the questions he himself put, as well as of the undertakings to which he pledged himself; and these he caused to be witnessed by the British consul at Genoa, who was present.

On the 8th of April the "Agamemnon," having shortly before left the fleet in San Fiorenzo Bay, anchored at Genoa; and the following morning the port saluted the broad pendant of the new commodore. The next day, April 10, Beaulieu attacked the French at Voltri. The "Agamemnon," with another sixty-four-gun ship, the "Diadem," and two frigates, sailed in the evening, and stood along the shore, by preconcerted arrangement, to cover the advance and harass the enemy. At 11 P. M. the ships anchored abreast the positions of the Austrians, whose lights were visible from their decks — the sails hanging in the clewlines, ready for instant movement. They again got under way the following day, and continued to the westward, seeing the French troops in retreat upon Savona. The attack, Nelson said, anticipated the hour fixed for it, which was daylight; so that, although the ships had again started at 4 A. M. of the 11th, and reached betimes a point from which they commanded every foot of the road, the enemy had already passed. "Yesterday afternoon I received, at five o'clock, a note from the Baron de Malcamp [an aid-de-camp], to tell me that the general had resolved to attack the French at daylight this morning, and on the right of Voltri. Yet by the Austrians getting too forward in the afternoon, a slight action took place; and, in the night, the French retreated. They were aware of their perilous situation, and passed our ships in the night. Had the Austrians kept back, very few of the French could have escaped." Whether this opinion was wholly accurate may be doubted; certain it is, however, that the corps which then passed reinforced betimes the positions in the mountains, which steadfastly, yet barely, checked the Austrian attack there the following day. Beaulieu wrote that the well-timed co-operation of the squadron had saved a number of fine troops, which must have been lost in the attack. This was so far satisfactory; but the economizing of one's own force was not in Nelson's eyes any consolation for the escape of the enemy, whose number he estimated at four thousand. "I beg you will endeavour to impress on those about the general," he wrote to the British minister, "the necessity of punctuality in a joint operation, for its success to be complete."

There was, however, to be no more co-operation that year on the Riviera. For a few days Nelson remained in suspense, hoping for good news, and still very far from imagining the hail-storm of ruinous blows which a master hand, as yet unrecognized, was even then dealing to the allied cause. On the 15th only he heard from Beaulieu, through the minister, that the Austrians had been repulsed at Montenotte; and on the 16th he wrote to Collingwood that this reverse had been inflicted by the aid of those who slipped by his ships. On the 18th news had reached him of the affairs at Millesimo and Dego, as well as of further disasters; for on that day he wrote to the Duke of Clarence that the Austrians had taken position between Novi and Alessandria, with headquarters at Acqui. Their loss he gave as ten thousand. "Had the general's concerted time and plan been attended to," he repeats, "I again assert, none of the enemy could have escaped on the night of the 10th. By what has followed, the disasters commenced from the retreat of those troops."

There now remained, not the stirring employment of accompanying and supporting a victorious advance, but only the subordinate, though most essential, duty of impeding the communications of the enemy, upon which to a great extent must depend the issues on unseen and distant fields of war. To this Nelson's attention had already been turned, as one of the most important functions intrusted to him, even were the allies successful, and its difficulties had been impressed upon him by the experience of the previous year. But since then the conditions had become far more onerous. The defeat of the Austrians not only left Vado Bay definitively in the power of the French, but enabled the latter to push their control up to the very walls of Genoa, where they shortly established a battery and depot on the shore, at St. Pierre d' Arena, within three hundred yards of the mole. Thus the whole western Riviera, from the French border, was in possession of the enemy, who had also throughout the previous year so multiplied and strengthened the local defences, that, to use Nelson's own words, " they have batteries from one end of the coast to the other, within shot of each other." Such were the means, also, by which Napoleon, the true originator of this scheme for securing these communications, insured the concentration of the flotilla at Boulogne, eight or ten years later, without serious molestation from the British Navy.

It may not unnaturally cause some surprise that, with the urgent need Nelson had felt the year before for small armed vessels, to control the coastwise movements of the enemy, upon which so much then depended, no serious effort had been made to attach a flotilla of that kind to the fleet. The reply, however, to this very obvious criticism is, that the British could not supply the crews for them without crippling the efficiency of the cruising fleet; and it was justly felt then, as it was some years later at the time of the Boulogne flotilla, that the prime duty of Great Britain was to secure the sea against the heavy fleets of the enemy. If, indeed, the Italian States, whose immediate interests were at stake, had supplied seamen, as they might have done, these could quickly have been formed to the comparatively easy standard of discipline and training needed for such guerilla warfare, and, supported by the cruising fleet, might have rendered invaluable service, so long as the system of coast defence was defective. How far the rulers of those States, trained heretofore to the narrowest considerations of personal policy, could have been induced to extend this assistance, is doubtful. They did nothing, or little.

Nelson measured the odds against him accurately, and saw that the situation was well-nigh hopeless. Nevertheless, there was a chance that by vigorous and sustained action the enemy might be not only impeded, but intimidated. He sought earnestly to obtain the co-operation of the Sardinians and Neapolitans in manning a flotilla, with which to grapple the convoys as they passed in shore. By this means, and the close scouring of the coast by the vessels of his squadron, something might be effected. He contemplated also using the crews of the British vessels themselves in gunboats and light-armed feluccas; but he said frankly that, important as was the duty of intercepting communications, the efficiency of the fleet was more important still, and that to divert their crews overmuch to such objects would hazard the vessels themselves, and neutralize their proper work. The resort, therefore, could only be occasional. The general political complexion of affairs in the Mediterranean depended greatly upon the presence and readiness of the British fleet, and its efficiency therefore could not be risked, to any serious extent, except for the object of destroying the enemy's naval forces, to which it was then the counterpoise.

Acting, however, on his determination to co-operate effectively, at whatever risk to his own squadron, — to the detachment, that is, which the commander-in-chief thought could safely be spared from his main force for the secondary object, — Nelson applied all his intelligence and all his resolution to the task before him. In words of admirable force and clearness, he manifests that exclusiveness of purpose, which Napoleon justly characterized as the secret of great operations and of great successes. "I have not a thought," he writes to the minister at Genoa, "on any subject separated from the immediate object of my command, nor a wish to be employed on any other service. So far the allies," he continues, with no unbecoming self-assertion, "are fortunate, if I may be allowed the expression, in having an officer of this character." He felt this singleness of mind, which is so rare a gift, to be the more important, from his very consciousness that the difficulty of his task approached the border of impossibility. "I cannot command winds and weather. A sea-officer cannot, like a land-officer, form plans; his object is to embrace the happy moment which now and then offers, — it may be this day, not for a month, and perhaps never." Nothing can be more suggestive of his greatest characteristics than this remark, which is perhaps less applicable to naval officers to-day than it was then. In it we may fairly see one of those clearly held principles which serve a man so well in moments of doubt and perplexity. At the Nile and at Trafalgar, and scarcely less at St. Vincent and Copenhagen, the seizure of opportunity, the unfaltering resolve "to embrace the happy moment," is perhaps even more notable and decisive than the sagacity which so accurately chose the proper method of action.

Nelson's deeds did not belie his words. Immediately after definite news of Beaulieu's retreat to the Po was received, Sir John Jervis appeared off Genoa with the fleet. The "Agamemnon" joined him, and remained in company until the 23d of April, when by Nelson's request she sailed on a cruise to the westward. From that time until the 4th of June she was actively employed between Nice and Genoa, engaging the batteries, and from time to time cutting out vessels from the anchorages. His attempts were more or less successful; on one occasion he captured a considerable portion of the French siege-train going forward for the siege of Mantua; but upon the whole the futility of the attempt became apparent. "Although I will do my utmost, I do not believe it is in my power to prevent troops or stores from passing along shore. Heavy swells, light breezes, and the near approach to the shore which these vessels go are our obstacles. . . . You may perceive I am distressed. Do you really think we are of any use here? If not, we may serve our country much more by being in other places. The Levant and coast of Spain call aloud for ships, and they are, I fancy, employed to no purpose here." The position was almost hopelessly complicated by the Genoese coasters, which plied their trade close to the beach, between the mother city and the little towns occupied by the French, and which Nelson felt unable to touch. "There are no vessels of any consequence in any bay from Monaco to Vado," he wrote to Jervis ; "but not less than a hundred Genoese are every day passing, which may or may not have stores for the French." "The French have no occasion to send provisions from France. The coasts are covered with Genoese vessels with corn, wine, hay, &c., for places on the coast; and they know I have no power to stop the trade with the towns. I saw this day not less than forty-five Genoese vessels, all laden, passing along the coast. What can I do?"

Although not definitely so stated, it is shown, by an allusion, that Nelson at this time entertained, among other ideas, the project of keeping afloat in transports a body of three thousand troops, which should hover upon the coast, and by frequent descents impose a constant insecurity upon the long line of communications from Nice to Genoa. The same plan was advocated by him against the Spanish peninsula in later years.[1] Of this conception it may be said that it is sound in principle, but in practice depends largely upon the distance from the centre of the enemy's power at which its execution is attempted. Upon the Spanish coast, in 1808, in the hands of Lord Cochrane, it was undoubtedly a most effective secondary operation; but when that distinguished officer proposed to apply a like method, even though on a much greater scale, to the western coast of France, against the high-road south of Bordeaux, it can scarcely be doubted that he would have met a severe disappointment, such as attended similar actions upon the Channel in the Seven Years' War. On the Riviera, in 1795, this means might have been decisive; in 1796, in the face of Bonaparte's fortified coast, it could scarcely have been more than an annoyance. At all events, the advocacy of it testifies to the acuteness and energy with which Nelson threw himself into the operations especially intrusted to him.

His letters during this period reflect the varying phases

[1] Naval Chronicle, vol. xxi. p. 60.

of hope and of discouragement; but, upon the whole, the latter prevails. There is no longer the feeling of neglect by his superior, of opportunity slipping away through the inadequate force which timid counsels and apathetic indolence allowed him. He sees that the chance which was permitted to pass unimproved has now gone forever. "As the French cannot want supplies to be brought into the Gulf of Genoa, for their grand army," he writes to the admiral, "I am still of opinion that if our frigates are wanted for other services, they may very well be spared from the Gulf." And again, "As the service for which my distinguishing pendant was intended to be useful, is nearly if not quite at an end, I assure you I shall have no regret in striking it." Sir John Jervis, he asserts with pride, has cruised with the fleet in the Gulf of Genoa, close to shore, "where I will venture to say no fleet ever cruised before — no officer can be more zealous or able to render any service in our profession to England;" yet from the decks of the flagship he and Nelson had helplessly watched a convoy passing close in shore, and directly to windward, but wholly out of reach of their powers of offence. At times, indeed, somewhat can be accomplished. For several days the "Agamemnon" "has kept close to shore, and harassed the enemy's troops very much. Field pieces are drawn out on our standing in shore. You must defend me if any Genoese towns are knocked down by firing at enemy's batteries. I will not fire first." Six weeks later he writes again: "Our conduct has so completely alarmed the French that all their coasting trade is at an end; even the corvette, gunboats, &c., which were moored under the fortress of Vado, have not thought themselves in security, but are all gone into Savona Mole, and unbent their sails."

This movement, however, which he notes under the date of June 23, proceeded probably less from fear than from the growing indifference of the French concerning their communications by water, now that their occupation of the line of the Adige River had solidified their control over the ample resources of Piedmont and Lombardy. At the very hour when Nelson was thus writing, he learned also the critical condition of Leghorn through the approach of a French division, the mere sending of which showed Bonaparte's sense of his present security of tenure.

Nelson had severed by this time his long and affectionate connection with the battered " Agamemnon." On the 4th of June the old ship anchored at San Fiorenzo, having a few days before, with the assistance of the squadron, cut out from under the French batteries the vessels carrying Bonaparte's siege-train, as well as the gunboats which convoyed them. There was then in the bay the " Egmont," seventy-four, whose commander had expressed to the admiral his wish to return to England. Jervis, therefore, had ordered Nelson to the spot, to make the exchange, and the latter thought the matter settled; but to his surprise he found the captain did not wish to leave the station unless the ship went also. This did away with the vacancy he looked to fill; and, as the " Agamemnon," from her condition, must be the first of the fleet to go home, it seemed for the moment likely that he would have to go in her with a convoy then expected in the bay. " I remained in a state of uncertainty for a week," he wrote to his wife; " and had the corn ships, which were momentarily expected from Naples, arrived, I should have sailed for England." The dilemma caused him great anxiety; for the longing for home, which he had felt in the early part of the winter, had given away entirely before the pride and confidence he felt in the new admiral, and the keen delight in active service he was now enjoying. " I feel full of gratitude for your good wishes towards me," he wrote to Jervis in the first moment of disappointment, " and highly flattered by your desire to have me continue to serve under your command, which I own would afford me infinite satisfaction." The following day he is still more restless.

"I am not less anxious than yesterday for having slept since my last letter. Indeed, Sir, I cannot bear the thoughts of leaving your command." He then proposed several ways out of the difficulty, which reduced themselves, in short, to a readiness to hoist his pendant in anything, if only he could remain.

No violent solution was needed, as several applicants came forward when Nelson's wish was known. On the 11th of June, 1796, he shifted his broad pendant to the "Captain," of seventy-four guns, taking with him most of his officers. Soon afterwards the "Agamemnon" sailed for England. Up to the last day of his stay on board, Nelson, although a commodore, was also her captain; it was not until two months after joining his new ship that another captain was appointed to her, leaving to himself the duties of commodore only. In later years the "Agamemnon" more than once bore a share in his career. She was present at Copenhagen and at Trafalgar, being in this final scene under the command of an officer who had served in her as his first lieutenant, and was afterwards his flag-captain at the Nile. In 1809 she was totally lost in the river La Plata, having run aground, and then settled on one of her anchors, which, upon the sudden shoaling of the water, had been let go to bring her up.[1] It is said that there were then on board several seamen who had been with her during Nelson's command.

On the 13th of June the "Captain" sailed from San Fiorenzo Bay, and on the 17th joined the fleet off Cape Sicie, near Toulon, where Jervis, six weeks before, had established the first of those continuous close blockades which afterwards, off Brest, became associated with his name, and proved so potent a factor in the embarrassments that drove Napoleon to his ruin. There were then twelve British ships off the port, while inside the enemy had

[1] An account of this disaster, said to be that of an eye-witness, is to be found in Colburn's United Service Journal, 1846, part i.

eleven ready for sea, and four or five more fitting. The
following day Nelson again left the fleet, and on the 21st
of June arrived at Genoa, where very serious news was to
be received.

The triumphant and hitherto unchecked advance of
Bonaparte had greatly encouraged the French party in
Corsica, which had been increased by a number of mal-
contents, dissatisfied with their foreign rulers. Owing to
the disturbed condition of the interior, the British troops
had been drawn down to the seacoast. Bonaparte, from
the beginning of his successes, had kept in view the deliverance of his native island, which he expected to effect by
the exertions of her own people, stimulated and supported
by the arrival upon the spot of Corsican officers and soldiers from the French armies. These refugees, proceeding
in parties of from ten to twenty each, in small boats, mov-
able by sail or oars, and under cover of night, could seldom be stopped, or even detected, by the British cruisers,
while making the short trip, of little more than a hundred
miles, from Genoa, Nice, and Leghorn. The latter port,
from its nearness, was particularly favorable to these enterprises; but, although neutral, and freely permitting the
ingress and egress of vessels belonging to both belligerents,
its facilities for supporting a Corsican uprising were not
so great as they would be if the place were held for the
French. For this reason, partly, Bonaparte had decided to
seize it; and he was still more moved to do so by the fact
that it was a centre of British trade, that it contributed
much to the supply and repair of the British fleet, and
that the presence of vessels from the latter enabled an eye
to be kept upon the movements of the Corsicans, and
measures to be taken for impeding them.

"The enemy possessing themselves of Leghorn," Nelson
had written in the middle of March, when expecting them
to do so by a coastwise expedition, "cuts off all our supplies, such as fresh meat, fuel, and various other most

essential necessaries; and, of course, our fleet cannot always [in that case] be looked for on the northern coast of Italy." Bonaparte had not, indeed, at that time, contemplated any such ex-centric movement, which, as things then were, would have risked so large a part of his army out of his own control and his own support; but in the middle of June, having driven the Austrians for the moment into the Tyrol, consolidated his position upon the Adige, established the siege of Mantua, and enforced order and submission throughout the fertile valley of the Po, which lay in rear of his army and amply supplied it with the necessaries of subsistence, he felt not only able to spare the force required, but that for the security of the right flank and rear of his army it had become essential to do so. The Papacy and Naples, although they had contributed little to the active campaigning of the allies, were still nominally at war with France, and might possibly display more energy now that operations were approaching their own frontiers. Should the British take possession of Leghorn with a body of troops, — their own or Neapolitan, — the port would remain a constant menace to the operations and communications of the French, and especially at the critical moments when the Austrians advanced to the relief of Mantua, as they must be expected to do, and actually did on four several occasions during the succeeding six months.

Bonaparte, as he was ever wont, diligently improved the opportunity permitted to him by the need of the Austrians to reorganize and reinforce Beaulieu's beaten army before again taking the field. Threatened, as often again in later years, by enemies in divergent directions, he with the utmost promptitude and by the most summary measures struck down the foe on one side, before the other could stir. Occupying Verona in the first days of June, he immediately afterwards detached to the southward a corps under Augereau to enter the Papal States; and at the same time another small division, commanded by General Vaubois, started from the upper valley of the Po, ostensibly destined to proceed against Rome by passing through Tuscany. The effect of Augereau's movement, which was closely followed by the commander-in-chief in person, was to bring both Naples and the Pope speedily to terms. An armistice was signed by the former on the 5th, and by the latter on the 24th of June. Vaubois, on the other hand, after passing the Arno below Florence, instead of continuing on to Siena, as the Grand Duke had been assured that he would, turned sharp to the westward, and on the 28th of June entered Leghorn, which was thenceforth held by the French. Thus within a brief month were the British deprived of two allies, lethargic, it is true, in actual performance, but possessed of a degree of potential strength that could not but enter largely into Bonaparte's anxieties; while at the same time they lost the use of a seaport that had heretofore been considered essential to their support.

Rumors of Vaubois' movement reached Nelson in Genoa at noon of June 23, but somewhat vaguely. "Reports are all we have here," he wrote to Jervis the same day, "nothing official from the armies;" but he thought the situation critical, and started without delay for Leghorn. Arriving there on the morning of June 27, after a passage rendered tedious by light airs and calms, he found the British merchant vessels that had been in the harbor, to the number of nearly forty sail, already under way, laden with British merchants and their property, and standing out under convoy of several ships of war; while in pursuit of them — a singular indication of the neutrality possible to small States like Tuscany and Genoa at that time — were a dozen French privateers, which had been lying beside them within the mole. One or two of the departing vessels were thus taken.

The first impression upon Nelson's mind was that the occupation of Leghorn was only the prelude to an invasion of Corsica in force. "I have no doubt," he wrote to the Viceroy, "but the destination of the French army was Corsica, and it is natural to suppose their fleet was to amuse ours whilst they cross from Leghorn." Thus reasoning, he announced his purpose of rejoining the admiral as soon as possible, so as not to lose his share in the expected battle. "My heart would break," he says to Jervis, "to be absent at such a glorious time;" but it is difficult to understand why he imagined that the French would transfer their army into the destitution of the Corsican mountains from the fertile plains of Lombardy, abandoning the latter to their enemy, and exchanging their assured communications with France for the uncertainties and irregularities of a water transit over seas commanded by the British fleet. The tenure of the island, as he well knew, depended upon the willing support of the Corsicans themselves; in the equal balance of the existing war, neither belligerent could maintain its control against the opposition of the natives.

This anticipation, in its disregard of the perfectly obvious conditions, was scarcely worthy of Nelson's real native sagacity, and shows clearly how much a man, even of genius, is hampered in the conclusions of actual life by the lack of that systematic ordering and training of the ideas which it is the part of education to supply. Genius is one thing, the acquirements of an accomplished — instructed — officer are another, yet there is between the two nothing incompatible, rather the reverse; and when to the former, which nature alone can give, — and to Nelson did give, — is added the conscious recognition of principles, the practised habit of viewing, under their clear light, all the circumstances of a situation, assigning to each its due weight and relative importance, then, and then only, is the highest plane of military greatness attained. Whether in natural insight Nelson fell short of Napoleon's measure need not here be considered; that he was at this time far inferior, in the powers of a trained intellect, to his younger competitor in the race for fame, is manifest by the readiness with which he accepted such widely ex-centric conjectures as that of an attempt by sea upon Leghorn at the opening of the campaign, and now upon Corsica by a great part, if not the whole, of the army of Italy.

"On the side of the French," says Jomini, speaking of Bonaparte at this very period, "was to be seen a young warrior, trained in the best schools, endowed with an ardent imagination, brought up upon the examples of antiquity, greedy of glory and of power, knowing thoroughly the Apennines, in which he had distinguished himself in 1794, and already measuring with a practised eye the distances he must overpass before becoming master of Italy. To these advantages for a war of invasion, Bonaparte united an inborn genius, and clearly established principles, the fruits of an enlightened theory."

Jomini doubtless may be considered somewhat too absolute and pedantic in his insistence upon definite formulation of principles; but in these words is nevertheless to be recognized the fundamental difference between these two great warriors, a difference by which the seaman was heavily handicapped in the opening of his career. As time passed on, responsibility, the best of educators, took under her firm and steady guidance the training of his yet undeveloped genius, gleams of which from time to time, but fitfully and erratically, illumine his earlier correspondence. The material was there from the first, but inchoate, ill-ordered, confused, and therefore not readily available to correct passing impressions, wild rumors, or even to prevent the radically false conceptions of an enemy's possible movements, such as we have had before us. Bonaparte, furthermore, whose career began amid the troubled scenes of a revolution which had shattered all the fetters of established custom, — so strong in England to impede a man's natural progress, — had enjoyed already for some time the singular advantage of being military adviser to the Directory, a duty which compelled him to take a broad view of all current conditions, to consider them in their mutual relations, and not narrowly to look to one sphere of operations, without due reference to its effects upon others.

As to the invasion of Corsica after the manner he had imagined, Nelson was soon undeceived. Bonaparte himself, after a hurried visit to Leghorn, again departed to press the siege of Mantua, having assured himself that for a measurable time he had nothing to apprehend from movements on his flank and rear. Orders were received from Jervis on the 2d of July to institute a commercial blockade of Leghorn, permitting no vessels to enter or depart. The conduct of this business, as well as the protection of British trade in that district, and the support of the Viceroy in securing Corsica against the attempts of French partisans, were especially intrusted to Nelson, whose movements during the following months, until the first of October, were consequently confined to the waters between Corsica and Tuscany, while the Riviera west of Genoa saw him no more. Leghorn became the chief centre of his activities. These redoubled with the demands made upon him; his energy rose equal to every call. A few weeks before, he had made a conditional application to the admiral, though with evident reluctance, for a short leave of absence on account of his health. "I don't much like what I have written," he confessed at the end of his diffident request, and some days later he again alludes to the subject. "My complaint is as if a girth was buckled taut over my breast, and my endeavours, in the night, is to get it loose. To say the truth, when I am actively employed, I am not so bad. If the Service will admit of it, perhaps I shall at a future day take your leave." The service now scarcely admitted it, and the active duty apparently restored his health; at all events we now hear no more of it. Everything yielded to the requirements of the war. "The Captain has wants, but I intend she shall last till the autumn: for I know, when once we begin, our wants are innumerable."

In his still limited sphere, and on all matters directly connected with it and his professional duties, his judgment was sound and acute, as his activity, energy, and zeal were untiring. The menace to Corsica from the fall of Leghorn was accurately weighed and considered. Midway between the two lay the since famous island of Elba, a dependence of Tuscany, so small as to be held readily by a few good troops, and having a port large enough, in Nelson's judgment, to harbor the British fleet with a little management. "The way to Corsica," he wrote to the Viceroy, "if our fleet is at hand, is through Elba; for if they once set foot on that island, it is not all our fleet can stop their passage to Corsica." The Viceroy took upon himself to direct that the island be occupied by the British. Nelson complied without waiting for Jervis's orders, and on the 10th of July a detachment of troops, convoyed by his squadron, were landed in the island, and took charge, without serious opposition, of the town of Porto Ferrajo and the works for the defence of the harbor. The measure was justified upon the ground that the seizure of Leghorn by the French showed that Tuscany was unable to assure Elba against a similar step, prejudicial to the British tenure in Corsica. The administration remained in the hands of the Tuscan officials, the British occupation being purely military, and confined to the places necessary for that purpose.

The blockade of Leghorn was enforced with the utmost rigor and great effectiveness. For a long time no vessels were allowed to go either out or in. Afterwards the rule was gradually relaxed, so far as to permit neutrals to leave the port in ballast; but none entered. The trade of the place was destroyed. Nelson hoped, and for a time expected, that the populace, accustomed to a thriving

commerce, and drawing their livelihood from its employ-
ments, would rise against the feeble garrison, whose
presence entailed upon them such calamities; but herein,
of course, he underestimated the coercive power of a few
resolute men, organized for mutual support, over a mob of
individuals, incapable of combined action and each uncertain of the constancy of his fellows.

The Austrian preparations in the Tyrol gradually
matured as the month of July wore on. Towards its end
Marshal Wurmser, the successor of Beaulieu, advanced for
the relief of Mantua and the discomfiture of Bonaparte,
whose numbers were much inferior to his opponents. The
projected movement was of course known to the British,
and its first results in raising the siege of Mantua, and
throwing reinforcements into the place, gave them great
hopes. Amid the conflicting rumors of the succeeding
days, the wonderful skill and success of Bonaparte, who
overthrew in detail forces greatly superior in the aggregate
to his own, escaped notice for the time; the superficial
incidents of his abandoning his previous positions alone
received attention, and nothing less than his retreat in
confusion was confidently expected. Nelson, justly estimating the importance of Leghorn, and over-sanguine of
the support he might hope from the inhabitants, projected
a sudden assault upon the town, by troops to be drawn
from the garrisons in Corsica, supported by seamen of the
squadron. Speaking of the steady intercourse between
that island and the mainland by way of Leghorn, he says:
"The only way is to cut at the root, for whilst Leghorn is
open, this communication must constantly be going on.
This moment brings to my eyes a body of about 200 men,
with the Corsican flag carrying before them; they are
partly from Nice, and joined by Genoese, &c., on the
road. The time approaches," he rightly forecasts, "when
we shall either have to fight them in Corsica or Leghorn."
The imminence of the danger was evident. " Our affairs

in Corsica are gloomy," he had already written to the
Duke of Clarence. "There is a very strong republican
party in that island, and they are well supported from
France; the first favourable moment, they will certainly
act against us."

The details of the intended assault upon Leghorn do
not appear, and it is probable that they never passed
beyond the stage of discussion to that of acceptance,
although he alludes to the plans as "laid." Clear-sighted
for the key of a situation, and ardent to strike "at the
root," as five years later in the Baltic he was eager to cut
away the Russian root of the Armed Neutrality, instead of
hewing off the Danish branch, Nelson urged the speedy
adoption of the measure, and pressed his own fitness to
harmonize the land and sea forces under one command, in
virtue of his rank as Colonel of Marines. "Leghorn is in
such a state," he writes to Elliot on the 5th of August,
"that a respectable force landed, would, I have every
reason to suppose, insure the immediate possession of the
town. Not less than a thousand troops should be sent, to
which I will add every soldier in my squadron, and a party
of seamen to make a show. In every way, pray consider
this as private, and excuse my opinions. I well know
the difficulty of getting a proper person to command this
party. Firmness, and that the people of Leghorn should
know the person commanding, will most assuredly have a
great effect. A cordial co-operation with me (for vanity
apart, no one is so much feared or respected in Leghorn as
myself) is absolutely necessary. I am going further: we
know the jealousy of the army against the navy, but I am
by the King's commission a Colonel in the army from June
1st, 1795." After discussing this difficult question of
professional susceptibilities, he concludes: "You will
consider, Sir, all these points, and form a much better
judgment than I can, only give me credit that the nearest
wish of my heart is to serve my King and my Country, at

every personal risk and consideration. It has ever pleased God to prosper all my undertakings, and I feel confident of His blessing on this occasion. I ever consider my motto, *Fides et Opera.*" [1]

Having, with true strategic insight, chosen the place where the blow ought to be struck for the preservation of Corsica, he pressed, with characteristic fervor, the necessity of taking risks. He discusses details indeed; he proposes no mere adventure, real as was his personal enjoyment of danger and action. What man can do, shall be done; but being done, still "something must be left to chance. Our only consideration, is the honour and benefit to our Country worth the risk? If it is (and I think so), in God's name let us get to work, and hope for His blessing on our endeavours to liberate a people who have been our sincere friends." Hearing at the same time that an army officer of general rank will have the command instead of himself, he adds: "Pray assure him there is nothing I feel greater pleasure in than hearing he is to command. Assure him of my most sincere wishes for his speedy success, and that he shall have every support and assistance from me." Truly, in generosity as in ardor, Nelson was, to use the fine old phrase, "all for the service."

The project upon Leghorn had the approval of the Viceroy and of Jervis; but the latter, while expressing perfect reliance upon "the promptitude of Commodore Nelson," was clear that the attempt must depend upon the continued advance of the Austrians. This was also Nelson's own view. "All will be well, I am satisfied, provided Wurmser is victorious; upon this ground only have I adopted the measure." This qualification redeems the plan from the reproach of rashness, which otherwise might have been applied to the somewhat desperate undertaking of carrying a fortified town by such a feat of hardi-

[1] This motto was subsequently adopted by Nelson, when arms were assigned to him as a Knight of the Bath, in May, 1797.

hood. It loses thus the color of recklessness, and falls into place as one part of a great common action, to harass the retreat of a beaten enemy, and to insure the security of one's own positions.

On the 15th of August, when the above words were written, Nelson was still ignorant of the Austrian defeats at Lonato and Castiglione, nearly two weeks before, and of their subsequent retreat to the Tyrol. A rumor of the reverse had reached him through Florence, but he gave it little attention, as the French in Leghorn were not claiming a victory. On the 19th he knew it definitely, and had to abandon the expectation, confided to his brother, that the next letter seen from him would be in the "Public Gazette." "An expedition is thought of, and of course I shall be there, for most of these services fall to my lot." "One day or other," he had written to his wife, apparently with this very enterprise in mind, "I will have a long Gazette to myself; I feel that such an opportunity will be given me. I cannot," he continued with prophetic self-reliance, "if I am in the field of glory, be kept out of sight."

During the remainder of the month he continued to be amused with those unfounded reports of victories, which are among the invariable concomitants of all wars, and which his sanguine temperament and peculiar readiness to trust others made him especially ready to accept. He was not wholly unaware of this tendency in himself, though he continued to repeat with apparent belief reports of the most startling and erroneous character, and never seems to have appreciated, up to the time of his leaving the Mediterranean, the astonishing quickness and sagacity with which Bonaparte frustrated the overwhelming combinations against him. "We hear what we wish," he says on one occasion. "The Toulon information is, as I always thought it, pleasant to know but never to be depended upon; all is guess. I have long had reason to suspect great part is fabricated in Genoa;" but he was continually deceived by it.

Throughout the discomfitures of the Austrians on shore, the purely naval part of the war continued to be successfully maintained. Jervis, with unrelaxing grip, kept his position before Toulon, effectually checking every attempt of the French fleet to escape unobserved into the open, while Nelson shut up Leghorn so rigorously that the enemy lost even the partial advantage, as a port of supply, which they had before drawn from its neutrality. But, during this pregnant summer, grave causes for anxiety were rolling up in the western basin of the Mediterranean. The attitude of Spain had long been doubtful, so much so that before Sir John Jervis left England, in the previous autumn, the ministry had deliberated upon the contingency of her declaring war, and a conditional decision had been reached to evacuate Corsica, if that event occurred. During the spring of 1796 reports of coming hostilities were current in the fleet. Nelson's first opinion was that, if they ensued, there was no object in remaining in the Mediterranean, except to preserve Corsica from the French. This, he thought, was not a sufficient motive, nor had the conduct of the natives entitled them to protection. With all the powers making peace with France, he hoped Great Britain would leave the Mediterranean. This, however, was but a passing expression of discouragement, whence he soon rallied, and, with a spirit worthy of his race, which was soon to face all Europe undismayed, his courage mounted continually as the storm drew nearer.

The summer of 1796 was in truth the period of transition, when the victories of Bonaparte, by bringing near a cessation of warfare upon the land, were sweeping from the scene the accessories that confused the view of the future, removing conditions and details which perplexed men's attention, and bringing into clear relief the one field upon which the contest was finally to be fought out, and the one foe, the British sea-power, upon whose strength and constancy would hinge the issues of the struggle. The British Navy, in the slight person of its indomitable champion, was gradually rising to the appreciation of its own might, and gathering together its energies to endure single-handed the gigantic strife, with a spirit unequalled in its past history, glorious as that had often been. From 1796 began the rapid ascent to that short noontide of unparalleled brilliancy, in which Nelson's fame outshone all others, and which may be said to have begun with the Spanish declaration of war, succeeded though that was by the retreat in apparent discomfiture from the Mediterranean, now at hand.

The approach of this extraordinary outburst of maritime vigor is aptly foretokened in the complete change, gradual yet rapid, that passed over Nelson's opinions, from the time when rumors of a Spanish war first assumed probability, up to the moment when the fact became tangible by the appearance of the Spanish fleet in the waters of Corsica. Accentuated thus in a man of singular perceptions and heroic instincts, it further affords an interesting illustration of the manner in which a combative race — for Nelson was through and through a child of his people — however at first averse to war, from motives of well-understood interest, gradually warms to the idea, and finally grows even to welcome the fierce joy which warriors feel, as the clash of arms draws near. "If all the states of Italy make peace," he writes on the 20th of May, "we have nothing to look to but Corsica; which in the present state of the inhabitants, is not, in my opinion, an object to keep us in the Mediterranean: we shall, I hope, quit it, and employ our fleet more to our advantage." "Reports here," on the 20th of June, "are full of a Spanish war. If that should be the case, we shall probably draw towards Gibraltar and receive large reinforcements."

On the 15th of August, however, he writes to Jervis,

betraying the incipient revulsion, as yet not realized, against abandoning the Mediterranean, which was already affecting the current of his thoughts. "I hope we shall have settled Leghorn before the Dons, if they intend it, arrive. I have still my doubts as to a Spanish war; and if there should be one, with your management I have no fears. Should the Dons come, I shall then hope I may be spared,[1] in my own person, to help to make you at least a Viscount." A few days later, having meantime heard of Wurmser's disasters at Castiglione: "Austria, I suppose, must make peace, and we shall, as usual, be left to fight it out: however, at the worst, we only give up Corsica, an acquisition which I believe we cannot keep, and our fleet will draw down the Mediterranean;" but at the same time, August 19, he writes to the Duke of Clarence with glowing hopes and rising pride: "I hope Government will not be alarmed for our safety — I mean more than is proper. Under such a commander-in-chief as Sir John Jervis nobody has any fears. We are now twenty-two sail of the line; the combined fleet will not be above thirty-five sail of the line. I will venture my life Sir John Jervis defeats them. This country is the most.favourable possible for skill with an inferior fleet; for the winds are so variable, that some one time in twenty-four hours you must be able to attack a part of a large fleet, and the other will be becalmed, or have a contrary wind." That the Duke trembled and demurred to such odds is not wonderful; but the words have singular interest, both as showing the clear tactical apprehensions that held sway in Nelson's mind, and still more, at the moment then present, as marking unmistakably his gradual conversion to the policy of remaining in the Mediterranean, and pursuing the most vigorous aggressive measures.

A fortnight after this letter was written, Genoa, under

---

[1] That is, apparently, from detached service, and ordered to the main fleet.

pressure from Bonaparte, closed her ports against British ships, interdicting even the embarkation of a drove of cattle, already purchased, and ready for shipment to the fleet off Toulon. Nelson immediately went there to make inquiries, and induce a revocation of the orders. While the "Captain" lay at anchor in the roads, three of the crew deserted, and when her boats were sent to search for them they were fired upon by a French battery, established near the town. Nelson, in retaliation, seized a French supply ship from under the guns of the battery, whereupon the Genoese forts opened against the "Captain," which had meantime got under way and was lying-to off the city. Nelson did not return the fire of the latter, which was kept up for two hours, but threw three shot into the French battery, "to mark," as he said, the power of the English to bombard the town, and their humanity in not destroying the houses and innocent Genoese inhabitants. In the communications which followed under a flag of truce, Nelson was informed, verbally, that all the ports of the Republic were closed against Great Britain. This stand, and the firing on the ship, being considered acts of hostility, the little island of Capraia, between Corsica and Genoa, and belonging to the latter, was seized by Nelson, acting under the counsel of the Viceroy of Corsica. This was done both as a retaliatory measure, and to put a stop to the use which French privateers and parties of Corsicans had hitherto made of it, under cover of Genoese neutrality.

As Jervis was already under apprehension of an outbreak of scurvy in the fleet, consequent upon the failure of supplies of live cattle following the French occupation of Leghorn, the closure of the Genoese ports was a severe blow. It was, however, but one among several incidents, occurring nearly simultaneously, which increased his embarrassments, and indicated the close approach of the long-muttering storm. To use his own words, "The lowering aspect of Spain, with the advanced state of the equipment of the French fleet in Toulon," impelled him to concentrate his force. Rear-Admiral Man, who had been blockading Cadiz since his detachment there by Hotham, in October, 1795, was ordered up to the main fleet. Swayed by fears very unlike to Nelson's proud confidence in his admiral and his service, he acted with such precipitation as to leave Gibraltar without filling with provisions, and arrived so destitute that Jervis had to send him back at once, with orders to replenish with stores and then to rejoin without delay. Under the influence of the panic which prevailed at Gibraltar, Man had also sent such advices to the coast of Portugal as caused the commander-in-chief to fear that expected supplies might be arrested. "Oh, our convoy!" cried Nelson; "Admiral Man, how could you quit Gibraltar?" Yet, as he wrote to Jervis, he had expected some such step, from what he had already seen "under his hand to you."

Thus, for the time at least, there were lost to the British seven of the ships-of-the-line upon which Nelson had reckoned in his letter to the Duke of Clarence. It was possibly on this account that Jervis wrote him to shift his commodore's pendant to a frigate, and send the "Captain" to the fleet. Nelson obeyed, of course, and at once; but taking advantage of the fact that no captain had yet joined his ship, he thought it "advisable to go in her myself." In this he doubtless was influenced chiefly by his unwillingness to miss a battle, especially against such great numerical odds. "I take for granted," he admitted to the Viceroy, "that the admiral will send me back in a cutter, but I shall give him a good ordered seventy-four, and take my chance of helping to thrash Don Langara, than which few things, I assure you, would give me more real pleasure." The particular emergency seems, however, soon to have passed; for after two days with the fleet he returned off Leghorn in the "Captain," somewhat comforted as to the

apprehensions of the British Cabinet. " Whatever fears we
may have for Corsica, it is certain Government at home
have none, by taking so very respectable a part of your
force away." A regiment had been transferred to Gibraltar
with Man's squadron, when the latter returned there.

These rising hopes and stirring expectations of brilliant
service were speedily dashed. On the 25th of September
Jervis received orders from the Admiralty to abandon
Corsica, to retreat from the Mediterranean, and to proceed
with the fleet to England. In pursuance of these instructions Nelson was directed to superintend the evacuation of
Bastia, the " most secret " letter to that effect reaching him
at that port on the 29th of September, — his birthday. The
purpose of the ministry filled him with shame and indignation. Confronted abruptly with the course which four
months before had seemed to him natural and proper, the
shock brought out the fulness of the change through which
he had passed meantime. He has no illusions about
Corsica. The inhabitants had disappointed all the expectations of the British, — " At a peace I should rejoice at
having given up the island." But the days passing over
his head had brought wider and maturer views of the
general policy of Great Britain, as well as increasing faith
in the powers of the fleet, vigorously used in aggressive
warfare. " Whilst we can keep the combined fleet in the
Mediterranean [by our own presence], so much the more
advantageous to us; and the moment we retire, the whole
of Italy is given to the French. If the Dons detach their
fleet out of the Mediterranean, we can do the same — however, that is distant. Be the successes of the Austrians
on the other hand what they may, their whole supply of
stores and provisions comes from Trieste, across the
Adriatic to the Po, and when this is cut off [as by our
uncovering the sea it must be], they must retire." Above
all he grieves for Naples. If a weak and vacillating ally,
there was no doubt her heart was with them. " I feel

more than all for Naples. The King of Naples is a greater
sacrifice than Corsica. If he has been induced to keep off
the peace, and perhaps engaged in the war again by the
expectation of the continuance of the fleet in the Mediterranean, hard indeed is his fate; his kingdom must inevitably be ruined." In the impression now made upon him,
may perhaps be seen one cause of Nelson's somewhat
extravagant affection in after days for the royal family of
Naples, independent of any influence exerted upon him by
Lady Hamilton.

With these broad views of the general strategic situation, which are unquestionably far in advance of the comparatively narrow and vague conceptions of a year, or even
six months before, and doubtless indicate the results of
independent command and responsibility, acting upon
powers of a high order, he at the same time shows his keen
appreciation of the value of the organized force, whose
movements, properly handled, should dominate the other
conditions. "When Man arrives, who is ordered to come
up, we shall be twenty-two sail of such ships as England
hardly ever produced, and commanded by an admiral who
will not fail to look the enemy in the face, be their force
what it may: I suppose it will not be more than thirty-
four of the line. There is not a seaman in the fleet who
does not feel confident of success." "The fleets of England," he says again, "are equal to meet the world in
arms; and of all fleets I ever saw, I never beheld one in
point of officers and men equal to Sir John Jervis's, who
is a commander-in-chief able to lead them to glory."

Reasoning so clearly and accurately upon the importance
to Great Britain's interests and honor, at that time, of
maintaining her position in the Mediterranean, and upon
the power of her fleet in battle, it is not strange that
Nelson, writing in intimate confidence to his wife, summed
up in bitter words his feelings upon the occasion; unconscious, apparently, of the great change they indicated, not

merely in his opinions, but in his power of grasping, in well-ordered and rational sequence, the great outlines of the conditions amid which he, as an officer, was acting. "We are all preparing to leave the Mediterranean, a measure which I cannot approve. They at home do not know what this fleet is capable of performing; anything, and everything. Much as I shall rejoice to see England, I lament our present orders in sackcloth and ashes, so dishonourable to the dignity of England." To the British minister at Naples his words were even stronger: "Till this time it has been usual for the allies of England to fall from her, but till now she never was known to desert her friends whilst she had the power of supporting them. I yet hope the Cabinet may, on more information, change their opinion; it is not all we gain elsewhere which can compensate for our loss of honour. The whole face of affairs is totally different to what it was when the Cabinet formed their opinion."

Nevertheless, although Nelson's perceptions and reasoning were accurate as far as they went, they erred in leaving out of the calculation a most important consideration, — the maintenance of the communications with England, which had assumed vital importance since the general defection of the Italian States, caused by Bonaparte's successes and his imperious demands. It would be more true to say that he underestimated this factor than that he overlooked it; for he had himself observed, six weeks earlier, when the approach of a Spanish war first became certain: "I really think they would do us more damage by getting off Cape Finisterre;[1] it is there I fear them," and the reason for that fear is shown by his reproach against Man, already quoted, for his neglect of the convoy. The position of the Spanish Navy in its home ports was in fact

---

[1] On the northwest coast of Spain, at the entrance of the Bay of Biscay, and therefore right in the track of vessels from the Channel to the Straits of Gibraltar.

intermediate — interior — as regarded the British fleet and the source of its most essential ˙supplies. So long as its future direction remained uncertain, it lay upon the flank of the principal British line of communications. Nelson did not use, perhaps did not know, the now familiar terms of the military art; and, with all his insight and comprehensive sagacity, he suffered from the want of proper tools with which to transmute his acute intuitions into precise thought, as well as of clearly enunciated principles, which serve to guide a man's conclusions, and would assuredly have qualified his in the present instance. Upon the supposition that the Spanish Navy, practically in its entirety, entered the Mediterranean and appeared off Corsica, — as it did, — Nelson's reasoning was correct, and his chagrin at a retreat justified; but, as he himself had wisely remarked to Beaulieu, it is not safe to count upon your enemy pursuing the course you wish. Had the Spanish Government chosen the other alternative open to it, and struck at the communications, such a blow, or even such a threat, must have compelled the withdrawal of the fleet, unless some other base of supplies could be found. The straitness of the situation is shown by the fact that Jervis, after he had held on to the last moment in San Fiorenzo Bay, sailed for Gibraltar with such scanty provisions that the crews' daily rations were reduced to one-third the ordinary amount; in fact, as early as the first of October they had been cut down to two-thirds. Whether, therefore, the Government was right in ordering the withdrawal, or Nelson in his condemnation of it, may be left to the decision of those fortunate persons who can be cocksure of the true solution of other people's perplexities.

In evacuating the Mediterranean, Jervis determined, upon his own responsibility, to retain Elba, if the troops, which were not under his command, would remain there. This was accordingly done; a strong garrison, adequately provisioned, thus keeping for Great Britain a foothold within the sea, at a time when she had lost Minorca and did not yet possess Malta. Nelson hoped that this step would encourage the Two Sicilies to stand firm against the French; but, however valuable Elba would be to the fleet as a base, if held until its return, it was useless to protect Naples in the absence of the fleet, and upon the news of the latter's proposed retirement that Kingdom at once made peace.

After the receipt of his orders for the evacuation of Bastia, and pending the assembling of the transports, Nelson was despatched by the admiral to Genoa, to present reclamations for injuries alleged to have been done to Great Britain, and to propose terms of accommodation. The little Republic, however, under the coercive influence of Bonaparte's continued success, was no longer in doubt as to the side which policy dictated her to take, between the two belligerents who vexed her borders. During this visit of Nelson's, on the 9th of October, she signed a treaty with France, stipulating, besides the closure of the ports against Great Britain, the payment of a sum of money, and free passage to troops and supplies for the army of Italy. Thus was Genoa converted formally, as she for some time had been actually, into a French base of operations. Returning from this fruitless mission, Nelson rejoined the commander-in-chief on the 13th of October, at San Fiorenzo, and the same afternoon left again for Bastia, where he arrived the following day.

During the fortnight intervening since he left the place, the fact that the Spanish fleet was on its way to Corsica had become known, and the French partisans in the island were proportionately active. It was impossible for the British to go into the interior; their friends, if not in a minority, were effectually awed by the preponderance of their enemies, on land and sea. Nelson, wishing to cross overland to San Fiorenzo to visit Jervis, was assured he could not do so with safety. In Bastia itself the municipality had wrested the authority from the Viceroy, and consigned the administration to a Committee of Thirty. The ships of war and transports being blown to sea, the inhabitants became still more aggressive; for, foreseeing the return of the French, they were naturally eager to propitiate their future masters by a display of zeal. British property was sequestered, and shipping not permitted to leave the mole.

Nelson was persuaded that only the arrival of the ships accompanying him saved the place. Except a guard at the Viceroy's house, the British troops had been withdrawn to the citadel. Even there, at the gates of the citadel, and within it, Corsican guards were present in numbers equal to the British, while the posts in the towns were all held by them. Arriving at early dawn of the 14th, Nelson at once visited the general and the Viceroy. The former saw no hope, under the conditions, of saving either stores, cannon, or provisions. "The Army," said Nelson in a private letter to Jervis, with something of the prejudiced chaff of a seaman of that day, "is, as usual, well dressed and powdered. I hope the general will join me cordially, but, as you well know, great exertions belong exclusively to the Navy." After the evacuation, however, he admitted handsomely that it was impossible to "do justice to the good dispositions of the general."

Between the heads of the two services such arrangements were perfected as enabled almost everything in the way of British property — public and private — to be brought away. By midday the ships, of which three were of the line, were anchored close to the mole-head, abreast the town, and the municipality was notified that any opposition to the removal of the vessels and stores would be followed by instant bombardment. Everything yielded to the threat, made by a man whose determined character left no doubt that it would be carried into execution. "Nothing shall be left undone that ought to be done," he wrote to Jervis, "even should it be necessary to knock down Bastia." From time to time interference was attempted, but the demand for immediate desistence, made, watch in hand, by the naval officer on the spot, enforced submission. "The firm tone held by Commodore Nelson," wrote Jervis to the Admiralty, "soon reduced these gentlemen to order, and quiet submission to the embarkation." Owing to the anarchy prevailing, the Viceroy was persuaded to go on board before nightfall, he being too valuable as a hostage to be exposed to possible kidnappers.

On the 18th of October a large number of armed French landed at Cape Corso, and approached the town. On the 19th they sent to the municipality a demand that the British should not be permitted to embark. Under these circumstances even Nelson felt that nothing more could be saved. The work of removal was continued actively until sunset, by which time two hundred thousand pounds worth of cannon, stores, and provisions had been taken on board. At midnight the troops evacuated the citadel, and marched to the north end of the town, where they embarked — twenty-four hours ahead of the time upon which Nelson had reckoned four days before. It was then blowing a strong gale of wind. Last of all, about six o'clock on the morning of the 20th, Nelson and the general entered a barge, every other man being by that time afloat, and were pulled off to the ships, taking with them two field-guns, until then kept ashore to repel a possible attack at the last moment. The French, who "were in one end of Bastia before we quitted the other," had occupied the citadel since one in the morning, and the Spanish fleet, of over twenty sail-of-the-line, which had already arrived, was even then off Cape Corso, about sixty miles distant; but the little British squadron, sailing promptly with a fair wind, in a few hours reached Elba, where every vessel was safely at anchor before night. On the 24th Nelson

joined the commander-in-chief in Martello Bay, the outer
anchorage of San Fiorenzo. Everything was then afloat,
and ready for a start as soon as the transports, still at
Elba, should arrive. The evacuation of Corsica was complete, though the ships remained another week in its
waters.

The Spanish fleet continued cruising to the northward
of the island, and was every day sighted by the British
lookout frigates. Jervis held grimly on, expecting the
appearance of the seven ships of Admiral Man, who had
been ordered to rejoin him. That officer, however, acting
on his own responsibility, weakly buttressed by the opinion
of a council of his captains, had returned to England contrary to his instructions. The commander-in-chief, ignorant of this step, was left in the sorely perplexing situation
of having his fleet divided into two parts, each distinctly
inferior to the Spanish force alone, of twenty-six ships,
not to speak of the French in Toulon. Under the conditions, the only thing that could be done was to await his
subordinate, in the appointed spot, until the last moment.
By the 2d of November further delay had become impossible, from the approaching failure of provisions. On that
day, therefore, the fleet weighed, and after a tedious passage anchored on the first of December at Gibraltar. There
Nelson remained until the 10th of the month, when he
temporarily quitted the "Captain," hoisted his broad
pendant on board the frigate "Minerve," and, taking with
him one frigate besides, returned into the Mediterranean
upon a detached mission of importance.

Nelson's last services in Corsica were associated with
the momentary general collapse of the British operations
and influence in the Mediterranean; and his final duty, by
a curious coincidence, was to abandon the position which he
more than any other man had been instrumental in securing.
Yet, amid these discouraging circumstances, his renown
had been steadily growing throughout the year 1796, which

may justly be looked upon as closing the first stage in the history of British Sea Power during the wars of the French Revolution, and as clearing the way for his own great career, which in the repossession of the Mediterranean reached its highest plane, and there continued in unabated glory till the hour of his death. It was not merely the exceptional brilliancy of his deeds at Cape St. Vincent, now soon to follow, great and distinguished as those were, which designated him to men in power as beyond dispute the coming chief of the British Navy; it was the long antecedent period of unswerving continuance in strenuous action, allowing no flagging of earnestness for a moment to appear, no chance for service, however small or distant, to pass unimproved. It was the same unremitting pressing forward, which had brought him so vividly to the front in the abortive fleet actions of the previous year, — an impulse born, partly, of native eagerness for fame, partly of zeal for the interests of his country and his profession. "Mine is all honour; so much for the Navy!" as he wrote, somewhat incoherently, to his brother, alluding to a disappointment about prize money.

Nelson himself had an abundant, but not an exaggerated, consciousness of this increase of reputation; and he knew, too, that he was but reaping as he had diligently sowed. "If credit and honour in the service are desirable," he tells his brother, "I have my full share. I have never lost an opportunity of distinguishing myself, not only as a gallant man, but as having a head; for, of the numerous plans I have laid, not one has failed." "You will be informed from my late letters," he writes to his wife, "that Sir John Jervis has such an opinion of my conduct, that he is using every influence, both public and private, with Lord Spencer, for my continuance on this station; and I am certain you must feel the superior pleasure of knowing, that my integrity and plainness of conduct are the cause of my being kept from you, to the receiving me

as a person whom no commander-in-chief would wish to
keep under his flag. Sir John was a perfect stranger to
me, therefore I feel the more flattered; and when I reflect
that I have had the unbounded confidence of three commanders-in-chief, I cannot but feel a conscious pride, and
that I possess abilities." "If my character is known," he
writes to the Genoese Government, which knew it well,
"it will be credited that this blockade [of Leghorn] will
be attended to with a degree of rigour unexampled in the
present war." "It has pleased God this war," he tells the
Duke of Clarence, "not only to give me frequent opportunities of showing myself an officer worthy of trust, but
also to prosper all my undertakings in the highest degree.
I have had the extreme good fortune, not only to be
noticed in my immediate line of duty, but also to obtain
the repeated approbation of His Majesty's Ministers at
Turin, Genoa, and Naples, as well as of the Viceroy of
Corsica, for my conduct in the various opinions I have
been called upon to give; and my judgment being formed
from common sense, I have never yet been mistaken."

Already at times his consciousness of distinction among
men betrays something of that childlike, delighted vanity,
half unwitting, which was afterward forced into exuberant
growth and distasteful prominence, by the tawdry flatteries
of Lady Hamilton and the Court of Naples. Now,
expressed to one who had a right to all his confidence and
to share all his honors, it challenges rather the sympathy
than the criticism of the reader. "I will relate another
anecdote, all vanity to myself, but you will partake of it:
A person sent me a letter, and directed as follows,
' Horatio Nelson, Genoa.' On being asked how he could
direct in such a manner, his answer, in a large party, was,
' Sir, there is but one Horatio Nelson in the world.' I am
known throughout Italy," he continues; "not a Kingdom,
or State, where my name will be forgotten. This is my
Gazette. Probably my services may be forgotten by the

great, by the time I get home; but my mind will not forget, nor cease to feel, a degree of consolation and of applause superior to undeserved rewards. Wherever there is anything to be done, there Providence is sure to direct my steps. Credit must be given me in spite of envy. Had all my actions been gazetted, not one fortnight would have passed during the whole war without a letter from me. Even the French respect me." After the conclusion of the campaign, when on the way to Gibraltar, he tells her again: "Do not flatter yourself that I shall be rewarded; I expect nothing, and therefore shall not be disappointed: the pleasure of my own mind will be my reward. I am more interested, and feel a greater satisfaction, in obtaining yours and my father's applause than that of all the world besides." The wholesome balance between self-respect and a laudable desire for the esteem of men was plainly unimpaired.

Though devoid of conspicuous events, the year 1796, from the opening of the campaign, early in April, up to the evacuation of the Mediterranean, had been to Nelson one of constant and engrossing occupation. There is therefore little mention by him of his private affairs and feelings. In the home correspondence there is no diminution in the calm tenderness of affection always shown by him towards his wife and father, who continued to live together; rather, perhaps, the expressions to Mrs. Nelson are more demonstrative than before, possibly because letters were less frequent. But there is nothing thrilling in the "assurance of my unabated and steady affection, which, if possible, is increasing by that propriety of conduct which you pursue." He is clearly satisfied to remain away; the path of honor has no rival in his heart; there is no suggestion of an inward struggle between two masters, no feeling of aloneness, no petulant discontent with uneasy surroundings, or longing for the presence of an absent mistress. The quiet English home, the "little but neat

cottage," attracts, indeed, with its sense of repose, — "I
shall not be very sorry to see England again. I am grown
old and battered to pieces, and require some repairs " —
but the magnet fails to deflect the needle; not even a per-
ceptible vibration of the will is produced.

Yet, while thus engrossed in the war, eager for personal
distinction and for the military honor of his country, he
apparently sees in it little object beyond a mere struggle
for superiority, and has no conception of the broader and
deeper issues at stake, the recognition of which intensified
and sustained the resolution of the peace-loving minister,
who then directed the policy of Great Britain. Of this
he himself gives the proof in a curious anecdote. An
Algerine official visiting the "Captain" off Leghorn,
Nelson asked him why the Dey would not make peace with
the Genoese and Neapolitans, for they would pay well for
immunity, as the Americans at that period always did.
His answer was: "If we make peace with every one, what
is the Dey to do with his ships?" "What a reason for
carrying on a naval war!" said Nelson, when writing the
story to Jervis; "but has our minister a better one for the
present?" Jervis, a traditional Whig, and opposed in
Parliament to the war, probably sympathized with this
view, and in any case the incident shows the close confidence existing between the two officers; but it also indicates how narrowly Nelson's genius and unquestionable
acuteness of intellect confined themselves, at that time, to
the sphere in which he was visibly acting.• In this he
presents a marked contrast to Bonaparte, whose restless
intelligence and impetuous imagination reached out in
many directions, and surveyed from a lofty height the
bearing of all things, far and near, upon the destinies of
France.

CHAPTER VIII.

DECEMBER, 1796 – JUNE, 1797.   AGE, 38.

"WHEN we quitted Toulon," wrote Nelson to his old
captain, Locker, while on the passage to Gibraltar, "I remember we endeavoured to reconcile ourselves to
Corsica; now we are content with Elba — such things are."
Even this small foothold was next to be resigned. Upon
reaching Gibraltar, Jervis received orders from the Admiralty to evacuate the island.

This was the duty upon which Nelson was so soon despatched again to the Mediterranean. Though "most important," wrote he to his wife, "it is not a fighting mission,
therefore be not uneasy." The assurance was doubtless
honestly given, but scarcely to be implicitly accepted in
view of his past career. Leaving the admiral on the evening of December 14, with the frigates "Blanche" and
"Minerve," his commodore's pendant flying in the latter,
the two vessels, about 11 P. M. of the 19th, encountered
two Spanish frigates close to Cartagena. The enemies
pairing off, a double action ensued, which, in the case of
the "Minerve," ended in the surrender of her opponent,
"La Sabina," at half-past one in the morning. Throwing
a prize-crew on board, the British ship took her late antagonist in tow and stood away to the southeast. At half-past
three another Spanish frigate came up, and, in order to
meet this fresh enemy on fairly equal terms, the "Minerve"
had to drop her prize. The second fight began at 4.30, and

lasted half an hour, when the Spaniard hauled off. With
daylight appeared also two hostile ships-of-the-line, which
had been chasing towards the sound of the guns. These
had already been seen by the "Blanche," which was by
them prevented from taking possession of her antagonist,
after the latter struck. The pursuit lasted through the
day, the "Minerve" being hard pressed in consequence of
the injuries received by all her masts during the engagement; but both British frigates succeeded in shaking off
their pursuers. "La Sabina" was recaptured; she had
already lost one mast, and the remaining two were seen to
go over the side as she was bringing-to, when the enemy
overtook her. It is interesting to note that her captain,
Don Jacobo Stuart, was descended from the British royal
house of Stuart. He, with many of his crew, had been
transferred to the "Minerve," and remained prisoners.

Nelson reached Porto Ferrajo a week later, on the 26th
of December. "On my arrival here," wrote he to his
brother, "it was a ball night, and being attended by the
captains, I was received in due form by the General, and
one particular tune was played:[1] the second was 'Rule
Britannia.' From Italy I am loaded with compliments."
Having regard to comparative strength, the action was in
all respects most creditable, but it received additional
lustre from being fought close to the enemy's coast, and
in full view of a force so superior as that from which
escape had been handsomely made, under conditions requiring both steadiness and skill. Though on a small
scale, no such fair stand-up fight had been won in the
Mediterranean during the war, and the resultant exultation was heightened by its contrast with the general depression then weighing upon the British cause. Especially
keen and warmly expressed was the satisfaction of the
veteran commander-in-chief at Lisbon, who first learned

[1] It is evident that this must have involved a compliment personal to
Nelson.

the success of his valued subordinate through Spanish sources. "I cannot express to you, and Captain Cockburn, the feelings I underwent on the receipt of the enclosed bulļetin, the truth of which I cannot doubt, as far as relates to your glorious achievement in the capture of the Sabina, and dignified retreat from the line-of-battle ship, which deprived you of your well-earned trophy; your laurels were not then within their grasp, and can never fade."

General De Burgh, who commanded the troops in Elba, had received no instructions to quit the island, and felt uncertain about his course, in view of the navy's approaching departure. Nelson's orders were perfectly clear, but applied only to the naval establishment. He recognized the general's difficulty, though he seems to have thought that, under all the circumstances, he might very well have acted upon his own expressed opinion, that "the signing of a Neapolitan peace with France ought to be our signal for departure." "The army," wrote Nelson to the First Lord of the Admiralty, "are not so often called upon to exercise their judgment in political measures as we are; therefore the general feels a certain diffidence." He told De Burgh that, the King of Naples having made peace, Jervis considered his business with the courts of Italy as terminated; that the Admiralty's orders were to concentrate the effort of the fleet upon preventing the allied fleets from quitting the Mediterranean, and upon the defence of Portugal, invaluable to the British as a base of naval operations. For these reasons, even if he had to leave the land forces in Elba, he should have no hesitation in following his instructions, which were to withdraw all naval belongings. "I have sent to collect my squadron, and as soon as they arrive, I shall offer myself for embarking the troops, stores, &c.; and should you decline quitting this post, I shall proceed down the Mediterranean with such ships of war as are not absolutely wanted for keeping open the communication of Elba with the Continent."

The necessary preparations went on apace. Vessels were sent out to summon the scattered cruisers to the port. A frigate was despatched to Naples to bring back Sir Gilbert Elliot, the late Viceroy of Corsica, who, since the abandonment of the latter island, had been on a diplomatic visit to Rome and Naples. It is to this incident that we owe the fullest account transmitted of the Battle of Cape St. Vincent; the narrator, Colonel Drinkwater, being then a member of the Viceroy's suite, and attending him upon his return with Nelson's squadron. The Spanish prisoners were sent to Cartagena in a cartel, Nelson restoring to the captain of the "Sabina" the sword which he had surrendered. "I felt this consonant to the dignity of my Country, and I always act as I feel right, without regard to custom." By the 16th of January all the naval establishment was embarked, ready for departure, though some of the ships of war had not yet returned, nor had the Viceroy arrived. The delay allowed the "Minerve" to be completely refitted, two of her masts and most of her rigging having to be renewed.

When Elliot came, it was decided in a consultation between him, Nelson, and De Burgh, that the troops should remain. The transports had been completely victualled, and so prepared that every soldier could be embarked in three days. With them were left two frigates and a few smaller ships of war. On the 29th of January, Nelson sailed with the rest of his force and the convoy, divided into three sections, which proceeded for the Straits by different routes, to diminish the chances of total loss by capture. Nelson himself, with another frigate, the "Romulus," in company, intended to make a round of the enemy's ports, in order to bring the admiral the latest information of the number of ships in each, and their state of preparation. "I hope to arrive safe in Lisbon with my charge," he wrote to his wife on the eve of sailing, "but in war much is left to Providence: however, as I have hitherto been most successful, confidence tells me I shall not fail: and as nothing will be left undone by me, should I not always succeed, my mind will not suffer; nor will the world, I trust, be willing to attach blame, where my heart tells me none would be due." The habit of taking risks had wrought its beneficial influence upon mind and temper, when he thus calmly and simply reasoned from the experience of the past to the prospective fortnight, to be passed in sight of a hostile coast, and in waters where he could meet no friendly sail. "It has ever pleased Almighty God to give his blessing to my endeavours," was his New Year greeting to his father at this time.

During this month in Elba a slight political reference shows how his views and purpose were changing with the rapidly shifting political scene. In this hour of deepening adversity he no longer looks for peace, nor seeks the reason for the current war, which a few months before he had failed to find. "As to peace, I do not expect it; Lord Malmesbury will come back as he went. But the people of England will, I trust, be more vigorous for the prosecution of the war, which can alone insure an honourable peace."

The "Minerve" and the "Romulus" looked first into the old British anchorage in San Fiorenzo Bay, which was found deserted. Standing thence to Toulon, they remained forty-eight hours off that port, in which were to be seen no ships in condition for sailing. From there they passed off Barcelona, showing French colors, but without succeeding in drawing out any vessel there lying. The wind not being fair for Minorca, where Nelson had purposed to reconnoitre Port Mahon, the frigates next went to Cartagena, and ascertained that the great Spanish fleet was certainly not there. As Toulon also had been found empty, it seemed clear that it had gone to the westward, the more so as the most probable information indicated that the naval enterprises of the French and their allies at that time were to be outside of the Mediterranean. Nelson therefore pushed ahead, and on the 9th of February the " Minerve " and " Romulus " anchored in Gibraltar. All three divisions from Elba passed the Straits within the same forty-eight hours.

The Spanish grand fleet had been seen from the Rock, four days before, standing to the westward into the Atlantic. Two ships-of-the-line and a frigate had been detached from it, with supplies for the Spanish lines before Gibraltar, and had anchored at the head of the bay, where they still were when Nelson arrived. On board them had also been sent the two British lieutenants and the seamen, who became prisoners when the "Sabina" was recaptured. Their exchange was effected, for which alone Nelson was willing to wait. The fact that the Spanish fleet had gone towards Jervis's rendezvous, and the continuance of easterly winds, which would tend to drive them still farther in the same direction, gave him uneasy premonitions of that coming battle which it would " break his heart " to miss. It was, besides, part of his ingrained military philosophy, never absent from his careful mind, that a fair wind may fall or shift. " The object of a sea-officer is to embrace the happy moment which now and then offers, — it may be to-day, it may be never." Regretting at this moment the loss even of a tide, entailed by the engagements of the Viceroy, whom he had to carry to Jervis, and therefore could not leave, he wrote, " I fear a *westerly* wind." The Providence in which he so often expresses his reliance, now as on many other occasions, did not forsake the favored son, who never by sluggishness or presumption lost his opportunities. The wind held fair until the 13th of February, when Nelson rejoined the commander-in-chief. That night it shifted to the westward, and the following day was fought the Battle of Cape St. Vincent.

Taken in its entirety, the episode of this nearly forgotten mission to Elba is singularly characteristic, not only of Nelson's own qualities, but also of those concurrences

which, whatever the origin attributed to them by this or
that person, impress upon a man's career the stamp of "fortunate." An errand purely of evasion, not in itself of
prime importance, but for an object essentially secondary,
it results in a night combat of unusual brilliancy, which
would probably not have been fought at all could the
British have seen the overwhelming force ready to descend
upon conqueror and conquered alike. With every spar
wounded, and a hostile fleet in sight, the "Minerve" nevertheless makes good her retreat. Solitary, in an enemy's
sea, she roams it with premeditated deliberateness, escaping
molestation, and, except in the first instance, even detection.
She carries the fortunes of a Cæsar yet unknown, who is
ready to stake them at any moment for adequate cause;
but everything works together, not merely for his preservation, but to bring him up just in time for the exceptional
action, which showed there was more to him than even his
untiring energy and fearlessness had so far demonstrated.
As when, in later years, burning anxiety pressed him to
hasten after Villeneuve, yet failed so to discompose him as
to cause the neglect of any preparation essential to due
provision for the abandoned Mediterranean; so now, with
every power at highest tension to rejoin the admiral, eager
not to waste a moment, he mars his diligence by no precipitancy, he grudges no hour necessary to the rounded
completion of the present task, — to see, and know, and do,
all that can be seen and done. He might almost have used
again, literally, the expression before quoted: " I have not
a thought on any subject separated from the immediate
object of my command."

Leaving the "Romulus" in Gibraltar, the "Minerve"
sailed again on the 11th. The Spanish ships-of-the-line followed her at once. The east wind blows in wild and irregular puffs upon the anchorages immediately under the lofty
Rock, where the frigate lay. Farther up, where the Spaniards were, it crosses the low neck joining the peninsula

to the mainland, and is there more equable and more constant. The "Minerve" was consequently at a disadvantage until she got fairly from under its lee, and the chase
through the Straits became close enough to draw the idlers
of the town and garrison in crowds to the hillsides. It
soon became evident that the leading ship-of-the-line was
gaining upon the frigate, and the latter cleared for action.
Nelson had but a poor opinion of the Spanish navy of his
day, and doubtless chose, before surrendering, to take his
chance of one of those risks which in war often give
strange results. He said to Drinkwater that he thought
an engagement probable, but added, "Before the Dons get
hold of that bit of bunting I will have a struggle with
them, and sooner than give up the frigate, I 'll run her
ashore."

About this time the officers' dinner was announced.
Drinkwater went below, and was just congratulating
Lieutenant Hardy, who had been captured in the "Sabina," upon his exchange, when the cry "Man overboard!" was heard. The party dispersed hurriedly, in
sympathy with the impulse which invariably causes a rush
under such circumstances; and Drinkwater, running to the
stern windows, saw a boat already lowering with Hardy in
it, to recover the man, who, however, could not be found.
The boat therefore, making signal to that effect, soon
turned to pull to the ship. The situation was extremely
embarrassing, not to say critical; on the one hand, the
natural reluctance to abandon any one or anything to the
enemy, on the other, the imminent risk of sacrificing the
ship and all concerned by any delay, — for the leading
Spaniard, by himself far superior in force, was nearly
within gunshot. Temperament and habit decide, in questions where reason has little time and less certainty upon
which to act; by nature and experience Nelson was
inclined to take risks. It was evident the boat could
not overtake the frigate unless the latter's way was les-

sened, and each moment that passed made this step more perilous, as the pursuer was already overhauling the "Minerve." "By God, I'll not lose Hardy!" he exclaimed; "back the mizzen-topsail." The ship's speed being thus checked, the boat came alongside, and the party scrambled on board. Singularly enough, the enemy, disconcerted by Nelson's action, stopped also, to allow his consort to come up, — a measure wholly inexcusable, and only to be accounted for by that singular moral effect produced in many men by a sudden and unexpected occurrence. The daring deed had therefore the happiest results of a stratagem, and the frigate was troubled no further.

Steering that night to the southward, to throw off her pursuers, the "Minerve" found herself unexpectedly in the midst of a fleet, which, from the signals made, was evidently not that of Jervis, and therefore must be hostile. The hazy atmosphere veiled the British frigate from close observation, and, by conforming her movements to those of the strangers, she escaped suspicion. Nelson was uncertain whether it was the Spanish grand fleet, or, possibly, a detached body proceeding to the West Indies. He had heard a rumor of such an expedition, and the impression was probably confirmed by these ships being met when steering southerly from the Straits; Cadiz, the known destination of the grand fleet, being north. As the British commercial interests in the Caribbean were of the first importance, and would be much endangered, he told Drinkwater, who lay awake in his cot, that, if he became convinced the ships in sight were bound there, he should give up the attempt to join the commander-in-chief, and should start at once for the Islands, to forewarn them of the approaching danger. The colonel was naturally startled at the prospect of an involuntary trip across the Atlantic, and represented the equally urgent necessity — as he thought — of Jervis and the British Cabinet getting the information, which Elliot was bringing, of the views and intentions of the Italian governments. This Nelson admitted, but replied that he thought the other considera- tion greater, and that — the condition arising — he must do as he had said. The incident illustrates the activity of his mind, in comprehending instantly the singular opportunity thrust unexpectedly upon him, as well as the readiness to accept responsibility and to follow his own judgment, which he showed on so many other occasions, both before and after this.

Later in the night the hostile ships went about, eviden- cing thereby a desire to keep to windward, which pointed much more toward Cadiz than to any western destination. The " Minerve " imitated them, but altered her course so as to edge away gradually from her dangerous neighbors. Nelson, some time after, again entered the cabin, and told Drinkwater and Elliot, the latter having also waked, that he had got clear of the enemy, but that at daylight the course would be altered so as to sight them once more, if they were really going west. Should it prove to be so, they must make up their minds to visit the West Indies. Nothing, however, being seen during the 12th, the commo- dore, satisfied at last that he had been in the midst of the grand fleet, hastened on, and towards noon of the 13th joined the admiral. Before doing so, some of the Spaniards were again sighted. They had been seen also by the regu- lar British lookouts, one at least of which had kept touch with them through the preceding days of hazy weather. Nelson, after an interview with Jervis, went on board the " Captain," where his broad pendant was again hoisted at 6 P. M.

At daybreak, the position of the two fleets was twenty- five miles west of Cape St. Vincent, a headland on the Portuguese coast, a hundred and fifty miles northwest of Cadiz. During the night the wind had shifted from the eastward to west by south, and, being now fair, the Span- iards were running for their port, heading about east-south-

BATTLE OF CAPE ST. VINCENT
FEBRUARY 14, 1797.

▶ BRITISH, 15 SHIPS
▷ SPANISH, 27 ,,

WIND   W. BY S.

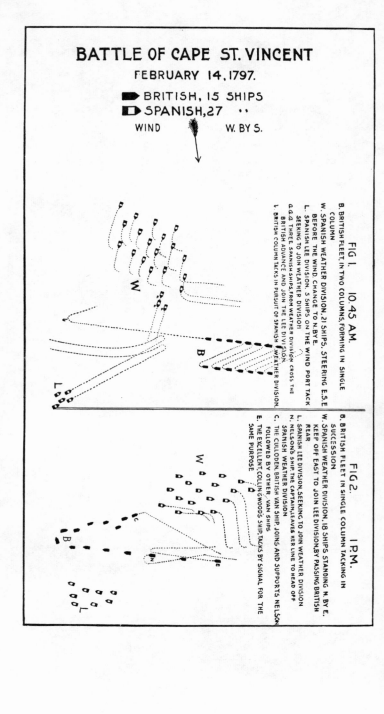

FIG 1.   10.45 A.M.

B. BRITISH FLEET, IN TWO COLUMNS, FORMING IN SINGLE
   COLUMN
W. SPANISH WEATHER DIVISION, 21 SHIPS, STEERING E.S.E.
   BEFORE THE WIND. CHANGE TO N. BY E.
L. SPANISH LEE DIVISION, 5 SHIPS ON THE WIND PORT TACK
   SEEKING TO JOIN WEATHER DIVISION
a.a.a THREE SPANISH SHIPS, FROM WEATHER DIVISION CROSS THE
   BRITISH ADVANCE AND JOIN THE LEE DIVISION.
ı. BRITISH COLUMN TACKS IN PURSUIT OF SPANISH WEATHER DIVISION.

FIG 2.   1 P.M.

B. BRITISH FLEET, IN SINGLE COLUMN TACKING IN
   SUCCESSION
W. SPANISH WEATHER DIVISION, 18 SHIPS STANDING N. BY E.
   KEEP OFF EAST TO JOIN LEE DIVISION BY PASSING BRITISH
   REAR
L. SPANISH LEE DIVISION, SEEKING TO JOIN WEATHER DIVISION
N. NELSONS SHIP, THE CAPTAIN, LEAVES HER LINE TO HEAD OFF
   SPANISH WEATHER DIVISION
C. THE CULLODEN BRITISH VAN SHIP, JOINS AND SUPPORTS NELSON
   FOLLOWED BY OTHER ,VAN SHIPS
E. THE EXCELLENT, COLLINGWOOD'S SHIP, TACKS BY SIGNAL FOR THE
   SAME PURPOSE.

east; but they were in disorder, and were divided into two principal fragments, of which the headmost, and therefore leewardmost, numbered six ships. It was separated from the other division of twenty-one by a space of six or eight miles. In the whole force, of twenty-seven ships, there were seven of three decks, the least of which carried one hundred and twelve guns; the remainder were principally seventy-fours, there being, however, one of eighty-four guns. Jervis's fleet consisted of fifteen ships-of-the-line, — two of one hundred guns, four of ninety-eight or ninety, eight seventy-fours, and one sixty-four. From the intelligence received the previous day of the enemy's proximity, the admiral kept the command throughout the night in two columns, in close order, a formation suited by its compactness to a hazy night, and at the same time manageable in case of encountering an enemy suddenly. The course was south by west, almost perpendicular to that of the Spaniards. The two fleets were thus running, one from the westward, and the other from the northward, to a common crossing.[1]

At daylight the enemy's fleet was partly visible to the leading ships of the British columns. As the morning advanced, and the situation developed, it was seen that the Spanish line was long and straggling, and the gap began to show. As the British were heading directly towards it, Jervis ordered a half-dozen of his ships, which were all still under moderate canvas, to press on and interpose between the enemy's divisions. An hour or so later he made the signal to form the single column, which was the usual fighting order of those days. The fleet being already properly disposed for manœuvres, this change of order was effected, to use his own words, " with the utmost celerity." Nelson's ship was thirteenth in the new order, therefore nearly the last. Next after him came the sixty-four, the " Diadem," while Collingwood, in the " Excellent," brought

[1] See Plate, Figure 1.

up the rear. Immediately ahead of Nelson was the "Barfleur," carrying the flag of one of the junior admirals, to whom naturally fell the command in that part of the line.

Three of the larger Spanish body succeeded in crossing ahead of the British column and joining the lee group, thus raised to nine ships. No others were able to effect this, the headmost British ships anticipating them in the gap. Jervis's plan was to pass between their two divisions with his one column, protracting this separation, then to go about in succession and attack the eighteen to windward, because their comrades to leeward could not help them in any short time. This was done. The lee ships did attempt to join those to windward by breaking through the British order, but were so roughly handled that they gave it up and continued to the south-southwest, hoping to gain a better opportunity. The weather ships, on the other hand, finding they could not pass, steered to the northward, — nearly parallel, but opposite, to the course which both the British and their own lee group were then following.

A heavy cannonade now ensued, each British ship engaging as its batteries came to bear, through the advance of the column to the south-southwest. After an hour of this, the admiral made the signal to tack in succession. This was instantly obeyed by the leader, the "Culloden," which was expecting it, and each following ship tacked also as it reached the same point. But as the Spaniards were continually receding from this point, which the British rear was approaching, it was evident that in time the latter would leave uncovered the ground that had so far separated the two hostile divisions. This the Spanish admiral expected to be his opportunity; it proved to be Nelson's.

At 1 P. M.,[1] by Nelson's journal, the "Captain," standing south by west, had come abreast the rearmost of the eighteen weather ships, having passed the others. He then noticed that the leaders of that body were bearing up be-

1 See Plate, Figure 2.

fore the wind, to the eastward, to cross behind the British column. If this were carried out unmolested, they could join the lee ships, which heretofore had been separated from them by the centre and rear of the British line, and at this moment were not very far distant, being still engaged with the British centre; or else, so Nelson thought, they might fly before the wind, making ineffective all that had been done so far. " To prevent either of their schemes from taking effect, I ordered the ship to be wore, and passing between the Diadem and Excellent, at a quarter past one o'clock, was engaged with the headmost, and of course leewardmost of the Spanish division. The ships which I know were, the Santissima Trinidad, 126; San Josef, 112;[1] Salvador del Mundo, 112;[1] San Nicolas, 80;[1] another first-rate, and seventy-four, names not known. I was immediately joined and most nobly supported by the Culloden, Captain Troubridge. The Spanish fleet,[2] from not wishing (I suppose) to have a decisive battle, hauled to the wind [again] on the larboard tack, which brought the ships afore-mentioned to be the leewardmost and sternmost ships in their fleet."

By this spontaneous and sudden act, for which he had no authority, by signal or otherwise, except his own judgment and quick perceptions, Nelson entirely defeated the Spanish movement. Devoting his own ship to a most unequal contest, he gained time for the approaching British van to come up, and carry on the work they had already begun when first passing these ships — before the moment of tacking. The British column being then in a V shape, — part on one tack, part on the other, the point of the V being that of tacking, — he hastened across, by a short cut, from the rear of one arm of the V to a position on the other side, toward which the van was advancing, but which it, being more distant, could not reach as soon as he, and

[1] Captured.
[2] That is, the weather division, — the eighteen ships.

therefore not to as good effect. To quote Jervis's words concerning this incident, " Commodore Nelson, who was in the rear on the starboard tack, *took the lead* on the larboard, and contributed very much to the fortune of the day." On the intellectual side, the side of skill, this is what he did; on the side of valor, it is to be said that he did it for the moment single-handed. The " Culloden," the actual leader, came up shortly, followed afterwards by the " Blenheim; " and the " Excellent " was ordered by Jervis to imitate Nelson's movement, and strengthen the operation which he had initiated. It was the concentration of these ships at the point which Nelson seized, and for a moment held alone, that decided the day; and it was there that the fruits of victory were chiefly reaped.

It must not be understood, of course, that all the honors of the day are to be claimed for Nelson, even conjointly with those present with him at the crucial moment. Much was done, both before and after, which contributed materially to the aggregate results, some of which were missed by the very reluctance of men of solid military qualities to desist from seeking enemies still valid, in order to enjoy what Nelson called the "parade of taking possession of beaten enemies." It seems probable that more Spanish ships might have been secured, had it not been for the eagerness of some British vessels to push on to new combats. But, while fully allowing the merits of many others, from the commander-in-chief down, it is true of St. Vincent, as of most battles, that there was a particular moment on which success or failure hinged, and that upon the action then taken depended the chief outcome, — a decisive moment, in short. That moment was when the enemy attempted, with good prospect, to effect the junction which Nelson foiled. As Collingwood afterwards summed up the matter: " The highest rewards are due to you and Culloden; you formed the plan of attack, — we were only accessories to the Dons' ruin; for had they got on the

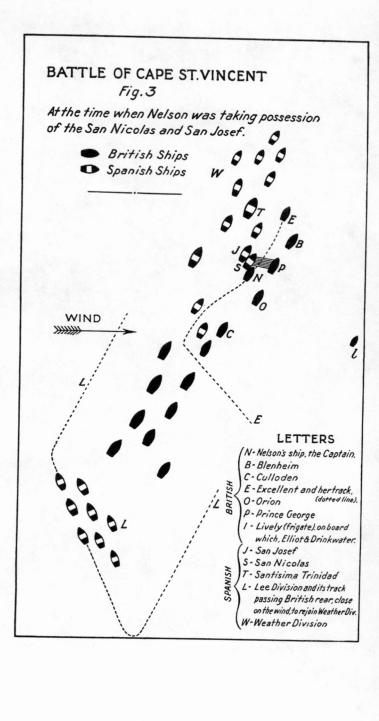

BATTLE OF CAPE ST.VINCENT
Fig.3

At the time when Nelson was taking possession of the San Nicolas and San Josef.

◖ **British Ships**
◐ **Spanish Ships**

WIND

LETTERS

N - Nelson's ship, the Captain.
B - Blenheim
C - Culloden
E - Excellent and her track, (dotted line).
O - Orion
P - Prince George
l - Lively (frigate), on board which, Elliot & Drinkwater.
J - San Josef
S - San Nicolas
T - Santisima Trinidad
L - Lee Division and its track passing British rear, close on the wind, to rejoin Weather Div.
W - Weather Division

BRITISH

SPANISH

other tack, they would have been sooner joined, and the business would have been less complete."

When Collingwood came up with the "Excellent," the "Captain" was practically disabled for further movement, had lost heavily in men, and was without immediate support. The "Culloden" had dropped astern, crippled, as had two of the Spanish vessels; the "Blenheim," after passing the "Culloden" and the "Captain," between them and the enemy, had drawn ahead. The "Excellent," steering between the two Spanish ships that had fallen behind, fired into both of them, and Nelson thought both then struck; but Collingwood did not stop to secure them. "Captain Collingwood," says Nelson, in his account, "disdaining the parade of taking possession of beaten enemies, most gallantly pushed up, with every sail set, to save his old friend and messmate, who was to appearance in a critical state. The Excellent ranged up within ten feet of the San Nicolas, giving a most tremendous fire. The San Nicolas luffing up, the San Josef fell on board her, and the Excellent passing on for the Santissima Trinidad, the Captain resumed [1] her situation abreast of them, and close alongside. At this time the Captain having lost her foretopmast, not a sail, shroud,[2] or rope left, her wheel shot away, and incapable of further service in the line, or in chase, I directed Captain Miller to put the helm a-starboard, and calling for the boarders, ordered them to board." [3]

The "Captain" fetched alongside of the "San Nicolas," her bow touching the lee (starboard) quarter of the Spanish vessel, her spritsail yard hooking in the other's mizzen shrouds. Commander Berry, a very young man, who had lately been first lieutenant of the "Captain," leaped actively into the mizzen chains, the first on board the enemy; he was quickly supported by others, who passed over by the spritsail yard. The captain of the ship was in

---

[1] That is, was left in.   [3] See Plate, Figure 3.

[2] Shrouds are large ropes which support the masts.

the act of following, at the head of his men, when Nelson stopped him. " No, Miller," he said, " *I* must have that honour ; " and he directed him to remain. One of the soldiers of the Sixty-ninth Regiment, who were serving on board as marines, broke open the upper quarter-gallery window of the " San Nicolas," and through this Nelson entered, with a crowd of followers, to find himself in the cabin of the enemy's ship. The doors being fastened, they were held there a few moments, while Spanish officers from the quarter-deck discharged their pistols at them ; but the doors were soon broken down, and the party, after firing a volley, sallied on the spar deck, which the enemy yielded to them, — a Spanish commodore falling by the wheel as he retreated. Berry had by this time reached the poop, where he hauled down the colors, while Nelson passed to the forward part of the ship, meeting on his way several Spanish officers, who, being by this time in the hands of British seamen, gave up to him their swords. The Spanish guns on the lower decks still continued firing for some moments, apparently at the " Prince George," which had passed to leeward of the ' Captain," and now kept her batteries playing upon the hull of the " San Nicolas " forward of the part where the " Captain " touched her.

At this moment a small-arm fire was opened from the stern galleries of the " San Josef " upon the British party in the " San Nicolas." Nelson caused the soldiers to reply to it, and ordered reinforcements sent to him from the " Captain." Parties were stationed at the hatchways of the " San Nicolas " to control the enemy and keep them below decks, and then the boarders charged again for the Spanish three-decker. Nelson was helped by Berry into her main chains ; but he had got no farther before a Spanish officer put his head over the rail and said they surrendered. " From this most welcome information," continues Nelson, in his narrative, " it was not long before I was on

the quarter-deck, when the Spanish captain, with a bow,
presented me his sword, and said the admiral was dying of
his wounds below. I asked him, on his honour, if the ship
were surrendered? he declared she was; on which I gave
him my hand, and desired him to call to his officers and
ship's company, and tell them of it — which he did;
and on the quarter-deck of a Spanish First-rate, extravagant as the story may seem, did I receive the swords of
vanquished Spaniards; which, as I received, I gave to
William Fearney, one of my bargemen, who put them with
the greatest sangfroid under his arm. I was surrounded
by Captain Berry, Lieutenant Pierson, 69th Regiment,
John Sykes, John Thomson, Francis Cook, all old Aga-
memnons, and several other brave men, seamen and soldiers: thus fell these ships." The firing from the lower
deck of the "San Nicolas" was by this time stopped, and
the "Prince George" was hailed that both the enemy's
vessels were in possession of the British. The "Victory,"
Jervis's flagship, passed a few moments later and cheered,
as did every ship in the fleet.

The dramatic and picturesque surroundings which colored the seizure of these two Spanish ships have doubtless
given an exaggerated idea of the danger and difficulty
attending the exploit. The impression made upon a sympathetic and enthusiastic eye-witness, Sir Gilbert Elliot,
who saw the affair from the decks of the frigate "Lively,"
has been transmitted to posterity with little diminution.
"Nothing in the world was ever more noble than the
transaction of the Captain from beginning to end, and the
glorious group of your ship and her two prizes, fast in
your gripe, was never surpassed, and I dare say never
will." Yet it may better be looked upon as another of
those "fortunate" occurrences which attend — and in
Nelson's career repeatedly attended — the happy meeting
of opportunity and readiness. Doubtless they were beaten
ships, but other beaten ships have escaped in general ac-

tions — did at St. Vincent. "I pretend not to say," wrote Nelson a week later, "that these ships might not have fell, had I not boarded them; but truly it was far from impossible but they might have forged into the Spanish fleet as the other two ships did." He was there, he could do nothing else, he saw with his rapid glance that he might do this, and he did it. And, after all, it was a big thing, — this boarding a first-rate ship over the decks of another hostile ship, not inaptly characterized in the fleet as "Nelson's patent bridge." We must mark, too, or we shall miss significant indications of character, that the same qualities which led him to the quarter-deck of the "San Josef" had led him but an hour before from the rear of the fleet to the van to save the fight, — the same quickness to see opportunity, the same promptness to seize it, the same audacity to control it. The brilliant crowning of the day may be but an ornament, but it sits well and fitly upon the knightly deed that rolled back the tide of battle in the hour of need.

Those Spanish ships of the weather division which were first encountered by Nelson, after he wore out of the line, bore the brunt of the fighting. As the whole division continued to stand on close to the wind, these ships, becoming crippled, dropped astern of their consorts, and so first received the broadsides of the British van as that arrived. Being also the leaders in the movement frustrated by Nelson, they became the most leewardly; and, as the British van on coming up passed to leeward, this contributed further to concentrate fire upon the same vessels. Among them was the "Santísima Trinidad," of four decks and one hundred and thirty guns, then the largest ship of war in the world. When Collingwood passed ahead of Nelson, he engaged her, but not as near as he wished, and could have done, had not the "Excellent's" rigging been so cut as to prevent her hauling close to the wind. She was also brought to action by Sir James Saumarez, in the

"Orion," and towards the close of her contest with the latter ship showed a British Union Jack, — a token of submission possibly unauthorized, as it was almost immediately hauled in again. Besides those boarded by Nelson, two other enemy's ships had already struck.

It was now after four o'clock, and the other Spanish division, of eight ships, was heading for the scene and near at hand. Although effectually blocked in their first attempt to pierce the British line, these had not received such injury as to detract seriously from their efficiency. Continuing to stand south-southwest, after the British began tacking, they at last gained ground sufficiently to come up to windward, the side on which their other division was. In view of the now inevitable junction of a great number of comparatively fresh ships, and of the casualties in his own vessels, Jervis decided to discontinue the action. He ordered his fleet to form on the starboard tack, covering the four prizes and the "Captain;" and with this done the firing soon ceased. The Spanish divisions united, and carried off their other disabled ships.

Nelson's account of the proceedings of the "Captain" on the 14th of February, having been published not long afterwards, apparently by his authority, was challenged as incorrect by Vice-Admiral William Parker, commanding the van, whose flag was on board the third British ship, the "Prince George." Parker claimed that the latter, with the "Blenheim" and "Orion," had been much closer to the "Captain" and "Culloden" than was implied in Nelson's narrative by the words, "For near an hour, I believe, (but do not pretend to be correct as to time,) did the Culloden and Captain support this apparently, but not really, unequal contest; when the Blenheim, passing between us and the enemy, gave us a respite." Parker labored under the misfortune of a singularly involved and obscure style, while in two separate papers he contradicted himself more than once on points of detail; but the tone of his letter to

Nelson was temperate and dignified, and he asserted that, "so different to your statement, very soon after you commenced your fire, you had four ships pressing on [Culloden, Blenheim, Prince George, and Orion], almost on board of each other, close in your rear; but " — and the admission following must be noted as well as the charge — "the ships thus pressing upon each other, and the *two latter not far enough ahead to fire with proper effect*,[1] besides having none of the enemy's ships left in the rear for our succeeding ships, at forty-three [2] minutes past one I made the signal to fill and stand on." Parker had also stated, in his log of the action, that the brunt fell upon the "Captain," the "Culloden," and the "Blenheim," but more particularly the two former, "from their being more in the van."

It appears to the writer probable that Nelson overestimated the period that he and Troubridge remained unsupported; time would seem long to the bravest man, when opposed to such heavy odds. Parker seems to have reckoned it to be about fifteen minutes, and he admits that it was impossible for him to open fire with proper effect for some time, although close on the heels of the "Captain" and the "Culloden," because he could not get abreast of the enemy. All the ships — Spanish and British — were moving ahead, probably at not very different rates of speed. The "Prince George" certainly became in the end actively and closely engaged, much of the time with the "San Josef," a ship of force superior to her own.

Nelson's account is a simple, if somewhat exultant, narrative of the facts as they passed under his observation; and, except in the statement to which Parker objected, they do not even inferentially carry an imputation upon any one else. There was a reflection, though scarcely in-

[1] The italics are the author's.
[2] In his letter to Nelson this is thirteen, but evidently a slip. His log of the action says forty-three.

tended, upon the van ships, which should have been, and
Parker says were, close behind the "Culloden;" but the
attack was upon the extreme rear of the enemy, and Nelson probably forgot that readers might not understand, as
he did, that the ships behind him must need some time to
get up, and that his own position, abreast the enemy's rear,
was in itself an obstacle to their reaching a place whence
their batteries could bear, with the limited train of broadside guns in those days.

Another and interesting illustration of the injustice a
man may thus unintentionally do, through inadvertence, is
afforded by Nelson's accounts of St. Vincent. There were
two drawn up on board the "Captain," — one by himself in
his own hand; the second simply signed by him, Miller,
and Berry. It is quite evident that the latter is based
upon the former, much of the phraseology being identical; but the whole is toned down in many points. The
instance of unintentional injustice is this. In his autograph account, Nelson, thinking only of himself,[1] speaks
of his going with the boarders, and makes no mention of
the captain of the ship, Miller, whose proper business it
would be rather than his. In the revision, Miller would
naturally feel that his failure to board should be accounted
for, and it contains accordingly the statement, "Captain
Miller was in the very act of going also, but I directed
him to remain." Berry's hand also appears; for whereas
Nelson's own account of boarding the "San Josef" simply
says, "I got into her main-chains," the published copy reads,
"Captain Berry assisting me into the main-chains."

So too with reference to Parker's controversy. In the
first draft there occurs the unqualified statement: "For
an hour the Culloden and Captain supported this appar-

---

[1] Both papers are headed: "A few remarks relative to myself in the Captain," etc. It is unfortunate that Nicolas, in giving these two papers, puts
first the one which, from internal indications, is (in the author's judgment)
the later in date.

ently unequal contest." The revision reads : "For near an hour, I believe, (*but do not pretend to be correct as to time,*)[1] did Culloden and Captain," etc. Parker quotes from the revision, which was therefore the one published, but does not quote the words italicized. Probably, if the "Blenheim" and the "St. George" had had a hand in this revision, there would have been more modification ; but Nelson did not realize where he was hurting them, any more than he did in Miller's case.

The love of glory, the ardent desire for honorable distinction by honorable deeds, is among the most potent and elevating of military motives, which in no breast has burned with a purer flame than in that of Nelson ; but it is better that officers leave the public telling of their own exploits to others, and it is evident that Nelson, when taken to task, realized uncomfortably that he had not exercised due thoughtfulness. Parker refrained from addressing him till he had received the printed account. This was not till July, and his remonstrance reached Nelson shortly after the loss of his arm at Teneriffe, when on his way home for what proved to be a tedious and painful recovery. He was then suffering, not only from pain and weakness, but also from discouragement about his professional future, which he thought threatened by disability, and for these conditions allowance must be made ; but for all this his reply did not compare favorably with Parker's letter, which had been explicit in its complaint as well as moderate in expression. He wrote curtly: "I must acknowledge the receipt of your letter of the 25th of July ; and, after declaring that I know nothing of the Prince George till she was hailed from the forecastle of the San Nicolas,[2] it is impossible I can enter into the subject of your letter."

This course was the more ungenerous, because no explanation, or even admission of involuntary wrong done,

---

[1] Author's italics.
[2] Hailed to stop firing, because the "San Nicolas" had surrendered.

could have detracted in the least from the abounding credit due and accorded to Nelson for his conduct at St. Vincent, which indeed did not depend upon the length of time he remained unsupported, but upon the rapidity and fearlessness with which he had acted aright at a very critical juncture. This had been done so openly, under the eyes of all men, that it could by no means be hid. Collingwood had borne witness to it, in words which have been quoted. Drinkwater and Elliot had watched the whole from the deck of their frigate. The latter had written to him: "To have had any share in yesterday's glory is honour enough for one man's life, but to have been foremost on such a day could fall to your share alone." The commander-in-chief had come out to greet him upon the quarter-deck of the flagship, — a compliment naval officers can appreciate, — had there embraced him, saying he could not sufficiently thank him, and "used every kind expression which could not fail to make me happy." Jervis had also insisted upon his keeping the sword of the Spanish rear-admiral who fell on board the "San Josef."

Before dropping this subject, which has the unpleasantness that attends all contentions between individuals about their personal deserts, it is right to say that Nelson had held from the first that Collingwood, Troubridge, and himself were the only ones "who made great exertions on that glorious day: the others did their duty, and some not exactly to my satisfaction." "Sir John Jervis," he continued, "is not quite contented, but says nothing publicly." He then quotes an anecdote which, if he had it from Jervis, confirms his own opinion about the support given. "Calder [the Chief of Staff] said, 'Sir, the Captain and Culloden are separated from the fleet, and unsupported: shall we recall them?' 'I will not have them recalled. I put my faith in those ships: it is a disgrace that they are not supported and [are] separated.'"

In his public letter Jervis refrained alike from praise and

from blame. He mentions but one name, that of Calder, as bearer of despatches, and only incidentally says that he has been useful to him at all times. In a private letter to the First Lord he was more explicit, yet scarcely adequately so. Whatever momentary expression of impatience escaped him, when anxious about the " Culloden " and " Captain," he knew that his own flagship could not get to them in time for efficient support, and he gives as the reason for reticence in his public letter that all had behaved well, and that he was " confident that had those who were least in action been in the situation of the fortunate few, their conduct would not have been less meritorious." He then mentions by name Troubridge, — who led the fleet, — Nelson, and Collingwood, and five ships (without the names of the captains), " Blenheim," " Prince George," " Orion," " Irresistible," and " Colossus," which " gallantly supported " Troubridge, though just where or when is not specified. " The ships' returns of killed and wounded," he says explicitly, " although not always the criterion of their being more or less in action, is, in this instance, correctly so." This would include the " Blenheim," whose casualties were in excess of any except the " Captain," and Parker's ship, the " Prince George," which lost not many less than Collingwood. The " Captain's " loss in killed, twenty-four, was double that of any other ship, and in killed and wounded nearly one-third that of the whole fleet.

An interesting anecdote of Jervis shows the importance conceded by him to Nelson's action. It rests on good authority, and is eminently characteristic of one who valued beyond most traits in an officer the power to assume responsibility. " The test of a man's courage," he used to say, " is responsibility." In the evening, while talking over the events of the day, Calder spoke of Nelson's wearing out of the line as an unauthorized departure from the method of attack prescribed by the admiral. " It certainly was so," replied Jervis, " and if ever you commit such a breach of your orders, I will forgive you also." Success covers many faults, yet it is difficult to believe that had Nelson been overwhelmed, the soundness of his judgment and his resolution would not equally have had the applause of a man, who had just fought twenty-seven ships with fifteen, because "a victory was essential to England at that moment." The justification of departure from orders lies not in success, but in the conditions of the case; and Jervis was not one to overlook these, nor hereafter to forget that only one man in his fleet had both seen the thing to do and dared the responsibility of doing it.

A victory so signal entailed, as a matter of course, a number of those rewards and titles with which Great Britain judiciously fostered the spirit of emulation in her Navy. These were to a considerable extent affairs of routine and precedent, and Nelson, knowing that junior flag-officers had on several previous occasions been made baronets, wished to avoid this hereditary dignity because inconsistent with his means. His love of distinction also prompted him to desire one of those Orders which carry with them the outward token of merit. Meeting Drinkwater the day after the battle, he expressed his reluctance to the baronetage, and upon the other's asking him whether he would prefer to be a Knight of the Bath, he replied, "Yes; if my services have been of any value, let them be noticed in a way that the public may know them." To Elliot, who was about to return at once to England, he wrote, asking him to make known his wishes to the Admiralty. "If you can be instrumental in keeping back what I expect will happen, it will be an additional obligation. I conceive to take hereditary honours without a fortune to support the dignity, is to lower that honour it would be my pride to support in proper splendour. There are other honours which die with the possessor, and I should be proud to accept, if my efforts are thought worthy of the favour of my King."

Elliot started for England a few days afterwards, and reached London at a time when the whole country was ringing with the news of the victory. Arriving at such a propitious moment, there could have been for Nelson no better advocate than this man, placed high in political councils, and having to give to the Ministry a long account of his career in the Mediterranean, throughout the whole of which the two had been in intimate contact and constant correspondence. Himself an eyewitness, and filled with enthusiasm for Nelson's latest exploit, Elliot knew better than any one that it was no sporadic outburst, but only a signal manifestation of the intuitive sagacity, the flashing promptness, and the sustained energy, whose steady fires he had known to burn, without slackening of force or change of motive, through two years of close personal association in public action to a common end. The government thus learned more of him than can easily transpire under ordinary service conditions, or be shown even by an incident like that at St. Vincent; and Elliot's admiration, free from all bias of professional partiality or professional jealousy, doubtless was more useful to Nelson than any narrative of his own could have been. Even the royal favor was conciliated, despite the obstinate temper which yielded prejudices with difficulty. "I must rejoice," wrote Nelson to the Duke of Clarence, who had mentioned to him the King's approval, "in having gained the good opinion of my Sovereign, which I once was given to understand I had no likelihood of enjoying."[1] It was to the honor of the monarch that he was thus as pliant to admit merit in an officer as yet only rising to distinction, as he was firm at a later day to stamp with the marks of his displeasure the flagrant moral aberration of the then world-renowned admiral.

The coveted Knighthood of the Bath was accorded on the 17th of March, "in order," wrote the First Lord, " to

[1] See *ante*, page 89.

mark the Royal approbation of your successful and gallant exertions on several occasions during the course of the present war in the Mediterranean, and more particularly of your very distinguished conduct in the glorious and brilliant victory obtained over the fleet of Spain by His Majesty's fleet, on the 14th of February last." Nelson's delight was great and characteristic. Material rewards were not in his eyes the most real or the richest. " Chains and Medals," he wrote to his brother, " are what no fortune or connexion in England can obtain ; and I shall feel prouder of those than all the titles in the King's power to bestow." To his wife he said : " Though we can afford no more than a cottage — yet, with a contented mind, my chains, medals, and ribbons are all sufficient." To receive honor was second to no possession, except that of knowing he had deserved it.

On the evening of the Battle of St. Vincent, soon after the firing ceased, Nelson shifted his commodore's pendant to the " Irresistible," of seventy-four guns, the " Captain " being unmanageable from the damage done to her spars and rigging. Her hull also had been so battered, that he wrote a few days later she would never be able to receive him again, which proved to be true ; for although, after she had been patched up, he returned to her temporarily, a newly fitted ship, the " Theseus," seventy-four, was assigned to his flag, as soon as a reinforcement arrived from England.

After a vain effort to reach the Tagus against contrary winds, with disabled ships, Jervis decided to take his fleet into Lagos Bay, an open roadstead on the southern coast of Portugal, and there to refit sufficiently to make the passage to Lisbon. While lying at Lagos Nelson became a Rear-Admiral of the Blue, by a flag-promotion dated on the 20th of February, although his flag was not hoisted until the first of April, when the official notification of his advancement was received by him. He was then thirty-

eight and a half years of age. In this rank he remained
until after the Battle of the Nile was fought, but it mattered comparatively little where he stood on the list of
flag-officers, while Jervis commanded; that he was an
admiral at all made it possible to commit to him undertakings for which he was pre-eminently qualified, but
which could scarcely have been intrusted to a simple
captain by any stretching of service methods, always —
and not improperly — conservative.

On the 23d of February the fleet sailed again, and on
the 28th anchored in the Tagus. The same day Nelson
wrote to his wife that he was to go to sea on the 2d of
March, with three ships-of-the-line, to look out for the
Viceroy of Mexico, who was reported to be on his way
to Cadiz, also with three ships-of-the-line, laden with
treasure. "Two are first-rates," said he, "but the larger
the ships the better the mark, and who will not fight for
dollars?" Foul winds prevented his getting away until
the 5th. From that date until the 12th of April he remained cruising between Cape St. Vincent and the coast
of Africa, covering the approaches to Cadiz; frigates and
smaller vessels being spread out to the westward, to gain
timely notice of the approach of the specie ships, upon
whose safe arrival Spain depended both for her commercial
affairs and her naval preparations.

But while thus actively employed, and not insensible to
the charm of dollars, the immediate business on board was
not in itself so engrossing, nor to him so attractive, as to
obtain that exclusiveness of attention which he prided
himself upon giving to matters more military in character, and more critical in importance. "The Spaniards
threaten us they will come out, and take their revenge,"
he writes to an occasional correspondent. "The sooner
the better; but I will not believe it till I see it; and if
they do, what will the mines of Mexico and Peru signify,
compared with the honour I doubt not we shall gain by

fighting an angry Don? They will have thirty sail of
the line, we twenty or twenty-two; but fear we shall have
a peace before they are ready to come out. What a sad
thing that will be!" His mind reverts to the troops in
Elba, which had been left in a most exposed position, and
were now about to withdraw under the protection of some
frigates, passing through a thousand miles of hostile sea
open to the line-of-battle ships at Toulon. He is more concerned about them than about his possible prize-money in
the rich ships from Vera Cruz and Havana, whose danger
from his own squadron was agitating all Spain. " Respecting myself," he writes to Jervis, "I wish to stay at
sea, and I beg, if line-of-battle ships are left out,[1] either on
this side the Gut, or to the eastward of Gibraltar, that I
may be the man. This brings forward a subject which
I own is uppermost in my mind, — that of the safety of
our troops, should they embark from Elba. The French
have a number of ships at Toulon. They may get two,
three, or four ready, with a number of frigates, and make
a push for our convoy. I am ready, you know, to go eastward to cover them, even to Porto Ferrajo, or off Toulon,
or Minorca, as you may judge proper."

This exposed detachment continued to occupy his
thoughts. A month later, on the 11th of April, he again
writes: " I own, Sir, my feelings are alive for the safety of
our army from Elba. If the French get out two sail of
the line, which I am confident they may do, our troops are
lost, and what a triumph that would be to them! I know
you have many difficulties to contend with, but I am anxious that nothing should miscarry under your orders. If
you think a detachment can be spared, I am ready to go
and do my best for their protection." In both letters he
apologizes for this freedom of urgency with his superior:
"I have said much, but you have spoiled me by allowing
me to speak and write freely. I trust you will not imagine

[1] That is, at sea, the main fleet being still in the Tagus.

that my taking the great liberty of thus mentioning my thoughts, arises from any other motive than affection towards you."

Jervis had already joined him on the 1st of April, before the second letter was written. His hesitation about sending the detachment suggested by Nelson had arisen, not from doubt as to the danger of the troops, but from the imminent expectation of the Spanish fleet coming out. The British force was already too inferior, numerically, to risk any diminution, in view of such a contingency. Confronted with divergent objects, Jervis would not be drawn into the snare of dividing his force; but after reconnoitring the port, he was satisfied that the Spaniards could not sail before Nelson had time to fulfil the proposed mission, and on the 12th of April he gave him the necessary orders. The latter transferred his own squadron to the command of Sir James Saumarez, and started at once. He had now returned to the "Captain," which had doubtless come down with Jervis. "She is little better than a wreck," he wrote to a friend; but the cripples had to be kept to the front, pending the arrival of fresh ships. Besides her, he had the "Colossus," seventy-four, and "Leander," fifty, with a suitable number of smaller cruisers. Passing within gunshot of Port Mahon in Minorca, he heard from several passing vessels that a French squadron of four ships-of-the-line was at sea, as he had anticipated; and these, he afterwards learned, were seen off Minorca only twenty-two hours before he passed. Fortunately a fresh northwest gale had carried them to the southward, and on the 21st of April, sixty miles west of Corsica, he joined the convoy, which carried over three thousand soldiers. He reached Gibraltar with it in safety in the early days of May, without adventures of any kind. "I observed a man-of-war brig evidently looking at us; but my charge was too important to separate one ship in chase of her, especially as three frigates had parted company; for until this garrison is safe down, I do not think our business is well finished." Its arrival completed the evacuation of the Mediterranean.

At Gibraltar several days were spent, evidently crowded with administrative details concerning the coming and going of convoys, for there is here an almost total cessation of Nelson's usually copious letter-writing. An interesting and instructive incident is, however, made known to us by one of the three letters dated during these ten days. The Consul of the United States of America had to apply to him for the protection of twelve American merchant ships, then at Malaga, against the probable depredations of French privateers lying in that port, which, under the edicts of the government of the French Republic, with whom the United States was at peace, were expected to overhaul and capture them when they sailed. Nelson at once complied, ordering a British frigate to go to Malaga and escort the vessels to the Barbary coast, and even out of the Straits, if necessary. In doing this, he wrote courteously to the Consul: "I am sure of fulfilling the wishes of my Sovereign, and I hope of strengthening the harmony which at present so happily subsists between the two nations."

On the 24th of May Nelson rejoined the admiral off Cadiz, and on the 27th shifted his own flag into the "Theseus." The day before he left the fleet, April 11th, Jervis had decided to institute a strict commercial blockade of Cadiz, with the object of distressing Spanish trade, preventing the entrance of supplies, upon which depended the operations of Spain against Portugal, as well as her naval preparations, and so forcing the Spanish fleet out to fight, in order to rid itself of such embarrassment. Nelson, as commander of the inshore squadron, had then issued the necessary notices to neutrals in the port, and to this charge he now returned. Under Jervis's intelligent partiality, he, the junior flag-officer, was thus intrusted with a command, which in the conduct of details, great and small, and in emergencies, was practically independent. Jervis, knowing his man, was content to have it so, reserving of course to himself the decision of the broad outlines of military exertion. The inshore squadron was gradually increased till it numbered ten sail-of-the-line. The boats of the fleet, which had been rowing guard off the harbor's mouth under the general supervision of the two senior flag-officers, were ordered, shortly after Nelson's arrival, to report to him; and upon him, indeed, devolved pretty nearly all the active enterprises of the fleet. It was his practice to visit the line of boats every night in his barge, to see by personal inspection of these outposts that his instructions were fully observed. "Our inferiority," he wrote about this time, "is greater than before. I am barely out of shot of a Spanish rear-admiral. The Dons hope for peace, but must soon fight us, if the war goes on."

Another motive, perhaps even more imperative than the wish to force the Dons out, now compelled Jervis to seek by all means to increase the activity of his fleet, and to intrust the management of such activities to his most zealous and capable subordinate. These were the months of the great mutinies of the British Navy, in which the seamen of the Channel fleet, and of the North Sea fleet, at the Nore, had taken the ships out of the hands of their officers. The details of Jervis's management, which was distinguished as much by keen judgment and foresight as by iron-handed severity, that knew neither fear nor ruth when it struck, belong to his biography, not to Nelson's; but it is necessary to note the attitude of the latter, a man more sympathetic, and in common life gentler, than his stern superior. Always solicitous for everything that increased the well-being and happiness of his crew, — as indeed was eminently the case with Jervis also, — he did not withhold his candid sympathy from the grievances alleged by the Channel fleet;

grievances which, when temperately presented to the authorities, had been ignored. " I am entirely with the seamen in their first complaint. We are a neglected set, and, when peace comes, are shamefully treated ; but for the Nore scoundrels," passing on to those who had rebelled after substantial redress had been given, and had made unreasonable demands when the nation was. in deadly peril, " I should be happy to command a ship against them." Jervis's measures received full support from him, clear-headed as ever to see the essentials of a situation. The senior vice-admiral, for instance, went so far as to criticise the commander-in-chief for hanging a convicted mutineer on Sunday. " Had it been Christmas Day instead of Sunday," wrote Nelson, " I would have executed them. We know not what might have been hatched by a Sunday's grog: *now* your discipline is safe." His glorious reputation and his known kindly character, supported by that of his captain, made mutiny impossible under his flag. It had not been up a month on board the " Theseus," which was lately from the Channel and infected with the prevalent insubordination, when a paper was dropped on the quarter-deck, expressing the devotion of the ship's company to their commander, and pledging that the name of the " Theseus " should yet be as renowned as that of the " Captain."

The stringent blockade, and the fears for the specie ships, weighed heavily on the Spaniards, who were not as a nation hearty in support of a war into which they had been coerced by France. Their authorities were petitioned to compel the fleet to go out. Whatever the event, the British would at least have to retire for repairs ; while if the Lima and Havana ships — to look for which the Cadiz people every morning flocked to the walls, fearing they might be already in the enemy's hands — should be captured, the merchants of Spain would be ruined. Better lose ten ships-of-the-line, if need be, than this convoy.

With rumors of this sort daily reaching him, Nelson's faculties were in a constant state of pleasing tension. He was in his very element of joyous excitement and expectation. "We are in the advance day and night, prepared for battle; bulkheads down, ready to weigh, cut, or slip,[1] as the occasion may require. I have given out a line of battle — myself to lead; and you may rest assured that I will make a vigorous attack upon them, the moment their noses are outside the Diamond. Pray do not send me another ship," he implores; "if you send any more, they may believe we are prepared, and know of their intention." "If they come out," he writes later to a naval friend, when he had ten sail under him, "there will be no fighting beyond my squadron."

To increase yet further the pressure upon the Spanish fleet to come out, a bombardment was planned against the town and the shipping, the superintendence of which also was intrusted to the commander of the inshore squadron. Only one bomb-vessel was provided, so that very extensive results could scarcely have been anticipated, but Nelson saw, with evident glee, that the enemy's gunboats had taken advanced positions, and intended to have a hand in the night's work. "So much the better," wrote he to Jervis; "I wish to make it a warm night in Cadiz. If they venture from their walls, I shall give Johnny[2] his full scope for fighting. It will serve to talk of better than mischief." "It is good," he writes to another, "at these times to keep the devil out of their heads. I had rather see fifty shot by the enemy, than one hanged by us."

The bombardment, which was continued upon two successive nights, did little direct harm; but it led to a sharp hand-to-hand contest between the British and Spanish boats, in which Nelson personally bore a part, and upon which he

---

[1] Cut, or let go, the cables, — leaving the anchor in haste, instead of raising it from the bottom.

[2] The British seamen.

seems afterwards to have dwelt with even greater pride and self-satisfaction than upon the magnificent victories with which his name is associated. " It was during this period that perhaps my personal courage was more conspicuous than at any other part of my life." On the first night the Spaniards sent out a great number of mortar gunboats and armed launches. Upon these he directed a vigorous attack to be made, which resulted in their being driven back under the walls of Cadiz; the British, who pursued them, capturing two boats and a launch. In the affray, he says, " I was boarded in my barge with its common crew of ten men, coxswain, Captain Freemantle, and myself, by the commander of the gunboats; the Spanish barge rowed twenty-six oars, besides officers, — thirty men in the whole. This was a service hand-to-hand with swords, in which my coxswain, John Sykes, now no more, twice saved my life. Eighteen of the Spaniards being killed and several wounded, we succeeded in taking their commander." In his report he complimented this Spanish officer, Don Miguel Tyrason, upon his gallantry. Near a hundred Spaniards were made prisoners in this sharp skirmish.

Not even the insult of bombardment was sufficient to attain the designed end of forcing the enemy's fleet out to fight. The Spaniards confined themselves to a passive defence by their shore batteries, which proved indeed sufficient to protect the town and shipping, for on the second night they got the range of the bomb-vessel so accurately that the British were forced to withdraw her; but this did not relieve the vital pressure of the blockade, which could only be removed by the mobile naval force coming out and fighting. So far from doing this, the Spanish ships of war shifted their berth inside to get out of the range of bombs. Nelson cast longing eyes upon the smaller vessels which lay near the harbor's mouth, forming a barricade against boat attack, and threatening the offensive measures to which they rarely resorted. " At present the brigs lie too close to each other to hope for a dash at them, but soon I expect to find one off her guard, and then — " For the rest, his sanguine resolve to persist in annoyance until it becomes unbearable, and insures the desired object, finds vent in the words: "if Mazaredo will not come out, down comes Cadiz ; and not only Cadiz, but their fleet."

This close succession of varied and exciting active service, unbroken between the day of his leaving Lisbon, March 5th, and the date of the last bombardment, July 5th, had its usual effect upon his spirits. His correspondence is all animation, full of vitality and energy, betraying throughout the happiness of an existence absorbed in congenial work, at peace with itself, conscious of power adequate to the highest demands upon it, and rejoicing in the strong admiration and confidence felt and expressed towards him on all sides, especially by those whose esteem he most valued. He complains of his health, indeed, from time to time ; he cannot last another winter; he is suffering for the want of a few months' rest, which he must ask for in the coming October, and trusts that, "after four years and nine months' service, without one moment's repose for body or mind, credit will be given me that I do not sham."

Bodily suffering was his constant attendant, to which he always remained subject, but at this time it was powerless to depress the moral energies which, under less stimulating conditions, at times lost something of their elastic force. They never, indeed, failed to rise equal to imminent emergency, however obscured in hours of gloom, or perplexity, or mental conflict; but now, supported by the concurrence of every favoring influence, they carried him along in the full flow of prosperity and exhilaration. Thanking Earl Spencer, the First Lord of the Admiralty, for a complimentary letter, he says: "The unbounded praises Sir John Jervis has ever heaped, and continues to heap on me, are a noble reward for any services which an officer under his command could perform. Nor is your Lordship less profuse in them." To his wife he writes: "I assure you I never was better, and rich in the praises of every man, from the highest to the lowest in the fleet." "The imperious call of honour to serve my country, is the only thing that keeps me a moment from you, and a hope, that by staying a little longer, it may enable you to enjoy those little luxuries which you so highly merit." "My late affair here[1] will not, I believe, lower me in the opinion of the world. I have had flattery enough to make me vain, and success enough to make me confident."

[1] The night conflict with the Spanish launches.

CHAPTER IX.

July, 1797 – April, 1798. Age, 39.

TOO much success is not wholly desirable; an occasional beating is good for men — and nations. When Nelson wrote the words with which the preceding chapter ends, he was on the eve of a sharp reverse, met in attempting an enterprise that had occupied his thoughts for more than three months. While cruising for the Viceroy of Mexico, before Jervis left Lisbon with the fleet, he had considered the possibility of the enemy's treasure-ships, warned of their danger, taking refuge in the Canary Islands, which belong to Spain. Meditating upon the contingency, he had formed a project of seizing them there, and probably had already suggested the matter to Jervis, taking advantage of the freedom permitted him by the latter in advancing opinions. However that be, immediately before he started to meet the Elba convoy, the commander-in-chief asked for his plan, which he submitted in writing, after talking it over with Troubridge, his intimate friend, upon whose judgment Jervis also greatly relied. Regarded as a purely naval expedition, Nelson pointed out that it was subject to great uncertainties, because, the land being very high, the wind could not be depended on. It might blow in from the sea, but if so it would be by daylight, which would deprive the attack of the benefits of a surprise;

while at night the land wind was too fitful and unreliable to assure the ships reaching their anchorage before the enemy could discover them, and have time for adequate preparation against assault.

For these reasons, certainty of success would depend upon co-operation by the army, and for that Nelson suggested that the Elba troops, over three thousand strong, already in transports and on their way, would provide a force at once available and sufficient. Save a naval dash by Blake, more than a century before, Teneriffe had never been seriously attacked. Probably, therefore, the heights commanding the town of Santa Cruz had not been fortified, and could be easily seized by the detachment designated; besides which, the water supply was exposed to interruption by an outside enemy. If only General De Burgh could be persuaded, Nelson was sure of success, and offered himself to command the naval contingent. Failing the consent of De Burgh, whom he and Jervis both thought deficient in moral courage to undertake responsibility, could not the admiral get assistance from O'Hara, the governor of Gibraltar, who would have at his disposal one thousand to fifteen hundred men? More would be better, but still with that number success would be probable. "Soldiers," regretted Nelson characteristically, "have not the same boldness in undertaking a political measure that we have; we look to the benefit of our Country and risk our own fame [not life merely] every day to serve her: a soldier obeys his orders and no more." But he thought O'Hara an exception, and then — could not the substantial advantages move him? The public treasure of Spain that might be seized would be six or seven millions sterling. Think what that sum would be, "thrown into circulation in England!" where specie payments had just been suspended. It was nearly a year's value of the subsidies which Great Britain was lavishing on the general war. Whatever the merits of Nelson's

judgment upon the soldiers of his day, this avowal of
readiness, for the nation's sake, to risk fame — reputation
— which was in his eyes the dearest of possessions, should
not be overlooked. It was the best he had to give; to
hazard life was but a vulgar thing compared to it. His
career, both before and after, fully bore out the boast.

While on the return with the Elba troops, in a despatch
sent ahead of the convoy, he jogs Jervis's memory about
O'Hara, having doubtless ascertained that De Burgh, as
they expected, would not deviate from his orders to proceed to Lisbon. "I hope you will press General O'Hara
about Teneriffe. What a strike it would be!" In a copy
of this letter forwarded to the Admiralty, presumably by
Jervis for its general information, these words were
omitted. Possibly he had already sounded O'Hara, and
found him unwilling, for he was not optimistic; possibly
Jervis himself thought that the fitting conditions had not
yet obtained, and did not care to let the idea get abroad
before the hour for execution arrived. For the time, the
commander-in-chief preferred to keep his fleet concentrated
before Cadiz, and to try to worry the enemy out to battle;
for which object, indisputably the most advantageous to
be pursued, he also naturally wished to use his most active
and efficient subordinate. Both blockade and bombardment having failed to provoke the enemy to action, and
intelligence having been received that a treasure-ship from
Manila had put into Teneriffe, it was decided in July to
make the attempt, which had only been postponed — never
abandoned. In words written by Nelson on the 18th of
June, the conditions determining Jervis's course are
clearly indicated. "I wish these fellows would come out,
and then, with the good ships we have left [after a
general engagement], we might be a little at liberty to
make dashes. I hope your design about Teneriffe will
not get wind, by making inquiries at the present moment.
Whenever I see it," he added characteristically, "ten

hours shall decide its fate." Although unable to obtain
the troops upon which he considered certainty to depend,
he felt little fear for the result. Two hundred additional
marines must be given, and certain specified artillery and
ammunition in excess of what he had. With these, "I
have no doubt of doing the job as it ought to be, the
moment the ships come in sight." "Under General
Troubridge ashore, and myself afloat, I am confident of
success."

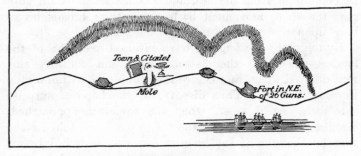

SKETCH OF SANTA CRUZ AND SURROUNDINGS.
(*From Nelson's Journal.*)

On the 14th of July he received his orders, which were
to seize Santa Cruz, the chief town, and hold the island to
ransom, unless all public treasure were surrendered to his
squadron, in which case the contribution on the inhabitants should not be levied. "God bless and prosper you,"
wrote Jervis, who, although he considered the enterprise
promising, was less sanguine than his junior. "I am
sure you will deserve success. To mortals is not given
the power of commanding it." On the 15th Nelson sailed,
having under his command three seventy-fours, a fifty-gun
ship, three frigates, and a cutter. Towards sundown of
the 20th the Peak of Teneriffe was sighted, distant fifty
or sixty miles. The following morning the landing-party,
a thousand strong, under the command of Captain

Troubridge, was transferred to the frigates. The intention was to keep the line-of-battle-ships out of sight, while the frigates, whose apparent force would carry no impression of menace, approached near enough to make a dash during the night. It was hoped that thus the assault might be so far a surprise as to enable the British to storm from the rear a fort on the heights, to the northeast of the town, and commanding it. Santa Cruz was then to be summoned. In the meantime the ships-of-the-line would be coming in from the sea, and upon arrival would support the shore movement by bringing their broadsides to bear upon the walls.

By midnight the frigates were within three miles of the landing-place; but there strong wind and contrary current delayed them, and before they could get within a mile the day dawned. Thus discovered, the hope of surprise was lost. At 6 A. M., when the squadron approached, Troubridge went on board the "Theseus" and told Nelson that he thought, if the heights over the fort, in its rear, could be seized, he could yet compel it to surrender. The landing-party was therefore put on shore at nine, but could not dispossess the enemy, who had recognized the importance of the position indicated by Troubridge, and had occupied it in force. The ships-of-the-line endeavored to get within range of the fort, to batter it, but could not come nearer than three miles. They were unable even to reach anchoring-ground, and, as it was blowing very fresh, they struck their topgallantmasts and stood off and on. At night Troubridge re-embarked his men on board the frigates, which had remained where they were. The following morning, July 23d, Nelson abandoned the attempt upon the fort, recalling the frigates; and, as the wind did not yet serve to approach the shore, he continued under sail during that day and the next. The members of the landing-party rejoined their proper ships.

Troubridge's failure to act at once upon his own judgment, and seize the heights above the fort, instead of waiting until he could communicate with the admiral, whereby were lost more than three invaluable hours, excites surprise, in view of the extremely high value set upon him as an officer by St. Vincent and Nelson; and is the more singular because the latter, in certain "Recommendations," dated July 17, had indicated the heights, as well as the fort, among the objects to be secured. It is, of course, possible that these Recommendations were not given out; but even so, the formal orders issued gave ample discretion. This hesitation was wholly contrary to Nelson's own readiness to assume responsibility, and probably accounts for his subsequent remark, in a private letter, that had he himself been present this first attempt would not have failed. Occurring in an officer of Troubridge's high standing, and contrasted with Nelson's action at St. Vincent, as well as on many other occasions, the incident serves to bring out forcibly the characteristic eminence of the latter, — the distinction between a really great captain and the best type of a simply accomplished and gallant officer. It may safely be said that had Nelson been in the frigates that morning, and thought as Troubridge thought, he would either have had the heights without waiting for orders, or, to use his own words on a former occasion, would have "been in a confounded scrape."

His first plan having miscarried, Nelson was nevertheless unwilling to forsake the enterprise wholly, without attempting a direct assault upon the town itself. Meantime the enemy was not idle, but employed the delay caused by the wind to collect a greater force, and to develop further the preparations to repel attack. At half-past five in the evening of July 24 the squadron reached an anchorage two or three miles north of Santa Cruz, and all boats were ordered prepared for a night expedition. Captain Freemantle, of the frigate "Seahorse," had with him his

wife, whom he had lately married; and with them Nelson,
who intended to lead the attack in person, supped that
evening. He was conscious of the imminent danger to
which he was about to expose himself and his followers; it
is indeed scarcely possible that he could, in undertaking
the adventure, have expected to succeed, except through
some happy accident skilfully improved, — the deserved
good fortune which had so often attended him. It was
not so much the hope of victory that moved him, as the
feeling that to retreat baffled, without a further effort,
would be worse than defeat. This in fact was the reason
which he afterwards gave. "Although I felt the second
attack a forlorn hope, yet the honour of our Country called
for the attack, and that I should command it. I never
expected to return." "Your partiality will give me
credit," he wrote to Jervis, "that all has hitherto been
done which was possible, but without effect: this night I,
humble as I am, command the whole, destined to land
under the batteries of the town, and to-morrow my head
will probably be crowned with either laurel or cypress. I
have only to recommend Josiah Nisbet [his stepson] to you
and my Country." He urged Nisbet not to go in the
boats, on the ground that his mother should not run the
risk of losing both husband and son in one night, and that
in the absence of Captain Miller, who was going in charge
of a division of men, Nisbet's duties with the ship
demanded his remaining. Nisbet steadily refused, and his
presence was the immediate means of saving the admiral's
life.

At eleven P. M. the boats shoved off, carrying a thousand
men. The orders were for all to land at the mole, the
intention being to storm it, and the batteries covering it, in
a body, and to fight their way, thus massed, to the great
square, which was designated as the place for rallying. A
considerable sea was running and the night dark, so that
the Spaniards did not discover the assailants till they were

within half gunshot. The bells of the place then began to ring, and a heavy fire opened, amid which the British pushed vigorously forward. Many, however, missed the mole. Nelson's own boat reached it with four or five besides, and the parties from these succeeded in carrying the mole itself, advancing to its head and spiking the guns; but there they were met with such a sustained fire of musketry and grape from the citadel and the neighboring houses, that they could get no farther. Many were killed and wounded, and the rest after a struggle had to retreat.

Troubridge, with a number of others who missed the mole, landed amid a heavy surf, which stove the boats on a rocky beach and tumbled the men into the water, whereby most of the ammunition was spoiled. In the midst of the turmoil the cutter "Fox" was struck by a shot under water, and went down, taking with her her commander and ninety-seven men. Although the scaling-ladders had all been lost in the general upset, those who here got on shore succeeded in climbing over the walls, and forced their way to the place of rendezvous in the great square. There Troubridge, having assembled between three and four hundred men, held his ground, awaiting Nelson and the party that might have entered by way of the mole.

It was in vain. Nelson had been struck by a grapeshot in the right elbow, as, with sword drawn, he was stepping from the boat to the landing. Bleeding profusely and faint, but clinging with his left hand to the sword, which had belonged to his uncle Maurice Suckling, he fell back into the arms of Josiah Nisbet, who managed with considerable presence of mind to bind up the shattered limb and stop the flowing of the blood. A few men being got together, the boat pushed off to take the admiral back to the ship. At this moment occurred the sinking of the "Fox;" upon which much delay ensued, because Nelson refused to abandon the men struggling in the water, and insisted upon looking personally to their being saved. At last the "Seahorse" was reached; but here again he would not go on board, saying that he would not have Mrs. Freemantle alarmed by seeing him in such a condition and without any news of her husband, who had accompanied the landing. When he got to the "Theseus," he declined assistance to climb to the deck. "At two in the morning," wrote Hoste, one of her midshipmen, who had been with him continuously since the "Agamemnon" left England, "Admiral Nelson returned on board, being dreadfully wounded in the right arm. I leave you to judge of my situation, when I beheld our boat approach with him, who I may say has been a second father to me, his right arm dangling by his side, while with the other he helped himself to jump up the ship's side, and with a spirit that astonished every one, told the surgeon to get his instruments ready, for he knew he must lose his arm, and that the sooner it was off the better."

At daylight Troubridge, who had collected some ammunition from Spanish prisoners, started from the square to try what could be done without ladders against the citadel; but, finding every approach blocked by overwhelming force, he had to retreat. Having neither powder nor provisions, and no boats with which to return to the ship, he sent a flag of truce to the governor to say that he was prepared to burn the place down with means at his disposal, but, being most reluctant to do so, was willing to treat, upon condition of the whole party being permitted to return to the ships, free and with their arms. One scarcely knows which most to admire, Troubridge's cool audacity in making such a demand, or the chivalrous readiness with which these honorable terms were at once granted to a man whose gallant bearing compelled the esteem of his enemies. Don Juan Gutierrez had repulsed the various attempts with such steadiness and watchfulness, had managed his business so well, that he could

Sir Thomas Troubridge

afford to be liberal. He agreed that Troubridge's men
should withdraw, carrying off with them all British equip-
ments, even to such boats as had been taken by the
Spaniards, but could still swim. On the other hand, it
was stipulated that no further attempt upon the town
should be made by Nelson's squadron. Prisoners on both
sides were to be given up. This arrangement having been
concluded, the governor directed that the British wounded
should be at once received into the hospitals, while the
rest of the party, with their colors flying, marched to the
mole, and there embarked.

Troubridge dwelt with evident pride upon his part in
this night's work, — a pride that was shared then by his
superiors, and will be justified in the eyes of military men
now. "The Spanish officers assure me they expected us,
and were perfectly prepared with all the batteries, and the
number of men I have before mentioned [8,000], under
arms: with the great disadvantage of a rocky coast, high
surf, and in the face of forty pieces of cannon, though we
were not successful, will show what an Englishman is
equal to." His conduct affords for all time an example
of superb courage in the face of extraordinary and unexpected difficulty and danger, and especially of single-
minded energy in carrying through one's own share of an
enterprise, without misplaced concern about consequences,
or worry as to whether the other parties were prospering
or not. Had Nelson reached the square he would have
found Troubridge there, and that was the one thing about
which the latter needed to care. Nelson's own words
recur to mind: "I have not a thought on any subject
separated from the immediate object of my command," — a
maxim eminently suited to the field and to the subordinate, though not necessarily so to the council chamber or
to the general officer. Troubridge that night proved himself invaluable as a subordinate, though the conduct of the
previous attempt seems to show a lack of that capacity to

seize a favorable moment, although in the presence of a superior, of which Nelson himself had given so brilliant an example at Cape St. Vincent.

The squadron remained off Teneriffe for three days after the assault, intercourse with the shore for the purpose of obtaining fresh provisions being permitted by the governor, between whom and the admiral were exchanged complimentary letters and presents of courtesy. On the 27th Nelson sailed for Cadiz, and on the 16th of August rejoined the commander-in-chief, now become Earl St. Vincent. The latter received him with generous sympathy and appreciation, which leave little doubt as to what his verdict would have been, had the gallant initiative taken by his junior at St. Vincent ended in disaster, instead of in brilliant success. Nelson's letters, sent ahead of the squadron by a frigate, had shown the despondency produced by suffering and failure, which had reversed so sharply the good fortune upon which he had begun to pride himself. "I am become a burthen to my friends and useless to my Country. When I leave your command, I become dead to the world; I go hence and am no more seen." "Mortals cannot command success," replied St. Vincent. "You and your companions have certainly deserved it, by the greatest degree of heroism and perseverance that ever was exhibited." Nelson had asked for his stepson's promotion, implying that he himself would not hereafter be in a position of influence to help the boy — for he was little more. "He is under obligations to me, but he repaid me by bringing me from the mole of Santa Cruz." "He saved my life," he said more than once afterwards. St. Vincent immediately made him a commander into the vacancy caused by the death of Captain Bowen, who had fallen in the assault. "Pretty quick promotion," wrote his messmate Hoste, who probably knew, from close association, that Nisbet had not the promising qualities with which he was then credited by his stepfather, from whom in later years he became wholly estranged.

On the 20th Nelson received formal leave to return to England in the "Seahorse," and on the 3d of September his flag was hauled down at Spithead. On the way home he suffered much. After amputation the ligature had been awkwardly applied to the humeral artery. As he would not allow the surgeon to examine the stump during the passage, this was not then discovered, but the intense spasms of pain kept him irritable and depressed. It is likely, too, that his discouragement was increased by brooding over the failure of his enterprise; believing, as he did, that had he been with the landing-party, the first attempt would have succeeded. He could scarcely fail now to see that, although it was strictly in accordance with service methods for the senior to remain with the ships, the decisive point in the plan, as first formed, was the seizure of the heights, and that there, consequently, was the true place for the one in chief command. Any captain, Troubridge especially, could have placed the ships as well as Nelson. It is self-accusation, and not fault-finding merely, that breathes in the words: "Had I been with the first party, I have reason to believe complete success would have crowned our efforts. *My pride suffered.*"

Whatever his mental distress, however, he always, from the time of receiving the wound, wrote to his wife with careful cheerfulness. "As to my health, it never was better; and now I hope soon to return to you; and my Country, I trust, will not allow me any longer to linger in want of that pecuniary assistance which I have been fighting the whole war to preserve to her. But I shall not be surprised to be neglected and forgot, as probably I shall no longer be considered as useful. However, I shall feel rich if I continue to enjoy your affection. I am fortunate in having a good surgeon on board; in short,

I am much more recovered than I could have expected. I beg neither you or my father will think much of this mishap: my mind has long been made up to such an event."

Immediately after quitting the "Seahorse" he joined his wife and father at Bath. For a time the wound seemed to be progressing favorably, but the unlucky complication of the ligature threw him back. "Much pain and some fever," he wrote to a friend soon after his arrival; and while he kept up fairly before his wife, who spoke of his spirits as very good, he confessed to St. Vincent, on the 18th of September, that he was then not the least better than when he left the fleet. "I have suffered great misery." This letter was dated in London, whither he had gone a few days before to be invested with the Order of the Bath, which was formally done by George III. in person on the 27th of September. He was graciously received by the King, who conversed with him after the ceremony, and by his manner throughout made a lasting impression upon the mind of Nelson, whose loyalty was intense. The Order of the Bath remained the most highly prized among his many decorations. At the same time was awarded him a pension of £1,000 a year.

He remained in London till near Christmas. Sir Gilbert Elliot, the late Viceroy of Corsica, who about this time became Lord Minto, saw him not long after his arrival there, as did also Colonel Drinkwater. Elliot found him looking better and fresher than he ever remembered him, although the continued pain prevented sleep, except by use of opium. He was already impatient to go to sea again, and chafed under the delay of healing, concerning the duration of which the surgeons could give him no assurance. The ligature must be left to slough away, for it was two inches up the wound, and if, in attempting to cut it, the artery should be cut, another amputation would be necessary higher up, which would not be easy, for the

Lady Nelson

stump was already very short. There was consequently
nothing for it but endurance. To his suffering at this
time an accomplished surgeon, who sailed with him shortly
before Trafalgar, attributed a neuralgic predisposition under which he then labored, and which produced serious
effects upon his general health.

A singular exhibition of his characteristic animation and
temperament was elicited by Drinkwater's visit. The
colonel saw him shortly before the naval battle of
Camperdown, fought on the 11th of October. "One of
the first questions which Nelson put to me was whether I
had been at the Admiralty. I told him there was a
rumour that the British fleet had been seen engaged with
that of Holland. He started up in his peculiar energetic
manner, notwithstanding Lady Nelson's attempts to quiet
him, and stretching out his unwounded arm, — ' Drinkwater,' said he, ' I would give this other arm to be with
Duncan [1] at this moment;' so unconquerable was the spirit
of the man, and so intense his eagerness to give every
instant of his life to the service."

Until the 4th of December his agony continued. On
that day the ligature came away, giving instant and entire
relief. In a letter to a friend, apologizing for delay in
replying, he said: "Truly, till last Monday, I have suffered
so much, I hope for your forgiveness. I am now perfectly
recovered, and on the eve of being employed." On Friday,
the 8th, he wrote to Captain Berry, who had led the
boarders to the "San Nicolas" at Cape St. Vincent, and
was designated to command the ship in which the admiral's
flag should next be hoisted, saying that he was well; and
the same day, with that profound recognition of a personal
Providence which was with him as instinctive as his
courage, he sent to a London clergyman the following request: "An officer desires to return thanks to Almighty

---

[1] The British admiral in command of the fleet which fought at Camperdown.

God for his perfect recovery from a severe wound, and also for the many mercies bestowed upon him. (For next Sunday.)"

As the close attention of the skilled surgeons in whose hands he had been was now no longer needed, he returned to Bath to await the time when his flagship should be completely equipped. St. Vincent had asked that the "Foudroyant," of eighty guns, should be prepared for him; but, after his sudden recovery, as she was not yet ready, there was substituted for her the "Vanguard," seventy-four, which was commissioned by Berry at Chatham on the 19th of December. In March she had reached Portsmouth, and Nelson then went up to London, where he attended a levee on the 14th of the month and took leave of the King. On the 29th his flag was hoisted, and on the 10th of April, after a week's detention at St. Helen's by head winds, he sailed for Lisbon. There he remained for four days, and on the 30th of the month, off Cadiz, rejoined St. Vincent, by whom he was received with open arms. The veteran seaman, stern and resolved as was his bearing in the face of danger, was unhopeful about the results of the war, which from the first he had not favored, and for whose ending he was eager. Now, at sixty-four, his health was failing, and the difficulties and dangers of the British cause in the Mediterranean weighed upon him, with a discouragement very alien from the sanguine joy with which his ardent junior looked forward to coming battles. His request to be relieved from command, on the score of ill health, was already on file at the Admiralty. "I do assure your Lordship," he wrote to Earl Spencer, "that the arrival of Admiral Nelson has given me new life; you could not have gratified me more than in sending him; his presence in the Mediterranean is so very essential, that I mean to put the "Orion" and "Alexander" under his command, with the addition of three or four frigates, and send him away, to endeavour to ascertain the real object of the preparations making by the French." These preparations for a maritime expedition were being made at Toulon and the neighboring ports, on a scale which justly aroused the anxiety of the British Cabinet, as no certain information about their object had been obtained.

Nelson's departure from England on this occasion closes the first of the two periods into which his career naturally divides. From his youth until now, wherever situated, the development has been consecutive and homogeneous, external influences and internal characteristics have worked harmoniously together, nature and ambition have responded gladly to opportunity, and the course upon which they have combined to urge him has conformed to his inherited and acquired standards of right and wrong. Doubt, uncertainty, inward friction, double motives, have been unknown to him; he has moved freely in accordance with the laws of his being, and, despite the anxieties of his profession and the frailty of his health, there is no mistaking the tone of happiness and contentment which sounds without a jarring note throughout his correspondence. A change was now at hand. As the sails of the "Vanguard" dip below the horizon of England, a brief interlude begins, and when the curtain rises again, the scene is shifted, — surroundings have changed. We see again the same man, but standing at the opening of a new career, whose greatness exceeds by far even the high anticipations that had been formed for him. Before leaving England he is a man of distinction only; prominent, possibly, among the many distinguished men of his own profession, but the steady upward course has as yet been gradual, the shining of the light, if it has latterly shot forth flashes suggestive of hidden fires, is still characterized by sustained growth in intensity rather than by rapid increase. No present sign so far foretells the sudden ascent to fame, the burst of meridian splendor with which the sun of his renown was soon to rise upon men's eyes, and in which it ran its course to the cloudless finish of his day.

Not that there is in that course — in its achievements — any disproportion with the previous promise. The magnitude of the development we are about to witness is due, not to a change in him, but to the increased greatness of the opportunities. A man of like record in the past, but less gifted, might, it is true, have failed to fill the new sphere which the future was to present. Nelson proved fully equal to it, because he possessed genius for war, intellectual faculties, which, though not unsuspected, had not hitherto been allowed scope for their full exercise. Before him was now about to open a field of possibilities hitherto unexampled in naval warfare; and for the appreciation of them was needed just those perceptions, intuitive in origin, yet resting firmly on well-ordered rational processes, which, on the intellectual side, distinguished him above all other British seamen. He had already, in casual comment upon the military conditions surrounding the former Mediterranean campaigns, given indications of these perceptions, which it has been the aim of previous chapters to elicit from his correspondence, and to marshal in such order as may illustrate his mental characteristics. But, for success in war, the indispensable complement of intellectual grasp and insight is a moral power, which enables a man to trust the inner light, — to have faith, — a power which dominates hesitation, and sustains action, in the most tremendous emergencies, and which, from the formidable character of the difficulties it is called to confront, is in no men so conspicuously prominent as in those who are entitled to rank among great captains. The two elements — mental and moral power — are often found separately, rarely in due combination. In Nelson they met, and their coincidence with the exceptional opportunities afforded him constituted his good fortune and his greatness.

The intellectual endowment of genius was Nelson's from the first; but from the circumstances of his life it was denied the privilege of early manifestation, such as was permitted to Napoleon. It is, consequently, not so much this as the constant exhibition of moral power, force of character, which gives continuity to his professional career, and brings the successive stages of his advance, in achievement and reputation, from first to last, into the close relation of steady development, subject to no variation save that of healthy and vigorous growth, till he stood unique — above all competition. This it was — not, doubtless, to the exclusion of that reputation for having a head, upon which he justly prided himself — which had already fixed the eyes of his superiors upon him as the one officer, not yet indeed fully tested, most likely to cope with the difficulties of any emergency. In the display of this, in its many self-revelations, — in concentration of purpose, untiring energy, fearlessness of responsibility, judgment sound and instant, boundless audacity, promptness, intrepidity, and endurance beyond all proof, — the restricted field of Corsica and the Riviera, the subordinate position at Cape St. Vincent, the failure of Teneriffe, had in their measure been as fruitful as the Nile was soon to be, and fell naught behind the bloody harvests of Copenhagen and Trafalgar. Men have been disposed, therefore, to reckon this moral energy — call it courage, dash, resolution, what you will — as Nelson's one and only great quality. It was the greatest, as it is in all successful men of action; but to ignore that this mighty motive force was guided by singularly clear and accurate perceptions, upon which also it consciously rested with a firmness of faith that constituted much of its power, is to rob him of a great part of his due renown.

But it was not only in the greatness of the opportunities offered to Nelson that external conditions now changed. The glory of the hero brought a temptation which wrecked the happiness of the man. The loss of serenity, the dark evidences of inward conflict, of yielding against conviction, of consequent dissatisfaction with self and gradual deterioration, make between his past and future a break as clear, and far sharper than, the startling increase of radiancy that attends the Battle of the Nile, and thenceforth shines with undiminished intensity to the end. The lustre of his well-deserved and world-wide renown, the consistency and ever-rising merit of his professional conduct, contrast painfully with the shadows of reprobation, the swerving, and the declension, which begin to attend a life heretofore conformed, in the general, to healthy normal standards of right and wrong, but now allowed to violate, not merely ideal Christian rectitude, but the simple, natural dictates of upright dealing between man and man. It had been the proud boast of early years: "There is no action in my whole life but what is honourable." The attainment of glory exceeding even his own great aspirations coïncides with dereliction from the plain rules of honor between friends, and with public humiliation to his wife, which he allowed himself to inflict, notwithstanding that he admitted her claims to his deferential consideration to be unbroken. In this contrast, of the exaltation of the hero and the patriot with the degradation of the man, lie the tragedy and the misery of Nelson's story. And this, too, was incurred on behalf of a woman whose reputation and conduct were such that no shred of dignity could attach to an infatuation as doting as it was blamable. The pitiful inadequacy of the temptation to the ruin it caused invests with a kind of prophecy the words he had written to his betrothed in the heyday of courtship: "These I trust will ever be my sentiments; if they are not, I do verily believe it will be my *folly* that occasions it."

The inward struggle, though severe, was short and decisive. Once determined on his course, he choked down

scruples and hesitations, and cast them from him with the
same single-minded resolution that distinguished his public
acts. "Fixed as fate," were the remorseless words with
which he characterized his firm' purpose to trample conscience under foot, and to reject his wife in favor of his
mistress. But although ease may be obtained by silencing
self-reproach, safety scarcely can. One cannot get the
salt out of his life, and not be the worse for it. Much
that made Nelson so lovable remained to the end; but into
his heart, as betrayed by his correspondence, and into his
life, from the occasional glimpses afforded by letters or
journals of associates, there thenceforth entered much that
is unlovely, and which to no appreciable extent was seen
before. The simple *bonhomie*, the absence of conventional
reticence, the superficial lack of polish, noted by his early
biographers, and which he had had no opportunity to
acquire, the childlike vanity that transpires so innocently
in his confidential home letters, and was only the weak
side of his noble longing for heroic action, degenerated
rapidly into loss of dignity of life, into an unseemly susceptibility to extravagant adulation, as he succumbed to
surroundings, the corruptness of which none at first
realized more clearly, and where one woman was the sole
detaining fascination. And withal, as the poison worked,
discontent with self bred discontent with others, and with
his own conditions. Petulance and querulousness too
often supplanted the mental elasticity, which had counted
for naught the roughnesses on the road to fame. The
mind not worthily occupied, and therefore ill at ease,
became embittered, prone to censure and to resent, sus-
picious at times and harsh in judgment, gradually tending
towards alienation, not from his wife only, but from his
best and earliest friends.

During the short stay of seven months in England,
which ended with the sailing of the "Vanguard," the
record of his correspondence is necessarily very imperfect,

both from the loss of his arm, and from the fact of his being with his family. Such indications as there are point to unbroken relations of tenderness with his wife. "I found my domestic happiness perfect," he wrote to Lord St. Vincent, shortly after his arrival home; and some months later, in a letter from Bath to a friend, he says jestingly: "Tell —— that I possess his place in Mr. Palmer's box; but he did not tell me all its charms, that generally some of the handsomest ladies in Bath are partakers in the box, and was I a bachelor I would not answer for being tempted; but as I am possessed of everything which is valuable in a wife, I have no occasion to think beyond a pretty face." Lady Nelson attended personally to the dressing of his arm; she accompanied him in his journeys between Bath and London, and they separated only when he left town to hoist his flag at Portsmouth. The letters of Lady Saumarez, the wife of one of his brother captains then serving with Lord St. Vincent, mention frequent meetings with the two together in the streets of Bath; and upon the 1st of May, the day before leaving the fleet off Cadiz for the Mediterranean, on the expedition which was to result in the Nile, and all the consequences so fatal to the happiness of both, he concludes his letter, "with every kind wish that a fond heart can frame, believe me, as ever, your most affectionate husband."

On the 2d of May the "Vanguard" quitted the fleet for Gibraltar, where she arrived on the 4th. On the 7th Nelson issued orders to Sir James Saumarez, commanding the "Orion," and to Captain Alexander Ball, commanding the "Alexander," both seventy-fours, to place themselves under his command; and the following day the "Vanguard" sailed, in company with these ships and five smaller vessels, to begin the memorable campaign, of which the Battle of the Nile was the most conspicuous incident.

CHAPTER X.

THE CAMPAIGN AND BATTLE OF THE NILE.

MAY – SEPTEMBER, 1798. AGE, 39.

BETWEEN the time that Nelson was wounded at Teneriffe, July 24, 1797, and his return to active service in April, 1798, important and ominous changes had been occurring in the political conditions of Europe. These must be taken briefly into account, because the greatness of the issues thence arising, as understood by the British Government, measures the importance in its eyes of the enterprise which it was about to intrust, by deliberate selection, to one of the youngest flag-officers upon the list. The fact of the choice shows the estimation to which Nelson had already attained in the eyes of the Admiralty.

In July, 1797, Great Britain alone was at war with France, and so continued for over a year longer. Portugal, though nominally an ally, contributed to the common cause nothing but the use of the Tagus by the British Navy. Austria, it is true, had not yet finally made peace with France, but preliminaries had been signed in April, and the definitive treaty of Campo Formio was concluded in October. By it Belgium became incorporated in the territory of France, to which was conceded also the frontier of the Rhine. The base of her power was thus advanced to the river, over which the possession of the fortified city of Mayence gave her an easy passage, constituting a permanent threat of invasion to Germany. Venice, as a separate power, disappeared. Part of her former do-

mains upon the mainland, with the city itself, went to
Austria, but part was taken to constitute the Cisalpine
Republic, — a new state in Northern Italy, nominally independent, but really under the control of France, to whom
it owed its existence. Corfu, and the neighboring islands
at the mouth of the Adriatic, till then belonging to Venice,
were transferred to France. The choice of these distant
and isolated maritime positions, coupled with the retention
of a large army in the valley of the Po, showed, if any
evidence were needed, a determination to assure control
over the Italian peninsula and the Mediterranean Sea.

The formal acquisitions by treaty, even, did not measure the full menace of the conditions. The Revolutionary
ferment, which had partially subsided, received fresh im-
petus from the victories of Bonaparte and the cessation of
Continental war; and the diplomacy of France continued
as active and as aggressive as the movement of her armies
had previously been. By constant interference, overt and
secret, not always stopping short of violence, French influence and French ideas were propagated among the weaker
adjoining states. Holland, Switzerland, and the Italian
Republics became outposts of France, occupied by French
troops, and upon them were forced governments conformed
to the existing French pattern. In short, the aggrandize-
ment of France, not merely in moral influence but in physical control, was being pushed forward as decisively in
peace as in war, and by means which threatened the political equilibrium of Europe. But, while all states were
threatened, Great Britain remained the one chief enemy
against which ultimately the efforts of France must be,
and were, concentrated. "Either our government must
destroy the English monarchy," wrote Bonaparte at this
time, "or must expect itself to be destroyed by the corruption and intrigue of those active islanders." The British ministry on its part also realized that the sea-power of
their country was the one force from which, because so

Nelson

manifold in its activities, and so readily exerted in many
quarters by reason of its mobility, France had most reason
to fear the arrest of its revolutionary advance and the
renewal of the Continental war. It was, therefore, the
one opponent against which the efforts of the French must
necessarily be directed. For the same reason it was the
one centre around whose action, wisely guided, the elements of discontent, already stirring, might gather, upon
the occurrence of a favorable moment, and constitute a
body of resistance capable of stopping aggressions which
threatened the general well-being.

When the British Government found that the overtures
for peace which it had made in the summer of 1797 could
have no result, except on terms too humiliating to be considered, it at once turned its attention to the question of
waging a distinctively offensive war, for effect in which
co-operation was needed. The North of Europe was hopeless. Prussia persisted in the policy of isolation, adopted
in 1795 by herself and a number of the northern German
states. Russia was quietly hostile to France, but the interference contemplated by the Empress Catherine had been
averted by her death in 1796, and her successor, Paul, had
shown no intention of undertaking it. There remained,
therefore, the Mediterranean. In Italy, France stood face
to face with Austria and Naples, and both these were
dissatisfied with the action taken by her in the Peninsula
itself and in Switzerland, besides sharing the apprehension
of most other governments from the disquiet attending her
political course. An advance into the Mediterranean was
therefore resolved by the British Cabinet.

This purpose disconcerted St. Vincent, who, besides his
aversion from the war in general, was distinguished rather
by tenacity and resolution in meeting difficulties and dangers, when forced upon him, than by the sanguine and
enterprising initiative in offensive measures which characterized Nelson. Writing to the latter on the 8th of Janu-

ary, 1798, he says: " I am much at a loss to reconcile the plans in contemplation to augment this fleet and extend its operations, with the peace which Portugal seems determined to make with France, upon any terms the latter may please to impose; because Gibraltar is an unsafe depot for either stores or provisions, which the Spaniards have always in their power to destroy, and the French keep such an army in Italy, that Tuscany and Naples would fall a sacrifice to any the smallest assistance rendered to our fleet." In other words, the old question of supplies still dominated the situation, in the apprehension of this experienced officer. Yet, in view of the serious condition of things, and the probable defection of Portugal under the threats of France and Spain, to which he alludes, it seems probable that the ministry were better advised, in their determination to abandon a passive defence against an enemy unrelentingly bent upon their destruction. As Nelson said of a contingency not more serious: " Desperate affairs require desperate remedies."

However determined the British Government might be to act in the Mediterranean, some temporary perplexity must at first have been felt as to where to strike, until a movement of the enemy solved the doubt. In the early months of 1798 the Directory decided upon the Egyptian expedition under General Bonaparte, and, although its destination was guarded with admirable secrecy until long after the armament sailed, the fact necessarily transpired that preparations were being made on a most extensive scale for a maritime enterprise. The news soon reached England, as it did also Jervis at his station off Cadiz. Troops and transports were assembling in large numbers at the southern ports of France, in Genoa, Civita Vecchia, and Corsica, while a fleet of at least a dozen ships-of-the-line was fitting out at Toulon. Various surmises were afloat as to the object, but all at this time were wide of the mark.

On the 29th of April, less than three weeks after Nelson left England, but before he joined the fleet, the Cabinet issued orders to St. Vincent to take such measures as he deemed necessary to thwart the projects of the Toulon squadron. It was left to his judgment whether to go in person with his whole fleet, or to send a detachment of not less than nine or ten ships-of-the-line under a competent flag-officer. If possible, the government wished him to maintain the blockade of Cadiz as it had been established since the Battle of St. Vincent; but everything was to yield to the necessity of checking the sailing of the Toulon expedition, or of defeating it, if it had already started. A speedy reinforcement was promised, to supply the places of the ships that might be detached.

Accompanying the public letter was a private one from the First Lord of the Admiralty, reflecting the views and anxieties of the Government. "The circumstances in which we now find ourselves oblige us to take a measure of a more decided and hazardous complexion than we should otherwise have thought ourselves justified in taking; but when you are apprized that the appearance of a British squadron in the Mediterranean is a condition on which the fate of Europe may at this moment be stated to depend, you will not be surprised that we are disposed to strain every nerve, and incur considerable hazard in effecting it." This impressive, almost solemn, statement, of the weighty and anxious character of the intended step, emphasizes the significance of the choice, which the First Lord indicates as that of the Government, of the officer upon whom such a charge is to devolve. "If you determine to send a detachment into the Mediterranean [instead of going in person with the fleet], I think it almost unnecessary to suggest to you the propriety of putting it under the command of Sir H. Nelson, whose acquaintance with that part of the world, as well as his activity and disposition, seem to qualify him in a peculiar manner for that service."

In concluding his letter, Earl Spencer summed up the reasons of the Government, and his own sense of the great risk attending the undertaking, for the conduct of which he designated Nelson. " I am as strongly impressed, as I have no doubt your Lordship will be, with the hazardous nature of the measure which we now have in contemplation; but I cannot at the same time help feeling how much depends upon its success, and how absolutely necessary it is at this time to run some risk, in order, if possible, to bring about a new system of affairs in Europe, which shall save us all from being overrun by the exorbitant power of France. In this view of the subject, it is impossible not to perceive how much depends on the exertions of the great Continental powers; and, without entering further into what relates more particularly to them, I can venture to assure you that no good will be obtained from them if some such measure as that now in contemplation is not immediately adopted. On the other hand, if, by our appearance in the Mediterranean, we can encourage Austria to come forward again, it is in the highest degree probable that the other powers will seize the opportunity of acting at the same time, and such a general concert be established as shall soon bring this great contest to a termination, on grounds less unfavorable by many degrees to the parties concerned than appeared likely a short time since." It may be added here, by way of comment, that the ups and downs of Nelson's pursuit, the brilliant victory at the Nile, and the important consequences flowing from it, not only fully justified this forecast, but illustrated aptly that in war, when a line of action has been rightly chosen, the following it up despite great risks, and with resolute perseverance through many disappointments, will more often than not give great success, — a result which may probably be attributed to the moral force which necessarily underlies determined daring and sustained energy.

As has appeared, the Government's recommendation had

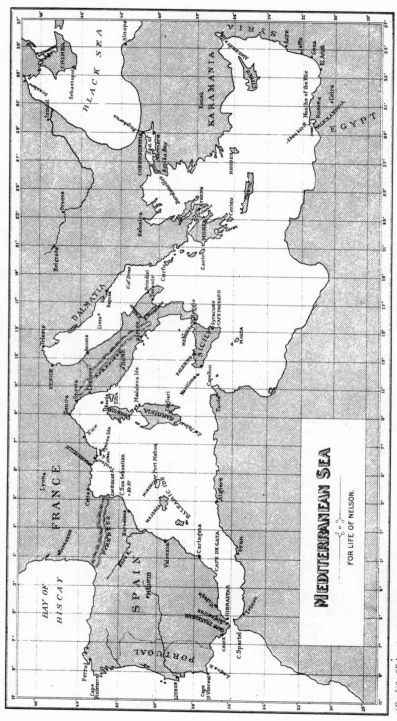

MEDITERRANEAN SEA

FOR LIFE OF NELSON.

(For Life of Nelson.)

been ratified beforehand by St. Vincent, in sending Nelson with three ships to watch Toulon. Upon receiving the despatches, on the 10th of May, the admiral's first step was to order Nelson to return at once to the fleet, to take charge of the detachment from the beginning. "You, and you only, can command the important service in contemplation; therefore, make the best of your way down to me." More urgent letters arriving from England, with news that a heavy reinforcement had left there, he, on the 19th, hurried off a brig, "La Mutine," commanded by Hardy, Nelson's former lieutenant, to notify the rear-admiral that a squadron of ten ships would be sent to him shortly from before Cadiz; and on the 21st this detachment sailed, under the command of Captain Troubridge.

The "Mutine" joined Nelson on the 5th of June. His little division had so far had more bad fortune than good. Leaving Gibraltar on the 8th of May, late in the evening, so that the easterly course taken should not be visible to either friend or enemy, he had gone to the Gulf of Lyons. There a small French corvette, just out of Toulon, was captured on the 17th, but, except in unimportant details, yielded no information additional to that already possessed. On the 19th Bonaparte sailed with all the vessels gathered in Toulon, directing his course to the eastward, to pass near Genoa, and afterwards between Corsica and the mainland of Italy. On the night of the 20th, in a violent gale of wind, the "Vanguard" rolled overboard her main and mizzen topmasts, and later on the foremast went, close to the deck. The succession of these mishaps points rather to spars badly secured and cared for than to unavoidable accident. Fortunately, the "Orion" and "Alexander" escaped injury, and the latter, on the following morning, took the "Vanguard" in tow, to go to Oristan Bay, in Sardinia. The situation became extremely dangerous on the evening of the 22d, for, the wind falling light, the sail-power of the "Alexander" was scarcely sufficient to drag both ships against a heavy westerly swell which was setting them bodily upon the Sardinian coast, then not far distant. Thinking the case hopeless, Nelson ordered the "Alexander" to let go the hawser; but Captain Ball begged permission to hold on, and finally succeeded in saving the flagship, which, on the 23d, anchored with her consorts under the Islands of San Pietro, at the southern extremity of Sardinia. The governor of the place sent word that they must not remain, Sardinia being allied to France, but added that, as he had no power to force them out, they would doubtless do as they pleased; and he supplied them with fresh provisions, — a line of conduct which illustrates at once the restrictions imposed upon British operations in the Mediterranean by French insistence, and at the same time the readiness of the weaker states to connive at the evasion of them, other instances of which occurred during this period. By the united efforts of the division, four days sufficed to refit the "Vanguard" with jury-masts, and the three ships again sailed, on the 27th, for an appointed rendezvous, to seek the frigates, which had separated during and after the gale.

This severe check, occurring at so critical a moment, — more critical even than Nelson knew, for he remained ignorant of the French sailing for some days longer, — was in itself disheartening, and fell upon one whose native eagerness chafed painfully against enforced inaction and delay. His manner of bearing it illustrated both the religious characteristics, which the experience of grave emergencies tends to develop and strengthen in men of action, and the firmness of a really great man, never more signally displayed than under the pressure of calamity and suspense, such as he continually had to undergo. The exceptional brilliancy and decisiveness of his greater battles — the Nile, Copenhagen, and Trafalgar — obscure the fact that each of them was preceded by a weary period of strenuous uphill work, a steady hewing of his way through a tanglewood of obstacles, a patient endurance of disappointments, a display of sustained, undaunted resolution under discouragements, nobler far than even the moments of triumphant action, into which at last he joyfully emerges and freely exerts his extraordinary powers. "I trust," he wrote to St. Vincent, "my friends will think I bore my chastisement like a man. I hope it has made me a better officer, as I believe it has made me a better man. On the Sunday evening I thought myself in every respect one of the most fortunate men, to command such a squadron in such a place, and my pride was too great for man." To his wife he wrote in the same strain: "I ought not to call what has happened to the Vanguard by the cold name of accident; I believe firmly that it was the Almighty's goodness, to check my consummate vanity."

Vanity was rather a hard name to call the natural elation of a young admiral, intrusted with an unusually important service, and proud of his command; but the providential interposition worked directly to his advantage. The delays caused by the repairs to the "Vanguard," and by the subsequent necessity of seeking the separated frigates at the rendezvous appointed for such a case, made possible the junction of Troubridge, of whose approach Nelson was totally ignorant. On the 2d of June Sir James Saumarez mentions speaking a ship, which a few days before had seen eleven sail-of-the-line, supposed to be English. "We are at a loss what conjectures to put on this intelligence." Five days before this, May 28, a vessel out of Marseilles had informed them of Bonaparte's sailing with all his transports. Nelson would doubtless have pursued them at once, in conformity with his instructions to ascertain the enemy's objects; but for such operations, essentially those of a scouting expedition, the frigates were too necessary to be left behind. On the 4th of June he reached the rendezvous, and, not finding the frigates, waited. The next morning, by the arrival of the

"Mutine," he learned that he was to expect the reinforcement, which converted his division into a fleet, and enlarged his mission from one of mere reconnoissance to the duty of overtaking and destroying a great maritime expedition.

Besides this good news, the "Mutine" brought word of another misfortune, more irretrievable than the loss of spars. She had fallen in with the frigates three days before, and the senior captain had told Hardy that he was going with them to Gibraltar, persuaded that the condition of the flagship, which he had seen, would necessitate her return to an arsenal for repairs. "I thought Hope would have known me better," commented Nelson, when he became aware of a step which materially affected, in fact probably entirely changed, the course of events, and most seriously embarrassed all his subsequent movements. This untimely and precipitate action, and his remark, illustrate conspicuously the differences between men, and exemplify the peculiar energy and unrelaxing forward impulse which eminently fitted Nelson for his present high charge.

The inconvenience and danger arising from the frigates' departure was instantly felt. "Nothing," wrote Saumarez, "can equal our anxiety to fall in with the reinforcement. Our squadron has been, these two days, detached in all directions, without falling in with them; and there is strong reason to fear they think us returned to Gibraltar" — from Hope s reports. Such were the risks springing from misplaced caution, more ruinous than the most daring venture, and which from beginning to end well-nigh wrecked the great attempt upon which the Admiralty, St. Vincent, and Nelson had staked so much. In further consequence, the line-of-battle ships became separated by stretching too far apart in their anxious care to find Troubridge, and when he joined the "Vanguard," on the 7th, the "Orion" and "Alexander" were not in sight.

The French having so long a start, and there being now with him eleven seventy-fours, Nelson with characteristic promptness would not delay an instant. The fifty-gun ship "Leander," which had come with Troubridge, was directed to wait forty-eight hours for the two absentees, with a memorandum of the course about to be followed. Confident that single ships would be able to overtake a squadron whose route they knew, the admiral at once pushed on for Cape Corso, the north point of Corsica, intending to pass between the island and Italy, seeking information as he went. The "Mutine" was all he had to replace the missing frigates.

June 7th thus marks the beginning of a chase, which ended only upon the 1st of August in the Battle of the Nile. During this miserable period of suspense and embarrassment, occasioned and prolonged beyond all reason or necessity by the want of lookout ships, the connecting and illuminating thread is the purpose of Nelson, at once clear and firm, to find the French fleet and to fight it the instant found. No other consideration draws his mind aside, except so far as it may facilitate the attainment and fulfilment of this one object. In this one light he sees all things. At the start he writes to St. Vincent: "You may be assured I will fight them the moment I can reach, be they at anchor or under sail." Three days later, he tells Sir William Hamilton: "If their fleet is not moored in as strong a port as Toulon, nothing shall hinder me from attacking them." "Be they bound to the Antipodes," he says to Earl Spencer, "your Lordship may rely that I will not lose a moment in bringing them to action, and endeavour to destroy their transports." Such expressions are repeated with a frequency which proves the absolute hold the resolution had upon his mind. When obstacles occur to him, or are mentioned, they do not make room for the thought of not fighting to be entertained; only Toulon suggests the idea of impossibility.

He raises difficulties diligently enough, but it is only that they may be the better overcome, not that they may deter. All possible conditions are considered and discussed, but simply in order that the best fighting solution may be reached. The constant mental attitude is such that the man is unprepared to recede before any opposition; he fortifies his mind beforehand with the best means of meeting and vanquishing it, but the attempt at least shall be made. "Thank God," he wrote at this moment, "I do not feel difficulties;" yet the avowal itself accompanies so plain a statement of his embarrassments as to show that his meaning is that they do not discourage. This characteristic appeared most strongly at Copenhagen, partly because the difficulties there were greatest, partly from the close contrast with a man of very different temper.

Being entirely without intelligence as to the real object of the French, there was nothing to do but to follow upon their track, with eyes open for indications. They were known to have gone southerly, towards Naples and Sicily; and these two points, parts of the Kingdom of the Two Sicilies, had been mentioned by Jervis as probable destinations. The "Orion" and "Alexander" rejoined in two or three days, and on the 14th of June information, second-hand but probable, was obtained that on the 4th the French armament had been seen off the west end of Sicily, steering to the eastward. "If they pass Sicily," said Nelson in his letter to Spencer written the next day, "I shall believe they are going on their scheme of possessing Alexandria, and getting troops to India — a plan concerted with Tippoo Saib, by no means so difficult as might at first view be imagined." Troubridge was now sent ahead in the "Mutine" to communicate with Sir William Hamilton, the British minister at Naples, and with Acton, the prime minister of that Kingdom. He took with him letters from the admiral, who wished to know what co-operation he might hope from the Court of Naples, in the matters of supplies, of frigates to act as lookouts, and of pilots for Sicilian waters.

On the 17th the squadron hove-to ten miles off Naples, and Troubridge rejoined. The Neapolitan Government sent assurances of good wishes, and of hatred to the French; supplies would be given under the rose, and Acton sent a written order to that effect, addressed to the governors of ports in the name of the King. Naples being at peace with France, assistance with ships could not be given, nor, to use the words of Nelson, "the smallest information of what was, or was likely to be, the future destination of the French armament. With this comfortable account I pushed for the Faro of Messina." Troubridge brought word, however, that the French fleet was off Malta, about to attack it, which served to give direction for the squadron's next move.

After leaving Naples Nelson wrote strong and clear letters to Sir William Hamilton upon the existing conditions. Why should Naples stand in shivering hesitation about taking a decided step in support of Great Britain? She had looked and prayed for the arrival of the fleet, as the one force competent to check the designs of the French. Sicily could be approached only by water, and the distance of Naples from Northern Italy rendered the control of the sea most advantageous, if not absolutely essential, to a French army attempting to hold the boot of the peninsula. Now the British fleet had come, in force adequate to neutralize the French Navy, and, in Nelson's belief, to defeat and destroy it, if properly supported. Did Naples expect to escape by a timid adherence to half measures, when by her notorious preference for the British she had already gained the ill-will of the French? "The French know as well as you and I do, that their Sicilian Majesties called for our help to save them — even this is crime enough with the French." Safety — true safety

— could be had only by strenuous and decisive action in support of Nelson's squadron. Did not the attack on Malta indicate a design upon Sicily? "Were I commanding a fleet attending an army which is to invade Sicily, I should say to the general, 'If you can take Malta, it secures the safety of your fleet, transports, stores, &c., and insures your safe retreat [from Sicily] should that be necessary; for if even a superior fleet of the enemy should arrive, before one week passes, they will be blown to leeward, and you may pass with safety.' This would be my opinion. . . . I repeat it, *Malta is the direct road to Sicily.*" If the French are overtaken, he continues, and found in some anchorage, it can scarcely be so strong but that I can get at them, but there will be needed things which I have not, fire-ships, bomb-vessels, and gunboats, when one hour would either destroy or drive them out. Without such aid, the British may be crippled in their attempt, and forced to leave the Mediterranean. In case of blockade — or necessity to remain for any reason — the fleet must have supplies, which only Naples can furnish. Failing these it must retire, and then Sicily and Naples are lost. Since, then, so much assistance must be given in time, why postpone now, when one strong blow would give instant safety? Why should not his own motto, "I will not lose a moment in attacking them," apply as well to the policy of an endangered kingdom as of a British admiral?

If this reasoning and advice took more account of the exigencies of the British arms than of the difficulties of a weak state of the second order, dependent for action upon the support of other nations, they were at least perfectly consonant to the principles and practice of the writer, wherever he himself had to act. But Nelson could not expect his own spirit in the King of the Two Sicilies. Even if the course suggested were the best for Naples under the conditions, it is the property of ordinary men, in times of danger, to see difficulties more clearly than advantages, and to shrink from steps which involve risk, however promising of success. The Neapolitan Government, though cheered by the appearance of the British fleet, had to consider danger also on the land side, where it relied upon the protection of Austria, instead of trusting manfully to its own arms and the advantages of its position, remote from the centre of French power. Austria had pledged herself to support Naples, if invaded without just cause; but it was not certain that she would interfere if the cause of attack was the premature admission of British ships into the ports of the kingdom, beyond the number specified in the still recent treaties with France. The Emperor was meditating war, in which he expected to assist Naples and to be assisted by her; but he did not choose to be hurried, and might refuse aid if an outbreak were precipitated.

Actually, what Naples did mattered little. Under some contingencies, such as Nelson was contemplating when he wrote his letter, it might have mattered much whether he received the abundant support of small armed vessels which he indicated; but in the end supplies only were required, and those he had orders from Jervis to exact at the mouth of his cannon from all powers, — friends or neutrals, — Sardinia only excepted. The fleet passed the Straits of Messina on the 20th of June, and continued south, keeping close to the Sicilian shore in hope of information, until the 22d, when it was off Cape Passaro, the southeastern extremity of the island. There a Genoese brig was spoken, which had left Malta the previous day. From her Nelson learned that Malta had surrendered to the French on the 15th, a week before, which was correct; but the information further stated, that, after landing a garrison, the expedition had sailed again on the 16th — it was thought for Sicily. This last news was untrue, whether by intention or not, for Bonaparte remained in Malta till the 19th; but upon it Nelson had to act. Had he seen the captain of the stranger himself, he might have found out more, for he was a shrewd questioner, and his intellect was sharpened by anxiety, and by constant dwelling upon the elements of the intricate problem before him; but the vessel had been boarded by the "Mutine," three hours before, and was now beyond recall.

At this season the winds in the Mediterranean prevail from the westward; therefore, with the six days' start the enemy was believed now to have, no time could be lost. Six days sufficed to carry the British squadron from its present position to Alexandria, which Nelson was already inclined to think the destination of the French. Yet, being dependent upon a wind then practically constant in direction, it would not do to yield a mile of ground, except upon a mature, if rapid, deliberation. Nelson's own mind was, by constant preoccupation, familiar beforehand with the bearings of the different conditions of any situation likely to occur, and with the probable inferences to be drawn; his opinions were, so to say, in a constant state of formation and development, ready for instantaneous application to any emergency as it arose. But he had, besides, exercised the same habit in the captains of the ships, by the practice of summoning them on board the flagship, singly or in groups; the slow movement of sailing vessels, particularly in the light summer weather of the Mediterranean, permitting such intercourse without materially affecting the progress of the fleet. Invitations or commands so to visit the flagship were common. "I have passed the day on board the Vanguard," notes Saumarez on one occasion, "having breakfasted and stayed to dinner with the admiral." "It was his practice during the whole of his cruize," wrote Berry, the flag-captain, "whenever the weather and circumstances would permit, to have his captains on board the Vanguard, where he would fully develop to them his own ideas of the different and best modes of attack, in all possible positions." That such conversations were not confined to tactical questions, but extended to what would now be called the strategy of the situation, is evident from allusions by Saumarez to the various surmises concerning the probable movements of the enemy. Nelson never yielded a particle of his responsibility, nor of his credit, but it is clear that such discussion would not only broaden his own outlook, but prepare his subordinates to give readier and sounder views upon any new conjuncture that might arise.

He now summoned on board four captains "in whom I place great confidence," Saumarez, Troubridge, — the two seniors, — Ball, and Darby, stated the case, and received their opinions. These seem to have been given in writing,[1] and from his letter to St. Vincent the results of the conference, as shown by his decision, may be summarized as follows. With the existing winds, it would be impossible for such a fleet as the enemy's to get to the westward. Had they aimed at Sicily, an object concerning which explicit disclaimers had been given by the French to the Neapolitan Government, some indication of their approach must have been known at Syracuse, the day before, when the British were off that city. Consequently, the expedition must have gone to the eastward. The size and nature of the armament must also be considered, — forty thousand troops, a dozen ships-of-the-line, besides a staff of scientific men, — all pointed to a great,

---

[1] The author is indebted to the present Lord De Saumarez for a copy of the opinion of Sir James Saumarez, written on board the "Vanguard" at this meeting : —

"The French fleet having left Malta six days ago, had their destination been the Island of Sicily there is reason to presume we should have obtained information of it yesterday off Syracuse, or the day before in coming through the Pharo of Messina — under all circumstances I think it most conducive to the good of His Majesty's service to make the best of our way for Alexandria, as the only means of saving our possessions in India, should the French armament be destined for that country.

"Vanguard, at sea, 22d June 1798.   JAMES SAUMAREZ."

distant, and permanent occupation. The object might be Corfu, or to overthrow the existing government of Turkey, or to settle a colony in Egypt. As between these, all equally possible, the last was the most direct and greatest menace to present British interests, and should determine his course. "If they have concerted a plan with Tippoo Saib, to have vessels at Suez, three weeks, at this season, is a common passage to the Malabar coast, where our India possessions would be in great danger."

Such was the conclusion — how momentous at the moment can only be realized by those who will be at the pains to consider a man still young, with reputation brilliant indeed, but not established; intrusted with a great chance, it is true, but also with a great responsibility, upon which rested all his future. On slight, though decisive, preponderance of evidence, he was about to risk throwing away an advantage a seaman must appreciate, that of being to windward of his enemy, — able to get at him, — the strategist's position of command. The tongues of envy and censure might well be — we now know that they were — busy in inquiring why so young an admiral had so high charge, and in sneering at his failure to find the enemy. "Knowing my attachment to you," wrote his old friend, Admiral Goodall, alongside whom he had fought under Hotham, "how often have I been questioned: 'What is your favourite hero about? The French fleet has passed under his nose,' &c., &c." Nelson was saved from fatal hesitation, primarily, by his singleness of purpose, which looked first to his country's service, to the thorough doing of the work given him to do, and only afterwards to the consequences of failure to his own fame and fortunes. At that moment the choice before him was either to follow out an indication, slight, but as far as it went clear, which, though confessedly precarious, promised to lead to a great and decisive result, such as he had lately urged upon the King of Naples; or to remain where he was, in an inglorious security, perfectly content, to use words of his own, that "each day passed without loss to our side." To the latter conclusion might very well have contributed the knowledge, that the interests which the Cabinet thought threatened were certainly for the present safe. Broadly as his instructions were drawn, no word of Egypt or the East was specifically in them. Naples, Sicily, Portugal, or Ireland, such were the dangers intimated by Spencer and St. Vincent in their letters, and he was distinctly cautioned against letting the enemy get to the westward of him. He might have consoled himself for indecisive action, which procrastinated disaster and covered failure with the veil of nullity, as did a former commander of his in a gazetted letter, by the reflection that, so far as the anticipations of the ministry went, the designs of the enemy were for the time frustrated, by the presence of his squadron between them and the points indicated to him.

But the single eye of principle gained keener insight in this case by the practised habit of reflection, which came prepared, to the full extent of an acute intellect, to detect every glimmer of light, and to follow them to the point where they converged upon the true solution; and both principle and reflection were powerfully supported in their final action by a native temperament, impatient of hesitations, of half measures, certain that the annihilation of the French fleet, and nothing short of its annihilation, fulfilled that security of his country's interests in which consisted the spirit of his instructions. His own words in self-defence, when for a moment it seemed as if, after all, he had blundered in the great risk he took, though rough in form, rise to the eloquence that speaks but of the abundance of the heart. "The only objection I can fancy to be started is, ' you should not have gone such a long voyage without more certain information of the enemy's destination: ' my answer is ready — who was I to get it from? The governments of Naples and Sicily either knew not, or chose to keep me in ignorance. Was I to wait patiently till I heard certain accounts? If Egypt was their object, before I could hear of them they would have been in India. To do nothing, I felt, was disgraceful; therefore I made use of my understanding, and by it I ought to stand or fall."

The destination of the enemy had been rightly divined, following out a course of reasoning outlined by Nelson a week before in his letter to Spencer; but successful pursuit was baffled for the moment by the wiliness of Bonaparte, who directed his vast armament to be steered for the south shore of Candia, instead of straight for Alexandria. Even this would scarcely have saved him, had Nelson's frigates been with the fleet. Immediately after the council, the admiral with his customary promptitude kept away for Egypt under all sail. "I am just returned from on board the Admiral," writes Saumarez, "and we are crowding sail for Alexandria; but the contrast to what we experienced yesterday is great indeed, having made sure of attacking them this morning. At present it is very doubtful whether we shall fall in with them at all, as we are proceeding upon the merest conjecture only, and not on any positive information. Some days must now elapse before we can be relieved from our cruel suspense; and if, at the end of our journey, we find we are upon a wrong scent, our embarrassment will be great indeed. Fortunately, I only act here *en second*; but did the chief responsibility rest with me, I fear it would be more than my too irritable nerves would bear." Such was the contemporary estimate of an eye-witness, an officer of tried and singular gallantry and ability, who shared the admiral's perplexities and ambitions, though not his responsibility. His words portray justly the immensity of the burden Nelson bore. That, indeed, is the inevitable penalty of command; but it must be conceded that, when adequately borne, it should convey also an equal measure of renown.

In the morning, before the consultation with the captains, three French frigates had been seen; but Nelson, warned by the parting of the "Orion" and "Alexander" a fortnight before, would not run the risk of scattering the squadron by chasing them. No time could now be lost, waiting for a separated ship to catch up. The circumstance of the fleet being seen by these frigates was quoted in a letter from Louis Bonaparte, who was with the expedition, to his brother Joseph, and was made the ground for comment upon the stupidity of the British admiral, who with this opportunity failed to find the armament. The criticism is unjust; had the frigates taken to flight, as of course they would, the British fleet, if not divided, would certainly not be led towards the main body of the enemy. Concentration of purpose, singleness of aim, was more than ever necessary, now that time pressed and a decision had been reached; but the sneer of the French officer reproduces the idle chatter of the day in London streets and drawing-rooms. These, in turn, but echoed and swelled the murmurs of insubordination and envy in the navy itself, at the departure from the routine methods of officialism, by passing over the claims of undistinguished seniors, in favor of one who as yet had nothing but brilliant achievement, and yet more brilliant promise, to justify committing to him the most momentous charge that in this war had devolved on a British admiral. A letter from one of the puisne lords of the Admiralty was read publicly on board the "Prince George," flagship of Sir William Parker, — the same who had the controversy with Nelson about the Battle of St. Vincent, — denouncing Lord St. Vincent in no very gentle terms for having sent so young a flag-officer.[1] "Sir William Parker and Sir John Orde have written strong remonstrances against your commanding the detached squadron instead of them," wrote St. Vincent to Nelson. "I did all I could to prevent it, con-

[1] Clarke and M'Arthur's Life of Nelson, vol. ii. p. 100.

sistently with my situation, but there is a faction, fraught
with all manner of ill-will to you, that, unfortunately for
the two Baronets, domined over any argument or influence
I could use: they will both be ordered home the moment
their letters arrive." It will be seen how much was at
stake for Nelson personally in the issue of these weeks.
Happy the man who, like him, has in such a case the clear
light of duty to keep his steps from wavering!

The night after Nelson made sail for Alexandria the two
hostile bodies crossed the same tract of sea, on divergent
courses; but a haze covered the face of the deep, and hid
them from each other. When the day dawned, they were
no longer within range of sight; but had the horizon of
the British fleet been enlarged by flanking frigates, chasing on either side, the immunity of the French from detection could scarcely have continued. For some days not a
hundred miles intervened between these two foes, proceeding for the same port. On the 26th, being two hundred
and fifty miles from Alexandria, Nelson sent the "Mutine"
ahead to communicate with the place and get information;
a single vessel being able to outstrip the progress of a
body of ships, which is bound to the speed of its slowest
member. On the 28th the squadron itself was off the
town, when the admiral to his dismay found that not only
the French had not appeared, but that no certain news of
their destination was to be had.

Preoccupied as his mind had been with the fear that the
enemy had so far the start that their army would be out of
the transports before he overtook them, the idea that he
might outstrip them does not seem to have entered his
head. Only three vessels had been spoken since Sicily
was left behind, — two from Alexandria and one from the
Archipelago; but these knew nothing of the French,
being doubtless, when met, ahead of the latter's advance.
That Nelson again consulted with his captains seems probable — indeed almost certain, from casual mention; but if

so, their opinion as to the future course does not appear. The unremitting eagerness of his temperament, the single-ness of his purpose, which saw the whole situation con-centrated in the French fleet, had worked together up to the present to bring him to the true strategic point just ahead of time; although, by no fault of his own, he had started near three weeks late.[1] These two high qualities now conspired to mislead him by their own excess. "His active and anxious mind," wrote Captain Berry, "would not permit him to rest a moment in the same place; he therefore shaped his course to the northward, for the coast of Caramania [in Asia Minor], to reach as quickly as pos-sible some quarter where information could probably be obtained."

To say that this was a mistake is perhaps to be wise only after the event. Had Nelson known that the French, when leaving Malta, had but three days' start of him, instead of six, as the Genoese had reported, he might have suspected the truth; it is not wonderful that he failed to believe that he could have gained six days. The actual gain *was* but three; for, departing practically at the same time from points equidistant from Alexandria, Bonaparte's armament appeared before that place on the third day after Nelson arrived. The troops were landed immediately, and the transports entered the port, thus making secure their escape from the British pursuit. The ships of war remained outside.

Meanwhile Nelson, "distressed for the Kingdom of the Two Sicilies," was beating back to the westward against the wind which had carried him rapidly to the coast of Egypt. Rightly or wrongly, he had not chosen to wait at the point which mature reflection had indicated to him as the enemy's goal, and the best course that now occurred to him was to do with his fleet the exploring duty that

---

[1] That is, counting from May 19, when Bonaparte left Toulon, to June 7 when Troubridge's squadron joined, and pursuit began.

frigates should have done. "*No frigates*," he wrote to Sir
William Hamilton; "to which has been, and may again,
be attributed the loss of the French fleet." On his return
he kept along the northern shore of the Mediterranean,
passing near Candia; but, though several vessels were
spoken, he only gathered from them that the French were
not west of Sicily, nor at Corfu. On the 19th of July,
he anchored the fleet at Syracuse, having, to use his own
words, "gone a round of six hundred leagues with an
expedition incredible," and yet "as ignorant of the situation of the enemy as I was twenty-seven days ago."

At Syracuse fresh disappointments awaited him, which
only the indomitable single-mindedness and perseverance of
the man prevented from becoming discouragements. The
minister at Naples had sent despatches to await him at
Cape Passaro; when he sent for these, thirsty for news
about the French, they had been returned to Naples. The
governor of the port, despite Acton's assurances to
Troubridge, made difficulties about the admission of so
many ships, and about supplying water, which they absolutely required. This Nelson resented, with angry contempt for the halting policy of the weak kingdom. "I
have had so much said about the King of Naples' orders
only to admit three or four of the ships of our fleet into
his ports, that I am astonished. I understood that private
orders, at least, would have been given for our free
admission. If we are to be refused supplies, pray send
me by many vessels an account, that I may in good time
take the King's fleet to Gibraltar. Our treatment is scandalous for a great nation to put up with, and the King's
flag is insulted at every friendly port we look at." "I
wish to know your and Sir William's plans for going
down the Mediterranean," he wrote to Lady Hamilton,
"for, if we are to be kicked in every port of the Sicilian
dominions, the sooner we are gone the better. Good God!
how sensibly I feel our treatment. I have only to pray I

may find the French and throw all my vengeance on them."

These words show the nervous exasperation superinduced by the tremendous strain of official anxiety and mortified ambition; for the governor's objections were purely formal and perfunctory, as was the Court's submission to the French. "Our present wants," he admitted at the same writing, "have been most amply supplied, and every attention has been paid us." Years afterwards Nelson spoke feelingly of the bitter mental anguish of that protracted and oft-thwarted pursuit. "Do not fret at anything," he told his friend Troubridge; "I wish I never had, but my return to Syracuse in 1798, broke my heart, which on any extraordinary anxiety now shows itself, be that feeling pain or pleasure." "On the 18th I had near died, with the swelling of some of the vessels of the heart. More people, perhaps, die of broken hearts than we are aware of." But the firmness of his purpose, the clearness of his convictions, remained unslackened and unclouded. "What a situation am I placed in!" he writes, when he finds Hamilton's despatches returned. "As yet I can learn nothing of the enemy. You will, I am sure, and so will our country, easily conceive what has passed in my anxious mind; but I have this comfort, that I have no fault to accuse myself of. This bears me up, and this only." "Every moment I have to regret the frigates having left me," he tells St. Vincent. "Your lordship deprived yourself of frigates to make mine certainly the first squadron in the world, and I feel that I have zeal and activity to do credit to your appointment, and yet to be unsuccessful hurts me most sensibly. But if they are above water, I will find them out, and if possible bring them to battle. You have done your part in giving me so fine a fleet, and I hope to do mine in making use of them."

In five days the squadron had filled with water and

again sailed. Satisfied that the enemy were somewhere in the Levant, Nelson now intended a deliberate search for them — or rather for their fleet, the destruction of which was the crucial object of all his movements. "It has been said," he wrote to Hamilton, "that to leeward of the two frigates I saw off Cape Passaro was a line-of-battle ship, with the riches of Malta on board, but it was the destruction of the enemy, not riches for myself, that I was seeking. These would have fallen to me if I had had frigates, but except the ship-of-the-line, I regard not all the riches in this world." A plaintive remonstrance against his second departure was penned by the Neapolitan prime minister, which depicts so plainly the commonplace view of a military situation, — the apprehensions of one to whom immediate security is the great object in war, — that it justifies quotation, and comparison with the clear intuitions, and firmly grasped principle, which placed Nelson always, in desire, alongside the enemy's fleet, and twice carried him, at every risk, to the end of the Mediterranean to seek it. "We are now in danger of a war, directly on Admiral Nelson's account; you see fairly our position; will Admiral Nelson run to the Levant again *without knowing for certain* the position of the French, and leave the Two Sicilies exposed in these moments? Buonaparte has absconded himself, but in any port he has taken securitys not to be forced. God knows where he is, and whether we shall not see him again in a few days, if we do not hear of what a course he has taken. I present all this to your consideration." To this letter, which oddly enough was written on the very day the Battle of the Nile was fought, Nelson might well have replied then, as he did in terms a year afterwards, "The best defence for His Sicilian Majesty's dominions is to place myself alongside the French fleet."

The fleet left Syracuse on the 25th of July, just one week before the discovery of the enemy in Aboukir Bay

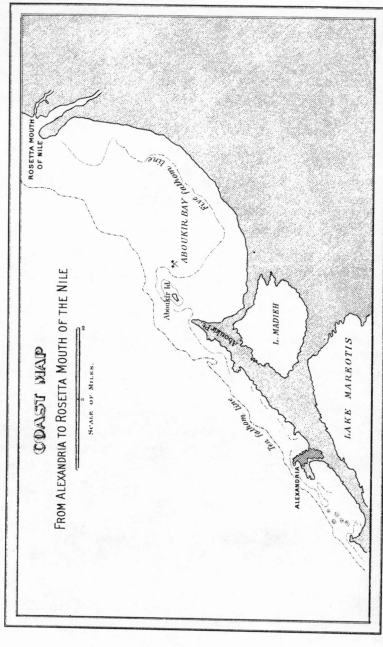

COAST MAP

FROM ALEXANDRIA TO ROSETTA MOUTH OF THE NILE

SCALE OF MILES.

5   10

ROSETTA MOUTH OF NILE

ABOUKIR BAY

Five fathom Line

Aboukir Id

ABOUKIR Pt.

L. MADIEH

Ten fathom Line

ALEXANDRIA

LAKE MAREOTIS

put an end to Nelson's long suspense. The course was first shaped for the southern capes of the Morea, and on the 28th Troubridge was sent into the Gulf of Koron for information. He returned within three hours, with the news that the French had been seen four weeks before from the coast of Candia, and were then steering southeast. This intelligence was corroborated by a vessel spoken the same day. Southeast, being nearly dead before the prevailing wind, was an almost certain clew to the destination of an unwieldy body which could never regain ground lost to leeward; so, although Nelson now learned that some of his missing frigates had also been seen recently off Candia, he would waste no time looking for them. It may be mentioned that these frigates had appeared off the anchorage of the French fleet, and had been recognized by it as enemies; but, so far from taking warning from the incident, the French admiral was only confirmed by it in a blind belief that the British feared to attack. Immediately after Troubridge's return, the fleet bore up under all sail, and at 2.45 in the afternoon of the 1st of August, 1798, the masthead lookout of the "Zealous" discovered the long-sought-for enemy, lying in Aboukir Bay, on the coast of Egypt, fifteen miles east of Alexandria.

Suspense was ended, but Nelson's weightiest responsibility had yet to be met. The enemy was still so far distant that he could not be reached till near nightfall, and it was possible that not only would the battle be fought in the dark, but that some at least of the ships would not have daylight to take their positions. The consequent difficulty and risk was in any event great; but in this case the more so, because the ground was unknown to every officer in the fleet. The only chart of it in possession of the British was a rude sketch lately taken out of a prize. There was no time now for calling captains together, nor for forming plans of action. Then appeared conspicuously the value of that preparedness of mind, as well as of purpose, which at bottom was the greatest of Nelson's claims to credit. Much had been received by him from Nature, — gifts which, if she bestows them not, man struggles in vain to acquire by his own efforts; but the care which he took in fitting himself to use those gifts to their utmost capacity is his own glory. The author of the first full narrative of these eventful weeks, Captain Berry, than whom no man had larger occasion to observe Nelson's moods, used his capitals well when he wrote, "The admiral viewed the obstacles with the eye of a seaman DETERMINED ON ATTACK." It was not for him, face to face with opportunity, to hesitate and debate whether he would be justified in using it at once. But this preparation of purpose might have led only to a great disaster, had it not received guidance from a richly stored intellect, which had pondered probable conditions so exhaustively that proper direction could be at once imparted and at once understood. The French admiral, indeed, by his mistaken dispositions had delivered himself into the hands of his enemy; but that might not have availed had that enemy hesitated and given time, or had he not instantly comprehended the possibilities of the situation with a trained glance which had contemplated them long before. "By attacking the enemy's van and centre, the wind blowing directly along their line, I was enabled to throw what force I pleased on a few ships. This plan my friends readily conceived by the signals." [1]

It was, therefore, no fortuitous coincidence that the battle was fought on a plan preconcerted in general outline, though necessarily subject to particular variations in detail. Not only had many situations been discussed, as Berry tells us, but new signals had been inserted in the signal-book to enable the admiral's intentions to be quickly understood. To provide for the case of the enemy being

[1] Nelson to Lord Howe.

met at sea, the force had been organized into three squadrons, — a subdivision of command which, while surrendering nothing of the admiral's initiative, much facilitated the application of his plans, by committing the execution of major details to the two senior captains, Saumarez and Troubridge, each wielding a group of four ships. Among the provisions for specific contingencies was one that evidently sprang from the report that the enemy's fleet numbered sixteen or seventeen of the line, — an impression which arose from there being in it four Venetian ships so rated, which were not, however, fit for a place in the line. In that case Nelson proposed to attack, ship for ship, the rear thirteen of the enemy. That he preferred, when possible, to throw two ships on one is evident enough — the approaching battle proves it; but when confronted with a force stronger, numerically, than his own, and under way, he provides what was certainly the better alternative. He engages at once the attention of as many ships as possible, confident that he brings against each a force superior to it, owing to the general greater efficiency of British ships over French of that date, and especially of those in his own squadron, called by St. Vincent the *élite* of the Navy.

The position of the French fleet, and the arrangements made by its commander, Admiral Brueys, must now be given, for they constitute the particular situation against which Nelson's general plan of attack was to be directed. Considering it impracticable for the ships-of-the-line to enter the port of Alexandria, Brueys had taken the fleet on the 8th of July to their present anchorage. Aboukir Bay begins at a promontory of the same name, and, after curving boldly south, extends eastward eighteen miles, terminating at the Rosetta mouth of the Nile. From the shore the depth increases very gradually, so that water enough for ships-of-the-line was not found till three miles from the coast. Two miles northeast of the promontory of Aboukir is Aboukir Island, since called Nelson's, linked with the point by a chain of rocks. Outside the island, similar rocks, with shoals, prolong this foul ground under water to seaward, constituting a reef dangerous to a stranger approaching the bay. This barrier, however, broke the waves from the northwest, and so made the western part of the bay a fairly convenient summer roadstead. The French fleet was anchored there, under the shelter of the island and rocks, in an order such that " the wind blew nearly along the line." Its situation offered no local protection against an enemy s approach, except that due to ignorance of the ground.

It was therefore Brueys's business to meet this defect of protection by adequate dispositions; and this he failed to do. Numerically his force was the same as Nelson's; but, while the latter had only seventy-fours, there were in the French fleet one ship of one hundred and twenty guns, and three eighties. In a military sense, every line divides naturally into three parts, — the centre, and the two ends, or flanks; and it is essential that these should so far support one another that an enemy cannot attack any two in superior force, while the third is unable to assist. Shallow water, such as was found in Aboukir Bay, if properly utilized, will prevent a flank being turned, so that an enemy can get on both sides of the ships there, or otherwise concentrate upon them, as by enfilading; and if, in addition, the ships are anchored close to each other, it becomes impossible for two of the attacking force to direct their fire upon one of the defence, without being exposed to reprisals from those next astern and ahead. These evident precautions received no illustration in the arrangements of Admiral Brueys. The general direction of his line was that of the wind, from northwest to southeast, with a very slight bend, as shown in the diagram. The leading — northwestern — ship was brought close to the shoal in thirty feet of water, but not so close as to prevent the British passing round her, turning that flank; and there were

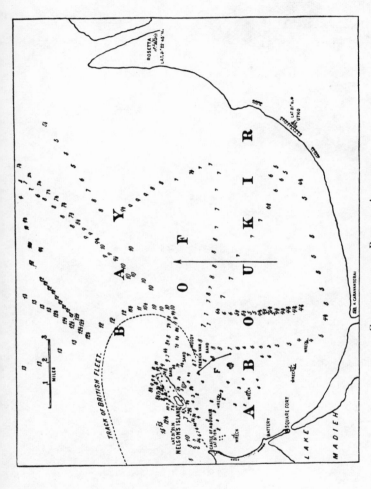

CHART OF THE BAY OF ABOUKIR.

FROM A SURVEY MADE BY THOMAS ATKINSON, MASTER OF H. M. S. THESEUS, 74, IN 1799.

(THE FIGURES REPRESENT SOUNDINGS IN FATHOMS.)

F. POSITION OF THE FRENCH FLEET (DRAWN TO SCALE), AS GIVEN IN THE TEXT.

between the successive ships intervals of five hundred feet, through any one of which an enemy could readily pass. Brueys had very properly accumulated his most powerful vessels at the centre. The flagship " Orient," of one hundred and twenty guns, was seventh in the order; next ahead and astern of her were, respectively, the "Franklin" and the "Tonnant," each of eighty. By a singular misconception, however, he had thought that any attack would fall upon the rear — the lee flank; and to this utter misapprehension of the exposed points it was owing that he there placed his next heaviest ships. Nelson's fore-determined onslaught upon the van accordingly fell on the weakest of the French vessels.

Such was the French order of battle. The proceedings of the British fleet, under its leader, show an instructive combination of rapidity and caution, of quick comprehension of the situation, with an absence of all precipitation; no haste incompatible with perfect carefulness, no time lost, either by hesitation or by preparations postponed. When the enemy were first discovered, two ships, the "Alexander" and "Swiftsure," were a dozen miles to leeward, having been sent ahead on frigates' duty to reconnoitre Alexandria. This circumstance prevented their joining till after the battle began and night had fallen. At the same moment the "Culloden" was seven miles to windward. She was signalled to drop the prize she was towing, and to join the fleet. To this separation was due that she went aground. The remaining ten ships, which had been steering about east, hauled sharp on the wind to enable them to weather with ample allowance the shoal off Aboukir Island. It was blowing a whole-sail breeze, too fresh for the lighter canvas; the royals were furled as soon as close-hauled. As the French situation and dispositions developed to the view, signals were made to prepare for battle, to get ready to anchor by the stern, and that it was the admiral's intention to attack the van and centre of the enemy. The captains had long been forewarned of each of these possibilities, and nothing more was needed to convey to them his general plan, which was intrusted to them individually to carry out as they successively came into action.

At about half-past five signal was given to form line of battle. This, for the ships of the day, was a single column, in which they were ranged ahead and astern of each other, leaving the broadside clear. As they came abreast the shoal, Nelson hailed Captain Hood, of 'the " Zealous," and asked if he thought they were yet far enough to the eastward to clear it, if they then headed for the enemy. Hood replied that he did not know the ground, but was in eleven fathoms, and would, if the admiral allowed, bear up and sound with the lead, and would not bring the fleet into danger. This was done, Hood leading all the fleet except the " Goliath," Captain Foley, which kept ahead, but outside, of the " Zealous." No close shaving was done, however, at this critical turn; and it is that steady deliberation, combined with such parsimony of time in other moments, which is most impressive in Nelson. So few realize that five minutes are at once the most important and the least important of considerations. Thus the British passed so much beyond the island and the shoal, before keeping away, that, as the long column swept round to head for the French van, the ships turned their port broadsides to the enemy, and were steering southwesterly when they finally ran down. " The English admiral," wrote the French second in command, " without doubt had experienced pilots on board; he hauled well round all dangers."

The " Goliath" still leading the fleet, followed closely by the " Zealous," the flagship was dropped to sixth in the order, — Nelson thus placing himself so that he could see what the first five ships accomplished, while retaining in his own hands the power to impart a new direction to the

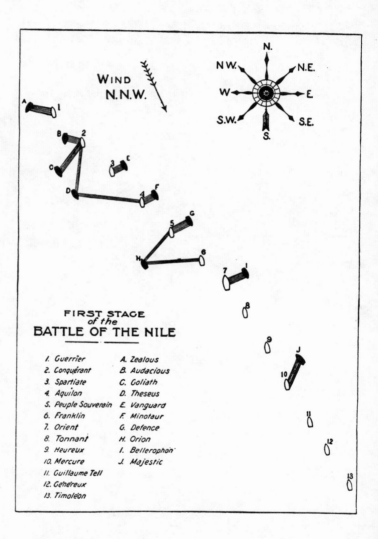

WIND
N.N.W.

N.
NW.   N.E.
W   E.
S.W.   S.E.
S.

FIRST STAGE
of the
BATTLE OF THE NILE

1. Guerrier	A. Zealous
2. Conquérant	B. Audacious
3. Spartiate	C. Goliath
4. Aquilon	D. Theseus
5. Peuple Souverain	E. Vanguard
6. Franklin	F. Minotaur
7. Orient	G. Defence
8. Tonnant	H. Orion
9. Heureux	I. Bellerophon
10. Mercure	J. Majestic
11. Guillaume Tell	
12. Généreux	
13. Timoléon	

remaining five of those then with him, should he think it necessary. Captain Foley had formed the idea that the French would be less ready to fight on the inshore side, and had expressed his intention to get inside them, if practicable. Sounding as he went, he passed round the bows of the leading vessel, the " Guerrier," on the inner bow of which he intended to place himself; but the anchor hung, and the "Goliath" brought up on the inner quarter of the "Conquérant," the second ship. The "Zealous," following, anchored where Foley had purposed, on the bow of the "Guerrier;" and the next three ships, the "Orion," "Theseus," and "Audacious," also placed themselves on the inner side of the French line.

The two leading French vessels were at once crushed. All the masts of the "Guerrier," although no sail was on them, went overboard within ten minutes after she was first attacked, while the "Conquérant" was receiving the united broadsides of the "Goliath" and the "Audacious," — the latter raking. Nelson therefore placed the "Vanguard" on the outer side, and within pistol-shot, of the third French ship, the "Spartiate," which was already engaged on the other side by the "Theseus," but at much longer range. His example was of course followed by those succeeding him — the seventh and eighth of the British engaging the fourth and fifth of the French, which were already receiving part of the fire of the "Orion" and "Theseus" on the inner side — the latter having ceased to play upon the "Spartiate" for fear of hitting the "Vanguard." Thus five French ships were within half an hour in desperate conflict with eight British, while their consorts to leeward looked helplessly on.

The ninth and tenth of Nelson's fleet were less fortunate, owing to the envelope of smoke and the growing darkness, which now obscured the scene. The "Bellerophon," missing the sixth French vessel, the "Franklin," brought up abreast the "Orient," whose force was double her own, and which had no other antagonist. The "Majestic," groping her way, ran into the ninth French, the "Heureux," where for some moments she hung in a position of disadvantage and had her captain killed. Then swinging clear, she anchored on the bow of the next astern, the "Mercure," and there continued a deadly and solitary action. Owing to the circumstances mentioned, the loss of each of these ships was greater, by fifty per cent, than that of any other of the British fleet. The movements so far described, and the resultant fighting, may be styled the first stage of the battle. Concerning it may be remarked the unswerving steadiness, rapidity, and yet sound judgment, with which all the movements were executed; and further, that not only was the first direction of the attack that prescribed by Nelson's signal, but that the second, initiated by his own ship, was also imparted by him. The incident of passing round the "Guerrier," and inside of the line, is a detail only, although one which cannot be too highly praised. "The van ship of the enemy being in five fathom," wrote Captain Hood, "I expected the Goliath and Zealous to stick fast on the shoal every moment, and did not imagine we should attempt to pass within her." It is difficult to exaggerate the coolness, intrepidity, and seamanlike care of Captain Foley, to whom is to be attributed, perhaps, the whole conception, and certainly the entire merit of the execution; but they no more detract from Nelson's honors than does the distinguished conduct of the other captains.

The battle had begun a little after half-past six, the "Guerrier's" masts falling at sundown, which was quarter before seven. It continued under the conditions already given until past eight o'clock — none of the ships engaged shifting her position for some time after that hour. It was, apparently, just before the second act of the drama opened with the arrival of the remaining ships — the "Alexander," "Swiftsure," and "Leander" — that Nelson was severely wounded; but the precise moment has not been recorded. He was struck upon the upper part of the forehead by a flying piece of iron, the skin, which was cut at right angles, hanging down over his face, covering the one good eye, and, with the profuse flow of blood, blinding him completely. He exclaimed, "I am killed! Remember me to my wife!" and was falling, but Captain Berry, who stood near, caught him in his arms. When carried below to the cockpit, the surgeon went immediately to him, but he refused to be attended before his turn arrived, in due succession to the injured lying around him.

The pain was intense, and Nelson felt convinced that his hurt was mortal; nor could he for some time accept the surgeon's assurances to the contrary. Thus looking for his end, he renewed his farewell messages to Lady Nelson, and directed also that Captain Louis of the "Minotaur," which lay immediately ahead of the "Vanguard," should be hailed to come on board, that before dying he might express to him his sense of the admirable support given by her to the flagship. "Your support," said he, "has prevented me from being obliged to haul out of the line."[1] From the remark it may be inferred that the French "Aquilon," their fourth ship, which became the "Minotaur's" antagonist, had for a measurable time been able to combine her batteries with those of the "Spartiate" upon the "Vanguard," and to this was probably due that the loss of the latter was next in severity to that of the "Majestic" and of the "Bellerophon." The inference is further supported by the fact that the worst slaughter in the "Vanguard" was at the forward guns, those nearest the "Aquilon."

After his wound was bound up, Nelson was requested by the surgeon to lie quiet; but his preoccupation with the events of the evening was too great, and his responsibility too immediate, to find relief in inactivity, — the

[1] G. Lathom Browne's Life of Nelson, p. 198.

physician's panacea. He remained below for a while, probably too much jarred for physical exertion; but his restlessness sought vent by beginning a despatch to the Admiralty. The secretary being too agitated to write, Nelson tried to do so himself, and it was characteristic that the few lines he was then able to trace, blinded, suffering, and confused, expressed that dependence upon the Almighty, habitual with him, which illustrated a temperament of so much native energy and self-reliance, and is more common, probably, among great warriors than in any other class of men of action. This first outburst of emotion, excited in him by the tremendous event wrought by his hands, was identical in spirit, and not improbably was clothed in the same words, as those with which began the despatch actually sent: "Almighty God has blessed His Majesty's arms."

While Nelson lay thus momentarily disabled, important events were transpiring, over which, however, he could have exerted no control. It has been mentioned that the "Culloden" was seven miles to the northward and westward of the fleet, when the French were first discovered. Doing her best, it was impossible to reach the main body before it stood down into action, and the day had closed when the ship neared the shoal. Keeping the lead going, and proceeding with caution, though not with the extreme care which led Hood and Nelson to make so wide a sweep, Troubridge had the mishap to strike on the tail of the shoal, and there the ship stuck fast, pounding heavily until the next morning. The fifty-gun ship "Leander" went to her assistance, as did the brig "Mutine," but all efforts to float her proved vain. Meanwhile the "Alexander" and "Swiftsure" were coming up from the southwest, the wind being so scant that they could barely pass to windward of the reef, along whose northwestern edge they were standing. The "Alexander," in fact, was warned by the lead that she was running into danger,

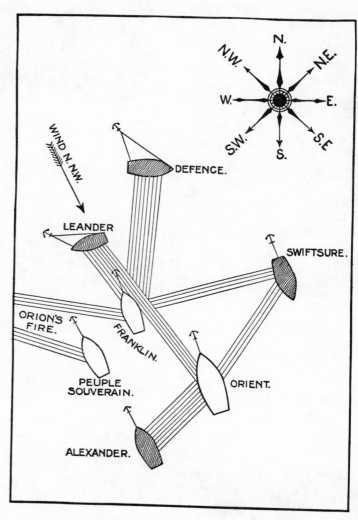

SECOND STAGE OF THE BATTLE OF THE NILE.
CONCENTRATION OF BRITISH RESERVE ON THE FRENCH CENTRE.

and had to tack. As they approached, Troubridge, by lantern and signal, warned them off the spot of his disaster, thus contributing to save these ships, and, by removing doubt, accelerating their entrance into action. As they rounded the stranded "Culloden," the "Leander" was also dismissed from a hopeless task, and followed them to the scene of battle.

The delay of the two seventy-fours, though purely fortuitous, worked in furtherance of Nelson's plan, and resulted, practically, in constituting them a reserve, which was brought into play at a most auspicious moment. The "Bellerophon," crushed by the preponderating weight of the "Orient's" battery, had just cut her cable and worn out of action, with the loss of forty-nine killed and one hundred and forty-eight wounded, out of a total of five hundred and ninety men. Her foremast alone was then standing, and it fell immediately after. The firing, which had been animated from the French left towards the centre, now slackened around the latter, at the point where the "Orient" and her next ahead, the "Franklin," were lying. For this spot, therefore, the captains of the two fresh British ships steered. The "Swiftsure," Captain Hallowell, anchored outside the enemy's line, abreast the interval separating the "Orient" and the "Franklin," between which he divided his fire. The "Alexander," Captain Ball, passed through the line, astern of the "Orient," and anchored close on her inner quarter. Just at this time a shot cut the cable of the "Peuple Souverain," next ahead of the "Franklin," and she drifted out of her place to abreast the latter ship, ahead of which a wide gap of a thousand feet was thus left. Into this the "Leander" glided, fixing herself with great skill to rake at once the "Franklin" and the "Orient."

These two French ships had already been much battered, and the "Franklin" was still receiving part of the fire of the "Orion," Sir James Saumarez, on her inner bow, as well as that of the "Defence," hitherto engaged by the "Peuple Souverain." This accumulation upon them of three fresh ships would doubtless have proved irresistible, even if a yet more dire calamity had not supervened. The new-comers took their positions soon after eight, and a little before nine a fire was observed on the poop of the "Orient." The British captains, seeing the flames fighting on their behalf, redoubled their efforts, directing their aim especially upon the scene of the conflagration, and thereby thwarting all attempt to extinguish it. The blaze spread rapidly, upward through the tarred rigging and the masts, downward to the lower decks, where her heroic crew, still ignorant of the approaching doom, labored incessantly at their guns. As the sublime sight forced itself upon the eyes of all about, friends and enemies alike busied themselves with precautions for their own safety in the coming catastrophe. The ships to windward held on; those to leeward for the most part veered or slipped their cables, the "Alexander" fiercely refusing to do so till assured that the "Orient's" destruction was inevitable. Captain Berry went below to report to the admiral this appalling climax to the night's work, and to his own long-sustained efforts in chase and battle. Nelson demanded to be led on deck, where he gave orders that the only boat still in condition for use should be sent with the "Vanguard's" first lieutenant, to help save the unhappy crew. He then remained watching the progress of the fire. At quarter before ten the "Orient" blew up. At this time the moon rose, and from her tranquil path looked down, through the clear Egyptian air, upon the scene of devastation.

Nelson was now persuaded to go to bed, but he neither got nor sought repose of mind. Throughout the night, and in the early morning, messages went from him to various ships to take this or that step, to garner in the fruits of the victory yet unculled. The fleet responded somewhat spasmodically, if not inadequately, to these

calls. Men in truth were worn out with labor and excitement. "My people were so extremely jaded," wrote
Captain Miller of the "Theseus," who obeyed a summons
to move, "that as soon as they had hove our sheet anchor
up they dropped under the capstan bars, and were asleep
in a moment in every sort of posture, having been then
working at their fullest exertion, or fighting, for near
twelve hours." Nelson, in common with other great
leaders, could not be satisfied with any but the utmost
results. To quote again his words of years gone by:
"Had ten ships been taken and the eleventh escaped, we
being able to get at her, I should never consider it well
done." His idea, Captain Berry tells us, was first to
secure the victory, and then to make the most of it, as
circumstances might permit. The expression is so luminous that it can scarcely be doubted that the words are
substantially those of the admiral himself.[1] First, the
great combination, which necessarily for the moment
neglects a part of the enemy in order to disconcert and
overwhelm the rest; afterwards, the unremitting pursuit,
which completes the triumph.

It was therefore perfectly characteristic of Nelson's
habit of thought, and not merely an egotistic expression
of baseless discontent with others, that he avowed his dissatisfaction with the results of the night's work, stupen-

[1] An interesting example of the illuminating effect of a sound maxim
upon different phases of a man's life and actions, and one illustrative of the
many-sidedness of this motto of Nelson's, occurs later in his career, and not
long before his death. When the frigates "Phœbe" and "Amazon" were
ordered to cruise before Toulon in October, 1804, "Lord Nelson gave Captains Capel and Parker several injunctions, in case they should get an opportunity of attacking two of the French frigates, which now got under way
more frequently. The principal one was, that they should not each single
out and attack an opponent, but 'that both should endeavour together to
take one frigate; if successful, chase the other; but if you do not take the
second, still you have won a victory, and your country will gain a frigate.'"
(Phillimore's Last of Nelson's Captains, p. 122.) When summarized, this
again is — Victory first; afterwards the results, as circumstances may permit.

dous and wholly unparalleled as they were. But his own condition, prostrated and with disabled head, was doubly typical of the state of his fleet after the "Orient" blew up. Not only were men overcome with fatigue, — from weariness as great men have been aroused by the inspiring call of a trusted chief, — but the guiding head of the body was dazed and incapacitated; that was gone which alone could sustain energy and give unity to movement. Although Nelson indulged in no metaphorical allusions, he had this figure of the head clearly enough in his mind, when he wrote four weeks later to Lord Minto: "I regret that one escaped, and I think, if it had pleased God that I had not been wounded, not a boat would have escaped to have told the tale; but do not believe that any individual in the fleet is to blame. In my conscience, I believe greater exertions could not have been, and I only mean to say, that if my experience could in person have *directed*[1] those exertions of individuals, there was every appearance that Almighty God would have continued to bless my endeavours." This opinion he reiterated to Lord Howe, even more positively, after four months' longer reflection, in a letter dated January 8, 1799; and, whether the result would or would not have equalled his belief, the traces are clear that what was wanted, during the remainder of that eventful night, was just that concord of action which the head imparts to the members. Messages went from ship to ship, captains consulted together and proposed to move together, and did move separately; there was no lack of good-will, nor, as Nelson says, of exertion; but men were not quite sure of what the other man would do, and felt no authority to command him; and there was hesitation over risks, and cautious delays about soundings and shaky spars, which, the author is persuaded, would not have deterred Nelson in such conditions, where victory was decisive, though not yet complete. Illustrations would perhaps be invidious,

[1] Author's italics.

as seeming to imply a blame upon individuals which Nelson expressly disavowed; blame that officers of exceptional professional capacity, concerning whom the measured professional opinion of Lord Howe affirmed that the Battle of the Nile "was unparalleled in this respect, that *every captain* distinguished himself," fell short of the peculiar excellence attained by Nelson only among the men of his day. Moreover, this work does not aim at a discussion of battles, except so far as they touch Nelson personally. It may, however, be permissible to remark, that the incident here under discussion suggests a doubt about the opinion, too easily current, that an admiral's powers of control cease when the battle joins. Under the circumstances, it is probable that Nelson, being so far incapacitated as he thought himself, should have transferred the direction of affairs, formally, to the next senior officer, with general orders to secure the best results attainable.

The following morning it was found that the leading six ships of the French had already struck their colors. The "Orient" having blown up, there were six survivors. Of these, one, the "Tonnant," next astern of the "Orient," though dismasted, was still afloat, a mile behind her former position, having dropped there to avoid the explosion. The "Heureux" and "Mercure," which had slipped their cables for the same reason, were ashore and helpless. The spars of the three rear ships, the "Guillaume Tell," "Généreux," and "Timoléon," were still standing, and they had received little injury. At about noon these vessels, commanded by Rear Admiral Villeneuve, got under way to go to sea; but the "Timoléon" cast with her head inshore, and, after an ineffectual attempt to wear, ran aground, bows on, her foremast going over the side as she struck. The crew escaped to the beach, and she was then set on fire by her captain, her colors flying as she burned. The two other ships escaped, with two frigates which accompanied them. Only one British ship, the

"Zealous," was in condition to follow, and she did so; but Nelson, seeing that she could not be supported, recalled her from the unequal contest.

It is upon the chance that these sole survivors of the great catastrophe might have been secured, by action during the night, that the validity of Nelson's regrets turns. Concerning this, it is impossible to affirm positively one way or the other; therefore his regrets were well grounded. It is not certainties, but chances, that determine the propriety of military action. Had Villeneuve, conscious that he had done nothing as yet, and not fully aware how the fight had gone, hesitated about running away, and had several British ships dropped to leeward together, which was all they had to do, and what the dismasted French had done, it was quite within the bound of possibilities that the "Généreux" and the "Guillaume Tell" would have been crippled at their anchors. "If" and "but," it may be objected. Quite so; it is on if and but, not on yea and nay, that military criticism justly dwells. A flash of lightning and a crash of thunder may be seen and heard; it is the still small voice that leads the hero to success. As regards Villeneuve, indecision was his distinguishing trait; and Bonaparte wrote that if any error could be imputed to him, it was that he had not got under way as soon as the "Orient" blew up, for by that time the battle was lost beyond redemption.

The extent of the victory was decided by this retreat, and Nelson, before devoting himself to the new duties entailed by his successes, paused an instant that he might first acknowledge his debt of gratitude to God and man. A memorandum was issued at once to the captains of the Squadron:

Vanguard off the mouth of the Nile, 2d August, 1798.

Almighty God having blessed His Majesty's arms with victory, the Admiral intends returning Public Thanksgiving for the same at two o'clock this day; and he recommends every ship doing the same as soon as convenient.

HORATIO NELSON.

To those under his command he at the same time issued a general order, congratulating, by explicit mention of each class, the captains, officers, seamen, and marines, upon the event of the conflict. "The Admiral desires they will accept his most sincere and cordial thanks for their very gallant behaviour in this glorious battle." It was this habit of associating to himself, in full recognition and grateful remembrance, those who followed and fought with him, that enthroned Nelson in the affections of his men; nor will it escape observation that the warmth, though so genuine, breathes through words whose quietness might be thought studied, were they not so transparently spontaneous. There is in them no appeal to egotism, to the gratified passion for glory, although to that he was far from insensible; it is the simple speech of man to man, between those who have stood by one another in the hour of danger, and done their duty — the acknowledgment after the event, which is the complement of the famous signal before Trafalgar.

The order closed with further words of commendation, which will not have the immortal response of the human heart to the other phrases; but which, uttered at such a moment, conveyed a salutary warning, justified as much by recent unhappy events in the British navy, as by the well-known disorganization and anarchy that had disgraced that of France. "It must strike forcibly every British seaman, how superior their conduct is, *when in discipline and good order*, to the riotous behaviour of lawless Frenchmen."[1] Captain Berry states that the assembling of the "Vanguard's" ship's company for the thanksgiving service strongly impressed the prisoners on board, — not from the religious point of view, which was alien from the then prevalent French temper, — but as evidence of an order and discipline which could render such a proceeding acceptable, after a victory so great, and at a moment of

---

[1] Author's italics.

such seeming confusion. No small amount of self-posses-
sion, indeed, was needed thus to direct the attention of
six hundred men, in the confined space of a ship, whose
shattered sides and blood-stained decks bore witness to the
hundred dead and wounded snatched from their number
within the few hours before; yet, on the other hand, nothing could have been better calculated to compose the
thoughts, or to facilitate the transition from the excitement of battle to the resumption of daily life.

If, by the escape of two ships-of-the-line, the British
triumph lacked something in technical completeness, the
disaster to the French was no less absolute. Victory, said
Nelson truly, is not the name for such a scene as I have
witnessed. There remained now to gather up the spoils
of the field, and to realize the consequences of the battle,
great and small, near and remote. The first was speedily
done; battered as they were, "only two masts standing
out of nine sail-of-the-line," within a fortnight six of the
nine prizes were ready to start for Gibraltar. Little by
little, yet with the rapidity of his now highly trained
intuitions, Nelson saw the greatness of what he had
effected, and with his full native energy struggled on,
amid mental confusion and bodily suffering, and in the
heat of an Egyptian August, to secure all the fruits of
success. With splitting head and constantly sick, a significant indication of the rattling shock his brain had
received, he was wonderfully helped, so far as the direction of his efforts was concerned, by the previous familiarity of his mind with the various elements of the problem.
First of all, the home government must be informed of
an event that would so profoundly affect the future.
Berry's orders, as bearer of despatches to St. Vincent off
Cadiz, were issued on the 2d of August; but there were
no frigates, and the "Leander," appointed to carry him,
could not sail till the 6th. For the same reason it was
not until the 14th that the "Mutine" could be sent off

with duplicates, to go direct to the Admiralty by way
of Naples, — a wise precaution in all events, but doubly
justified in this case; for the brig reached port, whereas
the fifty-gun ship was captured by the "Généreux." The
"Mutine's" account, though hastened forward without
delay, reached London only on the 2d of October, two
months after the action.

The news was received at the first with an applause and
a popular commotion commensurate to its greatness, and
promised for the moment to overflow even the barriers of
routine in one of the most conservative of nations. "Mr.
Pitt told me the day after Captain Capel arrived," wrote
his old admiral, Hood, to Nelson, "that you would certainly be a Viscount, which I made known to Lady Nelson.
But it was objected to in a certain quarter, because your
Lordship was not a commander-in-chief. In my humble
opinion a more flimsy reason never was given." Official
circles regained, or rather perhaps again lost, their senses,
and the victory, unquestionably the most nearly complete
and the most decisive ever gained by a British fleet, was
rewarded, in the person of the commanding officer, with
honors less than those bestowed for St. Vincent and
Camperdown. Nelson was advanced to the lowest rank
of the peerage, as Baron Nelson of the Nile. "In congratulating your Lordship on this high distinction," wrote
the First Lord, "I have particular pleasure in remarking,
that it is the highest honour that has ever been conferred
on an officer of your standing,[1] in the Service, and who
was not a commander-in-chief; and the addition [of the
Nile] to the Title is meant more especially to mark the
occasion on which it was granted, which, however, without any such precaution, is certainly of a nature never to
be forgotten." His Lordship's sense of humor must a
little have failed him, when he penned the platitude of
the last few words.

[1] "Rank" doubtless is meant by this singularly ill-chosen word.

To the sharp criticism passed in the House of Commons on the smallness of the recognition, the Prime Minister replied that Nelson's glory did not depend upon the rank to which he might be raised in the peerage; a truism too palpable and inapplicable for serious utterance, the question before the House being, not the measure of Nelson's glory, but that of the national acknowledgment. As Hood justly said, "All remunerations should be proportionate to the service done to the public;" and if that cannot always be attained absolutely, without exhausting the powers of the State,[1] there should at least be some proportion between the rewards themselves, extended to individuals, and the particular services. But even were the defence of the Ministers technically perfect, it would have been pleasanter to see them a little blinded by such an achievement. Once in a way, under some provocations, it is refreshing to see men able even to make fools of themselves.

Nelson made to the First Lord's letter a reply that was dignified and yet measured, to a degree unusual to him, contrasting singularly with his vehement reclamations for others after Copenhagen. Without semblance of complaint, he allowed plainly to appear between the lines his own sense that the reward was not proportionate to the service done. "I have received your Lordship's letter communicating to me the Title his Majesty has been graciously pleased to confer upon me — an Honour, your Lordship is pleased to say, the highest that has ever been conferred on an officer of my standing who was not a Commander-in-Chief. I receive as I ought what the goodness of our Sovereign, and not my deserts, is pleased to bestow; but great and unexampled as this honour may be to one of my standing, yet I own I feel a higher one in

---

[1] As General Sherman justly asked, "What reward adequate to the service, could the United States have given Grant for the Vicksburg campaign?"

the unbounded confidence of the King, your Lordship, and the whole World, in my exertions. Even at the bitter moment of my return to Syracuse, your Lordship is not insensible of the great difficulties I had to encounter in not being a Commander-in-Chief. The only happy moment I felt was in the view of the French; then I knew that all my sufferings would soon be at an end." To Berry he wrote: "As to both our Honours, it is a proof how much a battle fought near England is prized to one fought at a great distance."

Whatever was defective in the formal recognition of his own government was abundantly supplied by the tributes which flowed from other quarters, so various, that his own phrase, "the whole world," is scarcely an exaggeration to apply to them. The Czar, the Sultan, the Kings of Sardinia and of the Two Sicilies, sent messages of congratulation and rich presents; the Czar accompanying his with an autograph letter. The Houses of Parliament voted their thanks and a pension of £2,000 a year. The East India Company acknowledged the security gained for their Indian possessions by a gift of £10,000, £2,000 of which he, with his wonted generosity, divided at once among his father and family, most of whom were not in prosperous circumstances. Other corporations took appropriate notice of the great event; instances so far apart as the cities of London and Palermo, and the Island of Zante, showing how wide-spread was the sense of relief. Not least gratifying to him, with his sensitive appreciation of friendship and susceptibility to flattery, must have been the numerous letters of congratulation he received from friends in and out of the service. The three great admirals, — Lords Howe, Hood, and St. Vincent, — the leaders of the Navy in rank and distinguished service, wrote to him in the strongest terms of admiration. The two last styled the battle the greatest achievement that History could produce; while Howe's language, if more

measured, was so only because, like himself, it was more
precise in characterizing the special merits of the action,
and was therefore acknowledged by Nelson with particular
expressions of pleasure.

Besides the honors bestowed upon the commander of the
squadron, and the comprehensive vote of thanks usual on
such occasions, a gold medal commemorative of the battle
was given to the admiral and to each of the captains present.
The First Lord also wrote that the first-lieutenants of the
ships engaged would be promoted at once.   The word
"engaged" caught Nelson's attention, as apparently intended to exclude the lieutenant of the " Culloden," Troubridge's unlucky ship.   " For Heaven's sake, for my sake,"
he wrote to St. Vincent, " if this is so, get it altered. Our
dear friend Troubridge has suffered enough. His sufferings were in every respect more than any of us. He de-
serves every reward which a grateful Country can bestow
on the most meritorious sea-officer of his standing in the
service. I have felt his worth every hour of my command."   " I well know, he is my superior," he said on
another occasion; "and I so often want his advice and
assistance. I have experienced the ability and activity of
his mind and body: it was Troubridge that equipped the
squadron so soon at Syracuse — it was he that exerted
himself for me after the action — it was Troubridge who
saved the " Culloden," when none that I know in the service would have attempted it — it was Troubridge whom
I left as myself at Naples to watch movements — he is,
as a friend and an officer, a *nonpareil !* "   His entreaties
prevailed so far that the officer in question received
his promotion, not with the others, but immediately after
them; a distinction which Troubridge bewailed bitterly,
as a reflection upon himself and his ship.

On the 9th of August, Nelson sent a lieutenant to
Alexandretta, on the northern coast of Syria, to make his
way overland, by way of Aleppo, to India, with despatches

to the Governor of Bombay.   Resuming briefly the events
of the past months, and the numbers and character of the
French army in Egypt, he expresses the hope that special
care will be exercised against the departure of ships from
India, to convey this huge force thither by the Red Sea.
On the side of the Mediterranean, their fate is settled by
the recent victory.   They can receive nothing from France;
they cannot advance freely into Syria, as water transport
is essential for much of their equipment; even in Egypt
itself they are hampered by the difficulties of communication — on land by the guerilla hostility of the natives, and
now on the water through his own presence and control.
The Nile, through its Rosetta mouth, had been heretofore
the easiest communication between Cairo and Alexandria.
The garrison of the latter depended largely for daily bread
upon this route, now closed by the fleet in Aboukir Bay.
By land, nothing short of a regiment could pass over
ground where, even before the battle, the French watering-
parties from the ships had to be protected by heavy armed
bodies. He intended, therefore, to remain where he was as
long as possible.   " If my letter is not so correct as might
be expected," he concludes, " I trust for your excuse, when
I tell you that my brain is so shook with the wounds in
my head, that I am sensible I am not always so clear as
could be wished; but whilst a ray of reason remains, my
heart and my head shall ever be exerted for the benefit of
our King and Country."

It may be added here, that the scar left by this wound
seems to have been the cause of Nelson's hair being trained
down upon his forehead, during the later years of his life.
Prior to that it was brushed well off and up, as may be
seen in the portrait by Abbott, painted during his stay in
England, while recovering from the loss of his arm. After
his death, a young officer of the " Victory," who had cut
off some locks for those who wished such a remembrance
of their friend, speaks of "the hair that used to hang

over his forehead, near the wound that he received at the Battle of the Nile."

The perception of his control over the communications from Rosetta to Alexandria dawned rather late upon Nelson, for on the 5th of August he had announced his purpose of starting down the Mediterranean on the 19th. This he postponed afterwards to the first part of September, and again for as long as possible. While in this intention, most secret and urgent orders came on the 15th from St. Vincent, to return to the westward with his command, and to co-operate with an expedition planned against Minorca. Six prizes, with seven of the British ships-of-the-line, had started on the 14th for Gibraltar, under the command of Sir James Saumarez. The three remaining prizes were burned, and hasty temporary repairs, adequate only for a summer voyage, were put upon the "Vanguard," " Cullo-den," and " Alexander," the three most defective ships of his fleet. On the 19th he sailed with these three for Naples, which he had from the first intended to visit, in order to give them the complete overhauling they imperatively needed. On and after the 13th of August several frigates had joined him. Three of these, with three ships-of-the-line, were left with Captain Hood, to conduct the blockade of Alexandria, and to suppress the enemy's communications by water along the coasts of Egypt and Syria.

CHAPTER XI.

THE voyage of Nelson's small division from Aboukir
Bay to Naples occupied between four and five weeks,
owing partly to light and contrary winds, and partly to the
dull sailing of the "Culloden," which had a sail secured
under her bottom to lessen the dangerous leak caused by
her grounding on the night of the battle. This otherwise
unwelcome delay procured for Nelson a period of salutary,
though enforced, repose, which the nature of his injuries
made especially desirable. His mind, indeed, did not cease
to work, but it was free from harassment; and the obvious
impossibility of doing anything, save accept the present
easy-going situation, contributed strongly to the quietness
upon which restoration depended. Nor were there wanting matters of daily interest to prevent an excess of monotony. Now that frigates were no longer so vitally necessary, they and other light cruisers turned up with amusing
frequency, bringing information, and being again despatched hither and yonder with letters from the admiral,
which reflected instinctively his personal moods, and his
active concern in the future military operations.

The distress from his head continued for some time with
little abatement, and naturally much affected his tone of
mind. At the first he spoke of his speedy return to Eng-

land as inevitable, nor did the prospect occasion the discouragement which he had experienced after the loss of his arm; a symptom which had shown the moral effect of failure upon a sensitive and ambitious temperament. " My head is ready to split," he had written to St. Vincent before starting, "and I am always so sick; in short, if there be no fracture, my head is severely shaken." A fortnight after leaving the bay, he writes him again: " I know I ought to give up for a little while; my head is splitting at this moment; " and Nicolas remarks that the letter bears evident marks of suffering, three attempts being made to spell the word "splitting." Yet by this time the pain had become at least intermittent, for Saumarez, whose squadron fell in with the admiral's division several times, notes that on the 26th of August he spent half an hour on board the flagship, and found him in perfect health; and on the 7th of September Nelson himself writes to the British minister at Florence that he felt so much recovered, it was probable he would not go home for the present. A few days later he wrote to Hood, off Alexandria, that he relied upon the thoroughness of the blockade to complete the destruction of the French army. " I shall not go home," he added, " until this is effected, and the islands of Malta, Corfu, &c., retaken."

It is to the furtherance of these objects, all closely allied, and in his apprehension mutually dependent, that his occasional letters are directed. His sphere of operations he plainly conceives to be from Malta, eastward, to Syria inclusive. " I detest this voyage to Naples," he wrote to St. Vincent, two days before reaching the port. " Nothing but absolute necessity could force me to the measure. Syracuse in future, whilst my operations lie on the eastern side of Sicily, is my port, where every refreshment may be had for a fleet." The present necessity was that of refit and repair, to which Syracuse was inadequate. "For myself," he sent word to Sir William Hamilton, " I hope not to be

more than four or five days at Naples, for these times are
not for idleness." Not long after his arrival this conviction
as to the movements requiring his personal presence underwent an entire change; and thenceforth, till he left for
England two years later, it was only the presence of clear
emergency, appealing to his martial instincts and calling
forth the sense of duty which lay at the root of his character, that could persuade him his proper place was elsewhere than at the Court of Naples. It is only fair to add
that, upon the receipt of the news of his great victory, the
Admiralty designated to St. Vincent, as first in order
among the cares of the squadron within the Mediterranean,
"the protection of the coasts of Sicily, Naples, and the
Adriatic, and, in the event of war being renewed in Italy,
an active co-operation with the Austrian and Neapolitan
armies." Long before these instructions were received,
the very day indeed that they were written, Nelson had
become urgently instrumental in precipitating Naples into
war. Next in order of interest, by the Admiralty's letters,
were, successively, the isolation of Egypt and of Malta,
and co-operation with the Russian and Turkish squadrons
which, it was expected, would be sent into the Archipelago, and which actually did attack and capture Corfu.
The letter thus summarized may be taken to indicate the
general extent of Nelson's charge during the two following years.

It may be said, then, without error, that Nelson's opinion
as to the direction of his personal supervision underwent a
decisive change after his arrival in Naples. Before it, he
is urgent with that Court to support with active naval
assistance the operations against Malta, and to send bomb-
vessels, the absence of which he continually deplores, to
shell the transports in the harbor of Alexandria. He
hopes, indeed, to find on his arrival that the Emperor and
many other powers are at war with the French, but his
attention is concentrated upon Bonaparte's army. To the

British minister in Turkey he is yet more insistent as to what the Sultan should undertake. If he will but send a few ships-of-the-line, and some bombs, he will destroy all their transports in Alexandria; and an army of ten thousand men may retake Alexandria immediately, as the French have only four thousand men in it. Subsequent events showed this forecast of Nelson's to be as erroneous as those of Napoleon were at times in regard to naval prospects. "General Bonaparte," he continues, "only wants a communication opened by sea, to march into Syria, that the transports with stores, &c., for the army, may go alongshore with him." This he had learned from French officers who were prisoners on board, and we know it corresponded with the facts. "If the Sultan will not send anything, he will lose Syria." "Naples," he tells St. Vincent, "is saved in spite of herself. They have evidently broken their treaty with France, and yet are afraid to assist in finishing the vast armament of the French. Four hours with bomb vessels, would set all in a blaze, and we know what an army is without stores." This anticipation also proved deceptive; but the expressions quoted are fair examples of the general tenor of his letters between Aboukir and Naples, and show his feeling that the important points of his command lay to the east of Sicily.

The same tendency was shown upon the appearance of a Portuguese squadron of four ships-of-the-line, which entered the Mediterranean in July with orders to place themselves under his command. He first learned the fact upon this passage, and at once sent a frigate to Alexandria to beg the Portuguese admiral, the Marquis de Niza, to assume the blockade, as the most important service to be rendered the common cause. When the frigate reached its destination, Niza had come and gone, and Nelson then headed him off at the Strait of Messina, on his way to Naples, and sent him to blockade Malta. It may be added that this squadron remained under his command until December, 1799, and was of substantial utility in the various operations. Nelson professed no great confidence in its efficiency, which was not subjected to the severest tests; but he made a handsome acknowledgment to its commander when it was recalled to Lisbon.

On the 22d of September the flagship anchored at Naples. On the 15th her foremast had been carried away in a squall, and the "poor wretched Vanguard," as Nelson called her, having to be towed by a frigate, her two crippled consorts preceded her arrival by six days. The news of the victory had been brought three weeks before by the "Mutine," on the 1st of September. The Court party had gone wild with joy, in which the populace, naturally hostile to the French, had joined with southern vivacity of expression. Captain Capel, who commanded the brig, with Lieutenant Hoste, who was to succeed him when he departed with the despatches for England, had been at once taken to Court and presented. When they left the palace they were met by Lady Hamilton, who made them get into her carriage, and with characteristic bad taste and love of notoriety paraded them until dark through the streets of this neutral capital, she wearing a bandeau round her forehead with the words, "Nelson and Victory." "The populace saw and understood what it meant," wrote Hoste, "and ' Viva Nelson ! ' resounded through the streets. You can have no idea of the rejoicings that were made throughout Naples. Bonfires and illuminations all over the town; indeed, it would require an abler pen than I am master of to give you any account but what will fall infinitely short of what was the case."

By Nelson's orders the "Mutine" sailed in a few days to meet him with despatches, and on the 14th of September joined the division off Stromboli. With more important information, and letters from persons of greater consequence, she had brought also one from Lady Hamilton,

giving a vivid picture of the general joy, and in particular
an account of the Queen's state of mind, so highly colored
and detailed that Nelson could only hope he might not be
witness to a renewal of it, but which so impressed him
that he quoted it at length to Lady Nelson. When the
"Vanguard" approached the town, crowds of boats went
out to meet her, and His Sicilian Majesty himself came
on board when she was still a league from the anchorage.
He had been preceded by the British ambassador with
Lady Hamilton. The latter, having had only three weeks
to recover from the first shock of the news, was greatly
overcome, and dropped her lovely face and by no means
slender figure into the arms of the admiral, who, on his
part, could scarcely fail to be struck with the pose of one
whose attitudes compelled the admiration of the most exacting critics. "The scene in the boat was terribly affecting," he wrote to his wife. "Up flew her ladyship, and
exclaiming, 'O God, is it possible?' she fell into my arm
more dead than alive. Tears, however, soon set matters
to rights."

This was the beginning of an intimacy destined, in the
end, to affect profoundly and unhappily the future of
Nelson. Although Sir William Hamilton, in his own con-
gratulatory letter by the "Mutine," called him "our bosom
friend," they do not seem to have met since the summer
of 1793, when the young captain carried Hood's despatches
from Toulon to Naples; and Nelson, while acknowledging
on the present occasion the kindness of an invitation to
take up his quarters at the embassy, had expressed a preference for rooms at a hotel, on account of the business to
be transacted. This reluctance, however, was easily and
properly overruled, and immediately after anchoring he
went to live at the ambassador's house, which, under the
management of the celebrated woman who presided there,
became the social centre of the welcomes lavished not only
upon himself, but upon all the officers of the ships.

Lady Hamilton

Emma, Lady Hamilton, the second wife of Sir William, was at this time thirty-three years old, her husband being sixty-eight. Her name, when first entering the world, was Amy Lyon. Born in Cheshire of extremely poor parents, in the humblest walk of life, she had found her way up to London, while yet little more than a child, and there, having a beautiful face, much natural charm of manner and disposition, utterly inexperienced, and with scarcely any moral standards, — of which her life throughout shows but little trace, — she was speedily ruined, fell so far, in fact, that even with all her attractions it seemed doubtful whether any man would own himself responsible for her condition, or befriend her. In these circumstances, when not yet seventeen, she was taken up by a nephew of Sir William Hamilton, Mr. Charles Greville, who recognized not merely her superficial loveliness, but something of the mental and moral traits underlying it, which promised a capacity for development into an interesting and affectionate household companion. Upon her promises of amendment, in the matter of future relations with men, and of submission to his guidance and wishes in the general conduct of her life, he took her in charge, and the two lived together for nearly four years.

Greville bestowed a good deal of pains upon her training, and was rewarded, not only by gratitude and careful compliance with his directions, but by her sincere and devoted affection. The girl became heartily and fondly in love with him, finding both contentment and happiness in the simply ordered home provided for her. Her education, which hitherto was of the smallest, received attention, — her letters showing a very great improvement both in spelling and mode of expression by the end of their association. On the moral side, of course, there was not much development to be expected from one whose standards, with less excuse, were in no way better than her own. On this side Greville's teaching was purely utilitarian.

Her position was considered as a calling, — success in which demanded certain proprieties and accomplishments, only to be attained by the practice of habitual self-control, alike in doing and in not doing.

The future Lady Hamilton was affectionate and impulsive, good-humored, with generous instincts and a quick temper; but she was also ambitious and exceptionally clever. She loved Greville warmly; but she took to heart the hard truths of his teachings, and they sank deep in a congenial soil. Under the influence of the two motives, she applied herself to gain, and did gain, a certain degree of external niceness and self-control. Her affection for Greville made her willing, for his sake, because he was not rich, to live quietly, to accept modest surroundings, and to discard whatever was coarse in associates, or unbecoming in her own person or conduct. He, while relaxing none of his requirements, repaid her with courtesy and increasing admiration, than which nothing was dearer to her; for, if not appreciative of the satisfaction of self-respect, she was keenly alive to the delights of homage from others, though extorted by purely adventitious qualities. Glory was to her more than honor. This love of admiration, fostered, yet pruned, by Greville's shrewd precepts, was her dominant trait. To its gratification her singular personal advantages contributed, and they were powerfully supported by an unusual faculty for assuming a part, for entering into a character and representing its external traits. Thus gifted by nature, and swayed by vanity, her development was for the time regulated and chastened by the disinterestedness of her passion for her lover. Her worse qualities were momentarily kept in abeyance. Naturally lovable, not only in exterior but in temperament, she became more and more attractive. " Consider," wrote Greville, referring to her surroundings before she passed into his hands, " what a charming creature she would have been, if she had been blessed with the advantages of an early education, and had not been spoilt by the indulgence of every caprice."

Unfortunately the restraining influence, probably ephemeral in any event, was about to be rudely removed, permitting to flourish in unrestrained vigor the natural tendency to compel admiration and secure advantage by the spell of physical beauty, and by the exertion of natural aptitudes for pleasing in the only path to success open to her. In 1782 Hamilton's first wife died, and in 1784 he came to England on leave. There he met Amy Lyon, now known as Emma Hart, in the house provided for her by Greville. His admiration of her was extreme, and its tendency was not misunderstood by her. He returned to his post at Naples at the end of the year. In the course of 1785 Greville, who was now in his thirty-sixth year, decided that the condition of his fortune made it imperative for him to marry, and that as a first step thereto he must break with Emma Hart. Hamilton's inclination for her provided a ready means for so doing, so far as the two men were concerned; but her concurrence was not sure. After some correspondence, it was arranged that she should go to Naples in the spring of 1786, to live there under Hamilton's care, with the expectation on her part that Greville would join her a few months later. Placed as she then would be, it was probable that she would eventually accept the offers made her; though it would be less than just to either Greville or Hamilton, to allow the impression that they did not intend to provide sufficiently for her needs, whatever her decision.

In this way she left England in the spring of 1786, reaching Naples on the 26th of April. When the poor girl, after many of her letters to her lover remained unanswered, fully realized that the separation was final, her grief was extreme, and found utterance in words of tenderness and desolation, which, however undisciplined in expression, are marked by genuine pathos. But anger struggled with sorrow for the mastery in her soul. She was too keen-witted not to have had an inkling of the possible outcome of her departure from England, and of the doubtful position she was occupying at Naples; but her wishes had made her willingly deaf to any false ring in the assurances given her by Greville, and she resented not only the abandonment, but the deceit which she, justly or unjustly, conceived to have been practised, while her womanliness revolted from the cold-blooded advice given by him to accept the situation. The conflict was so sharp that for a time both he and Hamilton expected she would return to England; but Greville had not labored in vain at what he was pleased to consider her education. By the end of the year she was addressing Hamilton in words of very fairly assumed affection, but not until she had written to Greville, with a certain haughty desperation, " If you affront me, I will make him marry me." The threat was two-edged, for Hamilton intended Greville to be his heir; but the latter probably gave little heed to a contingency he must have thought very unlikely for a man of fifty-six, who had passed his life in the world, and held Hamilton's public position.

To effect this, however, Emma Hart now bent her personal charms, strong purpose, and the worldly wisdom with which Greville had taught her to assure her hold upon a man. Love, in its unselfishness, passed out of her life with Greville. Other men might find her pliant, pleasing, seductive; he alone knew her as disinterested. She followed out her design with a patience, astuteness, and consistency which attest the strength of her resolution, and her acute intellectual perception of the advantages at her disposal. Ambition, a natural trait with her, had been trained to self-control, in order to compass a lowly, colorless success. Unlooked-for opportunity now held before her eyes, distant and difficult of attainment, but not impossible, a position of assured safety, luxury, and prominence, which appealed powerfully to the love of pleasure, still dormant, and to the love of conspicuousness, which became the two most noticeable features of her character.

With all her natural advantages, however, the way was hard and long. She had to become indispensable to Hamilton, and at the same time, and by the same methods, an object the more desirable to him because of her evident attractiveness to others. Above all, she had to contend with her own temper, naturally lively and prone to bursts of anger, which the prolonged suspense of the struggle, acting upon a woman's nerves, tended peculiarly to exasperate. Hamilton was of an age when he might be enslaved by fondness, but not constrained by strength of passion to endure indefinitely household tempests, much less to perpetuate them upon himself by lasting bonds. In all this Emma Hart showed herself fully equal to the task. Tenderly affectionate to him, except when carried away by the fits of irritability which both he and Greville had occasion to observe, she complied readily with all his wishes, and followed out with extraordinary assiduity his plans for her improvement in education and in accomplishments. The society which gathered round them was, of course, almost wholly of men, who one and all prostrated themselves before her beauty and cleverness, with the same unanimity of submission as did the officers of Nelson's division after the Battle of the Nile. But, while giving free rein to coquetry, and revelling in admiration, she afforded no ground for scandal to the world, or dissatisfaction to Hamilton. In the attitude of outsiders towards her, he had reason to see only the general testimony to her charms and to his own good fortune. At the end of 1787 he wrote to Greville: " I can assure you her behaviour is such as has acquired her many sensible admirers, and we have a good man society, and all the female nobility, with the queen at their head, show her every distant civility."

Thus she persisted, keeping her beauty, and growing in

mental acquirements and accomplishments, but making little apparent headway towards the great object of her ambition. "I fear," wrote Hamilton towards the middle of 1789, when she had been three years with him, "her views are beyond what I can bring myself to execute; and that when her hopes on that point are over, she will make herself and me unhappy. Hitherto her behaviour is irreproachable, but her temper, as you must know, unequal." He underrated her perseverance, and exaggerated his own strength of reluctance, innate and acquired. Impossible as it would seem, with his antecedents and with hers, his friends and acquaintances became alarmed for the result, and not without cause. "Her influence over him exceeds all belief," wrote a mutual friend to Greville in March, 1791. "His attachment exceeds admiration, it is perfect dotage." Shortly after this letter was written the two went to England, and there they were married on the 6th of September, 1791. By the end of the year they were back in Naples, and did not again leave Italy up to the time of Nelson's arrival in 1798.

Lady Hamilton did not abuse the security of the place she had won with so much pains, nor on the other hand did her ambition and love of prominence permit her to settle down to inert enjoyment of it. The careful self-restraint with which she had observed the proprieties of her former false position facilitated the disappearance of prejudices naturally arising from it. Many English ladies of rank, passing through Naples, visited her, and those who refused to ignore the past of the woman, in the position of the British minister's wife, were by some sharply criticised. "She has had a difficult part to act," wrote Hamilton, six months after their return, "and has succeeded wonderfully, having gained, by having no pretensions, the thorough approbation of all the English ladies. The Queen of Naples was very kind to her on our return, and treats her like any other travelling lady of distinction; in short, we are very

comfortably situated here." "We dined yesterday with
Sir William and Lady Hamilton," wrote Lady Malmesbury,
whose husband was among the most distinguished diplo-
matists of the day. "She really behaves as well as possible, and quite wonderfully, considering her origin and
education."

This last phrase, used at the culmination of Lady Hamilton's good fortune and personal advance, was wholly good-
natured; but it sums up the best of the not very good that
can be said of her during the height of her prosperity, and
in later years. Although, as has been remarked, she did
not at this time abuse the security which as a wife she had
attained, — for policy too clearly dictated the continuance
of her previous circumspection, — the necessity for strenuous watchfulness, exertion, and self-restraint, in order to
reach a distant goal, no longer existed; and, although a
woman of many amiable and generous impulses, she had
not a shred of principle to take the place of the motive of
self-interest, which hitherto had been so peremptory in its
exactions. What she was in delicacy in 1791, that she
remained in 1796, — five years after the disappearance of
her social disabilities; a pretty fair proof that what she
possessed of it was but skin deep, the result of a diligent
observance of Greville's proprieties, for her personal advantage, not the token of a noble inner spirit struggling
from excusable defilement to the light. "She does the
honours of the house with great attention and desire to
please," wrote Greville's correspondent of 1791, before
quoted, "but wants a little refinement of manners, in
which, in the course of six years, I wonder she has not
made greater progress." "She is all Nature and yet all
Art," said Sir Gilbert Elliot, in 1796; "that is to say, her
manners are perfectly unpolished, of course very easy,
though not with the ease of good breeding, but of a bar-
maid; excessively good humoured, and wishing to please
and be admired by all ages and sorts of persons that come

in her way; but besides considerable natural understanding, she has acquired, since her marriage, some knowledge of history and of the arts, and one wonders at the application and pains she has taken to make herself what she is. With men her language and conversation are exaggerations of anything I ever heard anywhere; and I was wonderfully struck with these inveterate remains of her origin, though the impression was very much weakened by seeing the other ladies of Naples." "I thought her a very handsome, vulgar woman," curtly commented the lieutenant of a frigate which visited Naples in the summer of 1798, while hunting for Nelson in the game of cross-purposes that preceded the Nile.[1] Allowing for difference of observers, it is plain that the Lady Hamilton whom Nelson now met, had not improved in essentials over the Emma Hart of a half-dozen years before.

Two years afterwards, the verdict of these men was confirmed by Mrs. St. George,[2] a lady in London society, who viewed her possibly with something of the repugnant prejudice of a refined and cultivated woman, yet evidently measured her words calmly, even in her private journal. "I think her bold, daring, vain even to folly, and stamped with the manners of her first situation much more strongly than one would suppose, after having represented Majesty, and lived in good company fifteen years. Her dress is frightful. Her waist is absolutely between her shoulders." Nelson measured her by a different standard. "In every point of view," he tells herself, "from Ambassatrice to the duties of domestic life, I never saw your equal. That elegance of manners, accomplishments, and, above all, your goodness of heart, is unparalleled." The same lady describes her personal appearance, at the time when his devotion had reached the height from which it never declined. "Her figure is colossal, but, excepting her feet, which are

---

[1] Colburn's United Service Magazine, 1847, part ii. p. 52.
[2] Afterwards Mrs. Trench, the mother of Archbishop Trench.

hideous, well shaped. Her bones are large, and she is exceedingly *embonpoint*. The shape of all her features is fine, as is the form of her head, and particularly her ears; her teeth are a little irregular, but tolerably white; her eyes light blue, with a brown spot in one, which, though a defect, takes nothing away from her beauty or expression. Her eyebrows and hair (which, by the bye, is never clean) are dark, and her complexion coarse. Her expression is strongly marked, variable, and interesting; her movements in common life ungraceful; her voice loud, yet not disagreeable." Elliot's briefer mention of her appearance is at once confirmatory and complementary of that of Mrs. St. George: "Her person is nothing short of monstrous for its enormity, and is growing every day. Her face is beautiful."

To these opinions it may be not uninteresting to add the critical estimate of William Beckford, uttered many years later. Beckford was not an admirable character, far from it; but he had known good society, and he had cultivated tastes. Nelson accepted his hospitality, and, with the Hamiltons, spent several days under his roof, about Christmas time, 1800. In reply to the question, " Was the second Lady Hamilton a fascinating woman?" he said, " I never thought her so. She was somewhat masculine, but symmetrical in figure, so that Sir William called her his Grecian. She was full in person, not fat, but *embonpoint*. Her carriage often majestic, rather than feminine. Not at all delicate, ill-bred, often very affected, a devil in temper when set on edge. She had beautiful hair and displayed it. Her countenance was agreeable, — fine, hardly beautiful, but the outline excellent. She affected sensibility, but felt none — was artful; and no wonder, she had been trained in the Court of Naples — a fine school for an English woman of any stamp. Nelson was infatuated. She could make him believe anything, that the profligate queen was a Madonna. He was her dupe. She never had a child in her life."[1] As to this last assertion, Beckford was not in a position to have personal knowledge.

But along with this native coarseness, which, if not ineradicable, was never eradicated, she possessed an intuitive and perfect sense, amounting to genius, for what propriety and good taste demanded in the presentation of an ideal part, — the gift of the born actress. Of her powers in this way the celebrated "Attitudes" were the chief example, and there is no disagreement among the witnesses, either as to their charm or as to the entire disappearance of the every-day woman in the assumed character. "We had the attitudes a night or two ago by candle light," wrote Sir Gilbert Elliot in 1796. "They come up to my expectations fully, which is saying everything. They set Lady Hamilton in a very different light from any I had seen her in before; nothing about her, neither her conversation, her manners, nor figure, announce the very refined taste which she discovers in this performance, besides the extraordinary talent which is needed for the execution." "You never saw anything so charming as Lady Hamilton's attitudes," wrote Lady Malmesbury in 1791. "The most graceful statues or pictures do not give you an idea of them." "It is a beautiful performance," wrote Mrs. St. George, who saw her in 1800, when the Hamiltons and Nelson were travelling on the Continent, "amusing to the most ignorant, and highly interesting to the lovers of art. It is remarkable that although coarse and ungraceful in common life, she becomes highly graceful, and even beautiful, during this performance. It is also singular that, in spite of the accuracy of her imitation of the finest ancient draperies, her usual dress is tasteless, vulgar, loaded and unbecoming."

The stormy period of the French Revolution, which was about to burst into universal war at the time she was married, gave Lady Hamilton another opportunity to come yet

[1] Beckford's Memoirs, London, 1859, vol. ii. p. 326.

more conspicuously before men's eyes than she had hitherto done. It is not easy to say what degree of influence
she really attained, or what particular results she may have
effected; but she certainly managed to give herself so
much the air of a person of importance, in the political
intrigues of the day in Naples, as at the least to impose
successfully upon a great many, and to be accepted very
much at her own valuation. The French ambassador, writing to Bonaparte in 1798, says: " If the preponderance
which the French Republic ought to take here, removed
hence Acton and the wife of Hamilton, this country, without other changes, would be extremely useful for the execution of all your projects in the Mediterranean; " and Sir
William himself, who should have known, speaks of her
activity and utility, — " for several years the real and only
confidential friend of the Queen of Naples." Nelson,
writing to the Queen of Naples in 1804, after Hamilton's death, said: " Your Majesty well knows that it was
her capacity and conduct which sustained his diplomatic
character during the last years in which he was at Naples." [1]
Certainly, Nelson believed, with all the blindness of love,
whatever his mistress chose to tell him, but he was not
without close personal knowledge of the inside history of
at least two of those last years; for, in 1801, addressing
Mr. Addington, then Prime Minister, he used these words:
" Having for a length of time seen the correspondence
both public and private, from all the Neapolitan ministers
to their Government and to the Queen of Naples, I am perfectly acquainted with the views of the several Powers."
For her success Lady Hamilton was indebted, partly to
her personal advantages, and partly to her position as wife
of the British minister and chosen friend to the Queen.
Great Britain played a leading part everywhere in the
gigantic struggle throughout the Continent, but to a remote peninsular kingdom like Naples, protected by its

[1] Compare an equally strong assertion, Nicolas's Despatches, vol. vi. p 99.

distance from the centres of strife, yet not wholly inaccessible by land, the chief maritime state was the one and only sufficient ally. A rude reminder of his exposure to naval attack had been given to the King of the Two Sicilies, in 1792, by the appearance of a French fleet, which extorted satisfaction for an alleged insult, by threatening instant bombardment of his capital.

Sir William Hamilton, who had been minister since 1765, thus found himself suddenly converted from a dilettante and sportsman, lounging through life, into a busy diplomat, at the centre of affairs of critical moment. At sixty-two the change could scarcely have been welcome to him, but to his beautiful and ambitious wife the access of importance was sweet, for it led to a close friendship with the Queen, already disposed to affect her, even in the notorious position she had held before her marriage; and the Queen, a daughter of Maria Theresa and sister to Marie Antoinette, was much more of a man than the King. The intimacy became the talk of Naples, and the report spread, easily believed, because in the nature of things very likely, that the personal relations between the two women cloaked a great deal of underhand work, such as often accompanies diplomatic difficulties. Nor did Lady Hamilton lack natural qualifications for the position into which she undoubtedly wished to thrust herself. She was a brave, capable, full-blooded, efficient woman, not to be daunted by fears or scruples; a woman who, if only nerve and intelligence were required, and if distinction for herself was at stake, could be fairly depended upon. There was in her make-up a good deal of pagan virtue. She could appreciate and admire heroism, and, under the stimulus of excitement, of self-conscious magnanimity, for the glitter of effective performance and the applause of onlookers, she was quite capable of heroic action. It was this daring spirit, coarsely akin to much that was best in himself, and of which she made proof under his own eyes, that Nelson recognized; and this, in the thought of the writer, was the body of truth, from which his enthusiasm, enkindled by her charms and by her tenderness towards himself, projected such a singular phantasm of romantic perfections.

Such was the woman, and such the position in the public eye that she had gained for herself, when to Naples, first in the European continent, came the news which made Nelson for the moment the most conspicuous man of the day. He had achieved a triumph the most startlingly dazzling that had yet been gained, and over one who up to that time had excelled all other warriors in the brilliancy and extent of his victories. Bonaparte was not yet the Napoleon whom history knows, but thus far he had been the most distinguished child of the Revolution. That Lady Hamilton then and there formed the purpose of attaching Nelson to her, by the bonds which have sullied his memory, is most improbable; but it is in entire keeping with the career and the self-revelations of the woman that she should, instinctively, if not with deliberation, have resolved to parade herself in the glare of his renown, and appear in the foreground upon the stage of his triumph, the chief dispenser of his praises, the patroness and proprietor of the hero. The great occasion should shed a glamour round her, together with him. "Emma's passion is admiration," Greville had written soon after they parted, "and it is capable of aspiring to any line which would be celebrated, and it would be indifferent, when on that key, whether she was Lucretia or Sappho, or Scævola or Regulus; anything grand, masculine or feminine, she could take up."

Unhappily, Nelson was not able to stand the heady dose of flattery administered by a woman of such conspicuous beauty and consummate art; nor was his taste discriminating enough to experience any wholesome revolt against the rankness of the draught she offered him. The quick appreciation of the born actress, which enabled her when on the stage to clothe herself with a grace and refinement that dropped away when she left it, conspired with his simplicity of confidence in others, and his strong tendency to idealize, to invest her with a character very different from the true. Not that the Lady Hamilton of reality was utterly different from the Lady Hamilton of his imagination. That she ever loved him is doubtful ; but there were in her spirit impulses capable of sympathetic response to his own in his bravest acts, though not in his noblest motives. It is inconceivable that duty ever appealed to her as it did to him, nor could a woman of innate nobility of character have dragged a man of Nelson's masculine renown about England and the Continent, till he was the mock of all beholders ; but on the other hand it never could have occurred to the energetic, courageous, brilliant Lady Hamilton, after the lofty deeds and stirring dramatic scenes of St. Vincent, to beg him, as Lady Nelson did, "to leave boarding to captains." Sympathy, not good taste, would have withheld her. In Lady Nelson's letters there is evidence enough of a somewhat colorless womanly affection, but not a thrill of response to the greatness of her husband's daring, even when surrounded herself by the acclamations it called forth.

What Nelson had never yet found in woman Lady Hamilton gave him, — admiration and appreciation, undisguised and unmeasured, yet bestowed by one who had the power, by the admission of even unfriendly critics, of giving a reality and grace to the part she was performing. He was soon at her feet. The playful gallantry with which Ball, Elliot, and even old St. Vincent[1] himself, paid court to a handsome woman, greedy of homage, became in Nelson a serious matter. Romantic in temperament, he was all day in flattering contact with her. Worn out and ill from that "fever of anxiety," to use his own words, which he had endured since the middle of June, she attended and nursed

---

[1] St. Vincent at this time had not met her, at least as Lady Hamilton, but they exchanged occasional letters.

him. "Lady Hamilton," he exclaimed to Lady Nelson, with enthusiasm undiscriminating in more ways than one, "is one of the very best women in this world; she is an honour to her sex." A week later he tells her, with an odd collocation of persons: "My pride is being your husband, the son of my dear father, and in having Sir William and Lady Hamilton for my friends. While these approve my conduct, I shall not feel or regard the envy of thousands." The matter was passing rapidly into the platonic stage, in which Sir William was also erelong assigned an appropriate, if not wholly flattering, position. "What can I say of hers and Sir William's attention to me? They are in fact, with the exception of you and my good father, the dearest friends I have in this world. I live as Sir William's son in the house, and my glory is as dear to them as their own; in short, I am under such obligations as I can never repay but with my eternal gratitude." "Naples is a dangerous place," he sagely tells Lord St. Vincent, "and we must keep clear of it. I am writing opposite Lady Hamilton, therefore you will not be surprised at the glorious jumble of this letter. Were your Lordship in my place, I much doubt if you could write so well; our hearts and our hands must be all in a flutter." Matters progressed; within ten days the veteran seaman learned, among other concerns of more or less official importance, that "Lady Hamilton is an Angel. She has honoured me by being my ambassadress to the queen: therefore she has my implicit confidence and is worthy of it."

That such intimacy and such relations resulted in no influence upon the admiral's public action is not to be believed. That he consciously perverted his views is improbable, but that he saw duty under other than normal lights is not only probable, but evident. His whole emotional nature was stirred as it never had been. Incipient love and universal admiration had created in him a tone of mind, and brought to birth feelings, which he had, seemingly, scarcely known. "I cannot write a stiff formal public letter," he tells St. Vincent effusively. "You must make one or both so. I feel you are my friend, and my heart yearns to you." Such extravagance of expression and relaxation of official tone has no pertinent cause, and is at least noteworthy. The Court, or rather the Queen through Lady Hamilton, took possession of him. He became immediately one of the little coterie centring round Her Majesty, and he reflected its tone and partisanship, which, fostered probably in the intimate conversations of the two women, were readily transmitted to the minister by the wife whom he adored. The Queen, impetuous, enterprising, and headstrong, like her mother and sister, moved more by feminine feelings of hatred and revenge against the French than by well-balanced considerations of policy, not only favored war, but wished to precipitate the action of the Emperor by immediately attacking the French in the Roman territory. The decision and daring of such a course was so consonant to Nelson's own temperament that he readily sympathized; but it is impossible to admit its wisdom, from either a political or military standpoint. It was an excessively bad combination, substituting isolated attacks for co-operation, and risking results upon the chance of prompt support, by a state which would be offended and embarrassed by the step taken.

Under ordinary conditions Nelson might have seen this, but he was well handled. Within three days he had been persuaded that upon his personal presence depended the salvation of Italy. "My head is quite healed, and, if it were necessary, I could not at present leave Italy, who looks up to me as, under God, its Protector." He continually, by devout recollection of his indebtedness to God, seeks to keep himself in hand. "I am placed by Providence in that situation, that all my caution will be necessary to prevent vanity from showing itself superior to my gratitude and thankfulness," — but the current was too strong for him, and was swollen to a torrent by the streams of adulation, which from all quarters flowed in upon a temperament only too disposed to accept them. "Could I, my dearest Fanny," he writes to Lady Nelson, "tell you half the honours which are shown me here, not a ream of paper would hold it." A grand ball was given on his birthday, September 29; and a rostral column was "erected under a magnificent canopy, never, Lady Hamilton says, to come down while they remain at Naples." Within a week the conviction of his own importance led him to write to Lady Hamilton, evidently for transmission to the Queen, an opinion, or rather an urgent expression of advice, that Naples should at once begin war. It is only conjectural to say that this opinion, which rested on no adequate knowledge of the strength of the Neapolitan Kingdom, was elicited by the Queen through Lady Hamilton ; but the inference derives support from the words, "I have read with admiration the queen's dignified and incomparable letter of September, 1796," — two years before. That his views were not the simple outcome of his own unbiassed study of the situation is evident enough. "This country, by its system of procrastination, will ruin itself," he writes to St. Vincent, the very day after drawing up the letter in question; "the queen sees it and thinks " — not as I do, but — "as *we* do." That Lady Hamilton was one of the "we" is plain, for in the postscript to the letter he says: "Your Ladyship will, I beg, receive this letter as a *preparative for Sir William Hamilton*, to whom I am writing, with all respect, the firm and unalterable opinion of a British admiral," etc. Certainly these words — taken with those already quoted, and written just a week afterwards, "Lady Hamilton has been my ambassadress to the queen " — indicate that she was the intermediary between Nelson and the Court, as well as between him and her husband.

There is no record of any official request for this unoffi-

cial and irregular communication of the opinion of a British
admiral; and, of course, when a man has allowed himself,
unasked, though not unprompted, to press such a line of
action, he has bound himself personally, and embarrassed
himself officially, in case it turns out badly. Nelson very
soon, within a fortnight, had to realize this, in the urgent
entreaties of the Court not to forsake them; and to see
reason for thinking " that a strong wish for our squadron's
being on the Coast of Naples is, that in case of any mishap, that their Majesties think their persons much safer
under the protection of the British flag than under any
other; " that is — than under their own. They could not
trust their own people ; they could not, as the event proved,
trust their army in the field; and the veteran Neapolitan
naval officer, Caracciolo, whether he deserved confidence
or not, was stung to the quick when, in the event, they
sought refuge with a foreign admiral instead of with himself. That Nelson should not have known all this, ten
days after reaching Naples, was pardonable enough, and, if
formally asked for advice without such facts being placed
before him, he could not be responsible for an error thus
arising ; but the case is very different when advice is volunteered. He is more peremptory than the minister himself. " You will not believe I have said or done anything,
without the approbation of Sir William Hamilton. His
Excellency is too good to them, and the strong language
of an English Admiral telling them plain truths of their
miserable system may do good."

The particular position of Naples relatively to France
was this. French troops had for a year past occupied the
Roman Republic, which had been established by them upon
the overthrow of the Papal Government. Their presence
there was regarded by Nelson as a constant threat to the
Two Sicilies, and this to an extent was true ; but rather
because of the contagion of revolutionary ideas than from
the military point of view. From the latter, it should have

been obvious to a man like Nelson that the French must be deterred, under existing conditions, from entering Naples unprovoked; because the farther they advanced the more exposed was their army, in case war, which was darkly threatening, should be renewed in Upper Italy. They dared not, unless by folly, or because first attacked, prolong their already too extended ex-centric movement into Lower Italy. This was true, taking account of Austria only; but now that the British fleet was released by the entire destruction of the French at the Nile, and could operate anywhere on the coast, it would be doubly imprudent; and when the news that it had been done reached Egypt, Bonaparte, who had himself felt the weight of Naples as a possible enemy, remote and feeble as she was, exclaimed, "Italy is lost!" That Naples should co-operate in the general movement against France was right, although, as Nelson well knew, she had never dared do so under much more favorable conditions, — a fact which by itself should have suggested to him caution; but that she should act alone, with the idea of precipitating war, refusing to await the moment fixed by the principal states, was folly. This, however, was the course determined, under the combined impulse of the Queen, Lady Hamilton, and Nelson; and it was arranged that, after visiting the blockade off Malta, he should return to Naples to co-operate in the intended movement.

On the 15th of October Nelson sailed from Naples for Malta in the "Vanguard," with three ships-of-the-line which had lately joined him. He still felt, with accurate instinct, that Egypt and the Ionian Islands, with Malta, constituted the more purely maritime interests, in dealing with which the fleet would most further the general cause, and he alludes frequently to his wish to attend to them; but he promised the King that he would be back in Naples in the first week of November, to support the projected movement against the French. He remained off Malta, therefore, only one week, during which adequate arrangements were made for the blockade of the island, which had been formally proclaimed on the 12th of October, and was conducted for most of the following year by the Portuguese squadron ; the senior British officer, Captain Ball, acting ashore with the insurgent Maltese. These had risen against the French during the summer, and now held them shut up in La Valetta. The adjacent island of Gozo surrendered to the British on the 28th. Hood continued in charge off Alexandria with three ships-of-the-line ; while the Ionian Islands were left to themselves, until a combined Russian and Turkish squadron entered the Mediterranean a few weeks later.

On the 5th of November Nelson returned to Naples. "I am, I fear, drawn into a promise that Naples Bay shall never be left without an English man-of-war. I never intended leaving the coast of Naples without one ; but if I had, who could resist the request of such a queen?" He could ground much upon the Admiralty's orders, given when he was first sent into the Mediterranean, to protect the Kingdom of the Two Sicilies, and he had understood that the Emperor also would give his aid, if Naples attacked. This impression received strength from an Austrian general, Mack, — then of high reputation, but afterwards better known by his surrender to Napoleon at Ulm, in 1805, — being sent to command the Neapolitan army. Sir William Hamilton, however, writing on the 26th of October, was more accurate in saying that the Emperor only advised the King "to act openly against the French *at Malta*, as he would certainly support him ; " for, Naples having a feudal claim upon the island, action there could be represented as merely resistance to aggression. In consequence of this misunderstanding, great confusion ensued in the royal councils when a courier from Vienna brought word, on the 13th of November, that that Court wished it left to the French to begin hostilities ; otherwise, it would give no assurance of help.

Nelson was now formally one of the Council which deliberated upon military operations. In virtue of this position he spoke out, roughly enough. " I ventured to tell their Majesties that one of the following things must happen to the King, and he had his choice, — ' Either to advance, trusting to God for his blessing on a just cause, to die with *l'épée à la main*, or remain quiet and be kicked out of your Kingdoms.' " Thus rudely adjured, the King decided to be a hero after the pattern of Nelson.

On the 22d of November a summons was sent to the French to evacuate the Papal States and Malta, and a Neapolitan army marched upon Rome, commanded by Mack in person. At the same time Nelson took on board his squadron a corps of five thousand, to seize Leghorn, the possession of which, with control of the sea, was not unjustly considered threatening to the communications between the centre of French power, in Northern Italy, and the exposed corps at the foot of the peninsula. After landing this body, Nelson again went to Naples, leaving Troubridge in charge at Leghorn, with several ships ; directing him also to keep vessels cruising along the Riviera, and before Genoa, to break up the coastwise traffic, which had resumed great proportions since the absence of the British from the Mediterranean, and upon which the French army in Piedmont and Lombardy now greatly depended.

On the 5th of December the " Vanguard " once more anchored at Naples. Nelson's estimate of affairs as he now found them, is best told in his own words. " The state of this Country is briefly this : The army is at Rome, Civita Vecchia taken, but in the Castle of St. Angelo are five hundred French troops. The French have thirteen thousand troops at a strong post in the Roman State, called Castellana. General Mack is gone against them with twenty thousand : the event in my opinion is doubtful, and on it hangs the immediate fate of Naples. If Mack is defeated, this country, in fourteen days, is lost ; for the

Emperor has not yet moved his army, and if the Emperor will not march, this country has not the power of resisting the French. But it was not a case of choice, but necessity, which forced the King of Naples to march out of his country, and not to wait till the French had collected a force sufficient to drive him, in a week, out of his kingdom." It·is by no means so sure that no other course of action had been open, though Nelson naturally clung to his first opinion. By advancing, the King gave the French occasion, if they were seeking one ; and the Neapolitan army, which might well have deterred them, as it had embarrassed even Bonaparte in his time, had its rottenness revealed as only trial can reveal. When reviewed, it had appeared to Mack and Nelson a well-equipped force of thirty thousand of the "finest troops in Europe." Brought face to face with fifteen thousand French, in a month it ceased to exist.

Upon Mack's advance, the French general Championnet had evacuated Rome, into which the King made a vainglorious triumphal entry. The French retired to Castellana, followed by the Neapolitans ; but in the campaign that ensued the latter behaved with disgraceful cowardice. Flying in every direction, with scarcely any loss in killed, and preceded in their flight by the King, the whole force retreated in confusion upon the capital. There revolutionary ideas had spread widely among the upper classes ; and, although the populace both in city and country remained fanatically loyal, and hostile to the French, the King and Queen feared to trust their persons to the issue of events. Powerless through suspicions of those around them, apparently well founded, and through lack of any instrument with which to act, now that their army was destroyed, their one wish was to escape to Palermo.

To do this involved some difficulty, as the mob, like that of Paris, was bitterly opposed to their sovereign leaving the capital ; but by the management and determination of Nelson, who was greatly helped by the courage and presence of mind of Lady Hamilton, the royal family was embarked on board the " Vanguard" on the evening of December 21st. During several previous days treasure to the amount of two and a half millions sterling was being conveyed secretly to the ship. " The whole correspondence relative to this important business," wrote Nelson to St. Vincent, "was carried on with the greatest address by Lady Hamilton and the Queen, who being constantly in the habits of correspondence, no one could suspect." On the evening of the 23d the " Vanguard" sailed, and after a most tempestuous passage reached Palermo on the 26th. The youngest of the princes, six years old, taken suddenly with convulsions, died on the way in the arms of Lady Hamilton, whose womanly helpfulness, as well as her courage, came out strongly in this trying time. Nelson wrote to St. Vincent: " It is my duty to tell your Lordship the obligations which the whole royal family as well as myself are under on this trying occasion to her Ladyship." These scenes inevitably deepened the impression she had already made upon him, which was not to be lessened by her lapse into feminine weakness when the strain was over. To use her own words, in a letter to her old lover, Greville, " My dear, adorable queen and I *weep together*, and now that is our onely comfort." " Our dear Lady Hamilton," Nelson wrote again a few days later, " whom to see is to admire, but, to know, are to be added honour and respect; her head and heart surpass her beauty, which cannot be equalled by anything I have seen." Upon himself the brief emergency and its sharp call to action had had the usual reviving effect. " Thank God," he wrote to Spencer, " my health is better, my mind never firmer, and my heart in the right trim to comfort, relieve, and protect those who it is my duty to afford assistance to."

In Palermo Nelson again lived in the minister's house, bearing a large, if not a disproportionate, share of the expenses. When they returned to England in 1800, Hamilton was £2,000 in his debt. The intimacy and the manner of life, in the midst of the Neapolitan court, whose corruptness of manners both Nelson and Troubridge openly condemned, was already causing scandal, rumors of which were not long in reaching home. " I am quite concerned," wrote Captain Ball to Saumarez, when Nelson was about to quit the station, " at the many severe paragraphs which have been put in the newspapers respecting him and Lady Hamilton. I am convinced that there has not been anything improper between them — his Lordship could not fail being delighted with her accomplishments and manners, which are very fascinating." Lady Nelson, uneasy as a wife could not fail to be at reports affecting her husband's honor, and threatening her own happiness, quickly formed, and for a time entertained, the thought of joining him on the station; but, if she broached the idea to Nelson, he certainly discouraged it. Writing to her on the 10th of April, 1799, he said: " You would by February have seen how unpleasant it would have been had you followed *any* advice, which carried you from England to a wandering sailor. I could, if you had come, *only* have struck my flag, and carried you back again, for it would have been impossible to have set up an establishment at either Naples or Palermo." [1]

The scandal increased apace after his headquarters were fixed at Palermo. Lady Minto, writing from Vienna to her sister, in July, 1800, says : " Mr. Rushout and Colonel Rooke,[2] whom I knew in Italy, are here. Mr. Rushout is at last going home. He escaped from Naples at the same time as the King did in Nelson's ship, and remained six months at Palermo; so I had a great deal of intelligence

---

[1] Pettigrew, vol. i. p. 220.

[2] Lord Minto was at this time ambassador to Vienna. Rushout and Rooke were men well known on the Continent. Both are mentioned with some particularity in the Memoirs of Pryse Lockhart Gordon, another continental rambler.

concerning the Hero and his Lady. . . . Nelson and the Hamiltons all lived together in a house of which he bore the expense, which was enormous, and every sort of gaming went on half the night. Nelson used to sit with large parcels of gold before him, and generally go to sleep, Lady Hamilton taking from the heap without counting, and playing with his money to the amount of £500 a night. Her rage is play, and Sir William says when he is dead she will be a beggar. However, she has about £30,000 worth of diamonds from the royal family in presents. She sits at the Councils, and rules everything and everybody." Some of these statements are probably beyond the personal knowledge of the narrator, and can only be accepted as current talk ; but others are within the observation of an eyewitness, evidently thought credible by Lady Minto, who was a friend to Nelson. Mr. Paget, who succeeded Hamilton as British minister, mentions the same reports, in his private letter to Lord Grenville, the Secretary of State for Foreign Affairs. Hamilton had asked to see his instructions. " I decided at once not to do so, for he would certainly have been obliged to show them to Lady Hamilton, who would have conveyed them next moment to the queen. . . . Lord Nelson's health is, I fear, sadly impaired, and I am assured that his fortune is fallen into the same state, in consequence of great losses which both his Lordship and Lady Hamilton have sustained at Faro and other games of hazard." [1]

The impressions made upon Lord Elgin, who touched at Palermo on his way to the embassy at Constantinople, are worth quoting ; for there has been much assertion and denial as to what did go on in that out-of-the-way corner of the world, Lady Hamilton ascribing the falsehoods, as she claimed they were, to the Jacobinical tendencies of those who spread them. " During a week's stay at Palermo, on my passage here," wrote Elgin, " the neces-

[1] The Paget Papers, London, 1896, p. 185.

sity of a change in our representative, and in our conduct
there, appeared to me most urgent. You may perhaps
know from Lord Grenville how strong my impression on
that subject was." [1]   Troubridge, a pattern of that most
faithful friendship which dares to risk alienation, if it may
but save, wrote urgently to his chief: " Pardon me, my
Lord, it is my sincere esteem for you that makes me mention it. I know you can have no pleasure sitting up all
night at cards; why, then, sacrifice your health, comfort,
purse, ease, everything, to the customs of a country, where
your stay cannot be long? I would not, my Lord, reside
in this country for all Sicily. I trust the war will soon
be over, and deliver us from a nest of everything that is
infamous, and that we may enjoy the smiles of our country-
women. Your Lordship is a stranger to half that happens,
or the talk it occasions; if you knew what your friends
feel for you, I am sure you would cut all the nocturnal
parties. The gambling of the people at Palermo is publicly talked of everywhere. I beseech your Lordship leave
off. I wish my pen could tell you my feelings, I am sure
you would oblige me. I trust your Lordship will pardon
me: it is the sincere esteem I have for you that makes
me risk your displeasure." [2]   To this manly appeal Nelson
seems to have made no reply; none at least is quoted.

[1] The Paget Papers, London, 1896, p. 219.
[2] Clarke and M'Arthur, vol. ii. p. 355.

CHAPTER XII.

NELSON'S CAREER, AND GENERAL EVENTS IN THE MEDITERRA-
NEAN AND ITALY, FROM THE OVERTHROW OF THE ROYAL
GOVERNMENT IN NAPLES TO THE INCURSION OF THE FRENCH
FLEET UNDER ADMIRAL BRUIX.

JANUARY – MAY, 1799. AGE, 40.

THE four and a half months of unbroken residence in
Palermo, which followed the flight of the Court
from Naples, were full of annoyance and distress to
Nelson, independent of, and additional to, the disquieting
struggle between his passion and his conscience, which
had not yet been silenced. The disasters in Naples continued. The Neapolitan Navy had been left in charge of
one of the Portuguese officers, who soon found himself
compelled to burn the ships-of-the-line, to prevent their
falling into the hands of the revolutionists, — a step for
which he was severely, but apparently unjustly, censured
by Nelson. The peasantry and the lower orders of the
city took up arms, under the guidance of their priests,
and for some time sought, with rude but undisciplined
fury, to oppose the advance of the enemy; but such untrained resistance was futile before the veterans of France,
and on the 23d of January, 1799, Championnet's troops
entered the city. This was followed by the establishment of the Parthenopeian Republic, a name which reflected the prevailing French affectation of antiquity.
For all this Nelson blamed the Emperor, and formed
gloomy forebodings. "Had the war commenced in September or October," he had written amid the December
disasters, "all Italy would at this moment have been

liberated. Six months hence, when the Neapolitan Republic will be organized, armed, and with its numerous
resources called forth, I will suffer to have my head cut
off, if the Emperor is not only defeated in Italy, but that
he totters on his throne in Vienna." To this text he
stuck. Three months later, when the preparations of
Austria and Russia were complete, he wrote: "The
French have made war upon the Emperor, and have surprised some of his troops. Serve him right! why did he
not go to war before?" But the rapid, continuous, and
overwhelming successes of the Coalition, between April
and August, showed how untimely had been the step he
had urged upon the King of the Sicilies, disregardful of
the needed preparations and of the most favorable season
— February to August — for operations in Italy. Naples
never recovered such political equilibrium as she had possessed before that ill-advised advance. In Nelson's career
it, and its reverses, were to the Battle of the Nile what
Teneriffe was to St. Vincent; and it illustrates the inadequacy to success of merely "going ahead," unless both
time and method are dictated by that martial intelligence
which Nelson so abundantly possessed, but in this case
failed to use.

Not in Naples only did fortune now administer to him
rebuffs, which seemed singularly to rebuke the change of
direction and of base which he had been persuaded to give
to his personal efforts. Immediately upon his arrival in
Palermo, he heard from St. Vincent that a comparatively
junior captain, Sir Sidney Smith, had been sent out by
the Cabinet, bearing, besides his naval commission from
the Admiralty, one from the Foreign Office as envoy to
Turkey, conjointly with his brother, Spencer Smith.
This unusual and somewhat cumbrous arrangement was
adopted with the design that Smith should be senior naval
officer in the Levant, where it was thought his hands
would be strengthened by the diplomatic functions; but

the Government's explanation of its intentions was so
obscure, that St. Vincent understood the new-comer was to
be independent of both himself and Nelson. This impression was confirmed by a letter from Smith to Hamilton, in
which occurred the words, "Hood naturally falls under
my orders when we meet, as being my junior," while the
general tone was that of one who had a right, by virtue
of his commission alone, to take charge of such vessels,
and to direct such operations, as he found in the Levant.
This impression was fairly deducible from a letter of the
Secretary of State for Foreign Affairs, that Smith forwarded to Nelson; after which, without seeking an interview, he at once went on for Constantinople.

Nelson immediately asked to be relieved. "*I do feel, for
I am a man,*" he wrote to St. Vincent, "that it is impossible for me to serve in these seas, with the squadron
under a junior officer. Never, never was I so astonished."
With this private letter he sent an official application for
leave. "The great anxiety I have undergone during the
whole time I have been honoured with this important
command, has much impaired a weak constitution. And
now, finding that much abler officers are arrived within
the district which I had thought under my command, . . .
and, I flatter myself, having made the British nation and
our gracious Sovereign more beloved and respected than
heretofore; under these circumstances I entreat, that if
my health and uneasiness of mind should not be mended,
that I may have your Lordship's permission to leave this
command to my gallant and most excellent second in command, Captain Troubridge." In similar terms, though
more guarded, he wrote to Earl Spencer. At the same
time he took proper steps to prevent the official impropriety,
not to say rudeness, which Smith was about to commit by
taking from Hood his charge, without either the latter
or Nelson receiving personal instructions to surrender it.
He sent Troubridge hastily to Alexandria to take com-

mand there, with orders that, upon Smith's arrival, he should deliver up the blockade to him, and return to the westward. "I should hope," he wrote to Spencer, "that Sir Sidney Smith will not take any ship from under my command, without my orders;" but he evidently expected that he would, and was determined to forestall the possibility of such an affront.

Nelson's services had been so eminent, and were at this time so indispensable, and his exceptions to the manner in which Smith had been intruded into his command were so well founded, that the matter was rectified as rapidly as the slow round of communications in that day would permit. The Admiralty disclaimed any intention of circumscribing his control in the Mediterranean, and Smith received peremptory orders from St. Vincent to report himself to Nelson by letter for orders. The latter of course carried out the Admiralty's wishes, by intrusting to Smith the immediate direction of operations in the Levant, while retaining in his own hands the general outlines of naval policy. He kept a very tight rein on Smith, however, and introduced into the situation some dry humor, unusual with him. The two brothers, envoys, he addressed jointly, in his official letters, by the collective term "Your Excellency." "I beg of your Excellency," he says in such a letter, "to forward my letter to Sir Sidney Smith, Captain of the Tigre. I have this day received letters from Sir Sidney Smith, in his Ministerial capacity, I believe. I *wish* that all Ministerial letters should be written in your joint names; for it may be difficult for me to distinguish the Captain of the man-of-war from the Joint Minister, and the propriety of language in one might be very proper to what it is in the other." To the naval captain he writes: "I must *direct* you, whenever you have Ministerial affairs to communicate, that it is done jointly with your respectable brother, and not mix naval business with the other. I have sent you my orders,

which your abilities as a sea-officer will lead you to
punctually execute."

Nelson resented to the end this giving to a junior naval
officer, by a side-wind, an authoritative position in diplomatic affairs, which, on the naval side, properly belonged
to him. "Sir Sidney should recollect," he told Earl
Spencer, meaning doubtless that the latter also should
recollect, "how I must feel in seeing him placed in the
situation which I thought naturally would fall to me."
It was a singular step on the part of the Government,
justified neither by general practice, nor by particular
ability on the part of the person chosen; and all Nelson's
care and decision were insufficient to prevent the consequent evil, although he was perfectly clear in his intimation to "Your Excellency," the joint ministers, that they
should "upon all occasions, arrange plans of operations
with me," and not with Captain Sir Sidney Smith.
Smith was active and fought well; but, as far as he dared,
he did as he pleased in virtue of his diplomatic commission, looked only to the interests of his own small part of
the field, and, as will appear later, flatly disobeyed both
the spirit and the letter of Nelson's orders, as well as the
Government's purpose, concerning the French army in
Egypt. The general sound judgment and diplomatic
ability of Nelson, who was thus superseded, had on the
other hand been fully recognized — formally by the Government, explicitly by St. Vincent and Minto, both of
whom had personal experience of his conduct in such
matters. "What relates to co-operation with the armies
of the allied powers cannot be in better hands than yours,"
wrote the former. "You are as great in the cabinet as on
the ocean, and your whole conduct fills me with admiration and confidence." "There is one other point of excellence," said Minto in the House of Peers, "to which I
must say a single word, because I am, perhaps, the man
in the world who has had the best opportunity of being

acquainted with it. The world knows that Lord Nelson can fight the battles of his country: but a constant and confidential correspondence with this great man, for a considerable portion of time, has taught me, that he is not less capable of providing for its political interests and honour, on occasions of great delicacy and embarrassment. In that new capacity I have witnessed a degree of ability, judgment, temper, and conciliation, not always allied to the sort of spirit which without an instant's hesitation can attack the whole Spanish line with his single ship." Of Nelson's superior fitness in this respect, the unfortunate choice of Sidney Smith for his anomalous position was to furnish the Government an additional proof.

It was not in this matter only that maritime affairs in the East took a turn contrary to Nelson's wishes. Since he had persuaded himself that to bolster up the corrupt and tottering throne of Naples was the most important of his functions, he had become desirous that the isolation and blockade of the French army in Egypt, — a factor so decisive by its numbers, its brilliant efficiency, and the singular genius and renown of its general and his lieutenants, — should be assumed by some of the allies of Great Britain, although he was never slow to express his want of confidence in their navies. He was urgent, both with the joint ministers and with the representatives of Russia and Turkey, that the fleets of these two powers should relieve Hood off Alexandria, in order to strengthen his own hands on the coast of Italy and off Malta. Neither Russia nor Turkey was easily to be convinced. Egypt was no affair of the former's, except as it concerned the general cause; and from that point of view it was as much the business of Great Britain, already on the spot, as it was hers. With twenty thousand troops about to enter into a campaign in Northern Italy, as allies of Austria, Russia had undeniable interests there, as well as in the Ionian Islands, which commanded the entrance to the Adriatic, a sea important to communications between Austria and Lombardy. The islands also were, in the hands of France, a threat to the Turkish mainland. It was against these, therefore, that the Russo-Turkish forces directed their efforts, greatly to Nelson's disgust, and there they remained, chained by the obstinate resistance of Corfu, until the 1st of March, 1799, when it surrendered. The fifty-gun ship "Leander," which had been taken by the French seventy-four "Généreux," when carrying Nelson's despatches after the Nile, was here recaptured and restored to Great Britain.

Nelson viewed the progress and policy of Russia with a mind fully imbued with the distrust, which, for the last quarter of a century, had been supplanting gradually the previous friendly feeling of Great Britain toward that country. As soon as he heard of the intention to attack the islands, in November, 1798, he hurried off Troubridge to anticipate a seizure which he expected to be more easy than it proved. "You will proceed to sea without a moment's loss of time," his instructions ran, "and make the best of your way to the Island of Zante; and if the Russians have not taken possession of that island and Cephalonia, you will send on shore by the Priest I shall desire to accompany you, my Declaration. If you can get possession of the islands before named, you will send my Declaration into the Island of Corfu, and use your utmost endeavours to get possession of it. . . . Should the Russians have taken possession of these Islands and be cruizing near with the Turkish fleet, you will pay a visit to the Turkish admiral, and by saluting him (if he consents to return gun for gun) and every other mark of respect and attention, gain his confidence. You will judge whether he is of a sufficient rank to hold a confidential conversation with." It is evident that Nelson's action was precipitated by the news of the Russian movement, and its tenor dictated by a wish to sow distrust between

Turkey and Russia. The omission of any mention of a
Russian admiral is most significant. "Captain Troubridge
was absolutely under sail," he wrote to Spencer Smith,
"when I heard with sorrow that the Russians were there."
His eagerness in the matter is the more evident, in that
he thus detached Troubridge at the moment when he was
about to start for Leghorn, where his trusted subordinate
and his ship would be greatly needed.

"I was in hopes that a part of the united Turkish and
Russian squadron would have gone to Egypt — the first
object of the Ottoman arms," he tells the Turkish admiral.
"Corfu is a secondary consideration." To Spencer Smith
he writes: "I have had a long and friendly conference
with Kelim Effendi on the conduct likely to be pursued by
the Russian Court towards the unsuspicious (I fear) and
upright Turk. The Porte ought to be aware of the very
great danger at a future day of allowing the Russians to
get footing at Corfu, and I hope they will keep them in
the East. Our ideas have exactly been the same about
Russia. . . . Surely I had a right to expect that the
united fleets would have taken care of the things east of
Candia. I never wished to have them west of it." "The
Russians seem to me to be more intent on taking ports in
the Mediterranean than destroying Bonaparte in Egypt."

It was well known at this time that the Czar was look-
ing towards Malta and the restoration of the Order of the
Knights, of which he had been elected Grand Master the
previous October, immediately after Bonaparte's seizure of
the island became known. Nelson held that the King of
Naples was the legitimate sovereign, and he directed
Captain Ball, his own representative there, to have all the
Maltese posts and forces fly the Neapolitan flag; but he,
with Hamilton, got a note from the King, promising that
Malta should never be transferred to any other Power
without the consent of England. "Should any Russian
ships, or admiral, arrive off Malta," he instructed Ball,

"you will convince him of the very unhandsome manner of treating the legitimate sovereign of Malta, by wishing to see the Russian flag fly in Malta, and also of me, who command the forces of a Power in such close alliance with the Russian Emperor, which have been blockading and attacking Malta for near six months. The Russians shall never take the lead."

Three weeks later he authorized Ball, with the consent of the King, to preside over the meetings of the Maltese chiefs, and, by the desire of his Sicilian Majesty, the British flag was to be hoisted alongside the Sicilian in every place where the latter was flown, "side by side, that of England being on the right hand," to show that the island was under the special protection of Great Britain during the war. On the 23d of March he cordially congratulates the Russian admiral upon the fall of Corfu, news of which he has just received, and he mentions, meaningly, "The flag of his Sicilian Majesty, with that of Great Britain, is flying on all parts of Malta, except the town of Valetta, the inhabitants of which have, with his Sicilian Majesty's consent, put themselves under the protection of Great Britain." "I attach no value to it for us," he said explicitly to the First Lord, meaning, no doubt, for the purposes of the existing war. This opinion was perfectly consonant to the secondary importance he had latterly attributed to the presence of the British in the Levant, as compared to their duties towards Naples, but though he reiterated it in the later war, it was with the express qualification that, for the security of communication with India, not then in question, the value of the island was indisputable.

But if, positively, Malta was of little use to England, — "a useless and enormous expense," to use his own words, — yet, negatively, the consequences of its passing into the hands of a powerful rival were too serious to be permitted. "Any expense should be incurred rather than

let it remain in the hands of the French." The same
distrust of the Russians was suggested by his keen political insight. "You will observe what is said in the
despatches of the Consul at Corfu," he writes to St.
Vincent, "respecting the Russians being ordered to Malta.
I know this is a favourite object of the Emperor's, and is
a prelude to a future war with the good Turk, when Constantinople will change masters. This is so clear, that a
man must be blind not to see it." "I have just received
the Emperor of Russia's picture in a box magnificently
set with diamonds; it has done him honour and me a
pleasure to have my conduct approved;" "but," he tells
Ball, significantly, "this shall not prevent my keeping a
sharp look-out on his movements against the good Turk."

As regards Paul I., ferocious and half crazy as he was,
this imputation of merely interested foresight scarcely did
justice to the quixotic passions which often impelled him
to the most unselfish acts, but the general tendency was
undeniable; and Nelson's watchful attitude exemplifies
the numerous diplomatic, as well as military, responsibilities that weighed upon him. He was, practically, commander-in-chief in the Mediterranean, even if Government
refused to recognize the fact by reward, or by proper staff
appointments; for St. Vincent, autocratic as he was
towards others, could roll off upon Nelson all his responsibilities there, — "the uncontrolled direction of the naval
part," were his own words, — and sleep quietly. Despite
his objections to the island itself, and his enthusiastic
fidelity to the Neapolitan royal house, Nelson had evidently
the presentiment that Malta must come to Great Britain, a
solution which Ball and the Maltese themselves were urging
upon him. "A Neapolitan garrison would betray it to the
first man who would bribe him," he wrote; which, if true,
left to Great Britain no other alternative than to take it
herself. Neither he, Troubridge, nor the sovereigns, had
confidence in the fidelity of Neapolitan officers.

The blockade of Malta was maintained with great tenacity, and, coupled with the maritime prostration of France in the Mediterranean, resulted in a complete isolation of the French garrison in La Valetta by sea, the Maltese people hemming it in by land. By the 1st of May Ball had erected a battery at the head of the harbor, sweeping it to the entrance, so that the French ships, one of which was the "Guillaume Tell," eighty, that had escaped from Aboukir, had to be kept in the coves. These affairs of Malta brought Nelson into difficult diplomatic relations with the Barbary States, Tunis and Tripoli. The island not affording sufficient food, strenuous efforts had to be made by him and Ball to get grain from Sicily and elsewhere, a matter very difficult of accomplishment even were the transit unmolested; but these petty Mussulman states, for the purposes of piracy, kept themselves in formal war with Naples and Portugal, and frequently captured vessels under the Sicilian flag carrying corn to Malta. The British had too much on hand now to spare readily the force necessary to put down these depredators, at whose misdeeds they had winked in quieter days; and it required all Nelson's tact, combining threats with compliments, and with appeals to the prejudices of believers in God against those who denied Him, to keep the marauding within bounds. The irrepressible activity of Bonaparte's emissaries also stirred the Beys up to measures friendly to France. "The infamous conduct of the French during the whole war, has at last called down the vengeance of all true Mussulmen," he writes to the Bey of Tunis; "and your Highness, I am sure, will agree with me that Divine Providence will never permit these infidels to God to go unpunished. The conduct of your Highness reflects upon you the very highest honour. Although I have a squadron of Portuguese ships under my orders, I have prevented their cruizing against the vessels of war of your Highness. For at this moment all

wars should cease, and all the world should join in
endeavouring to extirpate from off the face of the earth
this race of murderers, oppressors, and unbelievers."

After these preliminary compliments, Nelson presents
his grievances. He has given the passports of a British
admiral to Sicilian vessels *bonâ fide* employed in carrying
grain to the besiegers of the French, and to such only;
and he must insist upon those passports being respected,
as the vessels bearing them are serving the great common
cause. He demands, also, that aid be not given to the
common enemy. "I was rejoiced," he writes the Bashaw
of Tripoli, "to find that you had renounced the treaty you
had so imprudently entered into with some emissaries of
General Bonaparte — that man of blood, that despoiler of
the weak, that enemy of all true Musselmen; for, like
Satan, he only flatters that he may the more easily destroy;
and it is true, that since the year 1789, all Frenchmen are
exactly of the same disposition." His Highness, however,
has relapsed into his former errors. "It is now my duty
to speak out, and not to be misunderstood. That Nelson
who has hitherto kept your powerful enemies from destroying you, can, and will, let them loose upon you, unless
the following terms are, in two hours, complied with.
. . . If these proper terms are not complied with, I can
no longer prevent the Portuguese ships from acting with
vigour against your Highness. Your Highness will,
without difficulty, write me a letter, the substance of
which will be dictated by the British consul."

The vehemence with which the French are here
denounced, though pitched in a key deemed harmonious
to the ears for which it was immediately intended, was
entirely consonant to the feelings which had lately taken
possession of Nelson. They were the result, probably,
in part, of the anxious rancor bred by the uncertainties
and worry of the pursuit of Bonaparte; in part, also, of
more direct contact than before with the unbridled license

which the French Government and its generals, impelled by
dire necessity and by an unquestionable lack of principle,
had given to the system of making war support war. The
feebleness and corruption of the Directory had relaxed the
reins of discipline from top to bottom, and a practice
which finds its justification only when executed with the
strictest method and accountability, had degenerated into
little better than disorganized pillage. " ' Down, down
with the French!' is my constant prayer." " ' *Down,
down* with the French!' ought to be placed in the council-
room of every country in the world." "To serve my
King, and to destroy the French, I consider as the great
order of all, from which little ones spring; and if one of
these little ones militate against it, I go back to obey the
great order and object, to *down, down* with the damned
French villains. Excuse my warmth; but my blood boils
at the name of a Frenchman. I hate them all — Royalists
and Republicans." Infidels, robbers, and murderers are
the characteristic terms. This detestation of the legitimate enemy spread, intensified, to those who supported
them in Naples, — the Jacobins, as they were called.
"Send me word some proper heads are taken off," he
wrote to Troubridge, "this alone will comfort me."
"Our friend Troubridge had a present made him the other
day, of the head of a Jacobin," he tells St. Vincent, "and
makes an apology to me, the weather being very hot, for
not sending it here!" Upon the copy of the letter accompanying this ghastly gift to him, Troubridge had written,
"A jolly fellow. T. Troubridge." The exasperation to
which political animosities had given rise may be gauged
by the brutal levity shown in this incident, by men of the
masculine and generous characters of Troubridge and
Nelson, and should not be forgotten in estimating the
actions that in due consequence followed.

The duties as well as the anxieties of his situation bore
heavily upon Nelson, and may help to account, in combi-

nation with the tide of adverse fortune now running strongly, for the depression that weighed upon him. "My public correspondence, besides the business of sixteen sail-of-the-line, and all our commerce, is with Petersburg, Constantinople, the Consul at Smyrna, Egypt, the Turkish and Russian admirals, Trieste, Vienna, Tuscany, Minorca, Earl St. Vincent, and Lord Spencer. This over, what time can I have for any private correspondence?" Yet, admitting freely that there is a limit beyond which activity may cease to please, what has become of the joyous spirit, which wrote, not four years before: "This I like, active service or none!" Occupying one of the most distinguished posts open to the Navy; practically, and almost formally, independent; at the very head and centre of the greatest interests, — his zeal, while preserving all its intensity, has lost all its buoyancy. "My dear Lord," he tells St. Vincent, alluding at the moment to his stepson Nisbet, "there is no true happiness in this life, and in my present state I could quit it with a smile." "My spirits have received such a shock," he writes some days after, to the wife of his early patron, Sir Peter Parker, "that I think they cannot recover it. You who remember me always laughing and gay, would hardly believe the change; but who can see what I have and be well in health? Kingdoms lost and a royal family in distress." "Believe me," he confides to his intimate friend Davison a month later, "my only wish is to sink with honour into the grave, and when that shall please God, I shall meet death with a smile. Not that I am insensible to the honours and riches my King and Country have heaped upon me, so much more than any officer could deserve; yet I am ready to quit this world of trouble, and envy none but those of the estate six feet by two." "I am at times ill at ease, but it is my duty to submit, and you may be sure I will not quit my post without absolute necessity." "What a state I am in!" he writes of one of those perplexities inevitable to an officer in his position. "If I go, I risk Sicily; as I stay, my heart is breaking." This is not the natural temper of a man to whom difficulties and perplexities had been, and were yet again to be, a trumpet call that stirred to animation, a stimulant that steadied the nerves, and sent the blood coursing with new life through heart and brain. Mingled as these expressions were with despondent broodings over his health, even if the latter were well founded, they are the voice of a mind which has lost the spring of self-content. The sense of duty abides, but dogged, cheerless; respondent rather to the force of habit than to the generous ardor of former days.

For over two months after the flight to Palermo, the condition of affairs for the Kingdom of the Two Sicilies was seemingly critical to the verge of desperation; for neither the preparations of the Coalition, nor the hollowness of the French successes, were understood, and news was slow to reach the remote city where the Court now dwelt. The republican movement extended, though superficially, to the toe of Italy, many of the towns in Calabria planting the tree of liberty, and the new flag flying on the islands along the coast. Sicily, though hostile to the French, was discontented with the existing government, and disaffection there was feared. In that, Nelson truly observed, lay the danger. "Respecting an invasion of the French, I have no alarms; if this island is true to itself no harm can happen." Nevertheless, "it is proper to be prepared for defence, and," if Calabria is occupied by the French, "the first object is the preservation of Messina."

For this purpose he ordered the Portuguese squadron there, immediately after he reached Palermo; and, when the outlook grew more threatening, appealed to the Turkish and Russian admirals to send a detachment to the Straits. General Stuart, commanding the troops in

Minorca, which had passed into the hands of Great Britain the previous November, was entreated to detail a garrison for the citadel of Messina, as no dependence was placed upon the Neapolitan troops. Stuart complied, and the citadel was occupied by two English regiments about the 10th of March. The danger, however, was considered sufficiently imminent to withdraw to Palermo the transports lying at Syracuse; a step which could not have been necessary had Nelson made Syracuse, as he at first intended, the base of operations for the British fleet, and suggests the idea, which he himself avows, that his own presence with the Court was rather political than military [1] in its utility, dependent upon the fears of their own subjects felt by the sovereigns. While these measures were being taken he endeavored, though fruitlessly, to bring matters to a conclusion at Alexandria and Malta, in order to release the ships there employed and fetch them to the coast of Naples. "The moment the Emperor moves," he wrote to St. Vincent, "I shall go with all the ships I can collect into the Bay of Naples, to create a diversion." Nothing certain can be said as yet, "whether all is lost or may yet be saved; that must depend upon the movements of the Emperor." Yet it was the hand of the emperor which he had advised the King of Naples to force, by his ill-timed advance.

Troubridge rejoined the Flag at Palermo on the 17th of March, having turned over the command in the Levant to Sir Sidney Smith, after an ineffectual attempt to destroy

[1] Palermo possessed a strategic advantage over Syracuse, in that, with westerly winds, it was to windward, especially as regards Naples; and it was also nearer the narrowest part of the passage between Sicily and Africa, the highway to the Levant and Egypt. With easterly winds, the enemy of course could not proceed thither; and at this time there was no enemy's force in the Mediterranean, so that westward movements had not to be apprehended. All dangers must come from the westward. These considerations were doubtless present to Nelson; but the author has not found any mention of them by him at this period.

the French shipping in Alexandria. By this time matters had begun to mend. Calabria had returned to its loyalty, and the insurrection of the peasantry against the French was general throughout the country, and in the Roman State. The Directory, taking umbrage at the advance of Russian troops to the frontiers of Austria, demanded explanations from the latter, and when these proved unsatisfactory directed its armies to take the offensive. The French advanced into Germany on the first of March, and in Italy towards the end of the month. But the action. of the French Government, though audacious and imposing, rested upon no solid foundation of efficiency in the armies, or skill in the plan of campaign. Serious reverses soon followed, and the fatally ex-centric position of the corps in Naples was then immediately apparent.

Before this news could reach Palermo, however, Nelson had sent Troubridge with four ships-of-the-line and some smaller vessels to the Bay of Naples, to blockade it, and to enter into communication, if possible, with the loyalists in the city. As the extreme reluctance of the King and Queen prevented his going in person, — a reason the sufficiency of which it is difficult to admit, — Nelson hoisted his flag on board a transport in the bay, and sent the flagship, in order not to diminish the force detailed for such important duties. Within a week the islands in the immediate neighborhood of Naples — Procida, Ischia, Capri, and the Ponzas — had again hoisted the royal ensign. On the 22d of April the French evacuated the city, with the exception of the Castle of St. Elmo, in which they left a garrison of five hundred men. In Upper Italy their armies were in full retreat, having been forced back from the Adige to the Adda, whence an urgent message was sent to Macdonald, Championnet's successor at Naples, to fall back to the northward and effect a junction with the main body, soon to be sorely pressed by an overwhelming force of the Austro-Russians, at whose head was the famous Suwarrow.   On the 29th the Allies entered Milan, and on the 7th of May the northern French, now under the command of Moreau, had retired as far as Alessandria, in Piedmont.   On this same day, Macdonald, having thrown garrisons into Capua and Gaeta, evacuated the kingdom of Naples, and hastened northward to join Moreau.   With the exception of these fortified posts and the city of Naples, the country was now overrun by the Christian army, the name applied to the numerous but utterly undisciplined bands of rude peasantry, attached to the royal cause, and led by Cardinal Ruffo.   The Jacobins in the city still held out, and had in the bay a small naval force under the command of Commodore Caracciolo.

Troubridge's successes continued.   A week later Salerno had been taken, and the royal colors were flying at Castellamare, on the opposite side of the Bay from Naples, and distant from it only twelve miles by land.   Nelson questioned Troubridge about the return of the King, whose most evident political conviction was that the success of the royal cause was vitally connected with the safety of the royal person.   "What are your ideas of the King's going into the Bay of Naples, without foreign troops? If it should cause insurrection [of the royalists] in Naples which did not succeed, would it not be worse? The King, if a rising of loyal people took place, ought to be amongst them; and that he will never consent to." "The King, God bless him! is a philosopher," he had said, repeating an expression of Lady Hamilton's, referring to the disasters which caused the headlong flight from Rome, through Naples, to Palermo; "but the great Queen feels sensibly all that has happened."   The Queen also was extremely fearful, and Nelson intimated to St. Vincent that a request would be made for British troops to protect the sovereigns.   "Their Majesties are ready to cross the water whenever Naples is entirely cleansed.   When that happy event arrives, and not till then, a desire will be expressed for the British troops to be removed from Messina into Naples to guard the persons of their Majesties." That Nelson should have considered it essential to maintain in power, by any means, sovereigns devoted to Great Britain, is perfectly comprehensible. What is difficult to understand is the esteem he continued to profess, for those whose unheroic bearing so belied the words he had written six months before: "His Majesty is determined to conquer or die at the head of his army." Under other conditions and influences, none would have been more forward to express dissatisfaction and contempt.

Withal, despite the favorable outlook of affairs and the most joyous season of the year, his depression of spirits continued. "I am far from well," he writes on the 3d of May, "and the good news of the success of the Austrian arms in Italy does not even cheer me." But in the midst of the full current of success, and of his own gloom, an incident suddenly occurred which threw everything again into confusion and doubt, and roused him for the time from his apathy. On the 12th of May a brig arrived at Palermo, with news that a French fleet of nineteen ships-of-the-line had escaped from Brest, and had been seen less than a fortnight before off Oporto, steering for the Mediterranean.

CHAPTER XIII.

FROM THE INCURSION OF THE FRENCH FLEET UNDER BRUIX TO
THE RESTORATION OF THE ROYAL AUTHORITY AT NAPLES. —
THE CARACCIOLO EXECUTION. — NELSON'S DISOBEDIENCE TO
ADMIRAL LORD KEITH.

MAY - JULY, 1799. AGE, 40.

THE intention of the French to send a fleet into the
Mediterranean had transpired some time before,
and the motive — to retrieve the destruction of their naval
power in that sea by the Battle of the Nile — was so
obvious that the attempt was regarded as probable. As
far back as the 7th of January, Nelson had written to
Commodore Duckworth, commanding the detachment of
four ships-of-the-line at Minorca, that he had received
notification of the force expected from Brest. If they got
into the Mediterranean, he was confident they would go
first to Toulon, and he wished to concert beforehand with
Duckworth, who was not under his orders, the steps
necessary to be taken at once, if the case arose. He did
not think, so he wrote to Ball, that they would venture a
squadron to Malta or Alexandria, in view of the certain
destruction which in the end must befall it, even if successful in reaching the port.

Both remarks show that he did not look for the number
of ships that were sent — nineteen, as the first news said,
twenty-five, as was actually the case. An emergency so
great and so imminent drew out all his latent strength,
acute judgment, and promptitude. The brig that brought
the news was sent off the same night to Naples, with
orders to proceed from there to Minorca and Gibraltar,

and to notify Duckworth and St. Vincent what Nelson intended to do. A cutter sailed at the same time for Malta. Troubridge and Ball were both directed to send or bring all their ships-of-the-line, save one each, to Minorca, there to unite with Duckworth. Troubridge's ships were to call off Palermo for further instructions, but not to lose time by coming to anchor there. Expresses were sent to the different ports of Sicily, in case any Russian or Turkish ships had arrived, to put them on their guard, and to request co-operation by joining the force assembling off Minorca, where Nelson reasoned Lord St. Vincent also would repair. To the latter he wrote: "Eight, nine, or ten sail of the line shall, in a few days, be off Mahon, ready to obey your orders (not in the port);" for his intention was that they should remain outside under sail. "You may depend upon my exertion, and I am only sorry that I cannot move [1] to your help, but this island appears to hang on my stay. Nothing could console the Queen this night, but my promise not to leave them unless the battle was to be fought off Sardinia."

The next day he wrote again in similar terms, seeking to reconcile his promise to the Queen with his impulses, and, it may be said safely, with his duty. "Should you come upwards without a battle, I hope in that case you will afford me an opportunity of joining you; for my heart would break to be near my commander-in-chief, and not assisting him at such a time. What a state I am in! If I go, I risk, and more than risk, Sicily, and what is now safe on the Continent; for we know, from experience, that more depends on *opinion* than on acts themselves. As I stay, my heart is breaking; and, to mend the matter, I am seriously unwell."

That evening, the 13th, at nine o'clock, a lieutenant arrived, who had been landed to the westward of Palermo by a sloop-of-war, the "Peterel," she not being able to

---

[1] That is, in person.

beat up to the city against the east wind prevailing. From him Nelson learned that the French fleet had passed the Straits, and had been seen off Minorca. The next day, the "Peterel" having come off the port, he went alongside, and sent her on at once to Malta, with orders to Ball to abandon the blockade, bringing with him all his ships, and to proceed off Maritimo, a small island twenty miles west of Sicily, where he now proposed to concentrate his squadron and to go himself. Troubridge, having already orders to come to Palermo, needed no further instructions, except to bring all his ships, instead of leaving one at Naples. Every ship-of-the-line in the squadron, including the Portuguese, was thus summoned to join the Flag, in a position to cover Palermo and the approaches to the eastern Mediterranean. To these necessary dispositions was owing that the senior officer left at Naples was Captain Foote, who afterwards signed the articles of capitulation with the insurgents, which gave such offence to Nelson, and have occasioned much controversy in connection with his subsequent action.

Troubridge, having sailed at once on receipt of his first orders, arrived on the 17th with three British ships and one Portuguese. A heavy gale prevented Nelson getting to sea till the 20th, when he sailed, and was joined the next morning by the fourth ship from Naples. The same day came a Portuguese corvette from Gibraltar and Mahon, with letters from St. Vincent and Duckworth. The former announced that the French had passed the Straits, and that he was about to start in pursuit. Duckworth, who also was asked to join off Maritimo, declined to do so, saying that he must await the commander-in-chief. Nelson had of course immediately communicated to the latter his change of plan. He hoped to collect ten sail-of-the-line, which, "if Duckworth reinforce me, will enable me to look the enemy in the face" — fourteen ships to nineteen; "but should any of the Russians or Turks be off Malta, I hope to get a force of different nations equal to the enemy, when not a moment shall be lost in bringing them to battle."

On the 23d of May he was off Maritimo with seven ships, Ball not having joined yet. His spirits were fast rising, as in thought he drew near the enemy. "Duckworth means to leave me to my fate," he wrote to Lady Hamilton. "Never mind; if I can get eleven sail together, they shall not hurt me." "I am under no apprehension for the safety of his Majesty's squadron," he said in a circular letter to his scattered vessels, designed to heighten their ardor; "on the contrary, from the very high state of discipline of the ships, I am confident, should the enemy force us to battle, that we shall cut a very respectable figure; and if Admiral Duckworth joins, not one moment shall be lost in my attacking the enemy." It must be mentioned that St. Vincent had expressed his opinion that the French were bound for Malta and Alexandria, and Nelson, when he wrote these words, was hourly expecting to see their sails appear on the horizon. He did not know yet, however, that they were twenty-five, instead of nineteen, of the line. To St. Vincent he expressed himself with the sober, dauntless resolution of a consummate warrior, who recognized that opportunities must be seized, and detachments, if need be, sacrificed, for the furtherance of a great common object. "Your Lordship may depend that the squadron under my command shall never fall into the hands of the enemy; and before we are destroyed, I have little doubt but the enemy will have their wings so completely clipped that they may be easily overtaken" — by you. In this temper he waited. It is this clear perception of the utility of his contemplated grapple with superior numbers, and not the headlong valor and instinct for fighting that unquestionably distinguished him, which constitutes the excellence of Nelson's genius. This it was which guided him in the great Trafalgar campaign, and the lack of which betrayed Villeneuve at the same period to his wretched shortcomings. Yet, as has before been remarked, mere insight, however accurate and penetrating, ends only in itself, or at best falls far short of the mark, unless accompanied by Nelson's great power of disregarding contingencies — an inspired blindness, which at the moment of decisive action sees, not the risks, but the one only road to possible victory.

Whilst thus expecting an engagement which, from the disparity of numbers, could be nothing short of desperate, he drew up a codicil to his will, making to Lady Hamilton a bequest, in terms that show how complete were the infatuation and idealization now in possession of his mind: "I give and bequeath to my dear friend, Emma Hamilton, wife of the Right Hon. Sir William Hamilton, a nearly round box set with diamonds, said to have been sent me by the mother of the Grand Signor, which I request she will accept (and never part from) as token of regard and respect for her very eminent virtues (for she, the said Emma Hamilton, possesses them all to such a degree that it would be doing her injustice was any particular one to be mentioned) from her faithful and affectionate friend." During this short cruise he wrote her almost daily, and at some length, in addition to the more official communications addressed to Hamilton. At this same period he was excusing himself to his wife for the shortness and infrequency of his letters: "Pray attribute it to the true cause — viz., that in truth my poor hand cannot execute what my head tells me I ought to do."

On the 28th of May Nelson received letters from St. Vincent, dated the 21st, off Minorca, which put him in possession of the movements of the enemy up to that date. The French fleet, under the command of Admiral Bruix, had appeared on the 4th of the month off Cadiz. It was then blowing a half-gale of wind, and the French admiral did not care, under that condition, to engage the fifteen

British ships-of-the-line which were cruising off the harbor, under Lord Keith, who had come out from England the previous autumn to be St. Vincent's second in command. The intended junction with the Spanish squadron in Cadiz being thus thwarted, Bruix passed the Straits on the 5th, and Lord St. Vincent, having recalled Keith, followed on the 12th with sixteen ships. On the 20th he joined Duckworth, and learned that the enemy, when last seen, were heading for Toulon. Keith's removal had uncovered Cadiz, and St. Vincent fully expected that the Spanish fleet would leave there for the Mediterranean, which it did, and on the 20th entered Cartagena, to the number of seventeen of the line, but much crippled from a stormy passage. This Nelson did not yet know, nor that Bruix had reached Toulon on the 14th of May, and sailed again on the 26th for the eastward.

Satisfied that the enemy would not at once come his way, and knowing that a vessel had passed up the Mediterranean from St. Vincent to put Sidney Smith on his guard, Nelson ordered Ball to resume the blockade of Malta with two ships-of-the-line. The rest of his squadron he kept massed, and took to Palermo, where he arrived May 29th. Lookout ships were stationed off the north end of Corsica and west of Sardinia. "My reason for remaining in Sicily," he wrote St. Vincent, "is the covering the blockade of Naples, and the certainty of preserving Sicily in case of an attack, for if we were to withdraw our ships, it would throw such a damp on the people that I am sure there would be no resistance."

On the 6th of June Duckworth arrived at Palermo from the main fleet, with four ships-of-the-line, among them the "Foudroyant," eighty. This ship had been designated originally for Nelson's flag, and he shifted to her from the "Vanguard" on the 8th. Duckworth brought a report that St. Vincent was about to give up

the command and go home, on account of ill-health. This
at once aroused Nelson's anxiety, for he had long felt
that few superiors would have the greatness of mind to
trust him as implicitly, and humor him as tenderly, as the
great admiral had done. It is not every one that can
handle an instrument of such trenchant power, yet delicate temper, as Nelson's sensitive genius. The combination in St. Vincent of perfect professional capacity with
masterful strength of character, had made the tactful
respect he showed to Nelson's ability peculiarly grateful
to the latter; and had won from him a subordination of
the will, and an affection, which no subsequent commander-
in-chief could elicit. He wrote to him: —

My dear Lord, — We have a report that you are going
home. This distresses us most exceedingly, and myself in particular; so much so, that I have serious thoughts of returning,
if that event should take place. But for the sake of our Country, do not quit us at this serious moment. I wish not to detract from the merit of whoever may be your successor; but it
must take a length of time, which I hope the war will not give,
to be in any manner a St. Vincent. We look up to you, as we
have always found you, as to our Father, under whose fostering
care we have been led to fame. . . . Give not up a particle of
your authority to any one; be again our St. Vincent, and we
shall be happy.

Your affectionate   Nelson.

This letter did not reach St. Vincent before he carried
his purpose into effect; but Nelson never quite forgave the
abandonment of the command at such a moment. In after
years he spoke bitterly of it, as a thing he himself could
not have done; failing, perhaps, to realize the difference in
staying power between forty-five and sixty-five.

On the 2d of June, being then seventy miles southwest
of Toulon, St. Vincent turned over to Keith the command
of the twenty ships-of-the-line then with him, and went
to Port Mahon. For the moment he retained in his own

hands the charge of the station, — continued Commander-in-chief, — with headquarters at Minorca, and two divisions cruising: one of twenty ships, with Keith, between Toulon and Minorca, and one of sixteen, including three Portuguese, under Nelson in the waters of Sicily. Friction between these two began at once. Lord Keith was an accomplished and gallant officer, methodical, attentive, and correct; but otherwise he rose little above the commonplace, and, while he could not ignore Nelson's great achievements, he does not seem to have had the insight which could appreciate the rare merit underlying them, nor the sympathetic temperament which could allow for his foibles. Nelson, exasperated at the mere fact of the other's succession to the command, speedily conceived for him an antipathy which Keith would have been more than mortal not to return; but it is to the honor of the latter's self-command that, while insisting upon obedience from his brilliant junior, he bore his refractoriness with dignified patience.

After St. Vincent left him, Keith continued to stand to the northward and eastward. On the 5th of June he received certain information that the French fleet, now twenty-two ships-of-the-line, was in Vado Bay. This word he at once sent on to Nelson. Next day his division was so close in with the Riviera, off Antibes, that it was fired upon by the shore batteries; but the wind coming to the eastward, when off Monaco, did not permit it to pass east of Corsica, and, fearing that the French would take that route and fall upon Nelson, Keith detached to him two seventy-fours, which joined him on the 13th of June.

At the moment of their arrival Nelson had just quitted Palermo for Naples, taking with him the whole squadron. The King of Naples had formally requested him to afford to the royal cause at the capital the assistance of the fleet, because the successes of the royalists elsewhere in the kingdom rendered imminent an insurrection in the city against the republican party and the French, which held the castles; and such insurrection, unless adequately supported, might either fail or lead to deplorable excesses. Lady Hamilton, whose irregular interference in State concerns receives here singular illustration, strongly urged this measure in a letter, written to the admiral after an interview with the Queen. Nelson consented, took on board seventeen hundred troops, with the Hereditary Prince, who was to represent the King, — the latter not wishing to go, — and was already clear of Palermo Bay when the two ships from Keith appeared. Gathering from their information that the French were bound for Naples or Sicily, in which his own judgment coincided, he returned at once into port, landed the Prince and the troops, and then took the squadron again off Maritimo, where he expected Ball and the two ships off Malta to join him without delay. "The French force being twenty-two sail of the line," he wrote in suppressed reproach to Keith, "four of which are first rates, the force with me being only sixteen of the line, not one of which was of three decks, three being Portuguese, and one of the English being a sixty-four, very short of men, I had no choice left but to return to Palermo."

With this incident of the insufficient reinforcement sent, began the friction with Keith which appears more openly in his correspondence with others. To St. Vincent, still commander-in-chief, he wrote: "I send a copy of my letter to Lord Keith, and I have only stated my regret that his Lordship could not have sent me a force fit to face the enemy: but, as we are, I shall not get out of their way; although, as I am, I cannot think myself justified in exposing the world (I may almost say) to be plundered by these miscreants. I trust your Lordship will not think me wrong in the painful determination I conceived myself forced to make," that is, to go back

Lord Keith

to Palermo, "for agonized indeed was the mind of your Lordship's faithful and affectionate servant."

Nelson appears to have felt that the return to Palermo, though imperative, in view of the relative forces of himself and the French, would not only postpone and imperil the restoration of the royal family, but would bring discredit upon himself for not seeking and fighting the enemy's fleet. "I shall wait off Maritimo," he wrote Keith, "anxiously expecting such a reinforcement as may enable me to go in search of the enemy's fleet, when not one moment shall be lost in bringing them to battle; for," he continues, with one of those flashes of genius which from time to time, unconsciously to himself, illuminate his writings, "I consider the best defence for his Sicilian Majesty's dominions is to place myself alongside the French." "My situation is a cruel one," he wrote to Hamilton, "and I am sure Lord Keith has lowered me in the eyes of Europe, for they will only know of 18 sail, [Ball having joined], and not of the description of them; it has truly made me ill." But, although not justified in seeking them, he had off Maritimo taken a strategic position which would enable him to intercept their approach to either Naples or Sicily, "and I was firmly resolved," he wrote with another of his clear intuitions, "they should not pass me without a battle, which would so cripple them that they might be unable to proceed on any distant service." "On this you may depend," he had written to Lady Hamilton, on the first cruise off Maritimo, three weeks before, "that if my little squadron obeys my signal, not a ship shall fall into the hands of the enemy; and I will so cut them up, that they will not be fit even for a summer's cruise."

On the 20th of June, off Maritimo, he received a despatch from St. Vincent that a reinforcement of twelve ships-of-the-line from the Channel was then approaching Port Mahon, and that Keith, having returned thither, had

left again in search of Bruix, whose whereabouts remained
unknown. He was also notified that St. Vincent had
resigned all his command, leaving Keith commander-in-
chief. Nelson was convinced — " I knew," was his expression — that the French intended going to Naples. He
determined now to resume his enterprise against the
republicans in the city; a decision which caused him
great and unexplained mental conflict. "I am agitated,"
he wrote Hamilton the same day, in a note headed " Most
Secret," "but my resolution is fixed. For Heaven's sake
suffer not any one to oppose it. I shall not be gone eight
days. No harm can come to Sicily. I send my Lady and
you Lord St. Vincent's letter. I am full of grief and
anxiety. I must go. It will finish the war. It will give
a sprig of laurel to your affectionate friend, Nelson." The
cause of this distress can only be surmised, but is probably
to be found in the fears of the Queen, and in the differences existing at the time between herself and the King.
Possibly, too, Lady Hamilton's sympathy with the Queen,
in a present fear for Sicily, may have led her, contrary to
the request so lately made for the admiral to go to Naples,
to second an entreaty that the island should not now be
exposed; and to refuse her may have caused him pain.
On the 21st he was at Palermo, and after two hours'
consultation with their Majesties and Acton, the Prime
Minister, he sailed again, accompanied in the " Foudroyant"
on this occasion by Sir William and Lady Hamilton, but
not by the Hereditary Prince, nor the Sicilian troops.
On the 24th, at 9 P. M., he anchored in the Bay of Naples.
Flags of truce were at that moment flying on the castles
of Uovo and Nuovo, which were in the hands of the
Neapolitan republicans, and upon the frigate "Seahorse,"
whose commander had been the senior British officer
present, before Nelson's own appearance.

On the passage from Palermo, Nelson had received information that the royalists, — with whom were co-operat-

ing some detachments of Russians and Turks, as well as
the British naval forces, under Captain Foote, of the
"Seahorse,"—had concluded an armistice with the French
and their Neapolitan allies, who were in possession of the
castles. The terms of the armistice, thus rumored, were
that the castles, if not relieved within twenty-one days,
should then be surrendered; the garrisons to march out
with the honors of war, and to be transported to Toulon in
vessels to be furnished by the King of Naples. This report
was erroneous in important particulars, especially as to the
period of twenty-one days. What really had happened
was, that a capitulation had been concluded, which provided that the Neapolitan insurgents should evacuate the
two castles held by them — Uovo and Nuovo — as soon as
the transports were ready to take them to Toulon, but not
before. The French, in the castle of St. Elmo, were not
included in the arrangement, their only part being that
it required the ratification of their commander before
becoming operative. This ratification was given, and,
when Nelson's squadron came in sight,[1] the treaty had
received the signature of all the parties interested; the
flags of truce indicating a cessation of hostilities until the
terms of the capitulation were carried into effect.

Nelson had been given full power by the King of the
Two Sicilies to act as his representative. He was also,
as commander of the fleet, the representative of the King
of Great Britain among the allied forces, which were
acting in support of the royalist cause. The double function introduces great confusion into the subsequent transactions, especially as there are on record no formal
credentials investing him with the authority he claimed to
have from the King of Naples. The omission probably

[1] The commandant of St. Elmo signed on the 3d Messidor, June 21.
Ruffo, with the Russian and Turkish representatives, had already signed.
The paper was then sent to Foote, who signed and returned to Ruffo on the
23d of June. The "Foudroyant" came in sight on the afternoon of the
24th.

arose from the extreme shortness of his stay in Palermo
on the 21st — only two hours and a half elapsing, by the
"Foudroyant's" log, between the entering of the ship and
her sailing again; a time sufficient for an interview and a
clear understanding, but scarcely for drawing up a regular
commission. The fact rests upon his own statement, adequately supported, however, by inferences reasonably to
be drawn from expressions in letters to him, both from the
King and from Acton, the Prime Minister. That his
power went so far as to authorize him to remove Cardinal
Ruffo, up to that time the King's representative, would
alone confirm the assertion of a man habitually truthful.
Sir William Hamilton also, writing to Greville, and alluding to his official despatch by the same mail, says, "We
had full powers." It may be accepted that Nelson himself was entirely satisfied that he was authorized at the time
to act for the King, when emergency required; and it is
certain that letters were speedily sent, empowering him to
appoint a new government, as well as to arrest Ruffo and
to send him to Palermo in a British ship.

Seeing the flags of truce flying, from the two castles
and the "Seahorse," and being under the impression that
has been stated as to the terms of an armistice, which he
called "infamous," Nelson immediately made a signal
annulling the truce, "being determined," he wrote to
Keith, "never to give my approbation to any terms with
Rebels, but that of unconditional submission." As the
execution of the capitulation depended upon the embarkation of the garrisons in the transports which were to be
provided, Nelson was entirely master of the situation, so
far as force went. Next morning, June 25th, he moved
his fleet of eighteen sail nearer in, mooring it in a close
line of battle before the city, and at the same time sent for
twenty-two gun and mortar vessels, then lying at the
islands, with which he flanked the ships-of-the-line. In
this imposing array, significant at once of inexorable pur-

pose and irresistible power, he sent to Ruffo his "opinion of the infamous terms entered into with the rebels," and also two papers, to be by him forwarded to the insurgents and to the French. From the latter, who had not treated, was required simply an unconditional surrender; but the message to the insurgents, sent, singularly enough, not from the representative of the King of Naples but from the British admiral, ran as follows:—

> His Britannic Majesty's Ship Foudroyant, Naples Bay,
> 25th June, 1799.
>
> Rear Admiral Lord Nelson, K.B., Commander of His Britannic Majesty's Fleet in the Bay of Naples, acquaints the Rebellious Subjects of His Sicilian Majesty in the Castles of Uovo and Nuovo, that he will not permit them to embark or quit those places. They must surrender themselves to His Majesty's royal mercy.
>
> NELSON.

Ruffo refused to send the papers in, and said decisively that, if Nelson saw fit to break the armistice then existing, between the signature of the capitulation and its execution, he would aid neither with men nor guns. Finally, he went on board the "Foudroyant;" but after an animated discussion, which rose nearly to an altercation, neither party yielded his ground. "I used every argument in my power," wrote Nelson, "to convince him that *the Treaty and Armistice was at an end by the arrival of the fleet,*" and this therefore may be taken to summarize his own position. He then gave the Cardinal a written opinion that the treaty was one that "ought not to be carried out without the approbation of His Sicilian Majesty." Neither his powers nor Ruffo's, he argued, extended to granting such a capitulation. Ruffo, indeed, had been expressly forbidden to do so; a fact which rendered the paper void from the first. "Under this opinion," reported Nelson to Keith, "the Rebels came out of the Castles;" "*as they ought,*" he wrote to his friend

Davison, "and as I hope all those who are false to their King and Country will, *to be hanged*, or otherwise disposed of, as their sovereign thought proper." They were then placed in transports, which were anchored under the guns of the fleet; and in the end many of them were put to death.

For his action in this case Nelson has been severely blamed. The point at issue is perfectly simple, however it may be decided. Disregarding subordinate considerations, of which there are many, such as the motives which induced Ruffo and Foote to grant terms, and the question whether they would have been justified, which Nelson denied, in conceding them under any conditions, the matter reduces itself to this: When an agreement has been made, one of the parties to which is acting only as a representative, not as a principal, nor accredited for the specific purpose, has the principal, in person or by proxy, a right to annul the agreement, provided, as in this case, it has not passed into execution, either total or partial? Nelson admitted that the persons of the insurgents would have been entitled to the immunity stipulated, if they had already delivered up the castles. They had not done so; the flags of truce marked only a cessation of hostilities, not the completion of the transaction. By the terms, the evacuation and embarkation were to be simultaneous: "The evacuation shall not take place until the moment of embarkation." The status of the opponents was in no wise altered by a paper which had not begun to receive execution. The one important circumstance which had happened was the arrival of the British squadron, instead of Bruix's fleet which all were expecting. It was perfectly within Nelson's competence to stop the proceedings at the point they had then reached.

[After writing the above, the author, by the courtesy of the Foreign Office, received a copy of Sir William Hamilton's despatch of July 14, 1799, giving his account of the events happening after June 20th, the date when

Nelson left Palermo for Naples. In this occurs a statement which would seriously modify, if not altogether destroy, the justification of Nelson's conduct in annulling the capitulation, which rests upon the condition that it had not received any substantial execution. Hamilton says: " *When we anchored in this Bay the 24th of June the capitulation of the castles had in some measure taken place.*[1] Fourteen large Polacks or transport vessels *had taken on board* out of the castles the most conspicuous and criminal of the Neapolitan Rebels, that had chosen to go to Toulon, the others had *already* been permitted with their property to return to their own homes in this kingdom, and hostages selected from the first royalist nobility of Naples had been sent into the castle of St. Elmo that commands the city of Naples, and where a French garrison and the flag of the French Republic was to remain until the news of the arrival of the Neapolitan Rebels at Toulon. . . . There was no time to be lost, *for the transport vessels were on the point of sailing for Toulon,* when Lord Nelson ordered all the boats of his squadron to be manned and armed, and to bring those vessels, with all the Rebels on board, directly under the sterns of his ships, and there they remain, having taken out and secured on board His Majesty's ships the most guilty chiefs of the rebellion."

Occurring in an official despatch, from a minister of Nelson's sovereign, his own warm personal friend and admirer, closely associated with him throughout the proceedings, and his colleague and adviser in much that was done, the words quoted, if they could stand accepted as an accurate statement of occurrences, would establish that Nelson had secured the persons of men who had surrendered on the faith of a treaty, and had held them, subject to the tender mercies of the King of the Two Sicilies. They were in his power (accepting Hamilton's statement), only because the King's Vicar-General, his representative so

[1] All italics in the quotations from this despatch are the author's.

far as they knew, had guaranteed their safety if they came out of the castles. The least they were entitled to, in such case, was to be restored to the castles — not yet evacuated — to be placed as they were before surrendering. It is true that, as the terms of the treaty made embarkation and evacuation coincident, and as the latter had certainly not taken place, it may be argued that they had no claim to immunity when they had precipitated their action, and left the castle of their own motion before the formal evacuation and embarkation; but one would prefer not to rest on such a technical plea the justification of a character generally so upright in his public acts as Lord Nelson.

Fortunately for his fame, there is adequate reason to believe — to be assured — that Hamilton's despatch is very inaccurate in details, and specifically in this one, so damaging as it stands. The incident of arming the boats and bringing out the vessels took place, according to the log of the "Foudroyant," not when the fleet moored, on the morning of June 25th, or even shortly afterwards, but on the morning of the 28th; two days after the castles, as shown by the logs of both the "Foudroyant" and "Seahorse," surrendered and were taken possession of. Miss Helen Maria Williams, whose account of the affair was strongly tinged with sympathy for the revolutionists, says: "While the two garrisons, to the number of fifteen hundred, *were waiting for the preparing and provisioning of the vessels* which were to convey them to France, Lord Nelson arrived with his whole fleet in the Bay of Naples [June 24–25]. On the evening of the twenty-sixth of June, the patriots evacuated their forts, and embarked on board the transports prepared for their conveyance to France. *The next day* [June 27], the transports were moored alongside the English fleet, each under the cannon of an English vessel."[1] These several witnesses may be confidently

---

[1] Nicolas, vol. iii. p. 511. Author's italics.

accepted, and prove that the embarkation and removal of the garrisons took place after Nelson's declaration to them, dated June 25th, in which he said "he would not permit them to embark or quit those places. They must surrender themselves to His Majesty's Royal mercy." Captain Foote, who had signed the capitulation that Nelson condemned, affords evidence which, though not conclusive, is corroborative of the above. Writing to Nelson at 7 A. M. of the 24th of June, fourteen hours before the fleet anchored, but only eight before he knew of its approach, he says: "the Republicans are about to embark," and again, "when the Capitulation is put into effect;" both which expressions show that up to that moment the agreement had not begun to receive execution. On the 22d of June Ruffo wrote to Foote that there were no vessels in Naples on which to embark the revolutionists, and requested him to furnish them; a request that Foote referred to Count Thurn, the senior Neapolitan naval officer, for compliance. It is therefore antecedently probable that the vessels could not have been collected from other ports, and prepared for an unexpected voyage of at least a week's duration, before Nelson arrived, forty-eight hours later.

Hamilton's despatch contains another mistake, affecting the order of events, so circumstantial that, taken with the one just discussed, it shows his accuracy on such points was more than doubtful. "Admiral Caracciolo," he says, was hanged, "the day after the King's squadron came to Naples;" the fact being that the squadron arrived on the night of June 24–25, and that Caracciolo was executed on the evening of the 29th. This error was not a slip of the pen, for he characterizes the alleged fact as "so speedy an act of justice" as to elicit loud applause from the concourse of spectators surrounding the ship in boats.

Hamilton was not only nearly seventy, but he was worn out in health and constitution. Writing a fortnight after the events, and having passed that time in the turmoil and confusion attending the re-establishment of order in Naples, it is not wonderful that he ran together incidents that happened in rapid succession, and failed to realize the importance which might afterwards attach to the date of their occurrence. "I am so worn out," he tells Greville, "by the long despatch I have been obliged to write to-day to Lord Grenville that I can scarcely hold my pen;" and again, "My head is *so confused* with long writing on this subject that I must refer you to my letter to Lord Grenville. . . . You will find me much worn and am little more than skin and bone, as I have very little stomach."

Although they were on board ship together, Nelson cannot have seen Hamilton's despatch, or he must have corrected a misstatement which directly contradicted his own account of June 27 to Lord Keith, as well as that he was sending by the same messenger, in a private letter to Earl Spencer. The latter ran thus: "Your Lordship will observe my Note (No. 1), and opinion to the Cardinal (No. 2). *The Rebels came out of the Castles with this knowledge*, without any honours, and the principal Rebels were seized and conducted on board the ships of the squadron. The others, embarked in fourteen polacres, were anchored under the care of our ships."

Hamilton's statement remaining uncorrected, and being so circumstantial, though erroneous, has made necessary a fuller discussion of the evidence on this point than otherwise might have been required.

Although, in the author's judgment, Nelson acted within his right in disallowing the capitulation, it is essential to note that a fortnight later, when fully cognizant of all the circumstances, he characterized it in a letter to Lord Spencer as "infamous." "On my fortunate arrival here I found a most infamous treaty entered into with the Rebels, in direct disobedience of His Sicilian

Majesty's orders."[1] Such an adjective, deliberately applied after the heat of the first moment had passed, is, in its injustice, a clear indication of the frame of mind under the domination of which he was. Captain Foote with his feeble squadron, and the commanders of the undisciplined mob ashore known as the Christian army, expected, as did Nelson himself, the appearance of the French fleet at Naples. In view of that possibility, it was at the least a pardonable error of judgment to concede terms which promised to transfer the castles speedily into their own hands. The most censurable part of the agreement was in the failure to exact the surrender of St. Elmo, which dominates the others. It is to be regretted that Captain Foote, who naturally and bitterly resented the word "infamous," did not, in his "Vindication," confine himself to this military argument, instead of mixing it up with talk about mercy to culprits and Nelson's infatuation for Lady Hamilton.]

On the 27th of June, the day following the surrender of Uovo and Nuovo, Troubridge landed with thirteen hundred men to besiege the French in St. Elmo, an undertaking in which he was joined by five hundred Russians and some royalists. Forty-eight hours later Nelson felt called upon, as representative of the King of the Two Sicilies, to take action more peremptory and extreme than anything he had hitherto done.

On the 29th of June, Commodore Francesco Caracciolo, lately head of the Republican Navy, was brought on board the " Foudroyant," having been captured in the country, in disguise. This man had accompanied the royal family in their flight to Palermo ; but after arrival there had obtained leave to return to Naples, in order to avert the confiscation of his property by the Republican government. He subsequently joined the Republicans, or Jacobins, as they were called by Nelson and the Court. His reasons for so doing

---

[1] Nicolas, vol. iii. p. 406.

are immaterial; they were doubtless perfectly sound from the point of view of apparent self-interest; the substantial fact remains that he commanded the insurgent vessels in action with the British and Royal Neapolitan navies, firing impartially upon both. In one of these engagements the Neapolitan frigate "Minerva" was struck several times, losing two men killed and four wounded. Caracciolo, therefore, had fully committed himself to armed insurrection, in company with foreign invaders, against what had hitherto been, and still claimed to be, the lawful government of the country. He had afterwards, as the republican cause declined, taken refuge with the other insurgents in the castles. When he left them is uncertain, but on the 23d of June he is known to have been outside of Naples, and so remained till captured.

It is not easy to understand in what respect his case differed from that of other rebels who surrendered unconditionally, and whom Nelson did not try himself, but simply placed in safe keeping until the King's instructions should be received, except that, as a naval officer, he was liable to trial by court-martial, even though martial law had not been proclaimed. It was to such a tribunal that Nelson decided instantly to bring him. A court-martial of Neapolitan officers was immediately ordered to convene on board the "Foudroyant," the precept for the Court being sent to Count Thurn, captain of the "Minerva," who, because senior officer in the bay, was indicated by custom as the proper president. The charges, as worded by Nelson, were two in number, tersely and clearly stated. "Francisco Caracciolo, a commodore in the service of His Sicilian Majesty, stands accused of rebellion against his lawful sovereign, and for firing at his colours hoisted on board his Frigate, the Minerva." The court assembled at once, sitting from 10 A. M. to noon. The charges being found proved, sentence of death was pronounced; and Caracciolo, who had been brought on board at 9 A. M., was at 5 P. M., by Nelson's orders, hanged at the foreyard-arm of the "Minerva." He was forty-seven years old at the time of his death.

The proceedings of the court-martial were open, but the record, if any was drawn up, has not been preserved. It is impossible, therefore, now to say whether the evidence sustained the charges; but the acts alleged were so simple and so notorious, that there can be little doubt Caracciolo had fairly incurred his fate. Even in our milder age, no officer of an army or navy would expect to escape the like punishment for the same offence; if he did, it would be because mercy prevailed over justice. As regards the technicalities of the procedure, it would seem probable that Nelson's full powers, especially when committed to a military man, included by fair inference, if not expressly, the right of ordering courts-martial; whereas he had not at hand the machinery of judges and civil courts, for proceeding against the civilians who had joined in the insurrection. Despite his fearlessness of responsibility, he was always careful not to overpass the legal limits of his authority, except when able to justify his action by what at least appeared to himself adequate reasons. The Portuguese squadron, for instance, was absolutely under his orders, so far as its movements went; but, when a case of flagrant misconduct occurred, he confined himself to regretting that he had not power to order a court. Anomalous as his position was in the Bay of Naples, before the arrival of the King, and regrettably uncertain as is the commission under which he acted, there is no ground for disputing that he had authority to order a court-martial, and to carry its sentence into execution, nor that Caracciolo came within the jurisdiction of a court-martial properly constituted. Having regard, therefore, to the unsettled conditions of things prevailing, no fatal irregularity can be shown either in the trial or execution of this prisoner.

But, while all this is true, the instinctive aversion with

which this act of Nelson's has been regarded generally is
well founded. It was not decent, for it was not necessary,
that capture should be followed so rapidly by trial, and
condemnation by execution. Neither time nor circumstances pressed. The insurrection was over. Except the
siege of St. Elmo, hostilities near Naples were at an end.
That Caracciolo's judges were naval officers who had recently been in action with him would be, with average
military men, rather in the prisoner's favor than otherwise ;
but it was very far from being in his favor that they were
men in whom the angry passions engendered by civil warfare, and licentious spoliation, had not yet had time to cool.
Neither the judges nor the revising power allowed themselves space for reflection. Nelson himself failed to sustain the dispassionate and magnanimous attitude that
befitted the admiral of a great squadron, so placed as to
have the happy chance to moderate the excesses which
commonly follow the triumph of parties in intestine strife.
But, however he then or afterwards may have justified his
course to his own conscience, his great offence was against
his own people. To his secondary and factitious position
of delegate from the King of Naples, he virtually sacrificed
the consideration due to his inalienable character of representative of the King and State of Great Britain. He
should have remembered that the act would appear to the
world, not as that of the Neapolitan plenipotentiary, but
of the British officer, and that his nation, while liable like
others to bursts of unreasoning savagery, in its normal
moods delights to see justice clothed in orderly forms,
unstained by precipitation or suspicion of perversion, advancing to its ends with the majesty of law, without
unseemly haste, providing things honest in the sight of
all men. That he did not do so, when he could have done
so, has been intuitively felt; and to the instinctive resentment thus aroused among his countrymen has been due the
facility with which the worst has been too easily believed.

Commander Jeaffreson Miles of the British Navy, writing in 1843, was one of the first, if not the very first, to clear effectually Nelson's reputation from the stigma of treachery, and of submission to unworthy influences, at this time. He has sought also to vindicate his hasty action in Caracciolo's case, by citing the swift execution of two seamen by Lord St. Vincent, at a time when mutiny was threatening. It cannot be denied that, for deterrent effect, punishment at times must be sudden as well as sharp; but the justification in each case rests upon attendant circumstances. In the instances here compared, we have in the one a fleet in which many ships were seething with mutiny, and the preservation of order rested solely upon the firmness of one man, — the commander-in-chief, — and upon the awe inspired by him. In the other, we see rebellion subdued, the chief rebels in confinement, the foreign enemy, except three small isolated garrisons, expelled beyond the borders of the kingdom six weeks before, and a great British fleet in possession of the anchorage. Punishment in such case, however just, is not deterrent, but avenging. True, Nelson was expecting the appearance of Bruix's fleet; but he himself characterized as "infamous" the capitulation granted by Ruffo and Foote, to which they were largely moved by the same expectation, when wielding a much smaller force than he did. The possible approach of the French fleet did not necessitate the hasty execution of a prisoner.

That Nelson yielded his convictions of right and wrong, and consciously abused his power, at the solicitation of Lady Hamilton, as has been so freely alleged, is not probably true, — there is no proof of it; on the contrary, as though to guard against such suspicion, he was careful to see none but his own officers during Caracciolo's confinement. But it is true that he was saturated with the prevalent Court feeling against the insurgents and the French, which found frequent expression in his letters. After living in the Hamiltons' house for four months, during which, to use his own expression, "I have never but three times put my foot to the ground, since December, 1798," in daily close contact with the woman who had won his passionate love, who was the ardent personal friend of the Queen, sharing her antipathies, and expressing her hatred of enemies in terms which showed the coarseness of her fibre,[1] Nelson was steeped in the atmosphere of the Court of Naples, and separated from that of the British fleet, none of whose strongest captains were long with him during that period. The attitude more natural to men of his blood is shown in a letter signed by the officers of the " Leviathan," Duckworth's flagship. Coming from Minorca, they were out of touch with Neapolitan fury, and they addressed Lady Hamilton, interceding for a family engaged in the rebellion; a fact which shows the prevailing impression — whether well founded or not — of the influence in her power to exert. " We all feel ourselves deeply impressed with the horrid crime of disaffection to one's lawful sovereign, . . . but when we consider the frailty of human nature," &c. " Advise those Neapolitans not to be too sanguinary," wrote Keith to Nelson, apparently immediately after receiving the news of Caracciolo's hanging.

[1] Mr. Pryse Lockhart Gordon, who was in Palermo in January, 1799, tells the following anecdote of Lady Hamilton. He had been dining at the ambassador's, and after dinner a Turkish officer was introduced. In the course of the evening he boasted that he had put to death with his own sword a number of French prisoners. " 'Look, there is their blood remaining on it!' The speech being translated, her Ladyship's eye beamed with delight, and she said, 'Oh, let me see the sword that did the glorious deed!' It was presented to her; she took it into her fair hands, covered with rings, and, looking at the encrusted Jacobin blood, kissed it, and handed it to the hero of the Nile. Had I not been an eye-witness to this disgraceful act, I would not have ventured to relate it." (Gordon's Memoirs, vol. i. p. 210.) The author, also, would not have ventured to adduce it, without first satisfying himself, by inquiry, as to the probable credibility of Mr. Gordon, and likewise testing his narrative. It bears marks of the inaccuracy in details to which memory is subject, but the indications of general correctness are satisfactory.

The abrupt execution of Caracciolo was an explosion of fierce animosity long cherished, pardonable perhaps in a Neapolitan royalist, but not in a foreign officer only indirectly interested in the issues at stake; and hence it is that the fate of that one sufferer has aroused more attention and more sympathy than that of the numerous other victims, put to death by the King's command after ordinary processes of law. It stands conspicuous as the act of an English officer imbued with the spirit of a Neapolitan Bourbon official. " Could it ever happen," he wrote to Acton, some months after this, " that any English minister wanted to make me an instrument of hurting the feelings of His Sicilian Majesty, I would give up my commission sooner than do it. . . . I am placed in such a situation — a subject of one King by birth, and, as far as is consistent with my allegiance to that King, a voluntary subject of His Sicilian Majesty — that if any man attempted to separate my two Kings, by all that is sacred, I should consider even putting that man to death as a meritorious act." [1] On the other hand, it must be considered that Nelson, though humane, tended even in his calmest moments to severity towards military offenders. Writing with reference to a captain convicted of misbehavior before the enemy, he said, " If a man does not do his utmost in time of action, I think but one punishment ought to be inflicted; " and it may be inferred that he would have approved Byng's execution, where cowardice was not proved, but grave military dereliction was.

On the 10th of July the King of the Two Sicilies arrived from Palermo in the Bay of Naples, and went on board the " Foudroyant," which, for the whole time he remained, — about four weeks, — became practically his seat of government. There the royal standard was hoisted, there the King held his levees, and there business of State was transacted. In and through all moved the figures of Sir Wil-

[1] Nelson to Acton, November 18, 1799. (Nicolas.)

liam and Lady Hamilton, the latter considering herself, and not without cause, the representative of the Queen. The latter had remained in Palermo, being out of favor with the Neapolitans, and with her husband, who attributed to her precipitancy the disasters of the previous December. The two women corresponded daily; and, if the minister's wife deceived herself as to the amount and importance of what she effected, there is no doubt that she was very busy, that she was commonly believed to exert much influence, and that great admiration for one another was expressed by herself, Hamilton, and Nelson, the " *Tria juncta in uno*," as the latter was pleased to style them. "I never saw such zeal and activity in any one as in this wonderful man [Nelson]," wrote she to Greville. "My dearest Sir William, thank God! is well, and of the greatest use now to the King." "Emma has been of infinite use in our late very critical business," said Hamilton to the same correspondent. "Ld. Nelson and I cou'd not have done without her. It will be a heart-breaking to the Queen of N. when we go" — back to England, as was then expected. "Sir William and Lady Hamilton are, to my great comfort, with me," wrote Nelson to Spencer; "for without them it would have been impossible I could have rendered half the service to his Majesty which I have now done: their heads and their hearts are equally great and good."

The execution of Caracciolo was shortly followed by another very singular incident, which showed how biassed Nelson had become towards the interests of the Neapolitan Court, and how exclusively he identified them — confused them, would scarcely be too strong a word — with the essential interests of the Allied cause and the duties of the British Navy. On the 13th of July the castle of St. Elmo was surrendered by the French, the whole city of Naples thus returning under the royal authority. On the same day, or the next, Troubridge, with a thousand of the best men that could be sent from the squadron, marched against

Capua, accompanied by four thousand troops. A letter had already been received from the commander-in-chief, Keith, to Nelson, intimating that it might be necessary to draw down his vessels from Naples to the defence of Minorca. " Should such an order come at this moment," wrote Nelson to the First Lord, forecasting his probable disobedience, " it would be a cause for some consideration whether Minorca is to be risked, or the two Kingdoms of Naples and Sicily? I rather think my decision would be to risk the former; " and he started Troubridge off with a detachment that seriously crippled the squadron. Capua is fifteen to twenty miles inland from Naples.

On the 13th — it is to be presumed after closing his letter to Spencer just quoted — an order reached him from Keith, in these words: " Events which have recently occurred render it necessary that as great a force as can be collected should be assembled near the island of Minorca ; therefore, if your Lordship has no detachment of the French squadron in the neighbourhood of Sicily, nor information of their having sent any force towards Egypt or Syria, you are hereby required and directed to send such ships as you can possibly spare off the island of Minorca to wait my orders." The wording was so elastic, as regards the numbers to be sent, as to leave much to Nelson's judgment, and he replied guardedly the same day : " As soon as the safety of His Sicilian Majesty's Kingdoms is secured, I shall not lose one moment in making the detachment you are pleased to order. At present, under God's Providence, the safety of His Sicilian Majesty, and his speedy restoration to his kingdom, depends on this fleet, and the confidence inspired even by the appearance of our ships before the city is beyond all belief; and I have no scruple in declaring my opinion that should any event draw us from the kingdom, that if the French remain in any part of it, disturbances will again arise, for all order having been completely overturned, it must take a thorough cleansing, and some little time, to restore tranquillity."

When Keith wrote this first order, June 27, he was at sea somewhere between Minorca and Toulon, trying to find Bruix's fleet, of which he had lost touch three weeks before, at the time he sent to Nelson the two seventy-fours, whose arrival caused the latter's second cruise of Maritimo. He had lost touch through a false step, the discussion of which has no place in a life of Nelson, beyond the remark that it was Keith's own error, not that of Lord St. Vincent, as Nelson afterwards mistakenly alleged; querulously justifying his own disobedience on the ground that Keith, by obeying against his judgment, had lost the French fleet. What is to be specially noted in the order is that Keith gave no account of his reasons, nor of the events which dictated them, nor of his own intended action. No room is afforded by his words for any discretion, except as to the number of ships to be sent by Nelson, and, though the language of the latter was evasive, the failure to move even a single vessel was an act of unjustifiable disobedience. To Keith he wrote privately, and in a conciliatory spirit, but nothing that made his act less flagrant. "To all your wishes, depend on it, I shall pay the very strictest attention."

Conscious of the dangerous step he was taking, Nelson wrote on the same day, by private letter,[1] to the First Lord

---

[1] Much confusion has been introduced into the times, when Keith's several orders were received by Nelson, by the fact that the original of this private letter to Earl Spencer is dated the 19th (Nicolas, vol. vii. p. clxxxv); while the secretary, copying it into the letter-book, wrote July 13th. (Nicolas, vol. iii. p. 408.) Nicolas considered the former correct, probably because it came last into his hands. The author considers the 13th correct, because the official letter to Keith bears that date, and reads, "I have to acknowledge the receipt of your Lordship's letter of June 27." (Nicolas, vol. iii. p. 408.)

The date of Troubridge's marching against Capua is similarly brought into doubt by these letters. The author believes it to have been July 13 or 14, from another official letter to Keith of the 13th. (Nicolas, vol. iii. p. 404.) "Captains Troubridge and Hallowell . . . march against Capua to-morrow of the Admiralty. "You will easily conceive my feelings," he said, "but my mind, your Lordship will know, was perfectly prepared for this order; and more than ever is my mind made up, that, at this moment, I will not part with a single ship, as I cannot do that without drawing a hundred and twenty men from each ship now at the siege of Capua, where an army is gone this day. I am fully aware of the act I have committed; but, sensible of my loyal intentions, I am prepared for any fate which may await my disobedience. Do not think that my opinion is formed from the arrangements of any one," an expression which shows that he was aware how talk was running. "*No;* be it good, or be it bad, it is all my own. It is natural I should wish the decision of the Admiralty and my Commander-in-chief as speedily as possible. To obtain the former, I beg your Lordship's interest with the Board. You know me enough, my dear Lord, to be convinced I want no screen to my conduct."

On the 9th of July, Keith wrote again, from Port Mahon, a letter which Nelson received on the 19th. He said that he was satisfied that the enemy's intentions were directed neither against the Two Sicilies, nor to the reinforcement of their army in Egypt; that, on the contrary, there was reason to believe they were bound out of the Straits. "I judge it necessary that all, or the greatest part of the force under your Lordship's orders, should quit the Island of Sicily, and repair to Minorca, for the purpose of protecting that Island during the necessary absence of His Majesty's squadron under my command, or for the purpose of co-operating with me against the combined force of the enemy, wherever it may be necessary." The commander-in-chief, in short, wished to mass his forces, for the neces-

morning." The odd Sea-Time of that day, by which July 13 began at noon, July 12, of Civil Time, also causes confusion; writers using them indiscriminatingly. The capitulation of St. Elmo was certainly signed on July 12. (Clarke and M'Arthur, vol. ii. p. 294.)

sities of the general campaign, as he considered them.
Nelson now flatly refused obedience, on the ground of the
local requirements in his part of the field. "Your Lordship, at the time of sending me the order, was not informed
of the change of affairs in the Kingdom of Naples, and that
all our marines and a body of seamen are landed, in order
to drive the French scoundrels out of the Kingdom, which,
with God's blessing will very soon be effected, when a part
of this squadron shall be immediately sent to Minorca;
but unless the French are at least drove from Capua, I
think it right not to obey your Lordship's order for sending down any part of the squadron under my orders. I
am perfectly aware of the consequences of disobeying the
orders of my commander-in-chief." It cannot be said that
the offensiveness of the act of disobedience is tempered by
any very conciliatory tone in the words used. The reason
for disobedience makes matters rather worse. "As I believe the safety of the Kingdom of Naples depends at the
present moment on my detaining the squadron, I have no
scruple in deciding that it is better to save the Kingdom of
Naples and risk Minorca, than to risk the Kingdom of
Naples to save Minorca." When he thus wrote, Nelson
knew that Bruix had joined the Spanish fleet in Cartagena,
making a combined force of forty ships, to which Keith,
after stripping Minorca, could oppose thirty-one.

None of Nelson's letters reached Keith until long after
he had left the Mediterranean, which probably prevented
the matter being brought to a direct issue between the two,
such as would have compelled the Admiralty to take some
decisive action. On the 10th of July the commander-in-
chief sailed from Port Mahon for Cartagena, following on
the tracks of the allied fleets, which he pursued into the
Atlantic and to Brest, where they succeeded in entering on
the 13th of August, just twenty-four hours before the British came up. The narrow margin of this escape inevitably
suggests the thought, of how much consequence might

have been the co-operation of the dozen ships Nelson could
have brought. It is true, certainly, as matters turned out,
that even had he obeyed, they could not have accompanied
Keith, nor in the event did any harm come to Minorca;
but there was no knowledge in Nelson's possession that
made an encounter between the two great fleets impossible,
nor was it till three days after his former refusal to obey,
that he knew certainly that Keith had given up all expectation of a junction with himself. Then, on the 22d of
July, he received two letters dated the 14th, and couched
in tones so peremptory as to suggest a suspicion that no
milder words would enforce obedience — that his commander-in-chief feared that nothing short of cast-iron orders
would drag him away from the Neapolitan Court. " Your
Lordship is hereby required and directed to repair to
Minorca, with the whole, or the greater part, of the force
under your Lordship's command, for the protection of that
island, as I shall, in all probability, have left the Mediterranean before your Lordship will receive this. Keith."
The second letter of the same date ended with the words:
" I therefore trust the defence of Minorca to your Lordship, and repeat my directions that the ships be sent for its
protection." On the receipt of these, though Capua had
not yet surrendered, Nelson at once sent Duckworth with
four ships-of-the-line to Minorca, detaining only their marines for the land operations.

It seems scarcely necessary to say that, while an officer
in subordinate command should have the moral courage to
transcend or override his orders in particular instances —
each of which rests upon its own merits, and not upon any
general rule that can be formulated — it would be impossible for military operations to be carried on at all, if the
commander-in-chief were liable to be deliberately defied
and thwarted in his combinations, as •Keith was in this
case. It does not appear that Nelson *knew* the circumstances which Keith was considering; he only *knew* what

the conditions were about Naples, and he thought that the
settlement of the kingdom might be prevented by the departure of several of his ships.   In this opinion, in the
author's judgment, his views were exaggerated, and colored
by the absorbing interest he had come to take in the royal
family and their fortunes, linked as these were with the
affections of a particular woman ; but, even granting that
his apprehensions were well founded, he was taking upon
himself to determine, not merely what was best for the
Kingdom of the Two Sicilies, but what was best for the
whole Mediterranean command.   It was not within his
province to decide whether Minorca or Naples was the
more important. That was the function of the commander-
in-chief. Had the latter, while leaving Nelson's force un-
changed, directed him to follow a particular line of operations in the district committed to him, it is conceivable
that circumstances, unknown to his superior, might have
justified him in choosing another; but there was nothing
in the conditions that authorized his assumption that he
could decide for the whole command.   And this is not the
less true, because Nelson was in the general a man of far
sounder judgment and keener insight than Keith, or because his intuitions in the particular instance were more
accurate, as they possibly were.   He defended his course
on the ground, so frequently and so erroneously taken,
that his intentions were right.   " I am so confident," he
wrote to the Admiralty, "of the uprightness of my intentions for his Majesty's service, and for that of his
Sicilian Majesty, which I consider as the same, that, with
all respect, I submit myself to the judgment of my superiors." Four years later, in 1803, he used the following
singular expressions concerning his conduct at this period:
" I paid more attention to another sovereign than my own;
therefore the King of Naples' gift of Bronté to me, if it is
not now settled to my advantage, and to be permanent, has
cost me a fortune, and a great deal of favour which I might

have enjoyed, and jealousy which I should have avoided. I repine not on those accounts. I did my duty, to the Sicilifying my own conscience, and I am easy." [1] "As I have often before risked my life for the good cause," he told his old friend the Duke of Clarence, "so I with cheerfulness did my commission: for although a military tribunal may think me criminal, the world will approve my conduct." With such convictions, he might, if condemned, as he almost inevitably must have been, have met his fate with the cheerfulness of a clear conscience; but no military tribunal can possibly accept a man's conscience as the test of obedience.

The Admiralty, who had sent Keith out knowing that St. Vincent, after three arduous years, meant soon to retire, could not of course acquiesce in Nelson's thus overriding the man they had chosen to be his commander-in-chief. "Their Lordships do not, from any information now before them, see sufficient reason to justify your having disobeyed the orders you had received from your Commanding Officer, or having left Minorca exposed to the risk of being attacked, without having any naval force to protect it." To this measured rebuke was added some common-sense counsel upon the pernicious practice of jeopardizing the *personnel* of a fleet, the peculiar trained force so vitally necessary, and so hard to replace, in petty operations on shore. "Although in operations on the sea-coast, it may frequently be highly expedient to land a part of the seamen of the squadron, to co-operate with and to assist the army, when the situation will admit of their being immediately re-embarked, if the squadron should be called away to act elsewhere [as Keith had called it], or if information of the approach of an enemy's fleet should be received, — yet their Lordships by no means approve of the seamen being landed to form a part of an army to be employed in operations at a distance from the coast, where,

[1] Nicolas, vol. v. p. 160.

if they should have the misfortune to be defeated, they might be prevented from returning to the ships, and the squadron be thereby rendered so defective, as to be no longer capable of performing the services required of it; and I have their Lordships' commands to signify their directions to your Lordship not to employ the seamen in like manner in future."

It was evident that the Admiralty did not fully share Nelson's attachment to the royal house of Naples, nor consider the service of the King of the Two Sicilies the same as that of the King of Great Britain. Earl Spencer's private letter, while careful of Nelson's feelings, left no room to doubt that he was entirely at one with his colleagues in their official opinion. Nelson winced and chafed under the double rebuke, but he was not in a condition to see clearly any beams in his own eye. " I observe with great pain that their Lordships see no cause which could justify my disobeying the orders of my commanding officer, Lord Keith;" but the motives he again alleges are but the repetition of those already quoted. He fails wholly to realize that convictions which would justify a man in going to a martyr's fate may be wholly inadequate to sap the fundamental military obligation of obedience. " My conduct is measured by the Admiralty, by the narrow rule of law, when I think it should have been done by that of common sense. I restored a faithful ally by breach of orders ; Lord Keith lost a fleet by obedience against his own sense. Yet as one is censured the other must be approved. Such things are." As a matter of fact, as before said, it was by departing from St. Vincent's orders that Keith lost the French fleet. Nor did Nelson's mind work clearly on the subject. Thwarted and fretted as he continually was by the too common, almost universal, weakness, which deters men from a bold initiative, from assuming responsibility, from embracing opportunity, he could not draw the line between that and an independence of action which would convert unity of command into anarchy. "Much as I approve of strict obedience to orders, yet to say that an officer is never, for any object, to alter his orders, is what I cannot comprehend." But what rational man ever said such a thing? "I find few think as I do, — but to obey orders is all perfection! What would my superiors direct, did they know what is passing under my nose? To serve my King and to destroy the French I consider as the great order of all, from which little ones spring, and if one of these little ones militate against it, I go back to obey the great order." There is so much that is sound in these words, and yet so much confusion might arise in applying them, that scarcely any stronger evidence could be given that each case must rest on its own merits; and that no general rule can supplant the one general principle of obedience, by which alone unity and concentration of effort, the great goal of all military movement, can be obtained.

During this period of agitation and excitement, Nelson's health did not show the favorable symptoms that usually attended a call to exertion. Much may be attributed to a Mediterranean summer, especially after the many seasons he had passed in that sea; but it can readily be believed that such exceptional responsibilities as he had just assumed could not but tell, even upon his resolute and fearless temper. "I am really sorry," wrote Troubridge to him, from the siege of St. Elmo, "to see your Lordship so low-spirited, all will go well;" and a few days later, "Your Lordship must endeavour to fret as little as possible — we shall succeed. His Majesty's arrival will relieve your Lordship; and if he punishes the guilty, the people will be happy." The day after he had refused to obey Keith's order, he wrote to him, "I am truly so very unwell that I have not the power of writing so much as I could wish;" and the next day, to the Admiralty, he makes the same excuse, adding, "I am writing in a fever, and barely possible to keep out of bed." "My dear friend," he tells Locker, "I am so ill that I can scarcely sit up; yet I will not let the courier go off without assuring you that all your kindnesses to me are fresh in my memory. . . . May God Almighty grant you, my revered friend, that health and happiness which has never yet been attained by your affectionate, grateful friend, Nelson." It cannot but be surmised that he did not feel that profound conviction of right, which had sustained him on previous occasions. The disquiet indicated resembles rather that attending the uncertainties of the Nile campaign. As Colonel Stewart noticed, two years later, "With him mind and health invariably sympathized."

END OF VOL. I.